A DIFFERENT KIND
OF VICTORY

A DIFFERENT KIND OF VICTORY

A Biography of Admiral Thomas C. Hart

BY JAMES LEUTZE

NAVAL INSTITUTE PRESS
Annapolis, Maryland

Library of Congress Cataloging in Publication Data
Leutze, James.
  A different kind of victory.
  Bibliography: p.
  Includes index.
  1. Hart, Thomas Charles.   2. Admirals—United
States—Biography.   3. United States. Navy—
Biography.   I. Title.
V63.H37L48   359'.0092'4   [B]   81–4005
ISBN 0–87021–056–4   AACR2

Printed in the United States of America

To the men of the Asiatic Fleet
who served with Admiral Hart
and who were served by him

CONTENTS

PREFACE

This is a multipurpose study. It is first and foremost the story of a naval officer and his times, times that were crucial in the history of the U.S. Navy. However, it is also the story of a man who, although the navy was the central, guiding factor in his life, was more than a naval officer. The connecting thread in these two stories is the character of Thomas C. Hart. If nothing else, Tommy Hart was a man of principle, and his principles and the actions they guide him to take are the theme of this work.

The central questions that are explored are: What forces and circumstances shaped Tommy Hart into an officer who was selected to be one of the U.S. Navy's four full admirals on the eve of World War II? How did he carry out the responsibilities assigned to him? How did he react to the fate that befell him in that conflict? Attempting to answer those questions requires some probing of his personality, but this is no psychological biography. The suggestions made in a psychological vein are few and, although framed after discussions with professionals, they are not intended to be in any way scientific; they are merely attempts to answer questions that are frankly beyond my capacity to answer otherwise.

While being of interest because of his fifty-two-year career that spanned three wars and his varied service in destroyers, submarines, battleships, industrial plants, academic institutions, a fleet command, the first Allied naval command, and the U.S. Senate, Thomas Hart is significant because of where he was between 1939 and 1942 and because he left a written record of his life and times. Aside from *Admiral Kimmel's Story*, which reads much like a defense lawyer's brief, and Admiral Ernest J. King's collaborative effort, *Fleet Admiral King*, there are no firsthand accounts of how the senior officers in the U.S. Navy saw the coming of the war or reacted in its early months. There are numerous valuable histories, including Samuel Eliot Morison's *History of United States Naval Operations in World War II*, that give overviews, and there are some first-person accounts, such as Captain Robert J. Bulkley's *At Close Quarters: PT Boats in the United States Navy*. Histories of the Asiatic Fleet, however, are narrow, novelistic, or shot full of inaccuracies. Unfortunately, from a historical point of view, the army and air forces participants in World War II were prolific writers and their actions have attracted much wider attention than anything written about the navy. The most obvious case in point is that of General Douglas MacArthur, who wrote his memoirs, whose aides wrote their memoirs, and about whom more than a dozen creditable books have been written, including a monumental study published in 1978 and a popular account published in 1979.

Not only was Hart in a position to observe events in the Far East and, through his correspondence, to keep up with developments in Washington, he also maintained a daily diary which gives a unique perspective on what was happening and how he was reacting to it. If that were not enough, immediately after returning to the United States in 1942, he wrote a lengthy narrative of events, to which he later added a supplement. Thus, he left a running account of developments in the Far East.

The period Hart spent in the Philippines and in Java was historically momentous and he was a controversial actor in the drama. Here it should be noted that, in writing this biography, I have attempted to avoid apologizing for Hart or defending him against his critics, unless apology and defense seemed to me justified. He never wrote a justification of his actions, nor would he, I believe, want anyone else to do so. When he was wrong he admitted it and accepted the consequences. This account attempts to follow that admirable example.

Tommy Hart's diary obviously was a valuable resource in charting his activities and feelings. Let me quickly add that I am aware of the pitfalls of relying too heavily on a personal diary; valid questions can be raised about why a person keeps such a record. My impression is that Tommy Hart did so in large part to vent reactions to people and events that would have been destructive if vented in any other way and equally destructive if kept locked inside himself. One thing is certain. He did not maintain the diary to apologize either for or to himself: in it he is fully as hard on himself as some suggest he was on them. The most amazing thing about the diary and the mass of other Hart material, which includes hundreds of letters between him and his trusted confidante, his wife Caroline Brownson Hart, and the invaluable series of oral history interviews he gave is that they are so consistent. If Hart says he said "so and so" to a superior on "such and such" a date, a check of the record proves *in every case* that that is precisely what he said and that it was said when he claims it was. His "geese" do not become "swans"; he does not tell one thing to one person and something else to another. His records are as honest and as straightforward as he was. He kept letters that praised him and, although it must have hurt like the devil, he also kept those that condemned him for making mistakes or losing the lives of loved ones. There was no cant about Tommy Hart, and while the perceptive historian who interviewed him for his oral history and later came to know him well observed that "he was not a transparent personality," the twin virtues of honesty and fairness do provide a constant guiding beam in charting the life of Tommy Hart.

A DIFFERENT KIND
OF VICTORY

1

CHILDHOOD AND YOUTH

On the surface it did not seem an unusual retirement ceremony. The ramrod-straight, white-haired admiral in the starched high collar stood awkwardly at the door, bidding a formal good-bye to sixteen younger officers. The first three or four filed past him without demonstrations of emotion, then a red-haired lieutenant commander grasped the older man's hand in both of his and said "Good-bye, Sir, you are the finest man I've ever known." The old admiral's eyes misted with tears and suddenly he was incapable of speaking to or even seeing the faces of the remaining men. Perhaps this scene requires closer observation; it is not a normal retirement ceremony: there is too husky a timbre in the voices, the participants are somehow too stiff, the atmosphere too highly charged. Moreover, the senior officer in question wears on his shoulders the four gold stars of a full admiral; the doorway is not in some officers' club, but in the Savoy Hotel, Bandung, Java; and the officers filing out into the night are the only ones who could be rounded up on short notice from the once-proud Asiatic Fleet to bid farewell to their commander. It is 14 February 1942, and Admiral Thomas C. Hart is stepping down as commander of the ABDA (American, British, Dutch, and Australian) naval forces, the first American ever to serve as commander of an allied naval force. "Oh, it was hard," he wrote that night; parting always made him sad, but leaving his friends out there in the face of a dangerous enemy and "commanded by God knows whom or how" was almost too much to bear.

The admiral who made that entry in his diary, "Tough Tommy"

Hart, as he was called by admirer and detractor alike, at sixty-four had served fifty-one years on active duty, but now he was returning home under a cloud. "Ill health" was the official explanation, but those who knew the situation realized, without having the details, that that was a contrived explanation. Even Admiral Hart did not know all the details and, though he had done nothing wrong, he sensed that it would be a long time before the record was set right. Being removed from command before the final stages of a battle that was going badly was not at all the way he had imagined ending his career. He had hoped to be commanding on the bridge and "catch a 14″ shell in the mid section," or so he had once said. That would have been more in keeping with the prior service of this strict, stern, extremely proper officer, who was known—even feared—throughout the navy for his "sundowner" discipline and compulsive dedication to duty. The irony could hardly have been greater. No one had shown more prescience about the coming of the war; no one had trained for it more arduously; no one had risked more in trying to gather intelligence about the Japanese naval force moving down the coast of Indochina before hostilities began; no one had prepared himself more rigorously, or examined more closely his own abilities to command. Now, with the war barely two months old, "Tough Tommy" was leaving the battle, returning home, probably to retirement on his farm in Connecticut where he could read about younger men, his younger men, getting swept from the bridge by 14-inch shells. "Oh, it was hard," he recorded, and the hardest part was that he probably did not have many years left to salvage his career or even to see the record set straight.

What was the record of the Asiatic Fleet in the Philippines and of the short-lived ABDA command? What had happened to bring this man to such an ironic denouement? Perhaps the time has now come when we can gain new insight both into what really happened and into the actual role of the "finest man" Lieutenant Commander Redfield Mason had ever known.

It all began on 12 June 1877 when Thomas Charles Hart was born in Davison, Michigan, the son of John Mansfield Hart and Isabella Ramsey Hart.[1] His father, who was thirty-seven years old at that time, had enlisted in the Union Navy as a landsman during the War between the States. His home of record was Bangor, Maine, although he actually came from the small community of Holden, and sailors from New England were in great demand. In

1865 John Hart was discharged from the navy where he had served in the frigate *Sabine* and soon, like many other veterans, made his way west.

Since, in the 1870s, Michigan was still on the frontier, it was a natural place for a Maine lumberjack to settle. Indeed, Bangor lumbermen were in great demand in the Michigan woods, so Hart moved up rapidly from lumberjack to crew chief to supervisor. This was boom time in the small lumber towns that sprang up and vanished with equal rapidity. There was no talk of environmental impact when the forests stretched to the horizon; the only charge was to put the trees on the ground. In 1888 four billion board feet of timber were cut in Michigan, and John Hart did more than his share.

In the course of the employment that took him all over northern Michigan, John Hart met Isabella Ramsey, the daughter of recent Scottish immigrants. Isabella was born in Scotland but now claimed the United States as home. After a short courtship the two were married. Thomas Charles Hart was their first and only child.

One day while Tommy, as he was always called, was still a baby, his father returned from work and in a normal burst of emotion Isabella ran across the yard to greet him. But then to John's horror, this common domestic scene turned into a nightmare. Before she reached her husband, Isabella lost consciousness and collapsed. Soon she was dead and John was a widower. So horrified was he that he seldom thereafter could bring himself even to reminisce about his wife or their life together. Thus, Tommy was robbed not only of association with his mother but also of any intimate knowledge of her. He did, however, as he grew older and gleaned some details of her death, learn an indelible lesson about the transitory nature of life and the suddenness with which a loved one could be swept away.

Before the turn of the century Michigan was a rather paradoxical environment in which to be raised. The natural beauty of the forests and the lakes was balanced by the scars left by man. The warm and sunny days of July and August were more than offset by the brutal cold of January and February. In fact, the Davison area was usually gray and bleak from November through May. And then there were the people—hardy, robust, pioneering types—but, behind the facade of physical wellbeing, there often lurked the debilitating effects of poor diet, hard work, and exposure to a harsh climate. Doctors were few and people had to rely mainly on home remedies or wait for infrequent trips to town.

A healthy man could prosper, but staying vigorous was a constant challenge. For a young boy there were the woods and streams to offer diversions but, as Bruce Catton recalls in *Waiting for the Morning Train,* there were also times when the brooding presence of the wilderness and the chilling reality that the north wind blew undeflected from the arctic, sent shivers, not of cold, down the spine. In this environment people worked hard, assumed little would come easily, and respected the man who kept his troubles to himself. Thus, it was natural for Tommy, despite his high spirits, to absorb a system of values more often associated with New England: thrift, prudence, self-reliance, and rugged individualism.[2]

No doubt John Hart mourned his young wife, but there was little outward sign of it. Within two years he was married again, this time to Mary Conklin. In some ways having a mother again was good for the growing Tommy, but his stepmother was never well and apparently made little effort to replace her predecessor. In the end it made no difference anyway since after only a year Mary Conklin Hart sickened and died. Again there was an interval without a woman in the house and then John Hart married for the third time. This stepmother, Amelia Sager Smith, was a widow with two daughters and for the first time since his natural mother died Tommy had someone who at least tried to fill the void. The problem was that after so little motherly attention Tommy was quite a handful to care for. According to his own stories, he was an active perhaps even devilish boy who, since his father was away supervising logging operations during most of the nonsummer months, required considerable looking after. When that looking after was neglected, high spirits and a sense of adventure took control—sometimes with serious consequences. For instance, there was the time Tommy and his friends burned down the hitching shed behind the church and another when a homemade bomb blew a chunk from a tree in the yard. His stepsister Maude Smith, with whom he became quite close, and other female relatives tell of high jinks that would have tried the patience of a saint, much more that of his inexperienced stepmother. Apparently his pranks did not endear him to his new mother who had her hands amply filled running her home and had not bargained on being warden to a young hellion. School officials as well took an unsympathetic view of the growing accumulation of indiscretions. The result was Tommy's suspension, a circumstance that would inevitably mean trouble when his father returned in the spring. The solution was simple, but not inexpensive: Tommy took his savings, bought a horse, and rode to school in a nearby community. It was an act of initiative, perhaps leavened with a pinch of desperation, and indicated a resourcefulness Thomas Hart would demonstrate often in the future.

The education he got in his newly chosen school and in the small rural schools that had preceded it was scarcely quality, or that was how it seemed when he looked back seventy-five years later. When Davison was incorporated as a town in 1889 it numbered only 456 people, so it is not surprising that the schools were of the one-room, one-teacher, all-classes-meet-together variety. Only two teachers, he said, had any impact on him. One was a man, a tough, stern, "intellectual," in Hart's words, who scared him but, he recalled, "I needed to be scared." The other was a woman whom he deeply respected and for whom he felt a sincere affection that inspired him to extra effort.[3] With those exceptions, his early school years were rather dreary; there was neither competition nor stimulation. Although he usually finished near the top of his class, he did not consider this standing an accomplishment. Later events suggest that Tommy's assessment of his academic achievement should not be taken too seriously, but we probably should accept his judgment that "I was rather a bad boy, taking it all together."[4]

At home John Hart—probably seeking some relief from his familial responsibilities and perhaps for his new wife—arranged to send Tommy east during the summers. John's family still lived in Maine and since he was one of nine brothers, there were plenty of relatives to welcome Tommy. These summers were perhaps the happiest times of his boyhood. There was always lots to do, many games to be played, animals to be tended and ridden, and places to be seen. There were some sobering times as well. The Harts were hardworking country people who apparently prayed the way they did everything else—fervently. Hence, during his summers in Maine Tommy got a thorough introduction into the formalities of the Methodist church. Maine meant variety, but religion meant boredom and, eventually, resistance. Partially as a result of his early exposure, he never became an avid churchman. But perhaps we should not be too hard on his well-meaning aunts and uncles. Tommy was not introspective or philosophical, so the long hours spent on hard benches in the white clapboard churches may have been simply painful and not necessarily formative.

In 1891 a change took place that had wide-ranging consequences in Tommy's life. His father sold his small business and his farm and moved into the relative urbanity of Flint, Michigan. Not only did this mean an end to the family's moving from town to town, but it also resulted in Tommy's entrance into the more sophisticated and competitive school system of Flint. Since this happened in his first year of high school, the subject matter was more difficult as well; so difficult that he rebelled, ending up, according to him, with a "rather dreary showing." Actually his grades were quite good; he made all 90s in his first semester and did only slightly less well in the spring of 1892.[5] The next year his grades were uniformly worse, but in the first semester he still scored in the high 80s or low 90s in all subjects. However, his lowest grade was an 83 in general history, which hardly seems to justify his comment that he was in jeopardy of having to repeat the grade. Still, he may have known something we do not, for it is curious that he received grades in only three subjects rather than the customary four. From what we know of his previous and future experiences, it would not be surprising to learn that he was having some disciplinary difficulties.

For whatever reason, when one afternoon in the spring of 1893 Tommy saw a notice in the local paper announcing that an appointment to the Naval Academy was available, prospects of escape beckoned. From hours spent with *Youth's Companion* and other literature for boys, he knew about West Point and Annapolis and they sounded exciting. When he showed the notice to his father, John Hart immediately dampened his enthusiasm. "You haven't any chance for that appointment," the elder Hart informed him. It seemed that Congressman David D. Aitken, who had the appointment, was a first-term Republican with whom the elder Hart was acquainted, but the acquaintance was not a happy one. John Hart knew that many boys would be after the appointment and, aside from having more influence with the congressman and better school records, they would be more mature than fifteen-year-old Tommy.

His father's reasoning seemed sound, so the subject was dropped until a few days later when Tommy heard that a competitive exam was to be held in Orchard Lake, Michigan, to ease Congressman Aitken's task of selection among the many applicants. With renewed hopes, Tommy asked his father for permission to go to Orchard Lake. It was something of a lark; several of his friends attended the military academy in Orchard Lake so he could see them, get out of school for two or three days and, of course, take a shot at the exam. No doubt he did not explain all

Thomas C. Hart, c. 1887. Courtesy of Mrs. T. C. Hart

this to his father who, though still dubious about his son's prospects, agreed to let him go.

It would have been hard to disagree with his father when, upon arrival at Orchard Lake, he checked out the competition. There were ten applicants for the appointment, three of them from the University of Michigan, and all older and better educated than the high-school sophomore from Flint. All hope seemed lost. But apparently the commandant of the school had turned the preparation of the examination over to an assistant who knew little about the academy curriculum. Consequently, the test was heavily weighted with basic subjects, "grammar school subjects," to quote Hart. Most of the competitors had forgotten a lot of that material, but Tommy Hart had covered it recently. He was especially lucky that the exam had many questions in his favorite subject, mathematics, and, joy of joys, a large part of that section consisted of trick questions in which he excelled. Finally it was over and the examiner left to correct the results. When he returned, he walked to the corner, where Tommy was seeking relative security, and put his hand on the shoulder of the new appointee to Annapolis—Thomas C. Hart.

Probably no one was more surprised than Congressman Aitken but, to his credit, he abided by the result. He presented Tommy with his letter of appointment and advised him to get to Annapolis quickly and begin prepping for the formal entrance examination which was only one month away. It is easy to imagine the scene and the emotion as Tommy was bundled aboard the train bound east. Emotions were surely mixed for his parents: sorrow at seeing him leave, pride, and relief that he was going off to get some discipline. For Tommy it meant leaving a not-totally-happy home, but what he knew of the academy must have included the fact that he was bound for a rigorous life, indeed. Fortunately, he had traveled alone before, because the anxiety of this leap into the unknown was almost overwhelming.

Things did not improve when he arrived at Werntz Preparatory School on the corner of Franklin and Cathedral Streets in Annapolis. The Naval Academy had just adopted new requirements, one of which was that applicants have a year of algebra. With that blow, Tommy was about to close his bags and return to Flint. One year of algebra! The mathematics he had had, although called *algebra,* was not nearly as advanced as the algebra in the entrance exam. No doubt his return would please Congressman Aitken and fulfill the dire predictions of other doubters. But Bobby Werntz, the headmaster of the school, persuaded him to stay by offering to give him private lessons. These were held in the evening at the Werntz home where, by patient coaching and careful handling, he was kept alert and awake so that the sessions could go on until midnight—and this after a full day of regular schooling. But it paid off. By examination day Tommy had completed the equivalent of one year of algebra and he passed on the first try. What a triumph, not only for Hart but for Werntz as well, who subsequently used the success story as an advertisement.

So now it was T. Hart, naval cadet. Looking at him in 1893, it would have been difficult to believe that he was ready for his first year of college. He was by far the smallest man admitted that year, standing only five feet, seven inches, and weighing ninety-eight pounds. He was promptly dubbed "Dad." He looked fresh-faced and he was, since he had not yet begun to shave. But he had gotten over the numerous hurdles placed in his way and, while he attributed his success to luck, one could perceive an inner toughness behind that shy, youthful look. In many ways he was young like those other young men who thirty years before had filled the ranks of the 24th Michigan and 20th Maine regiments and served so valiantly in the Civil War.

The winters in Michigan had toughened him, and his body, though slight, had known hard physical labor. He had traveled perhaps an unusual amount for a boy of that day and he had also adapted to numerous changes of school and surroundings. In addition, he had experienced separation from his family; from his mother permanently, and from his father for extended periods. Therefore, in some ways, going to school eight hundred miles from home at the age of fifteen was not as hard for Tommy Hart as it might have been for other boys. There is little indication that he and his father were unusually close; indeed, though always respectful of one another, there was a sense of distance between them. In many important ways the boy grew up without the usual family ties. No mother, only two stepsisters as siblings, and a father often absent. In these circumstances, the academy was bound to play an important formative role.

The Naval Academy that Tommy Hart entered in May of 1893 had changed surprisingly little since its founding forty-eight years before, so the dormitory occupied by Hart and his 91 classmates was already a relic.[6] With a total of only 263 cadets, there was little need for a big yard. The school had been through difficult times, as had the navy as a whole, during the decades following the Civil War and only the wise policies of Superintendent Francis M. Ramsay (1881–1886) and Superintendent William T. Sampson (1886–1890) saved it from what might have been a disastrous decline. Ramsay instituted a series of reforms and proposed still others that were epochal in the history of the academy; Sampson had the wisdom to conserve what had been done by his predecessor and expand upon it.

When Hart entered through the gates and walked down the tree-lined walks that May, Sampson had been succeeded by Captain Robert L. Phythian whose immediately preceding billet was superintendent of the Naval Observatory. Phythian followed in Sampson's path and changed few of the basic policies that were leading toward a rebirth of vigor in Annapolis. His methods were direct and kindly: "He believed in granting to the cadets all possible privileges which were consistent with the regulations and imposing no restrictions inconsistent with them and in taking advantage of the smooth-running discipline and scholastic work to cultivate more highly the social amenities of academic life."[7] This should not be taken to mean that discipline was lax or academic standards less than rigorous; the fact that only approximately 50 per cent of each entering class survived to graduation testifies to the contrary, but within certain limits Phythian tried to make life tolerable.

Tommy Hart was going to have little time to make extensive tours or observations of his new home, for as a member of the class accepted in May (the other three-quarters came in September) he soon found himself aboard the venerable sailing frigate *Constellation* preparing for a practice cruise. The cruise was the last extended service for the USS *Constellation,* launched just ninety-nine years before, and by all accounts it was a memorable one. It started out badly when, just after the midshipmen came on board, a sailor got his head crushed as a result of the youngsters helping to raise the anchor. With that as a start, the *Constellation* headed down the Chesapeake Bay and pointed her bow east toward the Azores and the Madeira Islands. Soon after she reached the open sea she ran into the first of a series of gales and, as could be expected, the midshipmen got seasick. As they wrote in the 1894 *Lucky Bag,* the academy's first year book: "Pell mell, slipping, sliding on the slanting deck, our faces distorted with the keenest anguish, we hurried to it (the rail), to give our tribute to old Ocean, and then to lie down and feel that death and dry land were the two finest things in the world." Added to these natural calamities was the devilment of the upper classmen who delighted in hazing their less experienced juniors. Hart does not say he got seasick, but almost surely he did; he does say, however, that "there was more concentrated misery in those three months than I've had all the rest of my life."[8]

The constant gales so weakened her rigging that for a time it appeared possible that the *Constellation* would be dismasted in mid-Atlantic. But even when that catastrophe was averted, there was inconvenience aplenty. For the 123 midshipmen on board there were five washbasins and a limited supply of fresh water. The upper classmen got first call on the basins—and on the water—the result being that the plebes were left to bathe, if at all, with sticky salt water. It is not surprising that Hart recalled years later that the "plebes became none too immaculate." Then there was the food—salt beef, codfish, sauerkraut, and canned pears. It was served to the midshipmen on the berth deck by black messmen who, slipping and sliding, seldom arrived below with full bowls.

But even under those conditions the midshipmen found, at least for a while, a way to entertain themselves. "During bad weather," Hart wrote, "a favorite sport was to coast on the mess stools between table and hatch covering—snatching a bit of food at each bump against the table. Not many had spirits enough to engage and the practice of it was soon stopped incident to one of their number toppling through a hatch. The consequent injury was a nuisance—the midshipman had to be cared for and someone had to do his work!" There was other excitement such as going aloft to man the yards, and one must simply imagine how exciting that was for a Michigan farm boy. There also was drill with the 8-inch smoothbore guns which had to be manually wrestled out of the gun ports and in again for reloading because the blank charges issued did not provide enough recoil.[9]

Eventually they reached the Azores, probably just in time for the plebes, every one of whom, according to Hart, had written out a letter of resignation. The islands provided opportunity to revisit terra firma and tour the sights. With these distractions most of the miseries were forgotten, as were the resignations. The return passage was made by the southern route which proved far more pleasant for the *Constellation*. By now the plebes were "salty 'sea-going' and proud of themselves." Nevertheless, they were delighted to enter the estuary of the Severn River and behold "the grounds of the Academy, looking like a forest of great trees, above whose all-enshrouding verdure appeared the slim white flag staff and the gray clock tower of New Quarters."[10]

Back in Annapolis, it was time to board the dismasted practice ship—and place of detention for unruly cadets—the *Santee,* moored permanently at the academy, and await the September plebes. And when they came, the May plebes had an opportunity to teach them some of the fun things the upper classmen had delighted in teaching them during the cruise. This entertainment was short-lived, though, because on 23 September they all moved to quarters, there to await the return of the upper classmen from September leave. On 1 October this tide broke over them "like a mighty deluge," for all plebes were alike to their seniors. "We bowed our heads to the torrent, and in time it abated its wild exhilaration," though it continued in abated form for the next nine months.[11]

Ironically, we know more about this opening phase of Tommy Hart's career at the academy than about the balance of his four years. He says in his oral history that his first year was extremely difficult for him academically and he was "anything but a success for the first two and a half years." The record more or less bears him out. In his first year, in a class of seventy-seven, he rated fortieth in algebra and geometry, fiftieth in English and history, and thirty-ninth in Spanish, French, and German. In his second year he improved his academic position, although his demerits rose. This rise was a direct result of his having more free time now that he had his studies under control.

It was this proclivity for impish diversion that brought him into contact with a man who made a significant impact on his life. In 1894 Captain Phythian was replaced as superintendent by Captain Philip H. Cooper. To tighten up discipline, Cooper brought with him Commander Willard H. Brownson, an officer of considerable experience and stern demeanor. Brownson was installed as commandant of cadets, the billet most immediately responsible for the cadets' training in military discipline and leadership.

Hart's class was very much in need of discipline and, apparently, Hart and several of his friends composed a group most definitely deficient. In the spring of 1894 four cadets, Hart and three others, formed a group called Coxey's Army, the sole purpose of which was devilment. They soaked upper classmen's beds and their occupants with water, pulled other tricks on upper classmen as well as their fellows, and caused late-night rackets. The identity of Coxey's Army was known to many of the cadets, but the instructional staff had yet to ferret them out.

Brownson arrived in November 1894 and within a month he had a confrontation with the "army" when Hart and his three friends decided to take on the authorities in a very direct way. The officer in charge of the quarters deck on which Hart's class lived was a lieutenant derisively called Savvy Dan. Dan was strict, devoid of humor, something of a prig, and had a trait that the midshipmen conceived of as "meanness." One afternoon after infantry drill Hart was presented with some seventy-five blank cartridges and told by his fellows to make a bomb with a slow-burning fuse. Coxey's Army was going to blow up Savvy Dan's desk, his pride and joy. Tommy did as directed, constructing a bomb in a half-pint ink bottle. At 3:00 a.m. this was duly set in a drawer of the desk. Soon, the entire dormitory was shocked into wakefulness by a tremendous roar.[12]

Obviously Brownson could not allow this challenge to authority to go unpunished, so he announced that the third class would mount two sentries on the floor all night in two-hour shifts. The class felt that damaging Savvy Dan's desk and reputation was worth this sacrifice, so after a few days Brownson increased the pressure. Letting it be known that he feared the culprits might be from outside the academy and capable of God knows what, he doubled the number of sentries. After a few days of this and the surmise that Brownson would continue the mathematical progression ad nauseam, Coxey's Army surrendered. Instead of dismissing them, which he could have done, the commandant had them quartered in the *Santee* for two months with no recreation time. No demerits were assigned, so none of the cadets suffered in their class standing, and Brownson told them he was confining them merely to guard against danger to life and property. This method of both finding the guilty and leavening justice with mercy, Hart later considered "a perfect example of correct handling of men in a matter of discipline" even though he suffered on the *Santee* for two months.

It should not be assumed, though, that Brownson had turned Thomas Hart into a model cadet. For instance, although he says that by his third year he had decided to straighten up and come around, he was enticed to go to a party one Saturday afternoon even though he was restricted to "barracks" for previous indiscretions. In this case he not only made the mistake of leaving the barracks but also of going to a party hosted by the daughters of Commander Edwin White, who had succeeded Brownson as com-

The class of 1897, U.S. Naval Academy. Naval Cadet Hart is immediately behind the man in the middle of the front row. Courtesy of Mrs. T. C. Hart

mandant of cadets. As if that were not bad enough, he made the fatal error of being so noteworthy that one of the hostesses mentioned him by name to her father. Commander White was not as accommodating as his predecessor had been. He ordered Hart and his roommate to account for themselves between the hours of 3:00 p.m. and 6:00 p.m. on that Saturday. When they did so, he gave them fifty demerits each and sent them back to the *Santee* for confinement.

Statistics probably best tell the story of Hart's career under academy discipline. In his youngster, or second, year he stood fifty-second out of seventy-seven in discipline; by his second-class year he had improved his conduct to stand thirty-first out of sixty; but in his first-class year, belying his comments about reforming, he stood thirty-second out of thirty-seven. What this means is problematic, but it is likely that Thomas Hart, who was only nineteen when he graduated, was full of boyish high spirits and they could not be dulled by the academy's rigid rules. Whether he was misbehaving to gain attention will be left to the psychologists. Hart later took some pride in the fact that throughout his career he was considered by superiors to be slightly insubordinate; there is no doubt that he displayed these traits early.

We also know that Thomas Hart did not follow the same erratic course in academic matters. At the start of his youngster year, he stood forty-second out of seventy-seven; the next year he stood twenty-sixth out of sixty; he went to thirteenth out of fifty-six the following year; and by graduation he was seventh out of thirty-seven. Considering the aggregate of the four years, he stood twelfth out of thirty-seven, with a score of 610.23 out of a possible 700. Thus Hart showed steady improvement in his classroom work. And here it should be stressed that, although the academy has always put primary emphasis on turning out line officers rather than intellectuals, the teaching methods were rigorous. Classes were very small, eight to ten cadets, and, since recitation was the pedagogical procedure rather than lecture, it was virtually impossible for a cadet to go to class unprepared—and get away with it. Hence one can assume that Hart's grades accurately reflected his knowledge. The subjects in which he did best were steam machinery, marine engines and boilers, physics and chemistry, history, international law, and seamanship. His worst subjects were French, calculus, mechanical drawing, trigonometry, and geometry.

But it was not all classroom work and inspections at the academy.

Since 1890 there had been a renewed interest in athletics. At the alumni gathering in that year Robert M. Thompson, of the class of 1868, pointed out that "however valuable scholastic attainments might be, all would be useless if, at the crucial moment of conflict, nerves and body failed."[13] This remark fell on receptive ears and the cadets' young bodies were soon being subjected to a full schedule of athletic events. Football was greeted with the greatest enthusiasm and the greatest spectacles were the contests between the two service academies. But that game became a victim of its own success and was not played for four years after 1894 "because of a supposed deleterious influence upon the class standing of the participants and the discipline of the academies."[14] One can fairly assume that Hart was one of those whose discipline was so affected. Although he was too small to participate in football, he found his niche in another sport revived in the athletic renaissance of the '90s—crew. "Dad" was just the right size to act as coxswain in the academy's eight-man shell and there he performed valuable service in 1895 and 1896. Then, partially in response to a "challenge from the New York Naval Reserves" and presumably at the urging of Superintendent Cooper, who wanted to see the cadets' athletic energies expended as much as possible in their natural element, the water, Hart and some associates organized a cutter crew. Lieutenant Albert W. Grant of the Mathematics Department helped, offering such sage advice as "If a man only put his blade in the water and pulled hard enough it did not matter if he feathered a few inches too high." Some of the academy crew were not paragons of physical prowess, but they had desire and they apparently took to heart Grant's suggestion that they put enthusiasm ahead of style. In the end they won the race with the reserves by a length, aided, as Hart said, "by their pluck and endurance."[15]

Evincing some of those same qualities, Tommy Hart made it to 4 June 1897 and graduation. There had been significant changes in him and in the school since his arrival a little more than four years before. He entered as a boy and was leaving at least well on his way to manhood. His knowledge had been increased and he had demonstrated an ability to master difficult academic subjects. His sense of decorum still left something to be desired, but at least he had learned the consequences of misconduct and, presumably, benefited from his punishment. He also had learned a number of practical things as a result of his athletic participation and his summer cruises. By the time he graduated, he had spent eight months and twenty-seven days afloat, most of that under sail. From these experiences he learned a life-long respect for seamanship and all manner of things to do with ships. Some of this may be attributed to the changes in the academy's curriculum, in that more and more emphasis was being placed on shiphandling. Physical changes were also taking place in Annapolis; acreage was added to the grounds and the Board of Visitors began agitating for some uniformity in architecture. The renaissance of the school's physical plant was yet to come, but like Naval Cadet Hart, the academy was poised to spring into a new and exciting period.

But first there was what should have been a triumphal return home on a short leave. However, as he would have been the first to admit, his activities at the academy, in things nonacademic, could hardly be pointed to with pride, and the results of some of his indiscretions could not be swept away with a diploma. Therefore, when Tommy Hart returned to Michigan he brought a sheepskin *and* a handful of bills for debts unwisely incurred. His father reached for the diploma and did not even look at the bills; they were Tommy's personal property. Hence Tommy Hart would have slowly to pay off his debts, and buy his meals, all on the ninety dollars per month he would earn for the next two years.

At this period in the navy's history, getting a commission took six years rather than four. This meant that Hart, now a passed midshipman, would spend two years at sea before taking his final examinations and receiving his commission. He always contended that luck played a large role in his career, and events during his two-year probationary period would seem to imply a reasonable share of good fortune.

The first happy stroke was his assignment to the battleship *Massachusetts,* sister ship of the *Oregon* and *Indiana.* These three were the most modern and heaviest ships in the newly augmented U.S. armada. Laid down in 1891, the *Massachusetts* displaced 10,288 tons and was capable of 16 knots. She boasted four 13-inch guns in two turrets, eight 8-inch guns, four 6-inch guns, and twenty 6-pounders. In addition, she was armed with numerous smaller weapons and six Whitehead torpedo tubes. For defense, she boasted an 18-inch steel belt and a 2¾-inch armored dec¹: to protect against plunging fire. Even during normal times, landing an assignment on the *Massachusetts* would be a plum, but the fall of 1897 was not a normal time. For tensions were increasing between Spain and the United States over that ancient European power's handling of troubles in Cuba.

The stage was small and although the resulting conflict would seem to present-day Americans to be minor, to students of international affairs the implications were vast, the change in the nation's course portentous. Participants would doubtless agree: it was the first real conflict since the Civil War more than a generation before; and while some may argue about the modernity of that struggle, there was no question that for the navy, at least, the Spanish-American War was far more modern than transitional.

The man elected president in 1896, William McKinley, was explicitly and emphatically opposed to war—at least so he had said during his campaign and privately afterwards. It is difficult to be entirely sure about McKinley, though, and historians continue to bicker about his strength of character, resolve, malleability, political acumen, and ultimately his room for maneuver.[16] One thing is certain, however: on 15 February 1898, his options became considerably more restricted. On that date the battleship *Maine,* sent to Havana presumably to protect American lives and property during the impending civil conflict, blew up and went to the bottom of Havana Harbor, the victim of a dastardly attack, or so the American press concluded.[17] A Naval Board of Inquiry rushed to Havana, where with full Spanish cooperation, an investigation was conducted. Meanwhile diplomatic negotiations went forward between the Spanish and the U.S. governments with the object of ending the rebellion in Cuba. The United States wanted the Spanish to take a series of steps and make guarantees; Spain believed the Americans were interfering in its internal affairs, but reluctantly and very slowly conceded point after point.

According to the Naval Board's findings, which were reported to Washington on 21 March, the *Maine* was sunk by an external explosion, most probably caused by a mine. The buckling of her plates and keel surrounding one of her bunkers pointed ineluctably to this conclusion. Pressure now was exerted in earnest against Spain, while the press and segments of the public went wild. "Remember the *Maine.* To hell with Spain" became the cry. Congress responded to the public clamor and McKinley either lost his will to resist the tide of emotion or decided to drift in the direction he wanted to go, anyway. Regardless of his intent, the result was demands that the Spanish felt compelled to reject. Albeit reluctantly, Spain declared war on the United States, and the United States responded similarly, albeit retroactively, on 25 April 1898, declaring war as of 21 April.

War! On 25 April 1898 the word raced through the 384-foot-long *Massachusetts* as she lay at anchor off Hampton Roads. The government had finally elected to take action and, since that was the case, there would surely be action for the modern battleship, but how and where? News soon arrived that Admiral Pascual Cervera was sailing for the Western Hemisphere from his base in the Cape Verde Islands.[18] While the more dramatically inclined considered it possible that he might bombard the Atlantic coast of the United States, the newly formed Naval War Board considered it far more likely that he would head for Cuba. The public furor was so intense, however, that it was decided to divide the North Atlantic Squadron in two. The force that retained the name "Atlantic Squadron" was sent to Key West under the command of Acting Rear Admiral William T. Sampson. Part of Sampson's job was to guard against an attack on Key West, but more importantly to prepare to take offensive action against Cuba or Puerto Rico. The remainder of the ships were christened the "Flying Squadron" and stationed at Norfolk under command of Commodore Winfield Scott Schley. Schley's job was to prepare for defensive action against an attack anywhere along the Atlantic coast.

Sampson, as his last name implies, was not inclined to passively await his opponent's moves; Cervera was at sea and the U.S. admiral wanted to intercept him at the earliest possible moment. Therefore, on 3 May he removed some of the ships from the blockade he had established two weeks earlier outside Havana Harbor and sailed east. Sampson calculated that Cervera and his fleet, which consisted of four cruisers and two destroyers, would duck into Puerto Rico for coaling. If Sampson could find him there, the U.S. force, which included the battleships *Iowa* and *Indiana,* the armored cruiser *New York,* two monitors, and a torpedo boat, should be able to end the naval war in the Atlantic very quickly. The problem proved to be finding the Spanish admiral, who figured things pretty much the way Sampson did. As Sampson arrived off Puerto Rico, Cervera was a thousand miles to the south, passing Martinique, whence he proceeded to Curaçao, and arrived at Santiago de Cuba on 19 May.

On that same day, Sampson, realizing the wily Spaniard had given him the slip, ordered Schley to sail for Cuba. Since the *Massachusetts* was part of Schley's Flying Squadron, Tommy Hart's first wartime action was about to begin. Within four days the squadron stood in to reconnoiter Cienfuegos Harbor. Since smoke was sighted, Schley considered it possible that Cervera lurked within, so he established a blockade four miles offshore. Amidst growing criticism of Sampson's inability to find Cervera, as well as indications that the Spanish fleet might be at Santiago, on 23 May Sampson ordered Schley to steam for that port. In a movement later condemned for its slowness, Schley sailed west. Hampered by bad weather, high seas, a declining supply of coal, and perhaps some doubt that Cervera was at Santiago, Schley did not arrive off that port and establish a picket line until 28 May. The next morning, much to his pleasure and no doubt the general excitement of his crew, the masts of the cruiser *Cristóbal Colón* were clearly sighted. At last the enemy had been found. Word was sent to Sampson, who arrived on 1 June, his force strengthened by the battleship *Oregon,* which had steamed from the Pacific, through the Strait of Magellan, to join the war.

So, the North Atlantic Squadron was now reunited, but what next? Cervera, extremely gloomy about his chances, was not ready to sail out and face the guns of a superior fleet. For Sampson, the prospect of entering the harbor to engage the Spanish ships was made unattractive by the narrowness of the harbor entrance: therefore, he did what the navy had done so much of during the Civil War—he established a blockade. As had been learned in that earlier conflict, sailing back and forth on blockade duty was not very stimulating. So the senior officers, eager for action, began to seek likely sites for a landing or for another way to get at the Spaniards. The best landing place would be on the western side of Santiago Harbor, but no one in the squadron was familiar with its topography. Therefore, it was decided to send in two cutters to scout the area: one was from the *New York* and was commanded by Hart's classmate and close friend Joseph W. Powell; the other was from the *Massachusetts* and put under Hart's command. The idea was to slip into Cabañas Bay in the early hours of 17 June, explore the shoreline for a possible landing spot, and then slip back out. They started into the bay at 4:45 a.m., but even in the pale light of predawn they were soon spotted and brought under heavy fire. So heavy and at such close range, much of it from approximately fifty yards, that the two cutters were forced to retreat. But before they could clear the harbor entrance they were struck seventeen times; miraculously there were no casualties. The official report of the action concluded: "The attempt though unsuccessful, deserves high praise for the coolness and courage shown by all aboard, particularly the conduct of young Powell and Hart."[19]

Since they could not get in and Cervera was not coming out of his own volition, there remained only one possibility; perhaps the army could be induced to force the Spanish fleet out by attacking Santiago from the land side. But getting the army to agree on an objective was almost as difficult as getting Cervera to do battle. Major General William R. Shafter had been given wide latitude by the War Department and since there was no one below the president who could impel the services to act in concert, the wisest thing seemed for Shafter and Sampson privately to conclude a cooperative agreement. Consequently, on 20 June when Shafter and his 16,000-man expeditionary force arrived off Santiago, a war council was held to lay plans. In view of the loose organizational structure, agreement came surprisingly easily. There was only one problem: each commander thought he had agreed to something different. The first move was for the army to land at Daiquirí, eighteen miles east of Santiago. Both services accepted that, but Shafter thought he had clearly stated that, after the landing, his objective would be the city of Santiago; Sampson understood Shafter's objective to be destruction of the batteries blocking entrance to the harbor.

But the first action was to be the landing at Daiquirí, and here Tommy Hart was to get his chance at martial glory. An amphibious assault against a defended coast was a hazardous undertaking and the short time between the commanders' meeting and D-day on 22 June did not provide much opportunity for planning. A naval force was quickly assembled under command of Captain Caspar F. Goodrich in the transport *St. Louis,* a converted passenger liner.

The *Massachusetts* had numerous boats, so it was decided that she should provide the expedition with ten rowboats of various sizes and a steam launch. The question was who to put in charge of the *Massachusetts*'s boats. Her executive officer, Lieutenant Commander Seaton Schroeder, doubtless thinking of the action four days earlier, nominated Midshipman Hart. Her captain, Francis J. Higginson, whom Hart believed did not like him, demurred, but after further consultation reluctantly agreed. Therefore, in the early morning hours of 22 June Tommy Hart found himself in a steam launch bobbing around amidst the assault force and in charge of the largest group of landing craft. The term *landing craft* is used loosely here; what he commanded were rowboats, the smallest capable of carrying thirty and the largest fifty combat-equipped infantrymen.

For the assault to begin at dawn on the twenty-second, Hart had to distribute his boats alongside several transports, including the *St. Louis,* and prepare to load assault troops after dark on the twenty-first. This task was duly accomplished and Hart was in place beside the *St. Louis* when the sun rose and the bombardment of the beachhead began. As he later recalled, "a large expenditure of ammunition ensued" but with little damage done except to trees on the beach, because the Spanish had chosen not to defend Daiquirí. It was just as well for the Americans, since the beach was open and considerable surf was running. Noting this, Hart decided to unload his boats at a small dock that projected out beyond the waves. Though a reasonable idea, this took considerable doing and the soldiers had to jump for handholds when the boats reached the top of the swells. Soon they were all scrambling up the rickety dock and Hart returned to the *St. Louis* for another load.

Other captains made directly for the beach with the result that a number of boats, especially the heavy metal ones from the transports, were stranded on the shingle. Because Hart had the largest, most powerful steam launch, Goodrich ordered him, upon his return to the *St. Louis,* to turn his landing boats over to someone else and go in and salvage as many metal boats as possible. This proved to be extremely difficult. Hart had only five men in the launch, so he had to rely on the soldiers on the beach for assistance in getting the "tin" boats waterborne. The method was to bring the launch to a point just beyond the surf, anchor, then have someone swim ashore with a line attached to a heavy rope. Once the man was ashore, the heavy rope would be pulled in and attached to the stranded boat.

All that sounds relatively simple, but here's what Hart has to say about it:

> Getting through the surf with the line took some doing. I found I had only one man besides myself who was a good enough swimmer for the job. He and I took turns at it and it took seven or eight hours to accomplish the task. We would swim through the surf, get our breath, call for help from the soldiers—and they were quite ready to give it, being bored by sitting in the bush all day long—and they would come out with plenty of manpower. Then they, by main strength, got the boat waterborne whereupon either I or the other swimmer got into her and off we went, the launch getting up her anchor and taking the salvaged boat where she belonged for further service.[20]

Having gotten very little sleep the previous night, Hart found this exertion grueling. By the end of the day he was virtually exhausted, so when he eventually brought his launch alongside the *St. Louis* he found the prospect of negotiating the accommo-

dation ladder almost more than he could handle; in fact he didn't
even have the strength to get off his launch. His men offered to
carry him, a suggestion which he refused. The prospect of that
indignity gave him the motivation to get from the launch to the
ladder "and there I stuck." A marine officer on board sized up
the situation and, without giving Hart the opportunity to refuse,
went down, threw him over his shoulder—all 105 pounds of him—
and carried him aboard.

Thus the army got ashore and thus Tommy Hart got his first
letter of commendation. Captain Goodrich wrote Higginson of
the *Massachusetts* about the "exceptional ability, skill and faith-
fulness" displayed by Midshipman Hart.[21] Goodrich noted specifically the seamanship that Hart had displayed when the launch's
anchor chain parted and she was swept broadside into the surf. At
that point the painter of the boat in tow got wrapped around the
screw of the launch and it looked as though the launch would
capsize with the possible loss of her crew. Yet Hart managed not
only to clear the screw but to bring the launch and the boat safely
out of the surf.

With the army ashore, the misunderstanding between the two
commanders soon became apparent. Instead of making for the
entrance to Santiago Harbor, Shafter drove inland and there was
little that Sampson could do to change the three-hundred-pound
general's mind or course. Nevertheless, it was essential that the
two commanders keep in close touch. For this purpose, the *Vixen,*
a converted yacht capable of 16 knots, was detailed as a dispatch
vessel. To augment her crew Hart was ordered from the *Massachusetts,* probably because of his skill in small-boat handling. It
was another stroke of good fortune. For one thing, at this stage
in the operations the *Vixen* had a far more active role to play than
did the larger ships. For another, her commanding officer, Lieutenant Alexander Sharp, Jr., took a liking to Hart and soon a
relationship, almost filial, developed between them.

Before the war Sharp served as naval aide to the assistant secretary of the navy, Theodore Roosevelt. Roosevelt and his Rough
Riders were with Shafter and this gave Hart an opportunity to
observe the future president at close, sometimes too close, quarters. The *Vixen* picked up the day's dispatches and took them to
Daiquirí or Siboney, then someone had to take them inland to the
army and bring back replies. As chance would have it, there was
only one officer-horseman on board the *Vixen.* Having gained
experience by riding to school in Michigan, Tommy Hart qualified

as a dispatch rider. Often Sharp would order Hart to take a message to Colonel Roosevelt and see if TR could come back to the *Vixen* for a chat. On at least four occasions there was enough of a lull on the battlefield to allow Theodore Roosevelt to accept the invitation. "He would be riding with an aide or two on each side," Hart recalled, "always talking, and I rode on behind. It was very hot in Cuba at that time. Mr. Roosevelt, as the world knows, was one of these men who perspire very freely, and he was not clean at all. In fact, riding behind, I could always smell him."[22]

As soon as Roosevelt arrived aboard he would disappear into the bathroom, which was still equipped as it had been by the yacht's wealthy former owner. Shortly, a pile of dirty clothes would be passed out and into the hands of waiting mess boys who would hustle them below decks for laundering. Then after much steam, soap, and scrubbing a glistening Theodore Roosevelt would appear, dressed in Alexander Sharp's clothes and ready for dinner. The wine stores were also much as the owner had left them, the *Vixen* having been very hastily commissioned. Sharp had the only key and never used it except when Roosevelt was on board, but his visits were deemed occasions worthy of vintage wines. The wine, the friendship, and no doubt the circumstance of sitting off an enemy coast in such palatial surroundings made these meals quite remarkable. "The talk," Hart recalled, was splendid, since "Sharp was a man of the world, the second officer was too," and Theodore Roosevelt was no mean raconteur. After dinner the future president would collect his clean clothes and disappear again into deepest Cuba. All in all these were memorable occasions for a young midshipman.

Soon Roosevelt and the rest of the army were bringing considerable pressure on the defenses of Santiago. Someone had to give and Admiral Cervera was ordered to do the giving. The admiral was distinctly unenthusiastic about his chances, but despite his grim foreboding, he chose 3 July 1898 to sally forth and do battle and possibly, just possibly, escape. Meanwhile, Sampson, in a final effort to reconcile his differences with the army, had sailed eastward in the *New York* to meet with Shafter and explain to him why the navy could not broach the mine-infested entrance to the harbor. With Sampson away, Schley was in tactical command at 9:35 a.m. when the *Infanta Maria Teresa, Vizcaya, Cristóbal Colón, Almirante Oquendo,* and two destroyers appeared in line, steaming out of the harbor. Schley, in the *Brooklyn,* much to his later regret and to the impairment of his reputation, turned east rather than in the direction of the enemy. He later claimed he was taking prudent evasive action, but to some his turn implied panic; whatever the case the *Brooklyn* was late in taking up the chase. All the other major U.S. ships, the *New York, Oregon, Texas, Iowa,* and *Indiana* moved immediately to pursue the fleeing Spaniards; only the *Massachusetts,* which was coaling at Guantánamo, missed the action. The speedy *Vixen* was in the midst of the fray, thus providing Hart with a view he would have been denied had he stayed with the *Massachusetts.* Soon the *Brooklyn* made up lost time and led the American battle line as they fired time after time at the Spanish ships. It was all very exciting as, one by one, the enemy ships either sank or were beached. The *Cristóbal Colón,* the fastest of Cervera's cruisers, was the last to give up. It had been a magnificent battle from the point of view of the Americans; they suffered only one man killed and one wounded, while the Spanish lost their entire fleet, and had 160 men killed and more than 1,800 captured. Although in the opening stages of the war the navy had been outmaneuvered by Cervera, the victory off Santiago swept all criticism from the public press, as editorialists and speakers outdid themselves in heaping praise on the gallant sailors. Only Schley's turn at the opening of the battle marred the surface of naval perfection.

With the victory over the Spanish fleet, the war was all but ended. Hemmed in on land and defeated at sea, the Spaniards had little choice but to surrender and on 16 July that course was chosen by General José Toral. On 10 December 1898 the Treaty of Paris was signed, formally bringing to a close the conflict known in some quarters as the "splendid little war." As a result of that conflict Spain was not only forced out of Cuba, but the United States gained a foothold in the Far East when Spain agreed to cede the Philippines in return for twenty million dollars.

That cession later proved fateful for Hart, but as of 1898 the war fought off Cuba was the most exciting time of his life. Letters of commendation and the notice he attracted among peers and superiors helped to burnish the image he had at the Naval Academy. The experience matured him as well, as was evinced when he returned to Annapolis to take his final examinations. In the final rankings, as of June 1899, with a mark of 809.01 out of a possible 1,000, he was seventh in his class of forty-seven members. His close friend, Harry E. Yarnell, with a mark of 856.64, stood at the top of the class. These final rankings were the ones that would count on the Navy List for assignment and future promotion. The long cruise in foreign waters had incidental benefits. For one thing, there was no place to spend money, so the budding young officer had a chance to catch up on his debts and began his formal naval career with a clean financial slate.

At twenty-one Tommy Hart still looked like an adolescent. The war had matured him, to be sure; however, his scrapbooks from these days contain many pictures of a sky-larking youngster posing for the camera surrounded by young men and a surprising number of young women, obviously having a wonderful time. But, as he later said, this was in many ways a lonely time for him. His salary did not allow many trips home and there was not much reason to go, anyhow. He had lots of childhood friends, but apparently felt little desire to see his father. Tommy had not spent even Christmas at home since he was fifteen. This separation from family left an impression on him that lasted well past his adolescence. One does not have to be a psychologist to know that all people have strong reactions to their parents. Tommy's problem was that he had no real mother first to love and then to break away from. His father was surely a figure of authority when he was present, but he was not present often. John Hart apparently wavered between punishing and indulging his son; he did very little counseling or advising in anything other than cursory, general terms. Psychologists tend to agree that if a boy has limited contact with his mother, and Tommy had virtually none, he will have an idealized concept of mothers and their role.[23] At the same time, men look for women like their mothers, or in Tommy's case, like he imagined his mother to be. As for the influence of his father, Tommy would naturally strive to emulate him to some degree and if possible to surpass him. Another psychological reaction about which we can safely hypothesize is that Hart would put great stress on the importance of family life and try to create for himself and for his own family what he had not had as a child.

So, as Tommy Hart approached maturity, he was deprived and seeking in one sense and blessed and satisfied in another. The academy and his profession had become a substitute for some of the things he had never had. After a rather rocky start, he had done well at Annapolis; his ability and courage had been tested in the face of battle. How far would he go, and how he would get there remained to be seen.

2

TOMMY HART'S SECOND WAR

For the next twenty years Hart was occupied in a variety of activities. He started his professional career, got married, and served in another war. He also set the pattern, at least in part, for the rest of his life. In dealing with this formative period, it is instructive to examine some fundamental questions. What were the influences and experiences that shaped Thomas Hart into a mature naval officer? How did he determine his career goals? Who was his model? How did he change from a rather callow youth of twenty-two into a serious, exemplary, professional of forty-two?

The beginning of the twentieth century found Tommy Hart at sea on a nineteenth-century ship whose name was synonymous with glory in a distant war. The wooden-hulled, steam-powered, but square-rigged sloop *Hartford*, Admiral David G. Farragut's flagship in the Battle of New Orleans (1862), was to be his home for the next three years. At this point the *Hartford* had been relegated to duty as a training ship, so Hart and the other young officers assigned to her worried about being diverted from the mainstream of naval professionalism. What was there to learn, they asked, in a Civil War relic? For Hart the answer was not quite as important as for others—he was having fun. At Annapolis he had acquired a love for distant places, and the *Hartford* offered the opportunity for travel to the Caribbean, Atlantic islands, and even some European ports, as well as for the practice of another of his enthusiasms, seamanship. Apparently he not only liked shiphandling, he was good at it. Almost all his fitness reports during this tour were in the excellent range.[1]

It was also during this period that Tommy was given a brief assignment that allowed him to demonstrate what he had learned about handling men. A group of sailors being mustered out of the navy needed to be returned from Norfolk to San Francisco, where they had enlisted.[2] The journey was to be made by rail, which meant that the accompanying officer would have to spend about a week supervising two carloads of rough, tough sailors, over whom the U.S. Navy's authority was about to expire. Naturally, this left plenty of time for trouble, particularly since the train made numerous stops, thus providing ample opportunity for obtaining alcoholic beverages, getting into fights, missing departures, and so on. Tommy Hart, assisted by a crusty old chief, was put in charge of the expedition. By this time Tommy had put on a little weight—he weighed approximately 120 pounds; he still stood, even when ramrod straight, less than six feet, and even though his boyish face was showing signs of the handsomeness that soon came, he still looked very young. What he lacked in age he tried to make up in bearing, and his voice, though seldom raised, had a penetrating quality that commanded attention. Still, he later admitted that the task ahead looked formidable.

When the group fell in on the train platform, Tommy outlined the journey to be made and a few simple rules about behavior, both on and off the train. Once they left the station, it quickly became apparent that many of the men did not have to get off the train if they wanted to drink. What they had not already ingested they were carrying in their seabags. Tommy had nothing against drinking, indeed he enjoyed a drink himself; furthermore, he rather expected seamen to drink, especially on a long trip such as this. What he could not accept was the rowdiness that he knew would erupt if stern action were not taken quickly to control the more boisterous members of the party. So, after they had been on their way for a few hours, he and the chief took a tour through the cars occupied by their charges. In the first car, several men had clearly had too much. Hart spoke to one who promptly calmed down, but another miscreant heard Tommy out and then ostentatiously took a long drag from his bottle. Swift action was called for, as all eyes were now on the slim ensign. Tommy reached past the man, grabbed his bottle, and threw it out the open window. The sailor uttered an oath and started to rise from his seat. At that point the chief's hairy fist passed over Tommy's shoulder and landed on the man's jaw. Dazed, the sailor sat back, and then started to rise again. This time Tommy unloaded on him with all he had. It was enough, not only for that sailor; word quickly passed that this officer was not to be trifled with. Consequently, the rest of the trip went smoothly and Tommy chalked up a successful land voyage.

When his tour in the *Hartford* was over, he learned that he was to be assigned duty at his alma mater. In 1902 the Naval Academy was looking for officers to help handle the rapidly expanding battalion of midshipmen, as the student body was designated in July 1902. Since on three occasions Lieutenant, Junior Grade, Hart had taken a drill team from the *Hartford* to Madison Square Garden for the military tournament, he seemed a natural choice for the post of infantry drill instructor. Captain Willard H. Brownson, the recently selected superintendent, spotted Hart's name on a list of officers available for duty. Despite his experience with Hart

Thomas C. Hart, officer of the deck, aboard the *Hartford* in 1900. Courtesy of Mrs. T. C. Hart

when the latter was a cadet, Brownson wrote the Navy Department that he would like to have Hart on the academy's faculty.[3]

Had Brownson closely observed the detail of sailors Hart took to the inauguration of President William McKinley in March 1901, he might have changed his mind. To keep his men dry outside during the long festivities in the rain, Hart ordered them to don rain gear under their uniforms. To keep them warm inside, he provided a considerable amount of rum. The sailors stayed dry and, by his own account, suspiciously warm.

But others did not notice, so Tommy Hart returned to Annapolis in the fall of 1902 with a fitness report that described him as "eminently fitted" for independent, important, and hazardous duties. Drilling midshipmen was hardly hazardous, but it was important and extremely taxing. With the decision to increase the size of the U.S. Navy, which Congress had made in the 1890s and which Theodore Roosevelt, who became president in 1901, was enthusiastically carrying out, came the need for more officers. To provide them, the academy's student body was to be doubled, from some four hundred to approximately eight hundred, and the bigger classes were to be admitted immediately, even before adequate quarters were available. This meant that Hart's duties, which included policing the corridors of the dormitories and the temporary structures where the midshipmen were housed, increased proportionately. The Navy Department underestimated the need for more officers to instruct the new classes, so Hart often found himself overworked. When the class of 1908 arrived in the summer of 1904, for instance, there was only one officer to instruct more than 275 midshipmen on shipboard and one to instruct them on shore. The man on shore was Lieutenant Hart. At the end of two months he had lost twelve pounds as well as his voice.[4]

Yet somehow he also found time to teach a class in ordnance and gunnery. In fact, he became so interested in the subject that he agreed to write a textbook on the subject in company with the department head, Commander William F. Fullam.[5] This book, unimaginatively titled *Ordnance and Gunnery*, was published in 1903 and was in use for many years. Hart also managed a full social life. He found he enjoyed dancing and squiring young ladies around the academy grounds. One young girl especially caught his eye. She was dancing at the time and the two long braids that hung down her back indicated that she had not yet reached maturity. But there was something special about Caroline Brownson, the superintendent's daughter, and Tommy Hart marked her down as someone he wanted to get to know. They talked together from time to time, but a seven-year gap in age was too much to span, at least at this time. Anyhow, there were lots of other girls, as his photo albums attest. The older he got the more handsome he became, and his talent on the dance floor made him eagerly sought after.

All in all it was an instructive time for Hart to be at the academy. Brownson was an exemplary officer, noted for his executive ability and leadership qualities. He was demanding, as will be recalled from Hart's days when Brownson was commandant of cadets, but he was fair. His appearance was always meticulously proper and his manner, though it might have struck some as overly aloof and aristocratic, was undeniably professional. Tough but fair would be a fitting characterization. If a young officer were looking for the epitome of a successful naval officer, Brownson would certainly do. The building going on at the academy was impressive as well. New buildings, like the chapel, the imposing superintendent's residence, Bancroft Hall, Mahan Hall, the officers' club, were springing up like mushrooms after a rain, in accordance with Ernest Flagg's ambitious plan.[6] If one wondered about the navy's dynamism, the academy between 1902 and 1904 was a good place to look for inspiration.

Hart apparently caught the mood of the place as well as the cut of Captain Brownson's jib; he was inspired by one and impressed by the other. Actually, Tommy was beginning to come of age. He saw plenty of future in this new navy; certainly it would provide him with a living better than those of his father and his relatives in either Michigan or Maine. Perhaps for this reason, or perhaps because it took a second dose of the academy really to sober him, Tommy began to become quite "military"; or maybe this was just his first chance to view the navy and its midshipmen objectively.

Hart began to look for ways to give his charges a more "military appearance." One improvement, he wrote in a memorandum, would be "to make the collars higher, according to the length of the individual's neck, coming close up under the chin . . ." The plebes, he continued, "generally get their first collars much too large, giving them an ungainly appearance, as young men of that age are inclined to have long thin necks which appear at their worst in loose low collars." He also wanted their uniforms to be better tailored, because he believed that pride and performance would be more likely in a midshipman who looked sharp.[7]

Although Brownson liked Hart well enough to object when his reassignment was being considered, he did not give him exceptionally high fitness reports. It is easy to imagine that the superintendent was a hard grader, so perhaps the fact that he gave Hart many "very good," rather than "excellent," evaluations should not be taken too seriously. On the other hand, as we shall see, Brownson had some reservations about Hart, at least for some assignments.

When he had been at the academy almost two years an emergency arose which required Hart's detachment for service in the new battleship *Missouri*. One of her gun turrets had exploded, killing two officers; Hart was sent as one of the replacements, a duty that, under the circumstances, could hardly be approached optimistically. Yet working with modern gunnery in a practical way allowed him to apply what he had written in his textbook. This was the beginning of his specialization in ordnance, an area in which, in one way or another, he spent much of his career. But hardly had he settled in the *Missouri* when another emergency, this one mingled with a measure of luck—a factor Hart came to feel was intimately involved in his career—called for his detachment elsewhere. The destroyer *Lawrence* needed a new skipper, and on very short notice.

So, in December 1905 at age twenty-eight he got his first command. The *Lawrence* was small and by the standards of the day quite fast. Furthermore, instead of heavy guns, her primary armament was torpedoes. How ideal for a man who enjoyed seamanship and working with any type of complicated ordnance. Steaming hither and yon over the sea and doing it right gave him a sense of independence and of something else to which he always gave considerable emphasis—fun. He later contended that this command did more to mature him than anything since the Spanish-American War.[8] In 1906 Lieutenant Commander E. A. Anderson, commander of his destroyer flotilla, wrote that Hart had brought the *Lawrence*'s torpedoes "to a very high state of efficiency" and had achieved a perfect score in autumn torpedo practice; overall, his performance was rated excellent.

Shortly after this report was made, there occurred something that on the surface, at least, appeared far from lucky. On 4 March 1907, the commander in chief of the Atlantic Fleet, Rear Admiral Robley "Fighting Bob" Evans, saw Hart lose his temper when addressing Lieutenant Commander Anderson. Hart did not approve of the way Anderson was handling the destroyers and after what he considered a display of bungled orders, he took it upon himself to tell Anderson what he thought. Admiral Evans investigated the incident and on 24 March 1907 recommended that Hart be removed from command of the *Lawrence* and a letter of admonition entered in his record. Hart accepted this judgment at the time although he later protested to Admiral Evans that his conduct, though disrespectful, was understandable and even proper under the circumstances. From this distance of time it is not possible to judge fairly Hart's contention, or even all the details. What we do know is that by 1909 Evans had changed his mind, or at least had come to see the merit in Hart's contention, and requested that his letter of admonition be removed from Hart's service record.[9]

In view of Hart's assignment after leaving the *Lawrence*, it is obvious that his conduct had not earned him universal condemnation. There was a vacant billet, previously filled by a rear admiral, at the Bureau of Ordnance. Since they wanted a young officer with experience and promise as a replacement, the job went to Lieutenant Hart. This was a real feather in his cap and, as he later admitted, it got his "head up" above his peers.[10] Much experimentation and modernization was going on in the bureau at this time, so Hart's practical experience was quickly applied. He liked the work and soon convinced his superiors they had made a good choice. Rear Admiral Newton E. Mason, chief of bureau, found him "especially loyal and subordinate"—so Hart *was* learning—as well as "extremely conscientious and painstaking" in the performance of his duty. Working with explosives, shells as well as torpedoes, was demanding, but Hart, who had always done well in engineering subjects and physics, excelled. It looked as though, with enough luck, good could come even out of adversity.

During this tour in Washington, two worlds were to meet. Rear Admiral Brownson, who had served as commander of the Asiatic Fleet after leaving the Naval Academy, had been selected as chief of the Bureau of Navigation, one of the most prestigious billets in the U.S. Navy. This meant that the Brownson family would be living in Washington, and the admiral rented a large, gracious house at 1736 M Street. To this house came the cream of Washington society. After all, Brownson was a cousin of William Howard Taft, President Theodore Roosevelt's secretary of war, as well as an intimate of such luminaries as Oliver Wendell Holmes, millionaire John R. McLean, and many of those influential Washington people known as "cave dwellers." Furthermore, he knew well all the military figures of the day, both in this country and abroad. This wide range of friends guaranteed that his home would be a busy, gay place, a place where his daughter Caroline, now twenty-three, could savor a Washington season in the company of the most prominent members of the legislative, executive, judiciary, and social branches of government, for then, as now, there were really four branches. For her it was a "kaleidoscope of luncheons, teas, receptions, dinners, and balls."[11] There were Sunday luncheons at expansive estates on the outskirts of town, receptions at the embassies, at Rauchers, Demonets, and the new Willard Hotel, theater parties at the National, the Poli, or the Belasco, cruises on the Chesapeake Bay in official yachts, hunts with the Chevy Chase hounds followed by lavish entertainments at country estates.

Thomas Hart brought to this bubbling world of Washington an entirely different background from that of Caroline Brownson, yet he was as welcome in it as she; he was thirty and a bachelor. Unattached males, especially males in uniform, were in great demand; in fact, he was sometimes called upon to be an aide at White House parties. During the round of festivities in the fall of 1908 he spotted the girl who had caught his attention when he saw her dancing with a midshipman in Annapolis. Now, however, she had put up her hair; without hesitation he went after her. As he later admitted, it was pretty difficult, holding down a responsible position and courting at the same time. Often it meant dancing till dawn and reporting for duty with very little sleep; as he later said, "I don't see how I lived."

Not only did he live, he prospered. He was successful in the bureau, and there is no question that Caroline responded to the charms of the trim, handsome, mature officer. The difficulty was with her father. Some of the reasons for Brownson's hesitance can only be guessed. Caroline, his youngest child, had become something of a playmate for the admiral; he could count on her for rides through Rock Creek Park, fishing expeditions in Canada, and even hunting trips. He may also have questioned the age difference between the two, and it is entirely possible that he did not consider Hart good enough for his daughter.

The admiral would not have had to be a snob to recognize that this young naval officer was not going to be able to maintain his daughter in the style to which she was accustomed. In addition to his naval pay, the Brownson family had a considerable fortune, as the way they lived implied. Hart had nothing, nor was there money or position in his background. There can be little question that the aristocratic Brownson put great stock in social amenities. It also will be recalled that Brownson did not give Hart the highest possible fitness reports when the lieutenant taught at the academy and he might even have remembered when Naval Cadet Hart was a member of the hell-raising "Coxey's Army." And navy channels had probably carried to Brownson's ears word of the recent insubordination by the commanding officer of the *Lawrence.*

On that issue there was a rather ironic twist. Brownson, the epitome of naval propriety, was himself involved that very fall in a case wherein the president of the United States accused him of disloyal conduct. The story need only be sketched.[12] President Roosevelt had let it be known that he intended to put medical officers in command of naval hospital ships. Brownson protested directly and indirectly that this was illegal, unwise, and prejudicial to the best interests of the service. What did doctors know about ships or, for that matter, about anything to do with the navy other than the insides of sailors? When Roosevelt persisted and made it clear that he was going to put his wishes in the form of an order, Brownson requested relief from the bureau. Roosevelt wrote a long official letter in which he said he considered this conduct childish, something done out of pique, and a "gross impropriety." Brownson said nothing in public. He considered his position regarding the medical officers the only one he could take with honor. As far as TR's outburst was concerned, the admiral confided to his diary: "I could not bandy words with the President." Had he, he would have reminded the president that "he had no right to administer a public reprimand to me except by sentence of a Court Martial." In Brownson's mind, and clearly that was the only thing that mattered to him, "My action in resigning . . . was due entirely to a sense of duty to the service to which I had been so devoted for forty-six years." The case, which got considerable public attention, was a striking example of insubordination based on principle. It made Hart's incident pale by comparison; that must have been clear to both the admiral and the lieutenant. But what self-sacrifice it must have been by the father of the woman he loved.

After his retirement the Brownsons left Washington in the spring of 1908, but they returned in the fall. Out of the navy, the admiral had time to pursue his other interests, such as hunting, fishing, shooting, and serving on a variety of boards both public and private. Tommy Hart again took up his own chase. The admiral remained dubious about the relationship, but by the spring of 1909 he could see that further protests were useless. In March, as Hart was preparing to go back to sea, Brownson relented and the engagement was announced.

Firmly established now as an ordnance specialist, Hart was assigned as a gunnery officer in the battleship *Virginia*. The commanding officer of the ship was his old mentor from Spanish-American War days, Alex Sharp, and the two took up their association where it had left off. As gunnery officer, Hart was charged with preparing the gun crews for the competitions, which were extremely heated, between the various battleships. His primary competitor was his classmate Luther M. Overstreet. For the year 1909 Overstreet's ship came in first and Hart's second, but Sharp described Hart as a "fine" even "splendid" officer. In recognition of these qualities Hart was promoted to lieutenant commander in August and a few months later he and Overstreet were reassigned from their old ships and ordered to two of the first U.S. dreadnoughts, the *North Dakota* for Hart and the *Delaware* for Overstreet. Hart continued to come in second, but his new commanding officer shared Sharp's high opinion of him, remarking specifically about his "great zeal" in working up the new ship's guns.

In March 1910 Hart returned to Washington for a day that he ever after considered the luckiest in his life. On the 30th of March, at the Brownsons' sizable new home, Caroline Robinson Brownson was married to Thomas Charles Hart by Chaplain H.D. Clark, who was Naval Academy chaplain during Brownson's and Hart's duty at Annapolis. The best man was Lieutenant Commander Leigh C. Palmer (class of 1896), and the groomsmen were Lieutenant Hugo W. Osterhaus (class of 1900), Lieutenant Commander Robert "Jock" Crank (class of 1892), and Lieutenant Commander Luther Overstreet (class of 1897) of battleship gunnery competition. It was a simple, but elegant, noon affair with some one hundred guests present. Navy predominated, but enough government officials and "cave dwellers" were sprinkled in to make it quite "social."[13]

The bride, who wore a gown of white satin trimmed with old lace, deserves our careful attention. Caroline Hart was five feet six and one-half inches tall, very slender, and portraits reveal dark brown eyes and an abundance of brown hair. She was not beautiful but was quite striking in the strength and character she exuded. Although not vivacious, neither was she shy, perhaps "reserved" would be a better word. In some ways she was the typical, upper-class, well-mannered, protected lady of the day. Her father did

Lieutenant Commander Thomas C. Hart, photographed, at the request of his future mother-in-law, before his marriage to Caroline Brownson in 1910. Courtesy of Mrs. T. C. Hart

not believe in formal higher education for women but she had the gentlewoman's knowledge of music, foreign languages, literature and, departing from the norm, history. She was a good dancer, a good horsewoman, a fair ice skater, and for that era, played a good game of tennis; the tennis champion, Bill Larned, was one of her best friends. Her familiarity with sports such as salmon-fishing was the result of her father's interest in the vigorous life. To say that she was better-rounded than the typical lady would be no exaggeration, nor would it be stretching the point to suggest that she was a person of exceptional strength, intelligence, and determination. She was a distinct asset as a naval wife. Caroline Hart knew the territory, so to speak, and was just the person to polish off any rough edges that might remain on her husband's exterior. There would seem to be little question that she and Tommy were beginning a marriage, love affair, and partnership in which they were willing to invest everything they had.

In Tommy's case there was not much other than his career and himself that he could contribute to the bargain, but of himself he was willing to invest without measure. The career, insofar as possible, would stay at the office and take care of itself. What Tommy was looking for, and found in Caroline, was a wife who would devote herself fully to him, who would provide stability and guidance to their children when they came, who would maintain a gracious home and haven to which he could return, who could hold her own with him in outdoor activities and at dinner parties, who had grace and style. In Caroline he had found someone who came closer to that ideal than he could really know in 1910. He was, as he later said so often, truly lucky in his choice of a mate.

While admitting the significant role that luck or fate played in the union, it is intriguing to speculate on what attracted Tommy to Caroline. Leaving aside all the important, but in the final analysis, superficial things like physical beauty, one comes down to several speculative, but rather safe factors that probably explain why he was drawn to her. For one thing, winning her must have seemed quite a challenge. As already mentioned, Caroline's world was far different from Tommy's and, at least in her father's view, which he made rather generally known, Hart was marrying out of his class. That naturally posed another challenge, that of proving her father wrong, at least regarding his promise within his chosen profession. Another factor influencing his attraction to Caroline must have been his respect for her good sense and stability. A man capable of violent outbursts of temper, or at least of invective, he generally held himself in rigid self-control. He wanted a woman with self-control and strength because he knew he would not be able to continue to love someone he could walk over. But in fact he had no interest in walking over her—he wanted an ideal love in which competition did not play a role. And, while everyone to a greater or lesser degree wants ideal love, Tommy was absolutely determined to be successful in his quest. It was the one big thing missing in his life and, when he thought back, he realized that it had always been missing. In Caroline he saw a chance to have the things he had never really had: a home, a family, and the warm, emotional glow that comes from knowing that you have created something permanent in the midst of a changing world. Caroline looked to Tommy like his kind of fellow architect.

After a short honeymoon at The Homestead in Hot Springs, Virginia, it was back to sea for the bridegroom. It may not have been luck but it was surely welcome when the chance arose to cut short his cruise. The navy was establishing a torpedo factory at what had been a small experimental plant in Newport, Rhode Island. Harry Yarnell, whom Hart highly esteemed, had done the initial work at Newport and had been asked to pick his successor. Apparently the regard was mutual, for Yarnell picked Hart to replace him as head of the Division of Maintenance and Repair. This meant returning to shore a year early, picking up where Yarnell left off; in short, completing and running an industrial plant charged with turning out and maintaining an extremely complex product. Despite the potential problems, Hart jumped at the chance.

Not only was it an opportunity to be with Caroline, it also was a challenge. Yarnell had done much toward developing the actual plant; production was going to be up to Hart. If dealing with new, challenging situations was what the navy was about, then it surely was good experience which Hart later said added a significant dimension to his professional development. For one thing, there was the torpedo itself—probably the most complicated weapon of the day. To produce it required precision of a high order even though the U.S. Navy was building the British-designed Whitehead torpedo. Hence Hart's engineers started with British specifications and drawings and added modifications to suit American requirements.

Early in 1911 orders were received for ninety-five torpedoes, twenty Mark V, Model 3s, and seventy-five Mark V, Model 5s.[14] It took until September to complete the first part of the order because the article being manufactured was novel. When they had finished, however, they had produced a weapon equal to or better and cheaper than any that could be bought elsewhere. Success only brought more orders; it was estimated that the workload increased almost 60 per cent over that of 1910.

Within one year after Hart arrived, most of the problems of propulsion and steering had been worked out; he next turned his attention to other matters. Warhead design, for instance. That required even more specialized skills with plenty of room for experimentation; this meant improvisation and it was here that

Hart excelled. There were fuses to compare, different metals to test, and even new designs to consider, while at the same time completing other necessary items like the 105,000 primers manufactured in 1912. One thing he worked on was designing a cutting device to be attached to warheads so that they could slice through submarine nets. And, of course, there was always the matter of explosives.

And, as if dealing with a very persnickety weapon were not enough, there were more mundane, but equally sensitive, aspects to the job. The factory was quite a large operation; in 1913 the total value of its manufactures was $973,491. To produce torpedoes and other items successfully, the station had to build up a civilian labor force. Relations between the navy and various groups of skilled workers, most particularly the Machinists' Union, were strained in the early decades of the century. At Newport, as at other naval manufacturing plants, profit was not involved, but great care was expended to ensure that costs were kept in line with comparable civilian operations. Hart was also supposed to reduce expenditures where possible, and he did. His plant reduced by 20 per cent the labor costs related to primer production. The obvious ways to accomplish such savings were to cut the labor force, keep wages down, or adopt the controversial Taylor system of scientific management. That system, which relied heavily on the time and motion concept complete with involved record-keeping, particularly aroused the ire of the labor unions, which saw it as "an acutely dangerous form of exploitation, on the grounds that it meant far more work at a lower unit rate of pay."[15] Not surprisingly, men like Hart found those very features appealing. The desire to keep costs down while pushing efficiency up naturally led to conflict between the Machinists' Union, which was interested in higher wages and more benefits, and the station's management, most notably Hart, who favored a Taylor-type approach. By December 1913 the conflict had reached crisis proportions, so Hart was ordered to temporary duty in Washington to deal with employee grievances at Newport.

The issue was handled at the Navy Department where Hart had his first contact with Franklin D. Roosevelt, serving at this time as assistant secretary of the navy. Roosevelt, appointed by President Woodrow Wilson, took a decidedly different view of unions from that of Hart. As one of his biographers has noted, dealing with the civilian workers in the navy's shore establishments "taught him relatively early in his political career the knack of getting along with the leaders of labor, and making himself popular with the rank and file."[16] Before very long Roosevelt had "learned to speak the language of the labor leaders, and mastered the sometimes intricate task of manipulating the labor vote." Tommy knew how to speak the language of labor, he had grown up around manual laborers, but his impression at this time was that the unions wanted their members to do less for more, an attitude with which he had little sympathy. He believed in an honest day's work for an honest day's pay—for himself or for anybody else; government workers were already being paid wages equal to or better than their counterparts who worked for civilian plants and, anyhow, he cared little what the union members thought of the navy or how they voted. His view seems a reasonable one, although it must be admitted that he was not inclined to be pro-union no matter what the circumstances, nor was he likely to be sensitive to the politician's approach since he had no interest in "manipulating the labor vote." Whatever the merits of the case, Hart apparently was ordered to be more conciliatory and, of course, he complied. But his manner must have indicated something short of total agreement or perhaps a hint of his real feelings about "political" administrators; in his service record was a note from Secretary of the Navy Josephus Daniels: "Do not assign Lt. Commander Hart at the Newport Torpedo Works or to service at Newport."[17] The secretary must have been referring to future assignments, for no move was made to replace him at that time.

In all probability that was because it could so easily be seen that Hart, despite his problems with some of his labor force, was making a significant contribution to the navy. Moreover, his immediate supervisors may have been aware that his experience at the torpedo station was making a significant contribution to Tommy's maturation. An important factor in any officer's success pattern is his ability as a manager, not only of such inanimate objects as ships, but also of men. It did not take great acuity to recognize that Tommy had the talent for that role; indeed the choice of him for the billet at Newport indicates that someone had sensed it quite early. Success in high command, or control over any large organization, is two parts management and one part charismatic leadership. Tommy was getting the management experience early and any charisma he lacked he would make up for in drive.

With the new year, Hart decided to undertake an important new enterprise: keeping a daily diary. In his second sentence he admits that he does not exactly understand why he is embarking on this course. He goes on to say, however, that he is sorry he had not done so earlier, which seemed as good a reason as any for starting when he did. After this speculation, he summarizes his life between the ages of sixteen and thirty-six. He says that the great turning point in his life was "blundering" into and through the academy. That started him on a better career than he would otherwise have had, but most importantly it brought him into contact with Caroline Brownson. Those two things, his career and his marriage, plus the birth of his two children, Isabella and Roswell, he sees as the only really important events of the previous twenty years. He doubts that anything correspondingly important will ever happen again. Still, "granting a continuance of health, I'm sure my present happy life will last and with the same hard work and luck, I expect a continuance of success in my profession—which thus far, I think has been at least average." Little did he know that he was starting a writing project that ultimately filled twenty-one volumes.

From 1 January 1914 on, his diary becomes a valuable part of what we know about his life and work. Most of the entries are not more than five or ten sentences; however, they give a distinct feeling for the man, because he records his reactions to many people and events. For instance, in his entry for 14 January 1914 he says that his sentiments are with the working man, but that he gets tired of the "constant search for benefits." On 15 February he refers to the administration in Washington as "Government by Demagogues," and on 28 March comments that he is "totally out of sympathy with the administration's business methods" and opines that it grows more "socialistic every day." On 22 June 1914, in discussing the ban on drinking that had just been forced on the navy by Josephus Daniels, he refers to the secretary as a "pot house politician from North Carolina." Interesting, too, are the insights into Hart's own personality. He frequently talks about his work, as on 3 April of the same year when he writes that he has spent the entire day on the range "watching five new torpedoes show how many different . . . ways there are of making bad runs." Other comments reveal him as a devoted family man who spends hours playing with his children, worrying about their illnesses, and agonizing over their behavior. One of the most frequently recurring strains in the diary is his idealization of Caroline. He constantly and lovingly praises her strengths, her numerous talents, and her capacity for dealing with domestic traumas. Never, in his view, does Caroline do anything wrong and seldom does she fall short of perfection. Simple things, like organizing birthday parties and handling Christmas festivities, bring forth paeans of praise; complex affairs, like childbearing, overtaxed his supply of laudatory phrases. The diary makes it abundantly clear that Caroline was all a woman could or should be and Tommy loved her without reservation. Any suspicion that he wrote these things so that she could read them is dispelled by the fact that she was not allowed to read the diary during his lifetime.

By the summer of 1914 Hart had been at the torpedo station for three years, so he knew that the happy period with his family would soon come to an end. They had been interesting, grueling, formative years. The work was not really naval, except that the plant was producing a naval weapon. That meant that he gained intimate knowledge of torpedoes and learned as well some other valuable lessons, including something about politics and politicians. On 4 September, as he prepared to move on to his next assignment, he admitted to being sorry to leave a place that was to some extent "my own creation" but he was leaving with pride in the fact that he had "delivered the goods." Although he requested another destroyer, he was sent as executive officer in the battleship *Minnesota*. This was not a command, but he could take some satisfaction in being the youngest executive officer in a "first-rate ship in the Navy." Revolution was raging in Mexico and almost immediately the *Minnesota* was ordered to Veracruz, where President Wilson had sent a force ashore to seize that vital customs port.

During his entire term in office, the president's foreign-policy concerns had been dominated by the Mexican Revolution. He wanted the bloody revolution to end, but more than that he wanted, as he said, to "teach the Mexicans to elect good governments." Not surprisingly, the government of General Victoriano Huerta resented Wilson's interference in Mexican affairs, thus inducing the U.S. president to throw his support behind Venustiano Carranza, who, with Pancho Villa, was in open revolt against Huerta. The whole situation reached a fever pitch in April 1914 when, after a confused embroglio involving the Mexican seizure of some American sailors, President Wilson decided to intervene directly by seizing Veracruz, thus denying the Huerta government the customs revenues that normally flowed through that major Caribbean port. Seizing Veracruz turned out to be another of Wilson's well-intentioned, though misguided, attempts to influence events south of the border.[18] When the Huerta government began—as anticipated—to topple, several competing factions arose to share the spoils and contend for power with Carranza. In short, Wilson had succeeded in making the revolutionary situation more, rather than less, confused.

For the American naval and military forces in Mexico the situation quickly deteriorated into a boring routine. Although the initial landing had been contested, once the American presence had been established neither of the contending factions in the revolution had the time or the energy to resist the "gringos." Action for the *Minnesota* therefore was minimal and for most of the crew there was not even much liberty ashore. But since Hart had the additional duty and title of chief of staff of Landing Force, U.S. Navy in Mexican Waters, he got ample opportunity to tour the U.S. shore establishments. What he saw did not impress him

Thomas C. Hart as chief of staff, Landing Force, U.S. Navy in Mexican Waters. Courtesy of Mrs. T. C. Hart

very much; the army and the marines seemed apathetic and unhappy, consequently they were "drinking a lot and generally going
to pot."

At first, Major General Frederick Funston, the field commander, impressed Hart as "quite a man from a business standpoint" but, after observing him during some evening drinking
bouts, Hart determined that the general did not have "the social
graces" that his position demanded.[19] Several weeks later Hart
came face to face with the general's drinking problem when, accompanied by a lady, he walked over to Funston's table during a
dance. Funston was so drunk that he had "to use both hands and
his teeth" to stagger to his feet. Then the general began what Hart
called a "maudlin conversation" and was in such a state "that there
was nothing to do but turn my back. I went straight for his Chief
of Staff with blood in my eye and said 'This is no place for your
General and he has got to get into his quarters as soon as it can
be done.'" While Hart tried to keep the curious away, the chief
of staff led the general away without too many people noticing.
It was not that Tommy was a prude, rather his sense of propriety
was offended by the sight of a senior officer demeaning himself
in public. A lot of the officers attending the function were far
senior to Lieutenant Commander Hart and they, apparently, were
not offended enough to take such peremptory action but, as it
later became increasingly clear, when setting his course, Tommy
often paid little attention to what others did. As to Funston personally, Hart's judgment was that "it all goes to prove that a man
who was pretty good at bush-whacking war-fare among Dagos and
who was above all an excellent press agent for himself doesn't
necessarily make a good General to represent us under such circumstances." It made Tommy mad and although he was aware that
letting people know how he felt would not make him popular,
particularly with the army, he thought he was right and, as he told
Caroline, "on the whole I don't think it will hurt me."

Tommy was far more impressed with his own commanding officer, Captain Roy Simpson, whom he considered "one of the
Navy's best." "He is an excellent seaman," Hart wrote, and that
is a quality he always looked for in a superior. As a leader of men,
Simpson was "a sympathetic but firm disciplinarian." That, too,
Tommy admired. Above all he was "a splendid gentleman" and
that put him at the top of Tommy's list as well as in marked contrast
to General Funston. But studying Simpson, fishing, and going on
shore occasionally was hardly enough to keep Hart satisfactorily

occupied. His frequent letters home make it obvious that he was bored and more than a bit lonely. He missed the children, whom he referred to as either "the livestock" or by their pet name "the Dee Dees," and most definitely he missed Caroline.

There often was not even much to say about the war; his letters on 27 November and 5 December, however, were exceptions. He had commented before about the Mexicans, for whom he had very little respect. In these letters, though, he gave a full picture of Veracruz, lapped by the effects of the revolution. The scenes in the city were to him something like a burlesque on the Latin-American military. With the *Minnesota* at anchor within a hundred yards of the principal pier for several days, Tommy had a seat in the dress circle. The pier swarmed with soldiers and their camp followers. The latter, he explained, among their other duties served as the quartermaster corps for the army. Each *soldadera* got a certain portion of the pay each month—when there was pay— to use for supplies and provisions in the barracks or in the field. The soldier took the rest of the money, drank it up, "beats the lady if he feels like it and all hands are happy." There were men and boys, women and girls, and swarms of horses, none of which were more than skin and bone—a fact that, as a horse lover, Tommy was quick to notice. Uniforms were chosen to suit the whim of the wearer with little uniformity, discounting the fact that all were dirty, wrinkled, and torn. In aggregate, the group presented a distinctly ragtag appearance. Of discipline there was little, of alcohol there was a sufficiency, of organization there was none. The sailors in the "Minnie" watched with ill-disguised humor, for instance, as the Mexican officers loaded, unloaded, and then loaded again two decrepit steamers, all, as Tommy wrote, "in the way of making up their minds."

Amazingly, there seemed to be relatively little trouble between the Mexican soldiers and the people of Veracruz, perhaps because the soldiers were too busy fighting among themselves. The revolutionary leader, General Carranza, "El Jefe," along with the leader of his army, General Alvaro Obregón, and his entire cabinet had arrived in town the day before Tommy wrote the above description. Word had it that before leaving Mexico City they had stripped the place pretty well clean, at least "we see train loads of automobiles (a particularly favorite variety of loot) and goods coming in." The money from Mexico City's banks was circulating freely around Veracruz except that which was being prepared for shipment to Paris and other points east. At a banquet held in his honor, Carranza was reported to have heartily applauded a speech in which it was proposed to rob and kill all foreigners. To Tommy this seemed hardly appropriate, since all the foreign consuls were present at the banquet, or likely, since Carranza did not need a war going on inside Veracruz when he still had so many enemies outside. In any case, it made for interesting speculation and fascinating viewing.

Several weeks later a chance came to get closer to the stage and he duly reported what he saw thereon to Caroline. The admiral allowed him an afternoon's shore leave and, even though he knew the town would be almost dead in the afternoon, Tommy leapt at the chance. What he found was a *very* dirty, very sleepy community absolutely crawling with Mexican soldiers. They were not acting like soldiers and most of them looked exactly like what they were—farmers carrying guns. They had set up housekeeping under the broad eaves of the warehouses along the waterfront. It was rudimentary housekeeping, to be sure: "no bedding—a serape [blanket] or two to break the wind—for it doesn't occur to them to put up screens to hide their *very* domestic and private affairs— one or two battered cooking utensils and that's about all." Most of the shops were shuttered because the merchants did not care to do business with the rabble, not because of their appearance or personal habits, but because of their method of payment. The money from Mexico City had apparently run out because now the army had set up a printing press which was turning out bills as the need arose. Obviously this "currency" had no present or future value, but it took real courage for a shopkeeper to tell that to a Mexican soldier.

Tommy did hear something about what had happened in Mexico City. It seems that when it became clear that the counterrevolutionaries under Pancho Villa and Emiliano Zapata were going to be successful in driving Carranza and the "constitutionalists" out of the capital, Carranza made a calculation of sorts. Why not pull out quickly and let Zapata, who was closer to the city than Villa, be the first "liberator"? Among the advantages was the fact that Zapata was renowned as a bandit, so he could be counted upon to rob and pillage indiscriminately. That being the case, or so the story went, before they left, the "constitutionalists" could commit whatever outrages they liked because the whole mess would ultimately be blamed on the Zapatistas. Therefore, the "constitutionalists" had taken as much loot as they could carry, only to find out later that the Zapatistas had behaved themselves admirably.

Tommy could not vouch for the truth of that story, but he did know that Veracruz was overrun with automobiles in all sorts of conditions. There seemed to be little mechanical talent in Carranza's army; when a problem arose with one of the cars they simply parked it. For about $200 Tommy was assured he could buy an excellent—eminently repairable—vehicle. One of his friends was offered a nearly new Packard for $750. The reason it was on the market? One blown-out tire, blown out when a friend of the present owner cut it with a knife.

To Hart it appeared that General Obregón was the real strong man and that El Jefe was just a figurehead. But there was still a lot of maneuvering for position. The United States was now supporting the bandit, Pancho Villa, but Tommy thought it unwise to intervene and try to squeeze the "constitutionalists" out of power. There seemed no leader who could command nationwide support and, in the vacuum, rival factions contended unceasingly. Somewhat contemptuously, Tommy noted that Secretary of State William Jennings Bryan "thinks he has handled this situation splendidly." On the other hand, he was sure that Woodrow Wilson knew "what a mess he has made of it—so bad that I find myself being sorry for him."

With all this going on, Tommy would have been hard pressed to be thoroughly bored. However, all he could do was watch, and that palled after a while. Hence, when in late December the *Minnesota* was ordered to the Philadelphia Navy Yard for replacement of her 8-inch and 12-inch guns, he was pleased.

This movement meant another dull period, the only redeeming factor being that there was frequent opportunity to see his wife and young family. Caroline had moved into her parents' big house at 1751 N Street, in Washington, so Tommy spent what weekends he could with them. When there, he found himself swept up in the round of dinners, plays, dances, and other entertainments that was so much a part of the Brownsons' life and with which he had become familiar five years before. By February the refit was complete, and the *Minnesota* sailed to the Caribbean for gunnery and torpedo practice. That Hart loved. Engine trouble, however, forced a return to Philadelphia, where the ship remained until the early summer of 1915. Tommy's birthday found him in that port, gloomily contemplating his present and his future. At thirty-eight, he was thinking often of old age and even considering himself a man of advanced years. "I realize," he wrote in his diary, "that I've about reached—or perhaps have passed—the zenith of my powers, mental, physical, nerves and all that, and must in the near future perceive the down-hill tendency. . . ."[20] This may have just been a bad time or an early midlife crisis, but it is indicative of the Tommy Hart who will appear again and again in the pages of his diary. Gone is the fun-loving, harum-scarum cadet; here is a somewhat sober, critical man confronting the problems of the world. The humor is still there, but it has been overlaid with a thick veneer of mature sobriety. By and large, the diary is filled with the serious reflections of a man who sees the world as a less than perfect place.

The rest of 1915 was spent in a variety of activities, including a leave at the Adirondack League Club on Little Moose Lake, in upstate New York. The countryside and the activities reminded Hart of his boyhood home in Michigan. There were fishing, tennis, and long tramps through the woods, and he thought if he could stay all summer "it would renew my long lost youth."[21] Neither a whole summer on leave nor a regained youth was possible, though. Fall meant putting Isabella and Roswell in school, so the Brownsons' home in Washington again became their home, too. This might not have been the most satisfactory arrangement, as Admiral Brownson had not yet fully accepted Tommy into the bosom of the family, but it was convenient for Caroline and since Tommy should be going to sea soon, it seemed practical.

In November, while the *Minnesota* was at Hampton Roads, Virginia, preparing to be put through full-power trials with her newly reworked engines, reports began to come in from Flint suggesting that Tommy's father was dying. He did not feel he should go to Flint until he heard something definite regarding his father's condition because, he said, he often denied his men leave unless their relative's death were imminent.

On 4 December John Hart died. Absorbing this blow, coupled with the guilty realization that he had been imprudent in not going home immediately, put Hart in a very low state of mind. "I haven't seen my father in the past ten months of his life and he has undoubtedly known that he was on his death bed and would have liked to see his only child before he went over the great divide," Hart wrote. "I've never been a very good son and I've failed lamentably in the end."[22] "My father," he went on, "was in many respects much more of a man than his son will ever be. He had only a common school education and was never of keen mentality. What he got came by hard work. He was positively determined, never 'quit' and never spared himself. All who knew him trusted him implicitly and respected his many excellent qualities. Yet he was always unlucky and his last few years were unhappy ones." He had lost what funds he had through unwise—"they were more than that, they really were foolish"—investments, and died almost penniless. Hart sent him some money, small amounts, but now he felt terribly guilty that he had not done more to make his father's last years easier.

When he arrived in Flint he found the family had already gathered and most arrangements had been made. The weather was bitter on the day of the funeral, with dark clouds and blowing snow. John Hart's friends from the Grand Army of the Republic managed the ceremony, which saw him laid to rest in a woodland cemetery outside of Davison where Tommy's mother was buried. "It was oh so cold bleak and dreary," Hart wrote. But finally the casket was lowered into the frozen ground.

The next two days he spent with his stepmother and her daughter's family, trying to get his father's affairs straightened out. As anyone who has been through this routine knows, it is sad under the best of circumstances. In this case, where there were few comforts or financial reserves to fall back on, it was especially poignant. He resolved to do what he could to assist the two women financially and provided what emotional support he could muster. Everything seemed so rough and barren compared with the life he had made for himself. The contrasts between Michigan and the East Coast were striking, between his new family and his old, between his luck and his father's lack of it.

It was with a sense of relief that on 10 December he boarded a train bound for Washington. He arrived home to find everyone thriving. With his father's death, he realized that he was "down to Caroline and the babies" but "no man, no matter how good he is, deserves more than that."[23] It must have made him even more guilty or at least apprehensive to see how blessed he was because he wrote in the next sentence, "This good luck of mine is due for an awful change." Whereas it seems somewhat unusual for a man to be referring to his good luck a week after his father has died, the pessimism is vintage Hart.

The relationship between a father and a son is obviously very important in determining the character of the son. In Hart's case, the slight contact there had been makes it extremely difficult to estimate what influences were exerted; however, certain reasonable suggestions can be made. There is often a feeling of guilt between children and parents and there surely was a measure of that here. On the other hand, there is an avoidance of responsibility evident in Tommy's attribution of "bad luck" as the cause of his father's poor showing in life. It is as though Tommy were denying that anyone, not his father, not himself, was responsible for the unhappy way things turned out. Perhaps the safest thing to say is that the relative lack of contact between these two people was the most important factor in their relationship. Away for long periods when Tommy was a child, distant and taciturn even when present, seldom visited or visiting during Tommy's years at Annapolis or after, John Hart had a slight impact on his son's life. Part of Tommy's immediate sadness may well have arisen from the recognition of opportunities missed and now lost forever. Whatever the case, it does not appear that he mourned for long.

Christmas was spent at the Brownsons' where a spirit of old-fashioned festivity prevailed, but it was becoming increasingly clear, as 1915 gave way to 1916, that world events might soon impinge on Hart's domestic preoccupation. On land the struggle for Verdun would begin within weeks, and eventually hundreds of thousands of men would be poured into the maw of battle. At sea a tenuous truce was being maintained following the sinking of the *Arabic*. Brilliant, committed young Americans were joining the Allied forces as volunteers and Teddy Roosevelt was stimulating the preparedness movement in the United States. Wilson was to run for president again in the fall, pointing with pride at his success in keeping America out of war. Yet the signs were ominous. Could the Allies hold on without aid from the United States? Did Americans have a "right" to travel where they wished on the high seas? Would the Germans really restrain their U-boats?

And what of America's submarines? Even after innumerable modifications as well as considerable help from the British, who were the leaders in the field, American boats continued to have trouble. On 25 March 1915 the *F-4* sank off Hawaii, with the loss of twenty-one lives, the first submarine disaster in the history of the U.S. Navy. Complicating the issue, the U.S. Navy's torpedoes were not performing properly. No one was quite certain whether the root of the difficulties rested with the submarines, the weapons, or the officers in command. One solution was to replace the three remaining F-boats at Pearl with four new K-boats; another was to assign an older, experienced officer and see what he could do in a troubled situation. The Navy Department decided that Hart, in part because of his familiarity with torpedoes, was just the man for the assignment. Thus it was that his detailer at the department asked him about taking a job with submarines. "No good," said Hart, "I'm too old to learn anything about submarines."[24] His superiors thought otherwise and after he realized that, with the *Minnesota* in reserve status for an indefinite time, the alternative was probably a shore billet, he became most enthusiastic about the prospects. On 1 February 1916 the orders came through designating him as commander of the Third Submarine Division, Pacific Torpedo Flotilla, based at Pearl Harbor. This was a command that counted as sea duty, yet he could take his family along. The only unpleasant note was a hint that he was being sent out to whip the division into shape; in other words, as a "tough guy," a designation he did not exactly relish.

The leave-taking was sad; the Brownsons had grown used to having the grandchildren and Caroline around, and it was Hart's guess that his wife's parents would be happy to "arrange my drowning" for taking them away. He made no comment about whether he thought they would miss him or not. The trip across the country and then across the Pacific was uneventful, and the Harts arrived in Honolulu on 22 February, just twelve days after leaving Washington. After a short but intensive search, the family rented a large rambling house in the Nuana Valley. It was surrounded by seventeen acres of jungle literally alive with flowers and other green growing things; unfortunately, the inside of the house had fallen into disrepair and also had green growing things in it. That problem he left in Caroline's capable hands, certain that she and the staff she would hire would soon have everything well in hand.

Hart's interests centered around the newly established base at Pearl Harbor which, even though barely functioning, was home for his submarines. He immediately concluded that the shore facilities offered far too attractive an alternative to sea duty for the health and welfare of his command. He decided, therefore, that the division would spend enough time cruising in local waters to ensure that his men did not become too comfortable. Naturally that included himself, and he went out in a submarine for the first time on 1 March. After a little consideration, he decided that this "first" should be kept a secret as it might detract from his influence were it known that the CO was not an old submariner in terms of experience afloat. Although conditions in the small submarines were crowded, smelly, and far from comfortable, down she went and up she came and Tommy's rites of passage were performed with no one being the wiser.

The first few weeks were anything but difficult to take, even though it rained hard, the "water coming down without the formality of forming rain-drops," and often. The family thrived and he was able to spend hours with them on weekends, playing, romping, motoring, and pursuing with particular enthusiasm his self-appointed duty of teaching his children the art of swimming. At first they just tumbled in the warm surf, but with the application of much time and effort he began to see results.

His personnel did leave something to be desired, so the "tough guy" role had to be played. His method was to move swiftly and summarily, thereby sending a clear signal that a new, firm hand was on the controls. One day he summoned several of the senior slackers into his office. He advised them that a transport had arrived in port that morning; it was leaving the next day. They were ordered to pack their gear and be on board. He went into no details, but the message apparently came across clearly because almost before the transport left the dock the word had spread through the command and performance began to improve.

The basic problem, he decided, was the division's lack of activity or at least its lack of practical experience. The solution was to take the submarines to sea, but the weather and the equipment just would not cooperate. The most difficult thing was to make torpedo runs when the seas were choppy, as they always seemed to be outside the confines of Pearl Harbor itself. Then there were "cranky" submarines; at times there was only one out of four available for service. But after dry-docking the boats, scraping their hulls, making short full-power runs, and giving his officers long pep talks on teamwork, Hart was ready to take the full division to sea for a week-long cruise. As an indication of how overdue this training was, it might be noted that it was the first time in four years that the tender *Alert* had been out of port overnight. The specific purposes of the cruise were to find a place to establish a torpedo practice range and to give the crews a view of the waters in which they might be operating during wartime. The first mission was accomplished when they found the protected anchorage off Lahaina ideal for measured torpedo runs. This meant the end of estimating distances, the method usually employed by the navy at this time. The other part of the mission was accomplished as well as it could be, given the fact that Hart could get no definitive word on exactly what role U.S. submarines in the Pacific were to play in case of war. Furthermore, the performance of his boats and the morale of his men showed signs of real improvement, so it appeared that his methods for "tautening up" the crews were paying off.

When at the base, Hart occupied himself trying to improve the rather primitive facilities at Pearl Harbor, participating in the requisite number of charitable and social functions, and getting about in Hawaiian society. Because the only facilities for servicing and maintaining the torpedoes were those in the submarines themselves, he devoted considerable energy to establishing a miniature torpedo station. It was Hart's impression that torpedoes had been accorded a rather low priority, well behind other mechanical devices on board. This was a "rather hopeless proposition," he thought, since it took more mechanical ability to maintain the torpedoes than anything else in the submarine business. His solution was to put the specialists together in one place and have them do the torpedo maintenance for all the submarines. Even though considerable improvisation was involved, the performance curve began to incline upwards.

Charity balls for such causes as Navy Relief could not be handled so rationally; they simply had to be gotten through. Most private social affairs seemed to fall into the same category. Hart found the island's society by and large to be provincial and composed of either colonials who had made lots of money by questionable means or missionaries who were far too sanctimonious for his taste. As for service society, that, too, struck him as narrow and inbred, particularly army society. There were exceptions, to be sure, but generally Hart judged his colleagues harshly; he weighed them and found them wanting.

By August he was well settled into life in the islands and into his command. In the competitions held at the end of that month, his boats came in first, third, fifth, and eighth out of the twenty-four competing. That made him mighty proud. Part of the reason for his success was, as he put it, that he had established a pattern of "crowding" his work rather than having "my work crowding me."[25] He also gave high marks to his subordinates because they were reacting positively to his methods.

Even when crowding his work, he found time for reading in preparation for the exams he had to take in connection with his promotion to full commander. The writings of Alfred Thayer Mahan formed a good part of his literary diet. "When a War College student reads such literature," he wrote in September, "he claims to be working." Tommy, however, found the first serious studying he had done perhaps since he left the Naval Academy, but certainly in the previous ten years, highly enjoyable. Mahan seemed to him to be preaching the gospel and it made him more eager than ever to work up a practical strategic plan for naval war in the islands. Why not try it, he asked himself. After expending considerable effort working on such a plan, he presented his product to his commanding officer only to find him uninterested. "As I might have expected," Hart grumbled, "we have very few men of that age who have kept their minds in training to *do* anything."[26]

He had the same gloomy reaction to the political campaign that was raging at home in that fall of 1916 between Woodrow Wilson and Charles Evans Hughes. Wilson won and Hart delivered himself of a blast:

> Well, we will have four more years of this same sort of administration—inefficient in its Federal Departments and most provincial. The Republicans have no better morals but they *are* efficient as far as they go. But the nation's wants and ideas are fairly well represented by either party—which are of scant patriotism and only sectionalism counts with them. We are *not* a real Nation—just an enormous and rather unhealthy fungus mass. Mr. Roosevelt is our only leader of broad enough view to steer us in our international relations—and he is not followed. Well, the *Navy* is to blame for its worst troubles; had we 500 thoroughly excellent officers in the upper half of our list, we could, and would do pretty well. As things look, I've scant hope for me.[27]

Things are relative, though, and he believed Americans, though not perfect, were more industrious than many other people. He found the native Hawaiians, for instance, lazy, shiftless, undependable workers. They worked only until they were paid and then did not return to work the next day. His conclusion? "The white and yellow races are the only ones with mainsprings."[28]

Despite all this negativism, and Hart did have more than a normal measure of it, he was personally very happy. On Thanksgiving, a day that had an almost religious significance for him, usually prompting some introspective comments in his diary, he wrote again about all he had to be thankful for. He had spent a successful year in his profession, had reasonably good health, healthy children, and "a dear wife who is still so misguided as to love me." In summation, his luck had continued, and he regretted that "I am so heathen that I know not how to thank."[29]

To ensure that his submarines continued on their positive course, he started the next month by taking them for a five-hundred-mile, ten-day cruise to Hilo. It was the first time such a lengthy training cruise had been attempted. There were exercises on and below the surface, practice maneuvers to attack or evade the tenders, which posed as enemy cruisers, and still other exercises pitting submarine against submarine. Not only was the cruise a success in itself, but it served to point up the excellent work that Hart had done. As the commander of the Pacific Torpedo Flotilla commented in his fitness report, "His work during this period deserves the highest commendation." As an officer, the report continued perceptively, he was "quiet, unassuming but thorough with a determined spirit to overcome all difficulties" and was not unwilling to "put up a fight" when necessary.

With this kind of commendation it is little wonder that Hart was on the promotion list published on 6 January 1917. His joy was muted somewhat by the knowledge that some good men and good friends had been passed over. Moreover, since he had been in grade for seven years, it was no real surprise that he was going up. He did note and privately agree with the selection board's decision not to promote his immediate commanding officer, Captain Clark, who had shown no interest in his strategic plan. It was an indication of Hart's tenacity that, despite that rebuff, he went ahead and developed a "campaign order" without Clark's support. He took his inspiration from the plans developed by German General Helmuth von Moltke, who had orchestrated the invasion of France in August 1914. On 17 January, when Hart finished his plans, he felt that the war could now begin and, like von Moltke, he would simply have to pull his orders from their pigeonhole, dispatch them to his ships, and all would roll automatically.

It was less than three months before that occasion arose, but before then Thomas Hart had his initiation in the war. The German gunboat *Geier* had been interned in the harbor at Honolulu since shortly after the war began in Europe.[30] During the intervening months her captain and two-hundred-man crew had the run of the city, where they were the toast of the large German community. Although the men of the Imperial Navy were slightly overbearing, relations with the U.S. Navy were good, both sides entering boat races and other competitions enthusiastically. But on 3 February 1917 the United States severed diplomatic relations with Germany. Early the next morning, smoke was seen billowing from the *Geier*: she was being scuttled by her crew lest she fall into unfriendly hands. She could not be allowed to sit at her commercial berth on the waterfront and burn, so Lieutenant Commander Hart was ordered to take a boarding party, put out the fires, and take over the ship.

It sounded risky, since there was reason to believe the ship's crew had set explosive charges. Quickly he boarded, giving the captain as his reason the fact that the ship was obviously endangering the waterfront; the U.S. Navy would take her over, he explained, and the crew would be interned ashore. But, he noted, he wanted all hands to stay on board until the ship had been searched for explosive charges and the harbor beneath her for mines. If there were to be an explosion, he wanted the Germans on hand for it.

The minesweeping took several hours and while it was going on Hart confronted another problem. What should be done about the Imperial German flag still flying at the *Geier*'s masthead? His boarding party clamored to haul it down, but did the United States, under international law, have the right to seize a German warship when she was not at war with Germany? Hart had not the foggiest idea. At that point he spotted his father-in-law, who was visiting the Harts and was on the waterfront watching the excitement. Knowing no one more likely to give sound advice, Tommy appealed to Admiral Brownson. "Don't haul down that flag!" the admiral immediately replied. That was good enough for Hart; the flag continued to fly even as he towed the *Geier* to Pearl Harbor for a permanent and safe internment. Her crew, with their pets, their tubas, their souvenirs, and their only slightly dampened Teutonic arrogance, were marched off to hastily improvised camps. It was a "rather ticklish job," Hart wrote, which did nothing to diminish his respect for Admiral Brownson's quick thinking and good judgment.

Early the next morning Caroline contributed her part to making February memorable by giving birth to Thomas Comins Hart, or Tom as he was called. There was little time for even becoming acquainted with his youngest before Tommy took off for San Francisco to take his written examinations for promotion to commander. All went well and, despite the discovery that he had very poor color sense, which he had known for years, he was duly promoted.

He was back in Hawaii by the time the United States declared war on 6 April. Because of the preparations he had made, all that remained to be done was to change the status of the interned German sailors to that of prisoners of war and put warheads on his torpedoes. Then he settled down to wait. It was a long wait and more than a trifle anticlimactic. There really was very little to do other than exercise to keep up efficiency and hope that a German raider would appear in the area to make life interesting. About the most warlike thing he did was set his crews to cultivating a victory garden.

Finally, in May, came orders that at least moved him closer to the scene of hostilities. He was assigned as commander of the submarine base at New London, Connecticut, with additional duty as chief of staff to the commander of the Atlantic Fleet's submarine force. Within three days the whole family was aboard a ship headed home. Hart was not happy with a shore detail, but to get it changed he would have to go to Washington. The chief of the Bureau of Navigation was his old friend and member of his wedding, L.C. Palmer, who heard him out patiently but could not, at the moment, offer him a more exciting billet.

The problem was that Hart was the victim of some rather sloppy detailing, which was to have long-range consequences. Since the previous commander of U.S. submarine forces, Rear Admiral Albert W. Grant, had not been moving as expeditiously as some would have liked to get American submarines into actual combat, he was to be replaced by Captain Samuel S. Robison.[31] But before Grant turned over the command and before Robison could choose his own chief of staff, Hart had been selected for the billet. It was more than slightly awkward. Robison brought his former executive officer, Commander Arthur Japy Hepburn, a classmate of Hart, with him and made it clear that Hart's duty commanding the base at New London was going to be his only duty. As Hart told Robison and Palmer, he was not qualified to command the major U.S. submarine base, since he really was not an experienced submarine officer, nor did he care to be stuck in the States with a war going on.

For the moment there was nothing to be done so he went, with what grace was possible, to New London, where he reported on 20 July. It was a big job, a sensitive situation, and, seemingly, a dead end. After plugging away unenthusiastically through the remainder of July and half of August, luck, or something much like it, came through. Either as a result of his continued pressure on Palmer, or possibly because Robison was as eager as Tommy to ease the personality situation, Hart was to be relieved. The Navy Department needed someone with long-range cruising experience in submarines to take an expeditionary force of boats across the Atlantic to conduct antisubmarine warfare against the Imperial

Navy in the waters off the British Isles. Hart qualified. They wanted a volunteer—Hart more than qualified. Tommy Hart was going to war again.

When he arrived at the Philadelphia Navy Yard on 30 August he found that his submarines were still undergoing refit and repairs. He was not pleased by this news, by the way the workmen in the yard approached their tasks, by the general efficiency of his own crews, or, for that matter, by the state of the nation. Everyone at the yard seemed to be rushing about throwing money at problems and building more facilities than were necessary, instead of paying attention to simple matters such as doing small tasks well. He stomped around in a dark-brown study for weeks.

Complaints to Captain Robison accomplished little, and before all was in readiness late summer had turned into early fall. The first consignment of U.S. submarines, four K-boats, accompanied by Commander Hart in the tender *Bushnell*, set sail for the Azores on 13 October 1917. The route was by way of Nova Scotia and thence across the North Atlantic to Ponta Delgada in the Azores. The submarines were supposed to be towed part of the way because they were not designed for eighteen-hundred-mile cruises across open ocean. Towing was fine when the weather was decent, but as any sailor knows, the North Atlantic can be treacherous in the fall. When winds and seas rise, as they did midway in the trip, tow lines part and problems multiply. However, after ten and a half days—a record—Hart and his charges arrived safely in the Azores.

With four submarines at least in the arena of the war, Hart turned back to pick up the rest of his command. With the experience of one crossing under his belt, he thought he would be able to make a quick turn-around voyage. He figured without the mediocre efforts of the workmen at the Philadelphia Navy Yard. When he arrived there, he found that the remaining submarines were not ready. For the next two weeks he fretted and stormed, trying to put some fire under the workmen in the yard. Whether this had any effect is hard to tell, but by 18 November his next detachment was ready for sea. When he had picked up more submarines at New London, his group consisted of seven submarines, three seagoing tugs, and the tenders *Bushnell* and *Fulton*. These boats plus the submarines already in the Azores were to base in the British Isles for the duration of the war, so there were serious good-byes to be said. Caroline, instead of breaking down in tears as she had every right to do, sent him off with a smile, a slap on the back, and a cheery "Good luck!" "Is there another woman who could thus have sent her man to war?" he wondered. As for himself, he was unable to speak.

This passage was a little different from the first. Hart decided to take the most direct route across the open Atlantic to make up lost time. Unfortunately he did not take enough account of two things: the shortcomings of the tugs and the weather. Bad weather set in four days out of New London. The barometric pressure dropped to 28.98 as Hart and his little fleet found themselves in the center of a real stem-winder of a gale, which served to point up the deficiencies of the tugs as well as of some of the submarines. Consequently, when Hart was forced to put in to Bermuda on 13 December, five of his submarines and two of his tugs were missing. He went through ten anguished days of searching before he found all but one of his charges: one of the tugs, perhaps prudently, had given up and returned to New York.

Hart and his detachment spent late December 1917 and early January 1918 in the Azores. Finally, after much muddling, which he attributed to the difficulties of operating an alliance, he was ordered to take his force to Queenstown, Ireland. This port proved unsatisfactory because it was also serving as headquarters of the surface patrol forces, so Hart's operation was transferred to the base at Berehaven in Bantry Bay.

The place might well have been called "Barrenhaven." Its shore line was surrounded by low peat hills broken here and there by rocky piles 800 feet to 1,000 feet high. The wind blew rain or snow from all points of the compass while heavy dark clouds usually obscured the sun. Technically Hart was serving under Rear Admiral William S. Sims, who commanded all American forces in European waters, but his immediate superior was Captain Martin E. Dunbar-Nasmith, RN. Hart soon became very fond of Nasmith who had an enviable war record, a quick wit, and a love of the outdoors that equaled his own. Rainy, blustery afternoons would often find the two captains—Hart's temporary promotion came through on 1 February 1918—tramping over the hills or clambering over the rock piles around the bay.

As commander of the only U.S. submarine flotilla in the European theater, Hart could hardly wait to send his boats into action. The British had found that a submarine with her low profile was much better able to approach another submarine undetected than was a larger vessel. Hence the game was to send one ship-killer in search of another. First, the American crews absorbed all they could from the experience of their British cousins, then they worked up their boats under Hart's stern eye, and finally they went out on their own. The first patrol was dispatched on 6 March, eleven months to the day after America entered the war. Much effort had gone into whipping the green crews with their cranky submarines into shape, so hopes were understandably high. Yet, time after time, opportunity passed just beyond their grasp. Sometimes they would not see the U-boat until she was already diving; sometimes they fired and missed; sometimes the boat commander forgot to fire a full spread of torpedoes. Despite the frustration of not chalking up any kills, they were gaining valuable experience.

Antisubmarine patrols were an exhausting, often unpleasant, way to learn a trade. They usually lasted eight days, long hours of which were spent submerged so as to avoid detection. "Arduous" was the term Admiral Sims later applied to his particular form of hazardous duty:

> Even on the coldest winter days there could be no artificial heat, for the precious electricity could not be spared for that purpose, and the temperature inside the submarine was the temperature of the water in which it sailed. The close atmosphere, heavily laden also with the smell of oil from the engines and the odors of cooking, and the necessity of going for days at a time without a bath or even a wash added to the discomfort. The stability of a submerged submarine is by no means perfect; the vessel is constantly rolling, and a certain number of the crew, even the experienced men, are frequently seasick. This movement sometimes made it almost impossible to stay in a bunk and sleep for any reasonable period; the poor seaman would perhaps doze off, but a lurch of the vessel would send him sprawling on the deck. One could hardly write, for it was too cold, or read, for there was little light; and because of the motion of the vessel, it was difficult to focus one's eyes on the page. A limited amount of smoking was permitted, but the air was sometimes so vitiated that only the most vigorous and incessant puffing could keep a cigarette alight. One of the most annoying things about the submarine existence is the fact that the air condenses on the sides as the coldness increases, so that practically everything becomes wet; as the sailor lies in his bunk this moisture is precipitated upon him like rain drops. This combination of discomforts usually produced, after spending a few hours under the surface, that mental state commonly known as "dopey."[32]

Hart considered the experience his commanders were getting and the work he was doing with the British were well worth the effort and sooner or later, he knew, would pay off. After two months of patrolling without success came a telegram from Admiral William S. Benson, the chief of naval operations, via Admiral Sims, giving Hart the additional duty of surveying British methods of conducting submarine warfare, including upkeep and administration. Previously, what detailed observation there was had concentrated on material features such as batteries, power plants, and so on. Hart was to look into the practical matter of how the British actually fought their submarines.

He turned over the operation of his flotilla to his executive officer so that he could spend the next six weeks touring the British submarine command. What he found was instructive and much to his liking. It appealed to his innate conservatism to find that the British were frugal, wasting little space or time on comforts for their crews. The command organizations also fitted his tastes, being so run that individual commanders had considerable latitude. In his view the bureaucracy seemed streamlined in comparison with the American system. By and large, the British submarine command appeared to Hart an efficient, tight, businesslike outfit, filled with hard-working sailors willing to put up with a minimum of creature comforts. And whereas the officers and men of the Royal Navy might have lacked the broad experience that characterized the U.S. Navy, because they changed assignments less regularly, they knew their specialties thoroughly and performed efficiently. By the time he was back on board the *Bushnell* to celebrate his twenty-five years of naval service on 19 May, he felt he had a thorough understanding of how the British fought their submarine war as well as some examples of how the U.S. service could become more efficient.

In June he had an opportunity to pass on some of what he had learned to Captain Robison, now an acting rear admiral, who, with his new chief of staff, Lieutenant Commander Chester W. Nimitz, was visiting American forces in England.[33] Robison and Nimitz were also trying to learn what they could of British fighting methods and operating procedures, so their talks were beneficial. Unfortunately, Hart could not yet tell them that his submarines had sunk a U-boat. "I'd pretty nearly give up my hope of future salvation if one of them would get (Fritz) before I have to leave here," he wrote in frustration on 19 June. The next day word came that he was not likely to be around if and when that happened. The Navy Department was rotating officers out of the war zone, bringing them home for debriefing, and then sending them back with newer ships. When Sims asked Hart to nominate an officer to go home and report on his observations of British methods, Tommy nominated himself, assuming that he would then get one of the new O-class submarines in the process. Sims and the navy accepted his nomination and, after a little less than five months in British waters, he was on his way home. On the evening of 20 June he set down his reflections in his diary:

> I was not proud of them [his men] for quite a while. They had long been spoiled, the *Bushnell* was nothing but a yacht and the submarine people were just tinkers who knew little about the sea and gave it scarcely a thought. For months I was clubbing them all about trying to make officers and seamen of them and to get into them some proper conception of what the job means. At times I nearly gave up hope. But the stuff was there and it has come out. They are now a good lot who may be depended upon to deliver the goods—and they are quiet and modest about it too.

While on his way to Liverpool to catch a ship home he visited several manufacturing plants, including Vickers Ltd. and Cammell Laird & Co., where British submarines were built. Although it was his general impression that they were turning out a product superior to ours, his conclusion was that the most helpful thing would be to capture a couple of the efficient German submarines and copy their designs.[34] Once on board the liner *Baltic*, his primary concern became avoiding those German submarines. There were plenty of them about, but the *Baltic*, at 23,000 tons and with lots of speed, was not assigned any escort. The voyage, however, passed uneventfully, 6 July marking his return to American soil after eight months out of the country. He went immediately with his family to Little Moose Lake, in the Adirondacks, since those plans had already been made by Caroline before she knew he was coming home. Although offered more leave, he felt he was needed in Washington, so after two days in the woods he reported to the Navy Department. There he received two shocks: he was not to get command of the O-boats and return to England, but was to stay in Washington in some yet-to-be-determined role: and, no one seemed vitally interested in picking his brain for information on the British submarine service. Washington was still in its wartime flurry, no one seemingly knowing who was doing what or why. There were rumors about the particularly bad state of the U.S. submarine forces. On 3 August 1918 Hart set up his desk in the Office of the Chief of Naval Operations and was advised by Admiral Benson that he, Hart, had full authority to make decisions on submarine matters in the name of the chief of naval operations. In short, Tommy was given carte blanche to run the submarine service as he saw fit. But the command relationship between his office, Admiral Robison, and the commanding officers of submarines in the field had yet to be resolved.

At this point Admiral Robison was running all U.S. submarine operations out of his office on board the cruiser *Chicago* at anchor off New London. As Hart would have been the first to admit, Robison had a tremendous load of work thrust on him by the war.[35] There were boats to be worked up, crews to be trained, maintenance to be done, and a constant flow of paper work. It did not make matters any simpler that Robison was also trying to run antisubmarine operations. Indeed, one of the first impressions Hart formed was that antisubmarine warfare could be handled more efficiently out of Washington and he could think of no one more qualified for the job than himself. He realized that this suggestion might well ruffle Robison's feathers, something that he was extremely loath to do, both because of his regard for Robison and because actuarial statistics showed that it was unhealthy for temporary captains to run counter to the wishes of admirals. However, in this case, Robison proved amenable, telling Hart that he viewed him as the submarine service's friend at court and agreeing to let him run some of the antisubmarine show. Tommy enthusiastically took on the task because U-boats were beginning to harry shipping off the East Coast. Furthermore, he was eager to apply some of what he had learned from the British. One scheme adopted was based on the idea of using decoys. As applied by Hart, a U.S. submarine would be mothered by a schooner or other such vessel, which would tow the silent submarine behind her. Should a U-boat spot the lone schooner and approach on the surface, the U.S. boat, lurking in wait, would be provided an attractive target.[36] It was a good idea and, given more time, it very likely would have borne fruit.

The submarines' friend at court had other ideas and they caused some disruption in the U.S. Navy. One day in a conference he mentioned that the commander of the British submarine service had found by experience that he could better control his command from London than from an outlying base. That idea was enthusiastically taken up by Captain William V. Pratt, the assistant chief of naval operations, in part because the Navy Department was eager to free Robison's flagship, the *Chicago,* for escort duty. Hart was asked to draft a memorandum on the British command establishment. He did so, and on the basis of that memorandum

Robison was told to haul down his flag and move to Washington. According to Hart, the admiral arrived "as full of ire as a man of his temperament could be" and doubtless blamed Hart for his unhappy state. His most immediate counter was to suggest that, since his office was to be in Washington, Hart should go to New London. Tommy, with the powerful assistance of Admiral Benson, resisted this ploy. The chief of naval operations was apparently very pleased with the work Hart was doing and wanted him in Washington. Tommy could see that terrible strains would be created by having overlapping submarine commands, but believed that he could most effectively apply what he had learned by operating out of the Office of the Chief of Naval Operations. The result was that Tommy stayed and, for several very awkward weeks, existed in a kind of no-man's-land, trapped between Benson and Robison. "It was a very disagreeable time for me," he recalled. In late October, tensions boiled over; there was some kind of a blowup involving Robison and Benson, the upshot of which was that Robison found himself out of the submarine service and on his way to France to take up a coastal command.

On 22 October Tommy moved formally into the billet that later became known as the director of submarines with considerable authority in determining policy and operations. For the next several weeks things worked smoothly; he had only one assistant but most of the bureaus of the Navy Department seemed willing to accept directions from the Office of the Chief of Naval Operations, so there was little bureaucratic obstruction. It was the calm before the chaos into which the Navy Department's internal structure was thrown when peace came. It was a short honeymoon; on 11 November 1918 the armistice was announced. Tommy Hart's second war was over.

3

THE 1920'S

With the war behind it the U.S. Navy was now going to have to fight yet another battle. The dream of a navy second to none was just within its grasp; all that was needed was completion of the 1916 building program. But serious objections began to be raised about the desirability of building such a navy: first, to build and maintain a large navy would take sizable capital expenditures and many people looked to the postwar period as a time for reducing the federal budget; second, there was a revulsion against war and the competition between nations that produced it. Those who were historically minded were haunted by the prospects of a new naval race if Britain, the United States, and Japan did not restrain themselves. These attitudes contributed to the calling of the Washington Naval Conference and the virtual naval building holiday that followed in the United States, and to more limited naval conferences that were held during the 1920s and early 1930s.

It was a difficult period for the U.S. Navy, one far different from the boom that had characterized the generation since the Spanish-American War. The resulting malaise was felt throughout the service with consequent loss of manpower and of clear concept of mission. With the German navy destroyed, Britain eliminated or unlikely as a foe, the only potential adversary was Japan, and war with her would mean a war in the vast reaches of the Pacific, a task that could be undertaken only by a fully manned, modern navy with bases from which to project its power. Because of public attitudes and those of Presidents Warren G. Harding, Calvin Coolidge, and Herbert Hoover, that navy did not exist in the 1920s, nor was the plan for fighting a war against Japan agreed upon by the various services that would have to cooperate in such an undertaking. In many ways it was a debilitating time to be in the service, especially when prospects on the outside looked bright. Hart did a lot of soul-searching over whether to stay in or get out, even after he reached the pinnacle of flag rank.

Tommy Hart's first postwar assignment grew out of the rather chaotic conditions existing in the early days of demobilization. As long as there was a war on, initiatives of the chief of naval operations and, consequently, of the director of submarines, were generally accepted. This willingness to accept centralized control lasted only long enough to allow Hart to get out orders to all his submarines telling them where to go and what actions to take upon arrival. But when that task was accomplished, bickering, backbiting, and foot-dragging became the order of the day. The primary reason seems to have been that the various bureaus, branches, and offices that worked smoothly under central control when the press of war was upon them reverted to resentment against the billet of chief of naval operations, which had been in existence only since 1915. In this situation Tommy Hart, whose only assistant, William H. Pashley, was soon taken from him but ultimately replaced by the capable Robert H. English, was very hard pressed to accomplish anything substantive. The situation was made worse when Admiral Benson departed for the Paris Peace Conference leaving Captain Josiah S. McKean as acting chief of naval operations. McKean did not alter Hart's assignment or duties but, according to Hart, "on occasions when he found that I was doing something which could be construed as being out of my bailiwick, I got severely bumped." Although he got bumped plenty, Hart got his way on many things; but whereas it had been easy, now it became very difficult.[1]

Still, Hart was very active in the submarine business during late 1918 and early 1919. There were many issues, particularly submarine design, to be resolved. He chaired the Submarine Design Board, for instance, which succeeded in killing the idea of building a steam-powered submarine. The board, of which submarine pioneer Chester Nimitz was a member, recommended building some large boats capable of long-range patrolling. Hart also helped to organize the Submarine Conference, a group of submarine officers who discussed a wide range of topics and advised the chief of naval operations on submarine policy. Although the conference was not formally recognized until 1926, it played a large role in the development of American submarines.[2]

The primary fight he got himself involved in during this period was the matter of bringing some captured U-boats to the United States for study. He believed very strongly that they were superior to U.S. submarines and that there was much to be learned from them. He presented this suggestion to the Office of the Chief of Naval Operations where it was met with monumental indifference. The only support he could find within the service hierarchy was from the experienced submariners. In frustration he turned to subterfuge and used his access to well-placed civilian functionaries to forward his project. The last Liberty Loan campaign was being organized so, without authorization, he went to the Washington head of the drive "with the suggestion that six German submarines be brought over, sent cruising along all our coasts and selling bonds from their decks." Delighted with this unique way of fund-raising, the civilian official took Hart's idea up the line; within twelve hours the secretary of the navy approved bringing the U-boats across the Atlantic.[3] The loan campaign prospered, as did Tommy's design-comparison project. After careful examination by U.S. design experts, and comparative trial runs, it was generally accepted that the U.S. Navy had much to learn. Still, there were those who opposed copying the German models, and Hart may have been overly impressed by them. Their habitability was certainly inferior to that of U.S. boats, but Tommy Hart believed that if the Germans could live and fight without what he liked to call "hotel accommodations" the Americans could, too. Furthermore, it is hard to avoid the impression that the lower cost of the U-boats, their more primitive creature comforts, and, consequently, the greater degree of dedication required to live aboard actually commended them to Tommy. He seldom, if ever, accepted the easier as being, ipso facto, the better way.

One of the reasons why the idea of copying U-boats was regarded as unsavory was that the German campaign against Allied merchant and passenger shipping was generally held to be immoral. Tommy agreed with this view, up to a point, but Germany's practice of "inhumane" warfare was "characteristic of the race," and not limited to her submarine service. Furthermore, he saw a real difficulty in differentiating between the inhumanity of using torpedoes, or mines, or gas, or bombs. He calculated that submarines were not responsible for more than 12,800 lives, total. And, as he said, "Many single days of the land warfare cost us a bigger loss of life than that and with far less decisive results." As far as the arms limitations being considered in 1919 were concerned, he wrote that he sincerely hoped they would be adopted, although he was aware that "national interest" and not "altruism" would determine what was proposed and accepted. In his view, the practical thing to do was to prohibit gas, mines, bombs, and submarines, because "unless thus included with other restrictions there seems no chance whatsoever of outlawing submarines."[4]

At this time, Hart was constantly being called upon to give his expert opinion on submarines, past, present, and future. He testified several times before the General Board, where he advocated building submarines that incorporated some German design features, and he lectured on submarines to various groups. The most detailed of his lectures was the one he delivered at the Army General Staff College in October 1919, a modified version of which he gave at the Naval War College in December 1920.[5] This lecture gives a good overview of Tommy's thoughts regarding the lessons of World War I. One of the points he emphasized was the small number of men and small percentage of resources that the Imperial Navy had devoted to U-boats. This was particularly noteworthy, given the high rate of success achieved by 10,000 submariners. In fact, he saw the Germans' decision not to put greater emphasis on the submarine war as "their greatest naval error and the only one that had a great influence upon final results."

He went on to point out that German submarines concentrated on merchant tonnage not because they were ineffective against warships, but because "the criterion of efficiency held up to them was the amount of tonnage put on the bottom; all the promotions, decorations, etc., were based on that." Since merchant ships were more numerous and safer to attack, the smart submarine commander naturally most frequently chose them as his target. Still, submarines accounted for 62 of the 134 surface warships that the British lost, even though the Germans did not seem to go "out of their way to make such attacks." As to the future, he saw the submarine playing a valuable role both offensively and defensively for the United States. He could not foresee the likelihood of there being any scientific or technological breakthrough that would effectively counter the scouting, the minelaying, or the torpedo-firing role of the submarine. And since Americans were loath to consider their submarines being used against merchant shipping, he felt it necessary to point out that, had German U-boat operations been directed only against Allied men-of-war, their effort would have been amply repaid. The United States could be equally successful without resorting to attacks on merchant ships, particularly if, during a future war, there were a long period of hostilities before the major fleet-to-fleet action, upon which most naval strategists planned. He concluded, as did many other submarine officers, that "if our Submarines and Submarine Service in general receives the necessary attention and development, in conjunction with air service and fast light surface craft, the Fleet action will never occur."

Those being his views, it is easy to understand why he had little tolerance for the suggestion sometimes put forward that the United States should unilaterally scrap its submarines.[6] It was hard to see how even those who did not accept his views on the offensive capability of the submarine, and many of the battleship admirals did not, could overlook the submarine's potential for filling some of the country's defensive needs. He laid out his views in a lengthy memorandum written for Admiral Benson. It was Hart's opinion that Japan was going to emerge as a power to be reckoned with and "its predatory instincts, backed by the discipline and militarism of its people and rulers will be directed at China." If this happened, the United States might well be drawn into a war in which the submarine would be its most effective weapon, at least for protecting the Philippines. "A sufficient force of submarines operating from Manila," he wrote, "would put Japan in the same position that the German submarines did the British Islands—if they were used to attack communications. . . ." However, "defense of the Islands is the consideration that is at least prior [primary?] and it needs no argument to show how completely relatively few submarines could preclude any successful attack in force by a Japanese Fleet and land expedition."[7] Ultimately Tommy had a chance to test that theory.

The more mundane questions regarding submarines in the U.S. Navy had to do with fitting them into the administrative hierarchy. As long as Admiral Benson was chief of naval operations, there was no insurmountable problem; he supported Hart and the office of director of submarines to the limit. There was, however, confusion over command and control because, while the commanders of the submarine units were willing to take orders from Hart, he was not their immediate superior and did not make out their fitness reports. Thus it often happened that Hart found himself in for an argument, or at least an open difference of opinion, when he visited a submarine base whose commander did not approve of his way of doing things. The situation became more acute after September when Admiral Benson retired and was replaced that November by Rear Admiral Robert E. Coontz who, to quote Tommy, was neutral concerning the office of director of submarines. Previously, Tommy had at least been able to count on the chief of naval operations for support of his various initiatives; from now on he would have to be prepared to defend himself against fire from both fore and aft. The idea of a centralized office for submarine matters was such a logical one and Hart's views usually so reasonable that he often got his way, but it took perseverance and a thick skin. There continued to be great dissension over mission, design, and the emphasis to be placed on submarine development, and these issues were in no way resolved by the simple expedient of having a director's office—it was something like throwing a spread over an unmade bed. The General Board spent a great deal of time on the subject of submarine design, but there was little agreement among the experts and, in some instances, apparently little sympathy for newfangled weapons like the submarine. The officer often brought before the board for interrogation was Hart. As he recalled:

> I think that I personally did very badly in all my appearances before the Board because the relations of my office with it were bad from the start. I cite that just as an illustration of what I had best say before I conclude . . . irrespective of my capacity for tact, I decidedly was not tactful during those days. I was hard worked, always irked by the time wasted in discussions, persuading people, etc., and as I now say, not at all in a good frame of mind for getting my way through tactfulness per se. In the end we did continue to exert a good bit of influence in the design and production of submarines though there are very many instances of great disappointment therein.[8]

What the appointment of a director of submarines did do was provide a person to whom complaints could be addressed. Looking back on it, Tommy said that after a while his "bark had been pretty well worn off."

This was not a very happy period for Hart, despite the fact that Benson supported him, writing in his fitness report for 1919, "I cannot sufficiently express my appreciation of the splendid work he has done and is doing with the submarines."[9] Benson saw to it that Hart was awarded the Distinguished Service Cross for his wartime tour in Europe with the submarine force. But everything moved so slowly, so inefficiently. Moreover, Hart saw many good men, enlisted and officer alike, leaving the navy for more lucrative, more rewarding professions. For the first time he found himself thinking that he too might be happier outside the navy. "It looks more and more like it were the proper step for me" he wrote in June 1919. "If the world straightens out in the immediate future I *guess* that there will never be a war in my time, the Navy is likely to atrophy for quite a time at least—so why stick?"[10] At the minimum he often found himself thinking of getting out of submarines.

All these factors led him to propose to Admiral Coontz in the spring of 1920 that he be released from submarine duty and sent to sea. It should be emphasized that Hart never intended to become identified as a submarine specialist or a submarine advocate; he was assigned to submarines, saw much room for improvement, and set about doing what was needed with his usual verve. He realized that many high-ranking naval officers did not welcome his preferment by the chief of naval operations, the vigor with which he defended submarines, or his determination to have German engineering and design advances incorporated into U.S. boats. Therefore, he assumed that Coontz would be delighted to have this submarine gadfly voluntarily step out of the picture. Instead, much to his surprise, Coontz demurred. He stated, rather sarcastically, that since Hart had spent a long time telling other people in the submarine service what to do, it might be a good thing for him to get out to the fleet and try applying his own advice. That attitude was not taken kindly by Tommy, nor did he like the prospect, but it looked as though that was what he would have to do if he wanted to go to sea. Since he was being sent out under more or less punitive conditions, the duty might as well be under the most satisfactory terms he could arrange. He talked with his friends in the Bureau of Navigation and managed to get command of the Third Submarine Flotilla with additional duty as commanding officer of the tender *Beaver*. That meant a sea command, and most satisfactorily a sea command far from the bickering and gloom of Washington. The only bright spot that spring was the birth of the Harts' second daughter, Caroline Brownson Hart, on 26 March 1920.

Harold M. "Cap" Bemis, with whom he had worked closely at Berehaven during the war, was the man Hart relieved on 31 July 1920. Cap assured him of the *Beaver*'s qualities as well as of the high morale of the submarine people. That was encouraging, but on 1 September disaster struck. One of his submarines, the *S-5*, sprang a leak while going through diving drills off Cape Henlopen, and ended up with fifteen feet of her stern out of water and the rest of her pointed at the bottom.[11] Hart in the *Beaver* got under way quickly and arrived on the scene to find that a hole had been cut in the submarine's hull and her thirty-eight-man crew rescued after suffering thirty-seven hours of terrible strain. The *Beaver* attached a cable to the stern of the *S-5* and tried to tow her to shoal water. When they had gone four or five miles, the cable parted and the *S-5* went to the bottom in 150 feet of water. There ensued weeks of investigations, discussions, plans, stops and starts, as the Navy Department tried to determine the best course to pursue. Finally it was decided to try to salvage the *S-5* and Hart was given the task of supervising the operation. After more weeks of rather lackluster efforts by poorly trained divers, the navy decided to reconsider. Then, after more disagreements, it was determined that the salvage operation would be called off. All of this backing and filling and finally the decision to do nothing was enough to send Hart to New York scouting out civilian job prospects. None developed.

The *Beaver* spent part of the winter in the Caribbean where Hart came down with a mild case of malaria. He was not too debilitated, however, to keep up the fight for the adoption of design features based on the German submarines. On 1 December he strongly endorsed a report on the German boats prepared by Lieutenant Commander Holbrook Gibson.[12] Gibson's conclusion was: "Comparing the German submarine to ours, taking item for item, machine for machine, equipment for equipment, I have not been able to find anything that is inferior to ours, but there are many, many cases where the German machinery and equipment is vastly superior. . . . The final result must be that the German boat is a more efficient fighting machine." Another experienced submarine officer, Captain Yates Stirling, wrote Hart in April 1921 and requested that Hart endorse Stirling's conclusions that appeared in a paper titled "Superiority of German Submarines over Vessels of the Type Designed in this Country."[13] Although he knew that getting further identified with this controversial matter would not help him, Tommy not only endorsed Stirling's findings, but also allowed Stirling to quote him in the body of the paper. "I cannot be hated any worse than is already the case" he noted. He went on to tell Stirling that he had requested relief from duty in the Office of the Chief of Naval Operations "because of the state of mind that over five years of this struggle to do things with submarines had gotten me into. One thing that had much to do with chafing my bark down to raw meat was the continued fighting to beg, cajole, and force the material Bureaus into learning something from the ex-German S/Ms."

Upon return from his winter cruise in tropic climates, Hart was assigned a task that thoroughly tested the endurance of some of those American submarines. He was provided with six new boats which he, in the *Beaver*, was to take on a fifteen-thousand-mile cruise from Portsmouth, New Hampshire, to Manila. He started for the West Coast on 31 May, arrived in California on 20 July, and on 2 September sailed for Hawaii. All boats arrived safely in Pearl Harbor on 15 September 1921, a little more than four years after Hart had left there on his way to the European theater. Considerable changes had been made in the submarine base, many of them by his friend Chester Nimitz, for whom he was developing the highest regard. After six weeks he was on his way again, bound for Guam, the longest run U.S. submarines had ever attempted. They arrived safely in spite of a few minor mishaps. Then it was on to Manila where they arrived on 1 December, six months after they started. On the eighth Hart was preparing plans for a war game, fighting for space in the harbor—he found that submarines had to fight for what they wanted wherever they were—and mak-

The USS *Holland* at anchor in San Diego Bay with two V-class submarines alongside. Courtesy of Mrs. T. C. Hart

ing a call on General Leonard Wood, who was serving as governor general. The primary preoccupation for the next several weeks was the drawing-up of war plans, in which the submarines were called upon to make a large contribution in defending the islands against attack.[14] From the navy's perspective, the defense of the islands was absolutely essential. In any war against Japan the Philippines would be the only practical advance base available for American forces. The army was not so sure it could hold the islands but its need to hold them was not as great as the navy's. The navy had a hard time visualizing a practical role for itself in a Pacific War, unless the Philippines could be held.

While the war planning was still in the preparatory stages, word came that Hart was to be relieved and assigned a shore billet. His orders read that he should return to the States in the army transport *Chaumont*. He could see little joy in that, so he arranged instead to take leave in order to go farther west before recrossing the Pacific. He wanted to visit Hong Kong, Shanghai, and Japan and then, having had a look at his potential allies and foes, head east toward San Francisco. He was relieved on 23 February and began his "educational" tour. His first discovery was the squalid conditions in which the Chinese in Hong Kong lived, "but I doubt they know any better." What impressed him in Shanghai was that "there are certainly a lot of white men who make a comfortable living off the Chinese."[15] His overall impression of Shanghai was: "cold rain, wind, mud, and leaden sky for climate. Much wastefulness on the part of the 'Europeans' whose code of morals and ethics would not do at home. For the Chinese only toil, misery and squalor." Japan he found much prettier, the people seemingly happier, more prosperous, more industrious; furthermore, foreigners were much less in evidence. He went to the usual places, Kyoto and Kobe, did the normal shopping and sightseeing, and generally enjoyed himself. Although Japan struck him as a far better place to visit than China, he concluded that "Mr. Jap" would be a formidable adversary. On 17 March he boarded the army transport *Thomas* which, after a stop at Honolulu, arrived in San Francisco almost ten months to the day from the time he started his submarines on their journey.

After a stop in Flint to check on the affairs of his stepmother, it was on to Washington and the family. A new daughter, Harriet, was born during his absence so there was much to catch up on. This separation of twelve months was the longest to date, which was lucky, considering Tommy had spent sixteen of his navy years at sea.

When he reported to the Navy Department he learned, with considerable satisfaction, that he was scheduled to enter the Naval War College with the next class in July. He had long felt that he should have been assigned to the War College, and the fact that he had not been probably contributed to his earlier thoughts about leaving the navy. There were none of these thoughts now; he even had the distinct pleasure of severing his connection with submarines, or so he thought. "Six years of submarining I've had—and that will be enough," he wrote in his diary on 12 April 1922.

He reported to the War College in Newport on 1 July 1922, having sold his house in Washington, bought one in Newport, and moved the whole family north. Tommy found the course work demanding if not always interesting, his fellow students stimulating, and the visitors who passed through a mixed bag. Assistant Secretary of the Navy Theodore Roosevelt, Jr., for instance, visited in mid-July and Admiral Sims, president of the War College, handled him "splendidly," Hart thought. Sims, he wrote, "showed all deference to the high office represented but made it entirely plain that the representative was— as compared to him—just a nice well-meaning boy—who has lots to learn."[16]

Tommy's educational program was a full one. There were lectures by staff and visiting experts, among whom was Stanley Hornbeck from the State Department, who lectured on China, short courses on international law and leadership psychology, theses to write, and always war games to play. To his surprise, Hart found that the games on the plotting board were quite realistic. Japan was usually the enemy and the students fought her off Hawaii, in the Aleutians, and in the Philippine Sea. They also on occasion fought Great Britain, as they did on 13 January 1923. The British Navy won, he carped, "as it usually does in these games and we conclude that we did not get equality as [a] result of that 'Limitation Treaty' of 1922." The educational program, in Hart's estimation, was well worthwhile and improved his capacity as a senior officer.

The question was what would be the assignment where he could make use of all he had learned. Since the War College program lasted only a year, when he was about six months into it, Tommy started scouting around for a suitable billet. What he wanted to do was to go back to the torpedo station, this time in command. Unfortunately, an officer with somewhat more pull than Tommy could muster had already spoken for that post. By late winter unconfirmed reports began to filter in that he might next go to the Army War College in Washington, D.C. He was not entirely pleased by that prospect because, as he put it, "it was taking me out of my own puddle."[17] In other words, the assignment, which was no feather in his cap, and which he got simply because he had done satisfactorily at the Naval War College and was available, might well cause him to lose ground in the competitive struggle for preferment. For several years the two schools had been exchanging students, which did stimulate interservice cooperation, and Hart was all for that, but a middle-aged officer could become sidetracked quite easily with too many assignments outside the main channel toward advancement. Therefore, when the rumor of his new assignment became a reality, he accepted it with more resignation than enthusiasm.

Graduation from the Naval War College was on 26 May 1923, when he was handed his sheepskin by Secretary of the Navy Edwin Denby. "Well, its been quite a hard pull," he wrote. "I began it at a little too advanced age, but on the whole held my end up. (I think). And I'm proud to confess that I am immensely benefitted and a far better officer than when I began the course." There also was great pleasure at being in Newport. There was time to swim, skate, and sled with his growing family. Visits to the torpedo station, where he and Caroline had their first real home and where Roswell, or "Brud" as he was called, was born, brought waves of nostalgia. And sooner or later all their friends passed through, among them Joe Powell, William D. Leahy, Willis McDowell, Harold R. "Betty" Stark, and, of course, the Brownsons. Now, with graduation behind him, there was a summer to spend more or less on leave.

One thing the Harts took time out to do was visit the Hotchkiss School in Lakeville, Connecticut, which they were considering for Brud and Tom. When Mrs. Brownson heard of this impending trip she recommended that they drive over from Lakeville to Sharon to see the family homestead built by Mrs. Hart's great-great-grandfather, George King, in the 1790s. This they did and to their great surprise found that the lovely old house at the end of the village green was for sale. The opportunity was too much to resist; they had no home and this house with the hundreds of acres of rolling farmland behind it would someday be ideal for a retired naval officer and his family. The negotiations were protracted, but within a year King House belonged to the Harts. It

was very satisfying to Tommy to add the ideal home to his lengthening list of familial pleasures.

The only snag was that he did not feel very well. There was no
specific physical symptom, he just felt dragged out and could not
get up much enthusiasm or pep for tackling the daily routine. He
had been bothered briefly by similar problems before, but in January he had passed out on the street one day. After examining
him very carefully, the doctors discovered that he suffered from
anemia and low blood pressure. They guessed it was an aftereffect
of the malaria he had contracted in Cuba. They found that he had
only 60 per cent of the red blood corpuscles he should have, and
that deficiency was causing "poor circulation, low blood pressure,
irregular heart and all."[18] Medication was prescribed, but it almost
made him feel worse. After reducing the dosage he seemed to
bounce back, but he concluded that he would just have to watch
himself carefully. And here it should be noted that for Tommy
Hart "watching himself closely" and "feeling dragged out" were
relative terms. His regular routine called for his getting up at 6:00
a.m. and exercising for fifteen minutes; then breakfast, followed
by walking to work, a light lunch, work, some form of physical
exercise such as tennis or horseback-riding, dinner, and in the
evening a play, the opera, a dance, or some other entertainment.
Bedtime was midnight or so. On weekends the routine was varied
by adding more sports, longer walks, and later hours. It was very
unusual for the Harts to spend more than two nights at home in
a row. So for Tommy, vitality, or lack of it, was hardly what a
normal person would think of when he used those terms. No
doubt Tommy felt less well than normal when his blood count was
low, but he was well enough to wear most people who tried to
keep up with him to a frazzle.

On 1 September 1923 he began the course at the Army War
College. In many ways, it was the Naval War College all over again
with different uniforms. Some new subjects were covered and
there was not nearly so much emphasis on war games; they did
go on field exercises, however, some of which, such as the one
to Gettysburg, turned out to be quite interesting. The curriculum
included more material on national resources, economics, and
other geopolitical issues. There were scores of visiting lecturers,
lots of papers to write, and visitors from the various branches of
army service. The ones Hart found the most difficult to take were
the aviators who seemed to him conceited and prone to poke fun
at the other branches. He was willing to concede that air weapons

had a future, yet the claims of many air advocates seemed to him outrageous and, as a group, the aviators struck him as pompous, or at best vain. Moreover, like many other military professionals, he could see a fight shaping up over the division of the scarce military appropriations.

The academic work, though unfamiliar, did not seem as demanding as what he had to do at Newport, but perhaps he was just getting into the scholarly habit. Apparently his superiors thought he was doing well, because in the spring of 1924 he was told that he was to remain at the War College for another year, this time as an instructor. There was usually one naval officer on the staff and Hart was to get that duty for the 1924–1925 term. Whereas going to the Army War College was not a sign of preferment, being requested by the army to serve on the faculty, which was the only way such assignments were made, was a distinct honor.

Even so, it was not exactly what Tommy wanted; he would have preferred going back to sea. Caroline, on the other hand, was pleased. They were living with her parents and leading the kind of life she loved. They went to the opera regularly, dined out often, entertained with what seemed to Tommy distressing frequency, and generally lived a "social" existence. Washington was a fascinating place, with embassy parties adding to the usual round of things to do. Calvin Coolidge had replaced Warren G. Harding, whom Hart genuinely liked, as president, and Tommy complained less about the nation's leadership than he did when Wilson was in office; furthermore, the Republicans also brought some Brownson family friends into the administration.

At the War College the new instructor found himself hard pressed, as most new instructors do, preparing to deliver lectures. It was not simply the matter of keeping ahead of the class; public speaking was hardly his forte, and going to the platform every day caused considerable agony, as he tried hard to overcome his natural reticence, while at the same time making his points. Most of his lectures were on naval topics; for instance, he gave one on submarines and the students also reviewed the naval lessons of the last war. Much impressed by the need for cooperation between the army and the navy, he cast around for a topic that would give a practical demonstration of how that cooperation could pay off. The topic he chose? Amphibious warfare. To put this in the proper academic framework, as well as to prove the feasibility of this kind of warfare, he did considerable research to find examples of successful amphibious operations. One of those he settled upon was the Anglo-French assault on Sevastopol in the Crimean War. The first difficulty was that very little information was available in this country on the subject, so he asked the British naval attaché in Washington to get him some books from London. Then, when he studied the matter carefully, he found that the Sevastopol landing was something less than a roaring success. However, having spent so much time on that operation, there was nothing for it but to continue, adding some other amphibious assaults to support his general thesis.

When he finally delivered his lecture, he got the impression that only a portion of the class was much impressed. That may have been because the landing at Sevastopol was flawed in many ways, but Hart tried to counteract the defects in his example by pointing out how successful were General James Wolfe's efforts in Canada in 1759 and how well Shafter's landing in Cuba had been executed, given the low state of the art at the time. Still, only a few in his class embraced the concept enthusiastically. Others either could not see much future in amphibious assaults, or, and this is possible, did not like Hart's presentation. In any case, he felt his efforts were justified in that he had at least tried to interest them in an area which he thought was on the very frontier of military technology. Moreover, the complexity of amphibious warfare, and he considered it to be "as complicated an operation as exists," demanded that both services give serious study to the prospect of conducting such operations in a future war.[19]

In the spring of 1925 he got word that his next assignment was to be command of the battleship *Mississippi,* then homeported on the Pacific coast. The route by which this determination was made illustrates that having friends in influential positions is not always, or at least in immediately observable ways, beneficial. His detailing officer was Bill Leahy, who had heard about Hart's health problems during the past several years.[20] The anemia had been handled without complications but he had suffered other minor, nagging ailments—sinusitis, a hernia, and rheumatism. Therefore, before making the assignment, Leahy questioned him closely to determine whether he was up to the rigors of commanding a battleship. Tommy assured him that he had recovered. Leahy was not totally convinced and in consequence chose him for the *Mississippi,* where morale was low as a result of a turret fire in which forty-eight men were lost. If Tommy could handle that assignment, Leahy and the rest of the navy would be convinced that he had recovered. Accordingly, in May Tommy started across the country to take over a more or less probationary command.

The "Missy" was a 33,000-ton battleship laid down in April 1915. Her main armament was twelve 14-inch guns, supplemented with twelve 5-inch and eight 3-inch antiaircraft guns, torpedo tubes, and a unit of float planes for reconnaissance. She was in all ways a modern battlewagon even though not in as tip-top shape as some of her sister ships in the battle line. The battlewagons were the glory of the navy, in spite of the attacks on their usefulness being made by Brigadier General William "Billy" Mitchell and others. Hart found it difficult to believe that the flimsy airplane was much of a threat to the awesome battleship, which was surely the most impressive-looking and effective weapon of the day.

After joining the *Mississippi* at Pearl Harbor on 5 June, he took her with the fleet to Australia and New Zealand, then back across the Pacific to San Pedro, California. He was there in November when orders came to proceed, in great secrecy, for Washington. When he arrived he was ordered to stay out of circulation until called to testify at the court-martial of Billy Mitchell on charges of insubordination. The purpose of this secrecy? So that Tommy could be a surprise witness who could discredit the general's character. In March 1925 Tommy discovered that an article by Mitchell in the *Saturday Evening Post* quoted extensively from a lecture on submarines delivered by Hart to the Army General Staff College in 1919. Not only had Mitchell lifted, verbatim, whole sections of Hart's lecture without attribution, but he had also violated security because the lecture was still classified as confidential. Hart reported this breach of regulations not only because he resented it, but because he was worried lest someone recognize the submarine material as his and conclude that he was one of Mitchell's devotees or was, at a minimum, providing him with propaganda to use against the "big ship" navy.[21] Tommy's report was filed away, but now the prosecution thought this example of Mitchell's duplicity might be germane as well as damaging.

On 9 December 1925 Hart was duly summoned to take the stand and testified that the words in the *Post* article were indeed his. Since Mitchell was on record as stating that he wrote everything that appeared under his name, Hart's testimony definitely challenged the general's veracity. The court, however, threw it out as irrelevant. It declared that the general was not on trial for plagiarism, nor was it interested in where he got the material for his books and articles. This did seem a bit lenient, since Mitchell had clearly violated a security classification, and it certainly was anticlimactic from Tommy's point of view. It appeared to him to be another example of how the court was leaning over backward to favor the defense. He also suspected that, privately, the army was overjoyed at Mitchell's attacks on the navy. They did not care, he guessed, how much he tore down the navy "thinking that all harm done the Navy will ultimately boom the Army."

After this abortive trip to the East Coast it was back to the fleet for winter maneuvers. Usually when the fleet exercised or conducted "wars" it was with many ships and many admirals—sometimes as many as eleven flags present at one time! The amount of rank multiplied the echelons through which a ship's captain had to go to get orders, and this often resulted in confusion. In February 1926 Hart wrote: "Much money and effort is required to bring all these forces together but, as ever, few results ensue. Never any follow-through to it—and there is an enormous quantity of Admirals and staff! Perhaps therein lies the trouble."

In this judgment Hart was joined by a number of critics in the service as well as in the political ranks. Even though the navy's strength was allowed to dwindle to some 80,000 men under President Coolidge, there were many politicians and their constituents who believed that it was over-officered. In fact, since the highest rate of attrition was in the lower ranks, the smaller the navy became as a whole the larger the proportion of high-ranking officers. Furthermore, there was a notable "absence of any pervading spirit of reform in the service." Despite press accounts documenting the deteriorating material condition of the navy, and calls for changes by such notable critics as Admiral Sims, little was done. One historian states the case bluntly: "By 1924 the condition of the fleet was thoroughly unsatisfactory. The supply of surplus war materials and salvaged parts was nearly gone. Ships limped around in need of repairs that Congress refused to provide. At times, war maneuvers and full speed tests of machinery were not held because of the cost of fuel."[22]

There seems little question that the navy was in a sorry state. No leadership from the president or the secretary of the navy, scandals surrounding leases of the naval oil reserves in Elk Hill, California, parsimony on the part of Congress, and bickering within the service about strategy and mission. The best place to be in these dolorous times was the battle line, as Tommy could recognize when he looked around and saw some of the top men in his class—William D. Leahy, Arthur J. Hepburn, and Clarence S.

Kempff—sharing battleship commands with him. Steaming with the battle line meant not only prestige but shiphandling and that he loved, especially on the rare occasions when he could get the "Missy" off by herself. But when the "Missy" was not on her own it was the competition between the ships that kept up his enthusiasm.

And despite his disagreements with Billy Mitchell he was learning how to use naval aircraft to the fleet's advantage. Things did not start off too well, as a story told by Vice Admiral Joseph J. "Jocko" Clark shows: Sometime in 1925 Clark, at this point a lieutenant commander, reported to Hart, whom he knew was "an old salt" with a peppery disposition. As Clark walked into Hart's office, Hart gave him a steely glare and announced "another one of those g.d. aviators. I want to tell you something—we got too many aviators on this ship already! Why, I can take you up on my quarterdeck, and show you oil marks, where the aviators have spilled oil on my quarterdeck!!" Clark was naturally taken aback and quickly left. He soon discovered that relations between the aviators on board who, by his own admission, were something less than perfect in manner and habit, and Hart were none too good. Since Hart soon demoted the senior aviator on board, Clark, the chosen successor, set about rectifying the matter, from the bottom up. He found that Hart responded well to the improved situation and even had a wry sense of humor. "How do you manage to fly without your music rolls?" chided the skipper when Clark appeared one day without the regulation puttees.[23] Eventually Hart came to win Clark's complete confidence; "he was one of our great naval officers of all time," Clark later said. And concurrently Hart came to trust Clark implicitly, on one occasion telling him "I'll fly anywhere with you." It would appear that, at least on a personal level, Hart was learning to appreciate aviators.

Partially because of that experience and partially because of his other shipmates, Hart loved his two years in the *Mississippi*. Not only did he prove that physically he was up to rigorous duty, but he improved the "Missy," her appearance and her performance, in the process. He later said that was his happiest assignment. One thing is certain; he was awfully blue when he turned over his command at Hampton Roads, Virginia, in late 1927. After giving his successor all the advice he seemed to want, Tommy went ashore with two hours to kill before the steamer for Washington left. He wandered around in the fog for a while and finally found himself sitting on a bench near the old soldiers' home, surrounded by old-timers. "My thought was that my useful and enjoyable life is over," he recalled. "I never will have anything again as good as those last two years. It was a doleful hour."[24]

His mood was not improved when he reported to the Navy Department and received news that he was going to spend several months marking time as superintendent of New York Harbor. In early fall, however, he got word that he was being considered for command of the torpedo station at Newport. In view of the unhappy comments his last tour there had elicited from Josephus Daniels, he advised the detail officer to check his service record to see if they still wanted him to take the command. The reply was affirmative and, as he noted, many people thought he had now accomplished his ambition, and to be sure he was happy to return to Newport. "It's going to be interesting," he wrote, "if only I find the health to get away with it."[25] In other words, he saw the task that lay ahead as potentially more exciting than command of a battleship and, despite his recent experience, he still had some doubts about his physical resilience.

Without dwelling on those familiar concerns, it is relevant to wonder why the task looked so demanding. Among the casualties of the Washington Naval Conference were the other manufacturing plants that provided either parts of, or completed, torpedoes. Since 1923 the Newport facility had been the only manufacturer of torpedoes. As the official history of the torpedo station suggests, after the Washington Conference "the handwriting was on the wall to reduce torpedo manufacturing activities." In other words, since it was assumed that sooner or later there would be restrictions on submarines, consolidation seemed a prudent, as well as an economical, step. Therefore, in July 1923 production was halted at the Washington Navy Yard, the Alexandria torpedo station, and at the E.W. Bliss Company. This left only Newport as a manufacturing facility, so when, in October 1927, Hart took over command there he was taking over *the* manufacturing of torpedoes for the U.S. Navy as well as the headquarters for torpedo research, design, overhaul, and testing.[26] This was a heavy responsibility made no easier by the fact that the station was just beginning to turn out the navy's first, independently produced torpedo. After years of work, 1926 saw some breakthroughs on the development of the Mark XI torpedo, which was to be used by submarines and destroyers. "The Mark XI," according to the official history, "had greater warhead capacity, better range-speed performance, greater accuracy, and was more rugged and reliable than any torpedo previously developed for our Navy. It also was the first torpedo to have the multispeed features (3 speeds) which had been undergoing development since 1924."[27] Later tests showed, however, that concentration on this design to the exclusion of others had serious disadvantages. Tommy was very proud to be manufacturing this "fine article," but it called for careful quality control by Hart's engineers and testing officers, and consequent strain on him.

As if this were not enough, he was under considerable pressure to reduce costs. Indeed, one of his primary objectives was to cut expenses to the bare minimum. He took two approaches to this end. The first thing he tried to do was bring about greater efficiency. The methods he employed were: providing better supervision, extending long-range planning, charting production and nonproduction expenditures on a daily basis, improving machining methods, instituting rigid quality control, coordinating personnel relations under one man, and reducing paper work so that supervisors could spend more time on the shop floor.[28]

The other way in which he reduced costs was by cutting back the civilian work force. Within days of his arrival he learned that the payroll for civilians was $186,000 per month while for the naval personnel it was $30,000. He soon decided that he would have to let some two hundred employees go; however, he was familiar with the trouble the Machinists' Union could make and added gloomily, "If I drop off 20 I'll be doing quite well."[29] Several days after writing this comment, he learned that civilian pay was to be raised, which made his problem all the more acute. In January of 1928 he informed forty-five men that they were being let go. It was not that he liked firing them, he said, his sympathies were with them, and it was "not pleasant to put them out in the cold," but they were redundant to the station's needs. He did get some satisfaction, though, from fighting the Machinists' Union and winning. When he got the work force down to just under one thousand, he still considered the station overmanned and continued to seek ways to reduce it.

The result of all his economy measures came clear just a year after he took over. It was November 1928 when Bill Leahy, now a temporary rear admiral and chief of the Bureau of Ordnance, came to the torpedo station for an inspection tour. When the admiral left, Hart sent with him some $600,000 that had been saved or would be saved in the near future. "I guess that is something that doesn't happen to them very often," noted Hart, "well its not too hard to do it."[30] Some of the work force might not have agreed with Hart's view on how easy it had been to accomplish those economies; however, Hart does seem to have tried, and to a certain extent succeeded, in maintaining good relations with his employees. He was constantly in the shop, available for consultation, met with the union regularly, and periodically gave "pep talks" to his people. The fitness report written on him by Admiral Leahy in March 1929 said that the station had been administered with "tact, economy, efficiency, and foresight. Material of superior quality is now being produced at a lower cost than heretofore by a contented, loyal and increasingly efficient working force. I consider Captain Hart an officer of superior professional attainments, possessing a high order of executive ability."[31]

Hart still was not satisfied that the station was turning out its product at the lowest possible cost. He was convinced that if the navy would spend some money in exchanging old machine tools for new ones, the savings would ultimately exceed the investment. "With up-to-date and fully efficient tools, properly laid out in a modern plant," said the official history, "the same men would produce much more with the same effort."[32] This was true not only in the area of torpedoes but also of primers, detonators, and igniters. Work in these complex fields included experiments with a new exploder known at that time, for security reasons, as the "index mechanism" and later as the famous, or infamous, Mark VI magnetic exploder. This device, which was intended to be activated as it passed under the maximum magnetic field of a ship, was thought to be the final word in torpedo efficiency. By the time Hart left Newport, the experiments had not been quite completed, but he had the satisfaction of knowing that this deadly device would soon be in the hands of U.S. submariners. Little did he know that the Mark VI exploder would come back to haunt him.

As 1929 began Hart knew that his tour would soon be up. Not only that, word had it that his name was near the top of the zone to be considered for promotion to flag rank. His diary entries leave no doubt that he wanted to be promoted. Deep down inside, he wrote, "I rather feel that I can be as good an Admiral as the list now averages—but," he added with true humility, "*not* as good a one as it [the navy] needs."[33] Rumors of his promotion continued to fly and some of the machinists thought this was the moment to push their demands. As one of his assistants recalled: "I informed you one morning that the Grievance Committee was coming to you with three ridiculous demands and that they felt 'with selection a month away he will not dare refuse, and if he does refuse his action will do him no good.' Your reply was: 'I have no friends on the Admirals' list and some enemies. Bring them in.' You turned them down on all counts."[34]

In March Hart started the ninth volume of his diary. "*This* is going to be *the* fateful volume of this diary which I started on this very island quite a few years ago," he wrote. "In it will be recorded whether I continue on this naval career, to the pinnacle, (or quite near enough to it to suit everyone—including me), or whether I terminate the active part of said career." Either way, he continued, "I have the situation very well 'discounted.' "[35]

On 14 June word came that the selection board had chosen him for promotion to rear admiral along with his classmates Orin G. Murfin, Arthur Hepburn, Walton R. Sexton, and Bill Leahy. He was no doubt pleased, but it would be very difficult to tell that from what he wrote. His next assignment was as Commander, Submarine Divisions, Battle Fleet, which meant he was to take over submarines in the Pacific, where he was to join them with all due speed. Within two weeks he was bound for Pearl Harbor. He arrived almost four years to the day after he had taken command of the *Mississippi* in that same harbor. This time he did not feel the same zest of impending competition. "Admirals don't compete," he knew. In his new command he realized "my subordinate officers and men will be looking to me for decent leadership" and that would "suffice to keep up the requisite steam in me." How well he would keep up that steam and what his prospects would be in 1930 remained to be seen; he and Caroline were still debating "shall I give up the Navy and all the rest of (or most of it), my life or shall it be otherwise disposed?"[36]

The tender *Holland* was his flagship and from her he observed his charges on maneuvers and practice shoots. It took him a little while to get reacclimated to submarines, but by August, when he convoyed six of them to the West Coast, he was feeling pretty well shaken down. Not that he thought all was well with the "silent service." On the contrary, the more he saw—particularly on the material side—the worse things looked. "Its all an infernal mess," he opined, "and even if I had the will to try to really 'reform' it, (as Caroline calls my usual endeavors), I wouldn't have the strength."[37] Nevertheless, he put considerable effort into trying to get his command in shape. There were some fine people in the submarine service, most notably Nimitz, who at this time was commanding Submarine Division 20 based at San Diego, but there just did not seem to be consensus as to whether submarines should be used offensively or defensively, with the fleet or independently. Consequently there was no unanimity on what kinds of boats to build.

Most of Hart's work was administrative, inspecting and otherwise overseeing, rather than actually running, his submarines. For one who enjoyed shiphandling more than paper work it was not too much fun. The primary reason he was pleased to be an admiral was because "if I had fallen by the wayside Caroline and the kids wouldn't be able to bear up so well."[38] In other words, he saw himself more or less as "background" for them, or so he said. If that was the case, he would be a bigger background soon. In yet another attempt to get a "handle" on submarines, Washington decided to put all submarines in both oceans under the command of one admiral. Tommy Hart was chosen to be that admiral. His orders called for him to report to New London by 14 May 1930. His title was to be Commander, Control Force, and, as such, he would be both more independent and more influential; furthermore, from a personal standpoint, he would be happier if he were based on the East Coast.

The actual work involved in this new assignment did not differ much from what he was doing as Commander, Submarine Divisions, Battle Fleet. He was closer to Washington and that meant occasional trips there to plead the case for submarines before the various bureaus in the the Navy Department and the General Board. He was not convinced that he made much impression even when lobbying with Secretary of the Navy Charles Francis Adams, with whom he established a close, personal rapport. "Hercules himself," wrote Hart in September, "is not man enough to clean up *that* mess."[39] Actually part of the problem was beyond the control even of Adams. The London Naval Conference, which lasted from 21 January to 22 April 1930, set parity for submarines at a total of 52,700 tons. This international agreement set off a great debate inside the U.S. Navy. Should it build a few large submarines or a larger number of small ones? And, if any boats were to be built, what precisely should be their design characteristics? While Hart was arguing for a balanced force of small submarines and multipurpose boats, the debate was abruptly terminated. On 11 October 1930 the Navy Department announced that 51 of the country's 106 submarines were to be decommissioned.[40] This would leave the navy with 55 submarines aggregating 51,050 tons, or 1,650 tons less than allowed by the London treaty. Furthermore, in view of the current economic difficulties, there was slight prospect of any new submarines being laid down soon. This was the darkness before a bright new dawn in submarine development, but to Tommy the sky looked a solid, leaden gray.

The only bright note was that he was to get to sea while he was in this command. His flagship, the tender *Camden,* was slated for decommissioning, but, before that happened, he was to take her and several divisions of submarines more than 7,500 miles to Hawaii, where he was to pick up twenty submarines that were to be decommissioned and return with them to the States; this meant a journey of some 15,000 miles with submarines and assorted small support vessels. Unfortunately, Hart did not feel in topnotch physical shape when the voyage started. He called in his medical officer, who, after a brief examination, declared that the admiral suffered from a chlorine or iodine deficiency not uncommon among people from the Great Lakes region. The treatment was doses of iodine, which Hart took with apparent good effect since he seemed to recover enough "pep" to make the journey in generally good humor.

When he was halfway home, Hart received word that he was to become superintendent of the Naval Academy in May of 1931. When the subject was first broached to him, he did not take it seriously because the "supe" was usually an older admiral, for whom the academy was the last assignment before retirement. The detailing officer, Frank Brooks Upham, told him that this time they were seeking a younger admiral and Hart, at fifty-three, might fit the bill. When the appointment was announced in January 1931 Tommy commented in his diary that he could not say he approached the task with "too much confidence." He and his fellow officers were critical of some of the academy's recent products, and he was not certain that he was up to the task of remedying the defects. Time would be the best measure of that; now he had to get ready to turn his submarine command over to Japy Hepburn and prepare to become an academic administrator.

The past eleven years had given Tommy Hart extremely diverse experiences. Two years on the staff of the chief of naval operations, two years in command of a submarine flotilla, three years of academic endeavor, two years in command of a battleship, two years in command of the torpedo station, and two years in command of submarines in both oceans: five years ashore and six years afloat.

He had crossed the Pacific, at least as far as Pearl Harbor, no fewer than five times, gone once to the Philippines and Australia, and visited China and Japan. Reflecting the navy's preoccupation with that island nation, there was no corresponding experience for him in the Atlantic. The life he lived during these various tours was probably typical of any naval officer's life. By and large, the work was not excessively taxing, there was a good deal of leisure time for golf, which he began to take up in lieu of tennis, incidental travel, and family activities. Where his life might have deviated from the typical was in the social sphere, particularly in Washington and Newport. The Harts were decidedly "society," which meant a constant round of entertaining and being entertained. Barely a week went by in port that there were not at least four nights of planned activities. Evenings at home with only the family were rare indeed.

His greatest professional contribution during this period was in submarines. He pioneered in the administration of the service; he helped organize the influential Submarine Officers Conference; he lobbied against the abolition of undersea weapons, unless coupled with a more sweeping disarmament measure; and he fought hard, and ultimately effectively, to get German design features incorporated into U.S. submarines. To be sure, some of those design features proved impractical or were superseded by engineering breakthroughs, and at least one submarine expert believes that the U.S. Navy went too far in trying to copy the U-boats.[41] Be that as it may, Hart's central point was that there was much to learn from the German designs and we should study them to see what could be incorporated to our benefit. There is no question but that the 1920s were a period of trial and error for U.S. submarines. It also seems obvious that having the *U–135* and her sisters as models was far more useful than not having them. Moreover, in the process of working the bugs out of U.S. submarines, progress was made in other ways. "Most significant of all," writes John D. Alden in *The Fleet Submarine in the U.S. Navy,* the navy had "trained a nucleus of competent design officers and a generation of eager submariners, and devised a mechanism, in the form of the Submarine Officers Conference, through which the talents of these diverse individuals could be harnessed constructively rather than dissipated in internal bickering. New ideas were in the air and the doldrums of slow trial and error were soon to be replaced by the winds of progress, ushering in a decade of rapid development."[42] Tommy Hart was in the forefront of the submariners' battle all along and could surely take considerable credit for these developments. He was not always right, but he was always in the center of the fray.

From Hart's perspective, the navy in general went through a low state during the 1920s. There seemed little direction from on high, little sense of purpose, and slight connection between the various activities in which he and others were engaged. He was not particularly critical of the high command, although he did not give top marks for leadership to many of the senior officers under whom he served, yet his diaries and letters exude a sense of drift, of slackness, of indolence. At the same time, the navy was being attacked by budget-cutters, by pacifists, by politicians, by air pioneers, and by the army. Actually, he had gained empathy with the army. Although he continued to criticize its officers for their lack of social grace, he liked many of those he met at the Army War College and he was in full sympathy with the concept of interservice cooperation. He was convinced that amphibious warfare represented the most practical application of the cooperative principle, but even if that were not at issue, he favored a policy of appreciation of one another's usefulness.

Family affairs had moved along satisfactorily, despite being considerably disrupted by his peripatetic existence. There were two happy periods at Newport when they all could be together, and when home he took every opportunity to mark out blocks of time to spend with the children. They naturally were sent to private schools and there were the usual fatherly concerns over manners, behavior, and futures. Isabella would soon graduate from the Dobbs School and Brud was thinking about Princeton. Tom was maturing quickly though he was chronically underweight. The two younger girls, known to each other and to Tommy as "nous," were still the babies and much adored. But no one was as greatly adored by Tommy as Caroline. In his eyes she was perfect. The perfect wife, the perfect mate, the perfect mother, the perfect hostess, the perfect whatever she chose to be. In Caroline Tommy found the mother he never had, the maker of the home he always wanted, the saintly woman he always idealized. Not surprisingly he judged that anticipation of her talents as superintendent's wife was one factor that led to his selection.

4

BACK TO THE ACADEMY

The years he spent as superintendent of the Naval Academy provided a good opportunity for gauging some important aspects of Tommy Hart's personality and his approach to the naval profession. He wrote a good deal about those years; men who were midshipmen during his tenure, though quick to admit they observed from afar, give a remarkably consistent view; and the academy's records and reports provide valuable information. Furthermore, in other assignments Hart was interested primarily in getting the task done well and achieving a good record, whereas at the academy he was trying to mold young men into officers who, whether modeled after himself or not, would seek and discharge command responsibility. To some of his charges he was the epitome of a flag, or at least a senior, officer; others found his apparent rigidity and taciturnity made it impossible to consider emulating him. But the unusually high number of officers from the classes of 1933 and 1934 who attained flag rank, won decorations, or were otherwise distinguished is a measure of the academy's effectiveness as a training ground. Those men were of the right age and seniority to fight and have command in World War II, as were the classes immediately before and immediately after. Tommy would be the first to give credit to his subordinates and to the students themselves for the brilliant record of the classes of '33 and '34, but it is only reasonable to assume that Admiral Hart also was doing something right.

The academy and the town of Annapolis that greeted Rear Admiral Thomas Hart were far different from what they had been when Naval Cadet Tommy Hart arrived there. Thirty-nine years can change a man and a place, and they surely did in this case. The immature, uncertain, more than slightly naughty teenager had grown into an adult who appeared self-assured and definitely gave no hint of naughtiness. On the contrary. Upon catching their first glimpse of the new superintendent, many midshipmen probably reacted as several admit they did, with a shiver of realization that this was a tough customer, indeed. Maybe not as rigid as he looked in his high starched collar, but obviously a man who intended to dispel the "slackness" he thought had been allowed to prevail.

The academy was almost ten times the size it was in 1892.[1] Its grounds now spread for almost two miles along the beautiful Severn River and upon them were many fine new buildings that housed the 2,200-man Regiment of Midshipmen and the faculty. Most of the faculty were professional naval officers, but approximately one-third were civilians, and Hart saw the maintenance of esprit de corps among this disparate group as one of his primary tasks. The social aspects of that task could be taken care of in the superintendent's residence, a commodious house completed in 1906 and intended both as a home and a place where official functions could be held. Those functions too had increased in frequency and size as the years passed. The modern roads that linked Washington and Annapolis made the academy an apparently irresistible lure for congressmen and other dignitaries who wanted to escape the heat, the lethargy, or the nonathletic atmosphere of the capital for a few hours. Particularly on weekends there was a stream of visitors, so many that Hart took to posting his sharpest lookout at the gate on Saturdays and Sundays to spot the unexpected personages, who, even though arriving unannounced, often insisted on every amenity that protocol required.

Some came for athletic events, or to lunch or dinner with the Harts, others simply to show off the academy to a visiting constituent. No doubt some came to look for waste or fat so that they could cut the academy's annual budget request. Adding to the usual budget-cutting zeal that many congressmen brought to any military expenditure in peacetime was the deepening depression. President Hoover had been coping grimly, too grimly some critics would say, with the financial crises for eighteen months when Tommy Hart came back to the Severn. Instead of improving, the unemployment statistics had risen, the bread lines grown longer; something more would have to be done. The grim shadow of government economy hung over the navy in general and the Naval

Academy in particular. The new superintendent would have to exercise all his instincts for economy and carry out whatever reforming plans he had with no more money, and possibly much less, than his predecessor had. And even then, if the national economy did not improve, other belt-tightening measures would have to be imposed, possibly by the Navy Department, possibly by the White House.

In some areas adjustments might well be desirable. Changes had been made in the life of the academy since Hart's last tour there in 1904, most notably reforms undertaken in the early 1920s intended, in the words of Jack Sweetman, the academy's most recent historian, to make "the transition between the cloistered academy of the nineteenth century and the open academy of today." Still the official description of the academy's mission remained:

> To mold the material received into educated gentlemen, thoroughly indoctrinated with honor, uprightness and truth, with practical rather than academic minds, with thorough loyalty to country, with a ground work of educational fundamentals upon which experience afloat may build the finished naval officer, capable of upholding, whenever and wherever may be necessary, the honor of the United States; and with all giving due consideration that healthy minds in healthy bodies are necessities for the fulfillment of the individual missions of the graduates; and that fullest efficiency under this mission can only be attained if, through just and humane yet firm discipline, the graduates carry into the Service respect and admiration for this Academy.[2]

Within this description the academy's critics, in whose ranks could be found many civilian educators and some distinguished officers like Vice Admiral Sims, found support for their charge that the academy was too narrow, too provincial, too professional, in short, a glorified trade school.[3]

An attempt was made to find out whether the charges being leveled at the academy in the early 1930s were valid. Questionnaires were sent to more than 1,200 men listed in the *Register of Alumni* as having graduated between the years 1931 and 1934. More than 900 of the recipients responded, the following reaction being typical:

> To me, coming from a poor family "on the other side of the tracks" it was just about "Heaven on Earth" and an unbelievable opportunity. I was poorly prepared as a student, not having graduated from high school, but almost everyone, instructors and stu-

dents, helped me get through. The instructional staff, both civilian and officer and enlisted, were excellent and deeply dedicated. The so-called "hazing" during plebe year has been vastly distorted. The seniors who were supposed to do the "hazing" actually helped me the most, both from a leadership viewpoint and scholastically. It was likened to a Big Brother relationship. Although the curricula was rather restricted when compared to the present, and the life was a bit spartan, it prepared us well for what was ahead. I am proud to have been a part of the great institution and fortunate to have had the privilege of serving with the graduates.[4]

Another officer had far less fond memories:

The life of a plebe was absolutely miserable. He was not allowed to have a radio or a phonograph. He was not allowed to *have a date*! Or ride in a car. Or leave the Naval Academy except for 5 hrs. on Saturday afternoon. He was required by first-classmen to learn reams of material gibberish and if he wasn't letter perfect they pounded his behind with brooms and subjected him to physical indignities you wouldn't believe. Plebes always sat on the last inch of their chairs at meals. They had to answer rapid-fire questions while they tried to eat. Inaccurate answers meant "sitting on infinity"—no chair, but sitting nevertheless and gobbling what food they could to keep from starving.

They had to take icy showers every morning, walk straight lines in Bancroft's corridors, eyes straight ahead and shoulders braced.

The list of things a plebe was forced to do is endless as well as unbelievable. And on top of all this endless torture the plebes had to master a full engineering curriculum as well as a full professional one (firing on the rifle and pistol ranges, handling small boats, endless infantry drill etc.) Plebes were forced to go out for some kind of athletics, too.

Their reward was $2 per *month* for spending money. As Superintendent, it was Admiral Hart's duty to know that these things were going on in his command but I don't think he did.

My opinion of plebe treatment? I would *never never* go through that again. But I was damned glad I had it. Fighting a war in a task force at sea was *fun* by comparison![5]

The schedule was arranged to fulfill the purposes outlined in the official description. Plebes arrived in June and for the next six months were subjected to physical training, classroom instruction, and hazing by the upper classmen. If asked what plebes were, the correct answer for a plebe to give was, "tough sons of bitches." And tough the life of a plebe was until Christmas, when there was a two-and-one-half-week vacation allowing those who could afford

it to go home. During the youngster and second-class summers
there were cruises in naval vessels and a three-week vacation in
September. The weekly routine was equally rigorous. After rising
at 5:30 a.m., the midshipmen were marched everywhere, to meals,
to class, to chapel. The class day ended at 4:30 p.m., at which
point they were under pressure, official and unofficial, to participate in some sport. Those who did not were derided as members
of the Radiator Club, because they supposedly sat on the radiators
in Bancroft Hall trying to soak up some extra warmth. Anyone
lucky enough not to have accumulated any demerits had liberty
on Saturdays and after compulsory attendance at chapel on Sunday.
Athletic events, especially football games, meant free time with
dances or other social events sometimes thrown in. For upper
classmen this might mean contact with one of those rare crea-
tures—members of the opposite sex. There were girls in Annapolis, of course, but for most midshipmen these "crabs," as they
were called, were only glimpsed from afar and fleetingly. A similarly cursory glance at *The Log,* the academy's humor magazine,
shows how immature was the midshipmen's consequent reaction
toward girls: the poems are sappy, the jokes sophomoric at best,
love, women, kissing, hugging, holding hands, beating hearts, all
idealized, dreamed about, and romanticized.

In class, all was business; the only amusement being the jokes
that could be made up about instructors or other officers. There
was "Whiskey Joe," "Wet Dream Willie," the "Iron Duke,"
"Asiatic Arthur," the "Beagle," the "Gallant Fox," "Ampere Pete,"
and so on. Lessons were learned by rote, and each student was
called upon daily to solve problems at the blackboard or repeat
what he had learned. "Any questions?" went the refrain. "All right,
gentlemen, man the boards." The instructors then gave grades for
every day's performance, acting more, the students said, as "score-
keepers" or "referees between the student and the book" than as
teachers. Exams were generally given at the end of each month,
grade sheets being watched anxiously because the correlation of
academic and professional scores determined the all-important
standing of a midshipman in his class.

There certainly was merit in the criticism some outsiders leveled
at the academy and there are graduates who, looking back, admit
that they gained little love for learning while storing up vast quan-
tities of useless knowledge. Some complain that there was too
little opportunity to pursue the humanities. One said, "I do not
think [the] USNA was a good educational institution. It was a

'trade school.' " Some graduates suggest that "the competency level" of the instructors was low. "Most of my instructors were naval officers back for a three-year shore duty from the Fleet," wrote one. Another suggested that "the instructor usually contributed nothing except to check off the answers and assign grades. In most cases he could not solve the problems he was grading."

A biting commentary was contributed by one officer:

Atmosphere: Antidiluvian. Having worked with farmers, construction crews, been used to servants and their care, the atmosphere for training leaders was unbelievably naive. L'audace, toujours l'audace!

Student body: Americans. Bigoted. Expiring patriots. Well-meaning, poor doing. Startled by anything different from Main Street. Striving for a high level of mediocrity. These were the days when Marine and seaman included college graduates in the ranks.

Instructional staff: Hot to trot, but who were they? What had they ever done? Rumors alone spread their reputation, if any. One duty officer "Screaming Greenman" [Captain William G. Greenman] probably was trying, but managed to get his ship plastered at Iron-Bottom Bay (?) French and Math profs were good.

Educational Institution: It was expensive, therefore it must have been good. It cost to select the students, therefore they were good. It was modeled after US institutions of higher learning, ah! so—

Bitter nostalgia clouds my thinking. With more infantry drill (close order, not combat) than the Military Academy, more math than MIT (I was told) and less seamanship than a troop of sea-scouts (my observation). I was stupid enough to try and find some information in the Library. That occupation was frowned on by the upper-classmen, and later, one's own classmates. Anyone who experimented, or wrote articles, was queer. Look at Lt. [Arthur A.] Ageton, and Dreisenstock [Joseph Y. Dreisonstok]! Wasting chances of promotion by getting their names on navigation tables— All I remember from the library was Sir Ian Hamilton's "Staff Officers Notebook" and Roger Ascham's "Toxiphilous." Hardly the latest in intelligent warfare.

The classroom work was rather structured, you had to have a burning thirst for knowledge to ask a question. You could learn what was in texts, but how in hell were you supposed to apply any of it? Practical work was merely orientation ashore.

The summer cruises were the only time of learning. And then aviation hit. One summer wasted. No, it convinced me that there was something that people better catch on to, but not me (until I got duty on a carrier).

Probably what I had in mind was Staff College, but I didn't know such a place existed. When it was talked about, it was a way to promotion, not a place to learn anything for your benefit or that of the Country.

The idea came across gradually that you were in a great fraternity. Regardless of the damage to your ship or country, don't let a classmate down! No matter how stupid. Some were disgusted and quit. Some tried to bore from within. The great mindless proletariat-lumpen just dug in and did their best.[6]

Despite the criticisms, most midshipmen loved the academy and look back on the experience happily. Moreover, these were tough days for those outside government service; jobs were difficult to find and employment was a rare and treasured commodity. Also, even outside the military, it was not the vogue to question authority in the early thirties. Anyone who criticized what authorities and those in command said, in anything other than a joking way, was marked as a maverick, a radical, a complainer. And, after all, the reputation of the academy around the country was high, there was stiff competition for entrance, and midshipmen at home or even in foreign countries could expect to be treated with respect. It was, as one graduate of that era said, "a completely different world" from that of today.

Entering into this atmosphere was difficult, to say the least, for a plebe, and even Hart, coming from a seagoing command, would have to make adjustments but he brought considerable enthusiasm to his new job. The primary duty of the academy, he believed, was to instill officerlike qualities in its students before they graduated. What did he mean by "officerlike qualities"? "It is presence, and personality, and looks; it is qualities of mind, proper reactions, all of those things, but particularly character, guts," he later said.[7] Tough Tommy Hart was chosen as superintendent because, in the eyes of many professional naval officers, those are the qualities that he epitomized. He was noted for "his high sense of duty and his inflexible discipline. He was just what the stricter 'ward room officers' in the Fleet thought the Academy needed."[8] Furthermore, there was a feeling among some in the naval hierarchy that Tommy's toughness was just the remedy needed to correct some of the slackness tolerated by his predecessors, including the most recent "supe," the capable, but fatherly and easygoing, Rear Admiral Robison ("Sammy" to the midshipmen). Robison, it will be recalled, was Hart's commander in the submarine service and there was some competition between the two after Hart returned from Europe. Tommy never made any comment about Robison's policies at the academy but, in light of their previous relationship, it would be reasonable to assume that Hart was neither inclined to emulate Robison's methods nor capable of doing so. The two men had different approaches. Robison, who had achieved distinction within the service, was what Tommy described as a "leader," while Tommy was, as he said, a "pusher." Apparently there was a body of opinion that held that the midshipmen needed some pushing or that academy procedure needed tightening. Tommy was fully prepared to tighten in some areas, but he wanted to loosen in others. For instance, he wanted to give the midshipmen more privileges in their last year and more say in ranking their peers. He also wanted to broaden, or "humanize," as he called it, the curriculum.

On a beautiful May afternoon Tommy Hart was installed as superintendent of the Naval Academy with all the pomp that very "pompish" place could furnish. Shutters clicked, swords flashed, and flags fluttered as officers and their ladies greeted the new superintendent and his lady. And while Caroline and Isabella fretted over all the cameras, the admiral prepared to face what he anticipated would be "one of the big adventures" of his life. He did not have long to wait. In less than two weeks the Board of Visitors arrived for their annual meeting. The board, made up of civilian appointees selected by the president, the vice president, and the speaker of the House of Representatives, was charged with overseeing the academy's operations, recommending budgetary changes, and advising on academic matters. Led by James Rowland Angell, president of Yale University, it wanted to see the curriculum broadened "to include subjects of a cultural nature."[9]

Angell was among the academy's early critics and he shared the view that its curriculum was too narrowly technical. Therefore, it is not surprising that this year the board's conclusion was that, in response to the burgeoning of technological information, the academy had become narrower by devoting more time than ever to training, particularly in engineering. That the humanities and the social sciences were being neglected had been noted by the boards of 1923 and 1924. But Angell and his colleagues were distressed to find that, while the midshipman received some courses in English, American history (primarily naval), and one foreign language, his education was "devoid of any economics, of any substantial course in government, of any biology, geology, ethics, or social science, or of any of the literature of foreign languages, or of any of the fine arts which play so large a part in the cultural life of all

Rear Admiral Thomas C. Hart taking command of the Naval Academy, 1931. Courtesy of Mrs. T. C. Hart

peoples." They did not consider themselves competent either to revise the curriculum or to recommend extension of the course of study by one or two years, nor were they confident that the academy, with its rotation of faculty, would be able soon to make sweeping revisions. They recommended, therefore, that a special commission be established to study the situation and make recommendations.

This action by the board presented Hart with a challenge he chose to accept rather than sidestep or study further, as his predecessors had done. It was his view that he and his staff "could

President Herbert Hoover visits the Naval Academy, 17 October 1931.
Courtesy of Mrs. T. C. Hart

reform ourselves better than it could be done by some outside commission which was bound to be in part civilian and perhaps somewhat political."[10] He also knew that several members of his staff had already studied the matter intensively and were in favor of some changes. There were two basic recommendations to be considered: (1) the provision of more cultural education, and (2) lengthening of the course of study, particularly in engineering. Then there was a suggestion, intended to assist in accomplishing (1) or (2) or both, that the four-year program should be extended by one year, or possibly two. After meeting several times with his staff and reviewing the relevant documents, Hart was ready to make some recommendations to his immediate superior, Rear Admiral Upham, chief of the Bureau of Navigation. His first recommendation was that the program not be extended to five or six years. It might have surprised some of his critics to know that he thought "four years are quite enough for anyone of the age of midshipmen to spend under such restraint as obtains here."[11] A longer period of strict routine and discipline would lead, in his opinion, to "staleness," would stifle the growth of initiative, and tend to develop "yes men."

Turning next to course content, he wrote that he thought too much emphasis was being placed on "applied education, particularly in engineering subjects," and this was what made it necessary to cut cultural subjects to the bone. The solution, in Hart's view, was to give up the effort to turn out ensigns fully qualified in all technical and professional areas. It would be far more reasonable and economical, as well as less destructive to the ensigns' ability to think independently, for the academy to broaden the curriculum, concentrate on teaching the principles of mathematics and engineering, and leave professional education to the postgraduate schools. Such a program would turn out ensigns educated in the humanities and better grounded in the "fundamentals which underlie all engineering."

Without agreeing wholeheartedly with this approach, which Hart realized would not go down well with many of his colleagues, the Bureau of Navigation gave him permission to go forward with his study. At times, Hart must have been sorry he had this permission, because not only was the work complicated and detailed, but he was out of his depth in dealing with academic subject matter. The object was to have a recommendation ready to present to the Board of Visitors in April 1932 and, after innumerable meetings, studies and revisions, that goal was met.

The board, meeting between 25 and 28 April 1932, approved the recommended changes in curriculum on the grounds that courses in "cultural subjects" like literature, history, economics, and government would "tend to develop a broader outlook on life, make for broader contacts, and hence make for leadership." When put into effect, the changes meant that "cultural subjects" would be allotted an additional three and one-half hours per week.

Obviously the changes could not be made without reorganizing the entire curriculum. The percentage of time devoted to cultural subjects increased from 21.6 to 31.6, while that devoted to mathematics and sciences decreased from 33.6 to 31.2, and to professional courses from 44.8 to 37.2.[12] Hart's Academic Board was guided throughout its deliberations by the concepts of stressing scientific fundamentals, of using laboratory, rather than classroom, hours for the factual aspects of professional subjects, and of ensuring that the demands on the time and energy of the midshipmen were not increased. The changes accepted by the Board of Visitors and the Navy Department were to be imposed gradually and to apply to all classes graduated after 1933. As they were being set in motion that fall of 1932, Hart wrote his friend Vice Admiral William H. Standley: "You may have read that we are making decided changes in the curriculum. That is all true, and furthermore, we are taking various liberties with the daily routine." It was Hart's guess that these changes would "make the old boys turn over in their graves." Whatever the reaction, he was prepared to take full responsibility, even though, as he admitted, he had started the process in the "valor of ignorance."[13]

Two years later, when the program was in full operation, it was still Hart's considered opinion that "no serious mistakes" had been made. To be sure, some degree of "professionalism" had been sacrificed, but he could not see that anything had been lost in such fundamentals as "readiness to keep watch, do boat duty," and so on. In return for the hours not spent on technical subjects there was "a decided improvement in the education," and coincidentally there came "a new life to the faculty under which teaching methods have bucked up tremendously."[14]

There were two other strictly academic reforms that Hart wanted to see instituted during his tenure, both aimed at improving the quality of the teaching. One was more careful selection of officer-instructors and longer tours for them, and the other was giving those officers better pedagogical preparation. Whether it was because, as Hart suspected, Admiral Upham wanted to compensate for having given him a difficult job, or whether it was because those reforms were logical, some adjustments along these lines were made. By 1933 senior officer-instructors were being assigned for three-year tours and the tours of some younger officers were being extended. This change caused or coincided with what Hart thought was a general improvement in faculty quality. Hart continued to plead, however, throughout his time as superintendent for more attention to be paid to selection and longer tours of duty, and to stress the importance of teaching. He argued, for instance, that more time should be spent on instruction and less on "manning the boards," and he urged that there be fewer classes in which monthly exams were given—he contended that the students forgot the material covered once the exam was over. In these quests he was successful, as he was in getting permission to send some modern-language instructors overseas for summer courses.

The reforms made hardly constituted an educational revolution and, as was foreseen, some of them, particularly those in the curriculum, were not popular throughout the navy. But they showed that Hart was hardly the crusty old conservative many people, especially among the midshipmen, thought he was. He was aware of and generally sympathetic with the criticism that the academy had gone too far toward being a trade school, that some of the faculty, particularly the officers, were competent in their subjects but were poor teachers; and that the answer to increasing technological sophistication lay not in constantly adding specialized courses or in extending the academic program to six years, but rather in stressing fundamentals and letting the more specialized courses be taught in postgraduate school. Moreover, his other comments reveal that he recognized that the atmosphere was not ideal for developing all officer-like qualities, most notably independent judgment, and he sympathized with some of the student desire for more control over their lives. What it meant as far as Hart's working days were concerned was that he always kept academics at the top of his calendar. As far as Hart knew, he was the first superintendent to make academics his number one priority. Since there was no dean in the academy organization, the academic work had to be handled by the superintendent with the assistance of the secretary of the Academic Board. The fact that there was just one set course of study simplified the task, but as Hart later reflected, "a good deal of dean-ish work has to be done right in these offices."[15]

But the most important thing was what Hart and his staff did when it came to teaching by example. Hart, and even some of the midshipmen, at least in retrospect, believed that Robison went too far in loosening discipline, so he set about turning the academy into a "tauter ship." The midshipmen soon recognized what Hart was doing and the statistics indicate that they adjusted their conduct accordingly. In 1931, Robison's last year as superintendent, seven members of the graduating class were required to resign before graduation because of misconduct.[16] In 1932, Admiral Hart's first year, twenty-four members of the graduating class were required to resign on the same grounds, and six were allowed to graduate before resigning. The next year, possibly because the midshipmen were adjusting to Hart's routine, only ten members of the graduating class were required to resign before and two after graduation. Interestingly enough, by 1934, Admiral Hart's last year, the number of forced resignations based on conduct was seven—the same number as in 1931. Obviously, not all the regiment made the adjustment, but Hart, and some of the midshipmen themselves, could see an improvement in morale and professionalism. Whether Hart ever reflected back on his own checkered career as a naval cadet, he does not say, although it would have been hard for him to avoid making analogies.

Two other questions that are not answered by the statistics are how Hart handled discipline and what methods he used to ferret out potential troublemakers. Hart totally accepted the concept behind the academy's strict discipline, especially in regard to honesty. No officer who would lie or cheat could be trusted in combat and any officer who could not obey regulations might, in combat, endanger himself and his ship. Hence Hart was intent upon enforcing the rules.

Sometimes he did this in ways that smacked of the martinet, infuriated the victim, and struck others as arbitrary and unfair. One graduate reported with bitterness the instance of a midshipman who was refused a commission "because he rode in a car before June Week to look at a house he wanted to rent for his relatives." In this case it was asserted that "Admiral Hart did not look into the circumstances enough to justify such a penalty."[17] According to another graduate:

> The atmosphere was tense. . . . For example, I lost my roommate in March of 1933, less than 90 days before graduation, because he exceeded the 150 demerits allowed for first class year. His last offense was falling in late by less than 3 minutes for a Sunday morning early church party. He would have been an outstanding naval officer and one of the type we could have used badly [*sic*] in World War II. I also lost two of my close first class friends, for the offense of falling out of the church party before it reached the dismissal area. They were placed on the disciplinary ship "Reina Mercedes" and kept there until the day before graduation at which time they were dismissed with a dishonorable discharge after they had passed successfully all the final exams for graduation. The atmosphere was a "dog eat dog" existence for academic survival.[18]

Not everyone agreed that Tommy always acted in a peremptory, or arbitrary, fashion:

> During the course of [a certain midshipman's] next academic year he was out on the town, and imbibed too deeply of the grape. Going through the gate adjacent to the superintendent's house he bumped into Admiral Hart, who noted that he was definitely drunk. Accordingly, he called the "Jimmy Legs" [gate guards] who took the midshipman in charge and to sick bay for examination, where he was pronounced drunk. At that time this offense was considered practically an automatic dismissal. However, the Admiral called in

my friend, stating that he now found himself in the role of arresting officer, judge, jury and prosecutor. He felt that this was definitely un-American, and should not be allowed. Therefore, he could not bring himself to dismiss the midshipman from the service but would, however, turn him back to the next class of 1934, but with the admonition that if the midshipman overstepped the line again with any major infraction of the rules, he would be on his way out immediately. I am glad to report that this midshipman did graduate with the class of 1934, and being in the lower half of the class took a commission in the reserve, and as such was back on duty in World War II, and had a very commendable career.[19]

A member of the class of 1933, Robert S. Riddell, recounts another incident that illustrates Hart's flexibility:

> One day, about three weeks before my graduation, I was late to formation, and, as was sometimes the custom, marked myself late, and as a result received three demerits, enough to put me over the top of 150 allowed for the year.
>
> Needless to say, I was not aware that I was that close to the top, or my actions might well have been different. Nevertheless it was done, and I was called before Admiral Hart where the situation was discussed. Finally he said, (and I'll never forget his words), "I'm sorry, Riddell, but your place will have to be filled by the man next below you!"
>
> I'm sure that I gulped and was stunned. However, somehow I was inspired to think, and say to him words to the effect that I felt sure that he, as well as the rest of the Academic Department, was aware that there were any number of First Classmen, as well as Second Classmen, who were late to formation, and who did not *mark* themselves late. "I think there is a question of honor in this."
>
> As soon as he heard those words he directed me back to the Commandant of Midshipmen. "Perhaps he may see fit to do something about this when you tell him of our conversation."
>
> He did see fit. Probation—no more demerits before the big day (and I lasted 30 years longer).[20]

It would seem that, while always stern, Tommy considered each case on its merits. If there were indications of serious flaws in character or judgment, he acted swiftly and seemingly without mercy. If, on the other hand, he believed an indiscretion to be an aberration arising more out of high spirits than moral deficiency, he could act with surprising leniency. Perhaps, unlike that meted out by Gilbert and Sullivan's Mikado, the punishment did not always fit the crime, but, contrary to the impression some people seem to have, Hart was not a "hanging judge."

And how did he feel about cases that came before him? There is no way of knowing in every instance, particularly since he apparently wore a mask of judicial inscrutability when dispensing sentences. However, time after time he confided to his diary how much he hated hurting some young man. His entry on 12 October 1931, where he says how much he wishes the midshipmen would not commit "crimes," is typical: three culprits were to come before him for offenses serious enough to require dismissal, "two of them are nice young chaps and it's pretty harrowing to show the required severity." But show it he very often did. He never really got used to having to punish good men. In November 1933, after a football game, he had to deal with an epidemic of scrapes involving midshipmen and liquor. "I *wish* they wouldn't," he wrote in his diary on the twenty-sixth, "for I'm getting very tired of firing them."

It was part of his philosophy that the midshipmen should learn to police and judge their peers. The course he followed was to turn the administration of the regiment over to the midshipmen officers for one week in 1932, while the commissioned officers acted only as advisers. So successful was this experiment that the period was lengthened to two weeks the next year. As nearly as he could observe, there was no decrease in efficiency or discipline and he was certain that it would improve the ability of the first classmen effectively to carry out their responsibilities upon graduation.

The route to getting all midshipmen to play a role in judging their peers was somewhat more complicated. Realizing that many instructors and officers were not aware of what individual midshipmen were really like, Hart decided to expand and regularize an already existing peer-rating system. Every man was required to rate the officerlike qualities of every other man in his battalion, except his roommates. That rating was then compared with one done by the faculty. This arrangement disclosed that there were two categories of midshipmen who had been previously overlooked: first, those who were self-effacing or shy and, therefore, were not noticed by the faculty but were known by their classmates to be of high quality; second, those who, although their indiscretions or weaknesses escaped the notice of the faculty, were well known as rascals by their peers. Hart and his staff realized that either they or the midshipmen could make errors in their judgments, but comparing the student ratings with those done by the faculty gave better knowledge of the student body than otherwise would have been possible. The peer-rating system also gave the midshipmen a real say in the life of the academy.

Thus, there was something of a paradox in Hart's career as superintendent: on the one hand, the austere, distant, cold disciplinarian, who set out to tighten up the regime of the academy; and, on the other hand, the sensitive, humane officer attempting to be just and to raise the morale of his institution. As has been seen before, he lacked the light touch that might have made him more approachable and even have eased the burden he so obviously felt. But, in a way, aloofness suited his concept of command responsibility; it was lonely at the top, he knew, and he seldom made any attempt to ease his loneliness. His consolation was his conviction that, had he been more lenient and more approachable, he would not have been able to turn out such mature, honest, responsible officers, well prepared to be lonely themselves some day. He had no doubt that he was serving the navy, his country, and his students well.

There were some harsh realities for which he could not prepare his midshipmen and which he could not change, or even mitigate. The depression continued to worsen and the academy could not long avoid its pinch. In 1932 congressional budget-cutters threatened to invoke a law that would result in commissioning only the top half of the graduating class. Naturally, this threat threw a pall over the nascent ensigns. Contingency plans were made, panicky letters written to potential employers, most of whom replied that opportunities were greater in the navy, and uniform orders delayed. In May came reprieve: the whole class would be commissioned—but there was no guarantee for the following year.

Indeed, the first rumor was that no commissions would be granted in 1933. What was soon apparent was a tightening of physical requirements for commissioning. Eyes, teeth, blood pressure, all were checked with special care to see if any decrepitude or weakness could be detected. The slightest deviation from the standards was sufficient to ensure that no commission would be granted. That was the policy of the Navy Department not of Hart. Then the Roosevelt administration announced that there would be a 15 per cent reduction in officers' pay, and finally the Navy Department ordered that this year only the top half of the class would be commissioned.

According to the midshipmen, the reaction of the students varied. Most of those who were safely in the upper 50 per cent were relieved, although a few admitted to envy of those who, through ineptitude, had an opportunity to consider a career other than the navy. The reaction of those firmly set in the lower half also varied. Some were resentful, dejected, angry, and felt betrayed; but most, having learned to accept the dictates of the service or the workings of a harsh world, grudgingly bent with the wind. The men most affected were those on the borderline. Where there was a chance, many of them studied until virtually exhausted, worrying as they did so about weakening their eyes, in hopes of displacing someone just a little bit farther up the line. Not surprisingly, this competition did not improve morale, as the midshipmen, in the language of one of them, "greased and gouged to graduate." Yet, some of them, looking back, believe that this competitiveness may have yielded a better product, and the wartime distinction later achieved by the class makes it difficult to argue the point. It was a tough way to acquire top-flight officers.

When June 1933 came around, only 250 of the graduating class received commissions, 13 resigned voluntarily, 41 were physically disqualified, and the other 127 were given honorable discharges and one year's pay, about seven hundred dollars, and let loose upon the world.

Although some of the midshipmen would never have known from his demeanor that Hart cared, others sensed that he did. "I had the definite feeling," wrote one, "that Admiral Hart was pulling for us, and that he would do anything in his power to help us." He was a perceptive midshipman, because Hart was deeply distressed by the problems created for individuals and worried about the impact that the practice would have upon his institution and the navy, should it be repeated. There was little he could do about the law or the depression, but he could help the uncommissioned graduates to find jobs, and this he set about doing. The U.S. Army Air Corps made available some thirty openings and the men who were accepted were sent to flight training at Randolph Field or Kelly Field. That left about ninety-seven, so Hart wrote steamship companies, engineering firms, the coast guard, and other government agencies that might possibly employ his graduates.[21] Courses were provided to help prepare students for the examinations required to qualify for licences as mates or pilots in the merchant marine. When he got a lead, and that was not often, he tried to match job to candidate and make arrangements to bring the two together. This one-man placement service was not too successful and he made plans so that, if the need should arise the next year, it could be better staffed and its procedures regularized.

In 1934, however, FDR changed course, as he began to see the need to enlarge the navy. Not only would all graduates get commissions but the 1933 graduates who had not been commissioned could reapply. Those who could still qualify physically and still wanted to go into the navy were commissioned as the class of '33B. That was a relief, but the tightened physical standards were still in force, and one who was forced to resign because of poor eyesight tells this story:

When I graduated from the Academy in 1934, diplomas were handed out by the Secretary of the Navy on a rostrum in Dahlgren Hall. As each graduate received his diploma, his name was called out over the public address system, and he proceeded across the rostrum and descended a ramp at the far end. Standing at the bottom of the ramp, ram-rod straight, was tiny Admiral Hart. In a quiet voice, intended only for the ears of the graduate, he called each by name and added something applicable only to that particular man. His comment to me was: "Bill Kisor, I regret that you have been forced to resign from the Service. Please hold yourself in readiness to re-join the Service if the need arises. As a nation we can ill afford the loss of the many fine men whose naval careers have been so abruptly terminated." Since there was a time lag between the calling out of a name and the time the graduate reached the bottom of the ramp, and due to the large number of men graduating, this final act of courtesy as each graduate received a firm, warm handshake and a few personal words, this quiet operation certainly took a lot of doing. Admiral Hart was one of a very few men who could have handled this without an error.[22]

It was not much of an incident and some people might dismiss it as purely pro forma. Nevertheless, Tommy Hart did take an interest in the careers of his midshipmen, whether they went on in the navy or turned to other fields. He could readily understand the view of those who decided not to go on in the service; he himself had seriously considered leaving it and some of his classmates, Joe Powell for instance, lauded the benefits of life on the outside. What Tommy did hate, though, was to see the decision forced on a capable young man. After all, he could see his own sons mirrored in many of them and, while Brud did not seem to favor a naval career, there was still Tom. Maybe, if he could pass the physical, he would choose to carry on the tradition.

While most of Hart's time was devoted to academic reforms,

discipline, and coping with reductions in the graduating class, there was always that other important aspect of academy life, sports. Even though the team did not win all the time, the star in the academy's crown and the premier sport was football, and here also Tommy found himself embroiled in controversy.

In June 1927 the superintendent of the Naval Academy, Rear Admiral Louis M. Nulton, with the consent of the Navy Department, decided unilaterally that there would be no more Army-Navy football games.[23] He had two basic reasons for making this decision: first, the Military Academy did not require a one-year residence at the school before a student could compete in varsity athletics—the Naval Academy did; second, the Naval Academy limited any student, even a transfer student, to three years of varsity athletic competition—the Military Academy did not. One result was that Army could, and did, recruit men who had played out their eligibility at some other school and allow them to play for four more years. Another result was that the Black Knights of the Hudson physically dominated Navy, defeating them with distressing regularity. Since the 1926 game ended in a 21-21 tie, 1927 probably seemed like a good time for Nulton to take action.

The Army-Navy football game was more than just a service contest. In the sports-mad twenties, it was a national institution. As Paul Gallico wrote, "it is the greatest military spectacle that this country has to offer." Every year it reminded Americans that while they were "a peace loving nation that does not indulge in weekly or even monthly parades of its military strength, somewhere in the country the best boys in the country are being trained to command the forces that may someday be called to a real defense of the republic."[24] Added to this "playing fields of Eton" fixation, was the fact that the color, the pageantry, and the rivalry rejuvenated the old graduates at least once each year. They and others brought pressure to bear on Nulton and his successors, but the "supes" stood more or less firm. "More or less firm," because a charity game was played in 1930 and there was a little wavering when the Military Academy ruled plebes ineligible, but there was no formal agreement to reinstate the game when Tommy took over as superintendent.

Hardly was he installed than pressure began to mount to hold a game for the benefit of the unemployed. At first Hart resisted, protesting that the only open date was so late in the year that it would interfere with the team's academic work. But letters urging that the game be held poured in. Finally Tommy relented and a game was scheduled for 12 December 1931. After that contest, which Army won 20-0, Hart wrote a warm letter to the superintendent of the Military Academy, Major General William D. Connor, in which he said he hoped that the games could soon be resumed as "annual affairs."[25] No doubt Hart was sincere in that desire, but he wanted Army to see that that hope would be realized only when Army adopted the three-year rule.

When 1932 began, requests started streaming in for another

Thomas C. Hart, superintendent of the Naval Academy, with Major General William D. Connor, superintendent of the Military Academy, at West Point. Courtesy of Mrs. T. C. Hart

charity game in Chicago, New York, or Philadelphia. Connor obviously was under the same pressure, as his letters to Hart revealed. By summer, the furor had become so great that there were meetings between the service chiefs and the two superintendents, all of whom were being politically pressured to make a decision. On 25 August Hart spent an hour and a half in Major General Douglas MacArthur's office supposedly "conferring" on the issue of athletic relations. Actually, for Hart, most of the time was spent "listening to a heretofore well known exposition of the Army position" by the army's eloquent chief of staff. What it came down to, in Hart's view, was that to the army "cooperation" meant "accepting their view—always."[26] Although the records do not make it clear who made the final decision, someone, probably the secretary of the navy, wanted Hart to accept the army's position. On 29 August Hart wrote in his diary: "Most unhappy. I seem to be in the situation of becoming the one who 'gives in' to the Army in the athletes' eligibility rule imbroglio. A predecessor of mine no doubt made a mistake, but I had to be the individual who backs water—licked. Am not used to that position." And the next day he added, "well, off to Philly, to meet the Army and eat crow, Damn!"

The night before the meeting Hart decided to make the best of a bad situation. He sat at his typewriter and hammered out the agreement that he proposed to sign and a press statement incorporating it. When he and Connor met on the thirty-first, the general proposed that they sign a five-year agreement. Hart demurred, his agreement called for three years, that was as far as he would go, and he made his point stick. After that, the meeting went smoothly. Despite this victory, Hart saw himself as trapped by the army and the politicians and he tried to surrender with "all due grace." He only hoped he had found the best way out of a bad situation.[27] The statement that was released to the press by Hart's aide, Lieutenant Commander Lynde D. McCormick, was dated 31 August 1932 and read: "Faced with a situation under which postseason football games are repeatedly played late in the year to the detriment of the academic work of both institutions, the Military and Naval Academies have decided to arrange a three-year series of athletic contests. The arrangement is made without change in existent policies under which each institution fixes its own eligibility rules but without prejudice to any future position which either Academy may take in the matter."[28]

To Hart's surprise, and probably relief, the press commentary was favorable. Sports writers were so glad to have the game back as a regular feature that they did not do much analysis of who had given in to whom. In fact, the resumption of the contest was front-page material. "I've worked hard on various improvements here for a year and a half," Hart complained, "but *that* is not noticed."[29] Be that as it may, as of the fall of 1932 "the game" was back as an annual affair and, as an added benefit, Hart had made a lifelong friend of General Connor. Time also eased some of his misgivings, so when he looked back on his "giving in" to the army he saw it "as a more advisable step than it seemed to be at the time."[30]

Thankfully, the superintendent's life was more than academics, sports, and discipline. As already noted, social activities occupied a high priority and took a large part of his time. The schedule was on occasion almost unbelievable. Naturally June Week, with its garden parties, balls, and receptions was taxing, but there also were other weeks when there were parties, dinners, dances, and special events, one right after the other for days on end. Hart found these activities, particularly when only naval people were involved, rather tiresome because it was the same group over and over again and conversation and interest were harder and harder to maintain. It was his impression, however, that his wife enjoyed these occasions, perhaps because she held up far better than he. Her happiness was vitally important to him and he put great store in her judgment, viewing her role as hostess as crucial to the success of his superintendency. He took special pride in the Wednesday receptions she organized. These "tea fights," as the midshipmen called them, were formal affairs attended by midshipmen, academy staff, their daughters, and sometimes young ladies from the community. Reactions among the midshipmen varied: some enjoyed the break in their routine and welcomed the opportunity to meet members of the opposite sex; some found the affairs depressingly formal and stiff; some avoided them like the plague; and some viewed those who attended as "greasers." The same varied reactions probably greeted the Sunday dinners and other affairs that the Harts gave in an attempt to entertain midshipmen officers. The simple fact is that Admiral Hart had somewhat the same quality as was noted in Herbert Hoover; when he tried to unwind he "creaked," which is unfortunate because Tommy enjoyed the company of young people and took a genuine interest in the lives of "his" midshipmen. It came as a distinct surprise to his charges, even those who had attended "tea fights," to find that he knew who they were and even years later could call them by name.

Not all midshipmen gave Mrs. Hart as high marks on the warmth scale as they gave to Mrs. Robison, or "Mazie," as they called her. Nevertheless, Caroline Hart knew her job and carried it off well. At official functions she was impeccable; she knew the tea ceremony perfectly; and at least one midshipman was so impressed by her that he sought a wife cast in her mold—and, to his enduring happiness, found one.

The schedule slowed down after June graduation. During the summer months, Caroline, accompanied by some or all of the children, went either to Connecticut or to The Adirondack League Club in upper New York State. If events allowed, the admiral would join them there for visits; although at no time during his three years at the academy did he feel free enough to take more than ten days' leave at a time. The rest of the summer he sweltered in the Annapolis heat. These summers in the big, empty superintendent's house he found very lonely. Not that he lacked for entertainment and visitors; it was just that he missed his family.

It was a decided relief, therefore, when September came round, the family was back in residence, the midshipmen returned from their cruises, and the routine began all over again. Fall meant football games, which the admiral attended regularly, whether they were played at home or away, and almost as regularly bemoaned the score, so the end of the season may have been as welcome as the beginning. After the football season came Christmas and for the Harts that meant a house full of children, grandparents, and usually a guest or two. Admiral and Mrs. Brownson, being in their eighties, were not always at their energetic best, but Christmas was always a very special family occasion. Winters were damp and cold in Annapolis and there was usually at least one significant snow. Sometimes, winter restricted the Harts' favorite family pastime, horseback-riding. For the midshipmen sports moved inside where a full range of events from basketball, which the admiral had never seen before, to rope-climbing, in which the academy led the nation, was vigorously pursued. With warmer weather came lacrosse, sailing, and the marvelous Maryland spring, which is nowhere more beautiful than along the Severn. Then it was June Week again as the annual round came full circle.

It was a happy time for the Harts. Brud graduated from Hotchkiss School, where he was followed by Tom, and went on to

Princeton. Isabella was often in residence in Annapolis; the younger girls, whom many of the midshipmen mistook for twins and nicknamed "Bad" and "Worse," lived with their parents. Tommy Hart enjoyed his children, they rode together, took long walks, and played games. There were worries about Brud's grades and the time when the girls disgraced the family by trying to cook under the bleachers with a group of other navy juniors. On this occasion, perhaps not surprisingly, Admiral Hart treated his girls as he would any other miscreants. He convened a court-martial, which found them guilty and sentenced them to thirty days' restriction to quarters. The sentence was carried out, even though it meant that they had to be escorted by the admiral to and from the gate on schooldays.

News of this incident contributed to the reputation of "Tough Tommy" Hart, about whom legends grew. The following, recounted by several students of those days, was one of the most popular:

> The scene is a lovely spring morning in 1931 [1932?] and the Admiral is taking a constitutional down Porter Row. He chances upon the poisonous male offspring (aged eight) of a bibulous instructor who had the nickname of "Whiskey Joe." The wretched child who answered to "Jimmy" was playing in the front yard of father's quarters.
>
> In an unwonted burst of joviality, induced by the weather, no doubt, the old man bade Jimmy a good morning.
>
> Glowering darkly the brat replied, "I'm not allowed to speak to you."
>
> "And why ever not?" asked the Admiral. "Because my father says you are an old s___ of a b___," replied the dear little boy.
>
> As I recall, Whiskey Joe and his family made an abrupt departure to other climes shortly after all this took place.[31]

Then, of course, there was the "Herbert Hoover" high collar he wore and his decree that a similar one be adopted by all midshipmen. This, along with having the uniform better tailored and changing the head gear, was intended to improve the midshipmen's appearance and, hence, self-esteem. He had been waiting since 1904 to introduce this clothing reform. On some it had the desired effect, but others resented the uncomfortable collars, quipped about "having a Hart," at which point they proffered their collars, and nicknamed the supe "Tall Collar" for T. C. Hart. Although most of them did not sense it, Hart took pleasure in being ribbed by the midshipmen.

In 1932 Tommy passed the forty-year in-service mark; at fifty-five he admitted to feeling his age, and his thoughts on reaching this milestone were not totally positive. How could they be? The navy was constantly cutting back on everything. The politicians, about whom he had had suspicions from afar, appeared no better from close up when he defended the academy's budget before congressional committees or discussed their academy appointees in Capitol Hill cloakrooms. Hoover was a "rugged individualist," the kind of president Hart could admire, but he appeared to have brought the nation to an unenviable state. So bad were things that Hart considered voting for Franklin D. Roosevelt and his running mate, John Nance Garner. In view of previous experience with FDR and the fact that he considered him to be "liberal if not radical," even thinking of such a thing indicated a fair degree of disillusionment with the Republicans.

He did not vote for Roosevelt; in fact, he probably did not vote, since he tended to observe the rule that military men should hold themselves aloof from politics. And actually, in the early part of FDR's administration, despite the pressures put on the academy to cut costs and graduating classes, it appeared that the White House was showing some favor toward the navy. But Roosevelt's concepts on redistribution of wealth appalled Hart. "Is it going to develop," he wondered in November 1933, "that frugality, decency, and forethought will turn out to be useless as far as providing some measure of security for the next generation is concerned?" It seemed that way at times to him. He realized, however, that Roosevelt was "experimenting" and on the anniversary of FDR's inauguration Hart opined that the results of those experiments would not be known "within my lifetime."[32]

The same was true of his own experiments with the curriculum. As if it were not bad enough having alumni criticizing him for diluting the naval tradition, at least one member of the 1933 Board of Visitors did not think he had gone far enough. Admiral Sims, seventy-five years old but just as ready for a fight as ever, believed that to ensure a better-rounded product the Naval Academy should accept only college graduates. These degree-holding young men would then be taught their professional skills at the academy. A more revolutionary change can hardly be imagined; Hart, among many others, was wholeheartedly against even considering such an idea. Sims arrived for the meeting that year prepared to "play h-1" and filled with what Hart considered "all kinds of pre-conceived and erroneous ideas." Part of the superintendent's task when the Board of Visitors came calling was to show off the institution, while also conducting the business meetings of the board. In April 1933 Sims's constant criticism of the way things were done made the visit difficult. After two days, Hart thought he had "sold" the place to some of the visitors who arrived "*very* doubting," but not to Sims. "He is quite impossible," wrote Hart, "to be brutal—he is a somewhat senile egotist." Sims got little support from the rest of the board, perhaps because they sensed the same negative tendencies Tommy did, so the old admiral had to content himself with drafting a minority report.[33] On 27 April Tommy was enormously relieved to see him go; "*hope* I was polite," he wrote, "even if I didn't feel like it." Except for a bitter fight over the appropriate number of civilian faculty members, Hart being in favor of reduction, this meeting with the board was the last severe test of Hart's academic policies.

When 1934 began it was time to think about a new assignment while the Navy Department looked around for a new superintendent. For Hart it was going to be back to sea; for the academy the selectee most favored was Rear Admiral David F. Sellers, who visited briefly during the spring. Hart immediately sensed a little tension; Sellers did not seem to be fully in sympathy with the way Tommy was running things. Tommy's own feelings on that subject were mixed. In April, when he was ending his third year, he wrote, "I wouldn't have missed them [the three busy years] for a lot. And I would not do them over again for a lot more."[34] As he noted two days later, the thing that made him the most unhappy was "ditching out" midshipmen, which he was still doing in May of 1934. In June he went through graduation for the last time. His efforts to line up a big-name speaker for the occasion failed, so he had to substitute. He was somewhat more satisfied with the result than he usually was. According to the graduates who were there, it was a short, but clearly memorable, speech, for many of them can still recall the burden of it. Tommy told them, much to the surprise of some, that, whereas they had been taught a great deal about technical and professional subjects, one tremendously important part of what made for a successful career had hardly been mentioned. To be successful in the navy, Hart said, took not only competence, intelligence, and character, but a very large measure of just plain "luck." That being the case, the best thing he could do for them was wish that the "fates" as well as their superiors smiled upon them. Many were impressed by this simple wish yet few could know how sincerely Tommy believed what he was saying.

The family left first, and Tommy stayed to turn over command and be of what help he could to Sellers. Most of the essential details about the academy were included in a twenty-three-page memorandum that Hart drew up because he doubted that Sellers would listen to what he had to say. It quickly became apparent that the new superintendent, as anticipated, had little interest in what wisdom Hart had to impart, and there is no indication that the memorandum was of much value to him.

On the night of his last day in Annapolis, Hart reflected on the job that some said he had done very well. "I agree," he wrote, "its better than some men have done but it might have been a lot better. But as I contemplate the paucity of natural equipment that I brought to the task I believe that I'm justified in the feeling of satisfaction that I really hold." On 18 June 1934 he formally turned over command in the rain, bundled into his car, and headed north. After crossing the Severn River, he stopped and looked back at the academy "through a cigarette." His reverie ended with this thought: "My alma mater; you made me absolutely, and are entirely responsible for most everything that I am today. And now, after 40 years, perhaps these last three years of my endeavor has paid you back in part."

Obviously, some of the actions Hart took as superintendent he took at the instigation of his superiors, and if he wanted advancement, which he did, he had better do what he was sent to do. The tightening of discipline was clearly a corrective sought by senior officers in the navy, a measure, it should be added, with which he was in wholehearted agreement. The fact that he was under severe economic pressure to be selective in terms of the midshipmen graduated was always there, in any case, if he ever wanted to waver. The same impetus and the same consensus in the senior ranks was not apparent for his other reforms, although he did get support from higher headquarters. That Admiral Sellers was among those who did not approve of Hart's curriculum changes became clear shortly after he took over, when he made it known that in his opinion the academy's "one justification for existence" was "to educate and train officers to fight the fleet." Moreover, in his opinion, "success or failure in battle with the fleet is in no way dependent upon a knowledge of biology, geology, ethics, social science, the literature of foreign languages or the fine arts."[35]

Hart seems to have sensed that Sellers was among the old graduates with whom his changes would not be popular. But, as has been seen before and will be again, he was not going to let his ambition for higher rank get in the way of doing things the way he thought best. Moreover, he undoubtedly hoped experience would show that his graduates were fully as able as those of earlier years to "fight the fleet."

The point is that the conservative, "Tough Tommy" Hart was not always and irreconcilably in favor of the ways of the past. He liked some new ideas, in fact he seemed always to be looking for a better way of doing things. It is certain that, though they did not know it, he liked the company and spirit of young minds and for this reason, if for no other, he was committed to making a better future for them if that was in his power. As far as he and other military officers were concerned, he did have some old-fashioned ideas. He was firmly convinced, for instance, that they should not curry favor with their subordinates—or their superiors, for that matter. Moreover, officers should expect to be held to a high standard, with admirals in his view especially harshly judged because they had reached the pinnacle and received their reward. Yet toward his subordinates he took a paternalistic, tolerant view. He expected, for example, that seamen would be drunk and disorderly while on liberty, and if they stayed out of trouble and out of his sight that was fine. If they got in trouble or came before him, he would, regretfully, punish them, and that he assumed they expected of him. Midshipmen apparently fell somewhere between the officer category and the seaman; they were not yet fully responsible for their actions, but they had to learn how officers would be treated by their superiors.

He believed orders and regulations might be fought or bucked through official channels, but until changed, had to be obeyed. As far as character was concerned, he was unbending; any deviation from a very high standard—to which he held himself—would be punished promptly and severely. Fairly, but severely. He wanted, but seldom got, his own approval; he also wanted the approval of his wife, of some close personal friends, and very probably of Admiral Brownson. Having the formidable Brownson as a frequent visitor at the academy, over which he had reigned almost thirty years previously, must have been an intimidating experience, to say the least. Whether or not it intimidated Tommy cannot be known; nor can it be known whether or not it occurred to the superintendent of 1934 that, in attitude and demeanor, he could easily have been mistaken for the superintendent of 1905.

5

CRUISERS AND
THE GENERAL BOARD

I n the next five years Tommy Hart's professional future would be determined. Would he go to the top or would he be diverted from what seemed like his destiny? Aside from having made enemies because of his independence and possibly having put some people off by his hard-bitten style, Tommy had had a very successful career, more than fulfilling the demands of each successive difficult assignment. Now his class, 1897, was moving into range for the navy's top commands and he was up there with the best of them. Would he go all the way to the top—Commander in Chief, U.S. Fleet (CinCUS)? The air on Olympus is very thin and the scramble to scale the slopes brings out many things in men; moreover, factors other than talent are often weighed in the balance. Did he have friends who would help him? Did he have enemies who would delight in passing him over? From a personal standpoint, the more important questions were: how would he go about gaining preferment and how would he accept defeat if his much vaunted luck did not hold?

After a brief vacation with the family at King House in Sharon, Connecticut, Hart set out for Providence, where he was to join the heavy cruiser *Louisville*, his flagship for the next nine months. His humor was good. He knew that he had done well in his last four assignments, or at least he knew that was what others thought. As he put it, he had "gotten away with things" during the past ten years. Now, as a senior rear admiral with seven years to go to retirement, he could see in the future, if he maintained a "proper humility," and if his "splendid luck" held, distinct possibilities. He resolved, however, simply to go on as he had been doing "if health holds out and *if* they continue to give me the ball." "But," he continued, "I'm not bothered by too much ambition and thought of self. I'm just racing along at normal gate [*sic*], will take things as they come—and expect to be satisfied with any outcome."[1]

On 18 July 1934 he assumed command of Cruiser Division 6. Initially he had been offered a division of battleships and, much to the surprise of the chief of the Bureau of Navigation, instead of jumping at it, he asked what other possibilities there were. There was a division of heavy cruisers available with approximately the same responsibility and promotion possibilities, he was told. "I'll take the cruisers," Hart replied. Why, he was asked, would he rather command 10,000-ton cruisers than glamourous 35,000-ton battlewagons? Because, Hart explained, battleships seldom got off on their own, and, anyway, he had already worked with the battle line for two years. Heavy cruisers, on the other hand, were a new type of ship and working with them would be stimulating, even challenging. Finally, he explained, "for a simple sailor like me, I saw more fun in fast ships." More "fun"? To the casual observer that would hardly seem a factor that would make much difference to Tommy Hart, but it surely did.[2]

As he began adjusting to his new assignment, he felt "woefully ignorant and green." Three years on shore had left him rusty, and when he reacted happily to the cruiser assignment as a "clean slate to write on" he did not know how clean it would really be. The only solution was to go over the ships from top to bottom and try to learn everything about them. He was amazed at the number of new gadgets and complex mechanical gear, much of which was in the gun turrets. Characteristically, he wondered whether all these firing aids were practical and necessary or just another way of wasting money. There also were manuals, plans, orders, instructions, doctrines, and directives on which he had to brush up. As he read until his eyes burned, he found the "digestion process" coming, albeit haltingly.[3] The best familiarization, of course, was to take the ships to sea and get a feel for what the "heavies" could do. That part he loved. By the end of August he had settled in, was sure he had made the right decision, and could write with conviction that he did not envy the commanders of the battleship divisions a particle because "theirs is a slow business of little interest."

At this time the U.S. Fleet consisted of the Battle Force, with the newer battleships, the carriers, two divisions of cruisers, and three or four squadrons of destroyers; the Scouting Force, with three divisions of cruisers and three squadrons of destroyers; the Submarine Force; and the Base Force. Cruiser Division 6 was part of the Scouting Force.

Early maneuvers were on the East Coast, at Newport, Rhode Island, and Hampton Roads, Virginia; fall meant a move to the Caribbean and then through the Panama Canal into the Pacific. The Scouting Force was based at San Pedro, where the division arrived in November. The weather off the Pacific coast was ideal—when there was not too much fog—for large-scale operations, which is how much time was spent that winter. The fact that Hart was glad to be in heavy cruisers should not be taken to mean that he was pleased with his handling of his division. On the contrary, he was much given to self-criticism in these first few months. His immediate superior, Vice Admiral Harris Laning, Commander, Cruisers, Scouting Force, however, recognized him as an "excellent officer [who] gets results, [is] well qualified for higher command and I recommend him for it." He went on, "Hart is a very high type flag officer, hardworking, capable and thorough, [he] has very high ideals and standards, which he lives up to himself and requires subordinates to do likewise."[4] The new year found Tommy philosophically realizing that his breaking-in period would take a little longer than he thought at the beginning. But that was all right, things were looking up, he even delivered himself of a rare burst of optimism. "Come on 1935," he wrote, "you and I are going to have a good time of it and fine things will happen."[5]

That anticipation was at least partially borne out in February when he replaced Laning as commander of the Scouting Force's cruisers. Unfortunately for Hart, no promotion came with his new responsibilities. He now had command of fourteen heavy cruisers, rather than three, with the additional duty of commanding one of the divisions, but he remained a rear admiral. His feelings were decidedly mixed about this development; it seemed that the depression was still pursuing him, as the navy, under congressional pressure to reduce the number of flag officers, chose the way the cruiser command was being handled as one means of complying. His steady progression up the promotion ladder had been stopped, or at least deferred. That did depress him a bit although he told himself that he had more luck and less ambition than most men.

After a little rumination he decided that he did not care much for the title "vice admiral," anyhow, as it had a rather "unsavory" sound to it, so he would just roll with the punches.

The big activity that spring was Fleet Problem XVI, a full-scale simulated war that was waged between Puget Sound, Hawaii, and the Aleutians. Late April found Hart in command of twenty assorted ships steaming west to assault Midway Island. That task was accomplished on 11 May when seven hundred marines Hart had brought out stormed ashore after the island had been properly "softened" up. It must have been a thrill to see the marines charging through the surf as fifty big patrol planes roared overhead. The big thrill for Hart, though, was yet to come. When the assault phase had been completed, roles were reversed and he was assigned three cruisers with the duty of attacking the force then holding Midway. His solution? Run in at night, launch his float planes, and strike an unsuspecting foe. His diary reflects the excitement he felt in going on the offensive. He described how impressive it was to see the three darkened cruisers plunging through the seas at high speed, looking like "three enormous wolfhounds stretched out at full speed and about to jump on their prey."[6] Jump they did and he described the attack in his diary: "We ran in and found the little island, in the moon-glare, turned, ran out a little and sent off our 12 stinging wasps at 1:30 a.m. [First time *that* has been tried]. Within half an hour we began to hear the enemy's frantic signals to turn the lights off, man their planes, etc. It was an utter surprise to them and with the . . . bombs and machine-gun fire poor enemy's planes must, figuratively, be about all in. The ships ran out as fast as they could go, the planes came out and found them and were recovered at dawn over 100 miles away from where we put the slug on friend Alf [Admiral Alfred W.] Johnson. He tried to retaliate but his planes, (which I suppose he wouldn't admit were sunk), couldn't find us. Well it was a good stunt—and very risky." It was also, by all measures, the most dramatic maneuver of the "war." He received plaudits for his accomplishment which he accepted with good grace while at the same time worrying lest too much emphasis be put on the potential of air power.

By June the fleet was back in California, but the summer months were as lonely as the time spent at sea because all the family was back East. They had been together only briefly since the cruiser assignment. Mrs. Hart went west in March, only to have her visit interrupted by her father's terminal illness. The old admiral, aged eighty-nine, died on 16 March 1935 at his apartment in the May-flower Hotel in Washington, D.C. His age and growing infirmity combined to soften the blow although he was sorely missed by all the Harts. This event added to Tommy's family responsibilities, which he already felt he was neglecting. When his birthday came around on 12 June it found him wondering whether he should serve the six years that remained before retirement. He had to think of his family, the burden of trying to prepare for an uncertain financial future, and, as he put it, "this being an Admiral brings me no great satisfaction anyhow."[7] Similar comments make it obvious that, no matter how negative his attitude toward the word *vice* might be, not having been promoted in February very definitely affected his thinking.

Good news for the family came in July and Hart's reaction shows that it was his career and not the service in general that he was down on. Anticipating the worst because of his weak eyes, young Tom was examined, found fit, and admitted to the Naval Academy in the class of 1939. He entered forty-two years and two months after his father, then a fifteen-year-old, had first glimpsed the gray stone buildings of the academy. In the view of one of Coxey's Army's finest, his son brought to the profession "much more, very much more, than I did . . . and can be expected to be a greater success." Although he told himself that it was only Caroline who was interested in seeing Tom follow in his footsteps, Tommy found himself extremely proud and very, very happy.

He was even happier when in early September his family arrived from the East Coast. He had rented a house in Pasadena, found a school for the two younger girls, Brownie and Harriet, and in other ways acted the dutiful parent. With much time spent in port, it was great to have family around to exercise with. As usual, he put much emphasis on strenuous activity; indeed, he claimed he felt "rocky" when he did not have it. Now, with plenty of playmates available there was lots of golf, about which he lost hope—every *other* week, horseback-riding, swimming, and tennis. There also was touring the girls about and going to PTA meetings, dances, dinners, and receptions. In short, the family's arrival and setting up housekeeping in no way brought relaxation, although it did improve his humor.

Nor did the fleet's being technically in home port during the fall and early winter mean no time at sea. There was gunnery practice in which his cruisers raised their short-range score by 20 per cent, and there were division, Scouting Force, and even fleet maneuvers. As can be imagined, Hart was happiest when cruising alone. It was not only that he liked being independent, but he did not have highest confidence in the Commander in Chief, U.S. Fleet, Admiral Joseph M. Reeves. Reeves often seemed to Hart imprecise about the purpose of a particular maneuver or, when precise, seemed more interested in experimenting with the fleet than in training it. "None of us seem to know anything about his tactical ideas," Hart wrote, "or how he intends to use the Fleet in battle." This may simply have been a matter of reticence, but Hart doubted that; he suspected that it indicated instead that Reeves was either not a good sailor, or not a good tactician, or possibly both. One thing Reeves was good with was aviation; in fact, he showed more interest in that part of the fleet than Hart thought healthy. Not that Hart did not respect the ability or usefulness of air power; he had demonstrated how effective it could be in the exercise at Midway. Nor was it that he did not respect his pilots; he thought that, as a group, the navy's airmen were the

Caroline Brownson Hart in her mid-fifties. Courtesy of Mrs. T. C. Hart

cream of the crop; Jocko Clark had convinced him of that. It was more that he wanted to see how the fleet would operate as a unit rather than always "choosing up" sides for some exercise or other. He liked Reeves as a man, and as overall commander he was fine, just erratic or, as Hart put it, his "gyro wobbles."

Hart's return to Washington in late November showed that whether Reeves was wobbly, or a sailor, or a tactician, he was making an impact on the Navy Department. Tommy's friends back East gave him the distinct impression that Reeves was running the Navy Department as well as the fleet, while the chief of naval operations, Admiral Standley, stood by ineffectually. Obviously, much of this was gossip, but he was left with the idea that much more politics was being played in the higher ranks than had earlier been the case. Perhaps the fact that Roosevelt had persuaded Congress to increase naval expenditures made high command more desirable. Or maybe it was that the still relatively small naval budget made every crumb more eagerly sought. The Vinson-Trammell Act of 1934 provided congressional authorization for obsolete ships to be replaced by new construction, with a gradual increase in tonnage to treaty limits. Nevertheless, the funds available were not unlimited. Hart did not expect that his fortunes would prosper in this atmosphere. He was not much of a "spender" nor did he have much stomach for political intrigue. "Perhaps my always having been a lone wolf will turn out badly in the end," he wrote, "but I can't see myself belonging to any clique—or being owned by anyone."[8]

This trip East more or less prepared him for who would be on the "slate" of top admirals published in January 1936. Japy Hepburn went to be Commander in Chief, U.S. Fleet, with four stars, and Vice Admiral Bill Leahy was promoted and chosen to command the Battle Force. Hart considered those two selections just and reasonable, but he did not feel the same way about Rear Admiral Frederick J. Horne being given three stars and made Commander, Aircraft, Battle Force, or about Rear Admiral Clarence S. Kempff being promoted to vice admiral in command of battleships in the fleet. In Horne's case it was a matter of someone else—namely Harry Yarnell—being more deserving, in Hart's view. Kempff's elevation he considered simply laughable, but a clear indication of Reeves's influence, since Kempff was one of Reeves's "boys." As for Tommy, he was left off, which came as no surprise to him. Yarnell thought as highly of Hart as Hart thought of him, and he wrote a letter of consolation on 24 January

1936. Don't feel too bad, he said, "you have worked for the efficiency of the Service and not for the advancement of No. 1"; furthermore, in Yarnell's opinion, Tommy had had "the guts to voice your honest opinion regardless of the consequences."[9] Others of his friends agreed that he had been badly treated but, somehow, he could not feel that way: he had a "grand experience" in heavy cruisers with "much fun and a great deal of satisfaction," which was about all that could be sought from any assignment.[10]

And satisfaction he continued to get. After tactical maneuvers that January, during which he again reflected on how much more he enjoyed cruisers than battleships, he gave a rare insight into why he found so much enjoyment in handling ships. "It is said that love of the exercise of power is a prime motivation of man," he wrote. Any man, he continued, could "get his thrill in a place like mine on seeing his ships with *their* enormous power respond instantly to the flicks of a few pieces of bunting displayed at his order. Grand and Glorious."[11]

His days of shiphandling were growing short; the time was coming for another shore assignment. On 23 January he found what that assignment was to be. He was going to the General Board, a body of which he had often been critical and by which in the past he had sometimes been roughly used. Surprisingly, he was quite pleased with this prospect, although he did see some irony in the fact that he, a maverick, would be a member of the rather stuffy board. It seemed to him that, after eleven years of being in command, serving on a board under someone else's command would be a relaxing change of pace. Thus, even though he did not hold the board in very high esteem, this would at the very least be a break from the pressure of command. And, demonstrating that his philosophical acceptance of not being given a command that carried the rank of vice admiral was not a matter of being resigned to remaining a rear admiral, he wrote in his diary that from the General Board in Washington he would be free to "jump for anything good that turns up."[12] Since he was hearing many rumors that his name was being bruited about for the navy's top command, "anything good" might really be worth jumping for.

Although the assignment was announced in January it was not until June that he actually turned over his command. In the interim there were the usual maneuvers, with which he had become familiar, and the fleet exercise. On Fleet Problem XVII, one of his younger friends commented that Hart did a "great job" of showing what cruisers could do. "I know little of war," Lieutenant Commander William Ward "Poco" Smith continued, "but it seems to me that six battleships heavily engaged by nine of the enemy would be made uncomfortable if teed by a line of cruisers dropping 8″ shells into their steering [spaces], engine rooms, and through the backs of their turrets."[13] That Admiral Hepburn agreed is shown in this extract from a fitness report:

> As Commander Cruisers, R. Admiral Hart brilliantly fulfills the promise of his long standing service reputation, both as a seaman and as an administrator. I am particularly impressed by his intense and unselfish devotion to high standards in promoting Service interests. A cold blooded analyst of both personnel and material conditions he is at the same time considerate, reasonable and just. His command is never unconscious of the steady pressure from above for continuous improvement.

Much to Hart's surprise and pleasure, his staff, which he considered to be the best he ever had, demonstrated in various ways that they had similar regard for him. There was an engraved cigarette box, a surprise birthday celebration, and many comments implying that they anticipated his early return from Washington to command the fleet. The final verse of a song they composed for his birthday ran:

> Washington calls our Tommy now—
> They need him there to show 'em how
> He'll do it, too, for he can't be beat
> And then he'll come back to take the Fleet.[14]

That anticipation was obviously pleasing, but it was the expression of personal warmth and regard that most clearly touched him. Although he did not let it show, he was quite overcome with emotion. He was not accustomed to his juniors letting him know the way they felt, as did Lieutenant Commander John W. Wilcox, Jr. "Your knowledge of the job," Wilcox wrote to Hart, "your interest, your example, your consideration of those under you, and last but not least, your perfect handling of the force at all times" contributed to the force's high morale and respect for its commander. "I shall always feel," Wilcox concluded, "that you are the man the Navy has been looking for to command the Fleet."[15]

All Hart's officers might not have agreed with Wilcox who, however, as executive officer, had a good opportunity for observation. Hart's style of leadership was very direct, and somewhat formidable, as the following story illustrates. Once, when Tommy was leading his cruisers in to San Pedro Harbor, the navigator of his flagship made the required course calculation and relayed it to the admiral. When he rechecked his figures, the navigator found he had made an error and recommended to the admiral that the course be changed. Again rechecking the figures, the navigator discovered to his horror that indeed his first calculation was correct. When this news reached the bridge, Hart bellowed: "This ship does not jump around like a jack rabbit sir! Which course is right?" The navigator replied that the original one was correct. When the anchor went down, Hart summoned the officer and barked, "What happened?" Knowing from fleet gossip that Hart hated alibis, the navigator answered simply, "I busted, sir." "All right," bellowed Hart and promptly dropped the matter.[16] Actually Hart seldom raised his voice, but its penetrating quality may have made it seem like a bellow. Be that as it may, Hart was a no-nonsense fellow who preferred an honest admission of error to an involved explanation. That approach may not have been appreciated by everyone who felt the lash of his tongue, but it did save time and psychic energy.

That Hart had the saving grace of humor is illustrated by another episode that took place while he was Commander, Cruisers, Scouting Force. An ensign who graduated from the academy during Hart's tenure as superintendent was considerably unnerved when he heard that Hart was the admiral who was coming to inspect his ship. When Hart came onto the bridge, he seemed just as formidable as ever and, to test the alertness of the engine-room crew, he walked over to the voice tube and shouted into it: "If eggs are five cents apiece, how much would a dozen cost?" To the horror of the ensign, the reply came back: "Shut up, you dumb S.O.B. Don't you know we're being inspected?" Hart showed just a twitch at the corners of his mouth. "They are alert," he announced.[17]

Even though Hart accepted the loneliness of command, one of the things he loved most about having a command at sea was the opportunity to spend some time with his young officers. When at sea or on shipboard in port, he invited small groups of young officers to dine with him in his mess whenever possible. Many of the youngest of them were students at the academy during his superintendency, so these occasions sometimes took on the atmosphere of a college reunion. At one such gathering, a student whose career had been rather checkered saw for the first time that Tommy had a sense of humor as well as an ability to judge character:

I was a very unmilitary inmate of the Academy. Academics caused me small concern and I determined to learn as much as I could in matters that interested me whilst keeping as low a profile as possible. I never intentionally broke a rule; I just ignored the ones I did not agree with. This inevitably led to some difficulty with the executive (disciplinary) department and saddled me with an undeserved reputation as a rebel. This is to explain that although I was charged with a serious offense, I was (for once) completely innocent.

A classmate got the bright idea of teaching some plebes to sing *The Internationale* while he raised a red rag in the mess hall. I happened to be seated at the same table but knew nothing of this project before or after commission. It was supposed to be a joke. At that time none of us had much idea about communism and it was just a sort of a crackpot outfit, the Wobblies, etc. Needless to say we were scooped up forthwith and hustled to nearest confinement. My reputation as a non-conformist had me in real trouble for a while. My protestation of innocence was scoffed at until . . . I finally had to appear before the Superintendent. I was petrified. Admiral Hart was reputed to be absolutely (you should pardon the expression) heartless. He was perfectly calm (where others had raged and threatened). He asked me some questions which I answered as truthfully as I ever answered anything. At the end he smiled slightly, admonished me about being foolish and dismissed me. That is the last I ever heard of the matter. The point is he believed me where no one else had, and he was so easy to talk to.

After the Admiral had been aboard [the USS *Minneapolis*] a few days he invited about seven of the younger officers to have dinner with him. The dinner was pleasant and the old man was friendly. We were flattered and pleased. During the meal he turned to me and said, "Howard, I remember seeing you while you were a midshipman, but I can't recall the exact circumstances. What was it you came up before me for?" Man, I spilled my guts; I recited the whole story while he sat there and nodded pleasantly. Everybody got a yuk out of the incident. As we left I hung back and, when the others had exited, I asked how he had remembered the incident with all his duties. He smiled and said, "Oh, I didn't remember it. I just looked at all of you young men and decided you were the one most likely to have been to my office and it might make a good story."[18]

There would be little opportunity for this kind of camaraderie in Tommy's next assignment, and he found himself once again sad at leaving a command afloat, this time there being an added twinge because he realized that he might never again have an independent command at sea.

The General Board of the Navy, established in 1900 by Secretary of the Navy John D. Long, with Admiral George Dewey as its first chairman, was part of the reorganization that went with becoming a rival to Great Britain on the high seas. In a sense it was a contemporary of Tommy Hart, having grown and matured just as he had. Chaired by Admiral Dewey until 1917, it came to have considerable influence through the judicious exercise of its advisory function to the secretary of the navy. A later secretary, Josephus Daniels, described it as "composed of officers of mature experience and eminent professional accomplishment, constituting a deliberative body to consider all matters of naval development, naval strategy, tactics, etc."[19] In the early days, with President Theodore Roosevelt as commander in chief expressing an expansionist foreign policy and ships coming down the ways with satisfying frequency, the General Board performed an invaluable function. After 1915, it became the primary vehicle for implementing the national policy of building a "navy second to none." Over the years, however, as the internal administrative mechanisms of the navy, such as the Office of the Chief of Naval Operations, became more vigorous, the board declined in importance. That factor, combined with what amounted to a building freeze during the twenties and early thirties, left it with very little upon which to advise. True, it did play a role in the various disarmament conferences as well as make recommendations on building programs and other important matters, but its golden years were clearly behind it by the time Hart assumed his seat. After all that is said, since the General Board made recommendations concerning ships' characteristics and the composition of the fleet, the work before it in the late thirties, when more money began to flow from Congress, was of much more significance than had been the case since the Washington Naval Conference.

That the work would be of some moment was satisfying, yet Hart still hoped that the rumors about his name being in for some higher command would soon be verified, so he viewed himself as something of a transient member. That was another function of the board; it served as a holding ship, or temporary billet, for senior officers for whom there was no appropriate permanent billet at the moment. When he reported to the board on 10 July 1936 he was not overwhelmed with the talent assembled. To be sure, there were some senior admirals: Frank Brooks Upham, the chairman, Joseph M. Reeves, Walton R. Sexton, Adolphus E. Watson, John W. Greenslade, and Alfred W. Johnson; the obvious problem was that few of them had experience in materiel procurement. Since much of the board's effort was directed toward that end, this deficiency seemed serious. The board had the power to call on any experts whom they believed could provide relevant information, but still, the lack of expertise and the constant changing of the board's composition bothered him.

The work was interesting in that a wide variety of matters came before the board, but Hart's diary is filled with references to the fact that, in his view, it did not seem to work very hard or very efficiently on any of them. The basic issue each year was to determine what the composition of the fleet should be two years hence; for instance, in 1936 they set building plans for 1938. In addition, they considered such disparate items as fleet organization and command, minesweepers, antisubmarine devices, policy relating to lighter-than-air ships, the expediting of naval shipbuilding, motor torpedo boats, aircraft building programs, and selection. On this last subject Hart had some very strong opinions. He had long been frustrated by the lack of accurate information available to selection boards. In February 1936 he wrote an unsolicited letter to the General Board suggesting that since there seemed to be no way to ensure that officers would fill out the "remarks" section of the evaluation forms accurately, there needed to be some new system for providing selection boards with information.[20]

Among other things, he recommended that health be given very serious consideration, especially when it came to officers being promoted to top commands. In general, he favored a system similar to that being advocated by Admiral Sims. Under the Sims plan, if, for example, there were slots for forty new commanders, all serving commanders would be asked to list, in order of competence, the top forty lieutenant commanders in the service. After that, arriving at the names of the men who should be promoted would be a relatively simple, mathematical procedure. Some new method had to be adopted because the navy was simply not getting the kind of officers it needed and, every time Hart was put on a selection board, he was convinced that the reason for it was the kind of biased, incomplete information upon which promotions were based. The board did not share his unhappiness with the current procedure, so he was left to worry about what he saw as the profession's unprofessional promotion methods.

In November he had reasons to be even less happy about promotion procedures. Admiral Standley was preparing to retire from the navy and William Leahy was slated to take his place as chief of naval operations. Although they were classmates and good friends, Hart's reaction to the nomination of Leahy was that "politics and favoritism" would be playing an increased role during the next several years.[21] Leahy's closeness to Roosevelt, combined with Hart's developing cynicism about how things ran in Washington, no doubt contributed to this reaction. A few days later, word of the flag command changes that were to occur in January 1937 was made public. All rumors to the contrary—he said he had put little stock in them anyhow—Hart was not going back to sea in command of the fleet; Japy Hepburn was going to keep that job. Hart said that Japy's selection did not bother him; he did speculate, though, that his own command possibilities had been distinctly narrowed; now almost the only way he could go back to sea was as CinCUS. As his years of active service grew fewer, the stakes in the game of professional preferment rose.

He was again going to be promoted, in a way. Admiral Reeves, who had taken over from Upham, as chairman of the General Board, was stepping down as of 30 November 1936. On 1 December Tommy Hart would replace him as chairman. Hart felt neither honored nor elevated; he wrote, "guess it's because I'm used to seeing one of the dug-outs in that seat." "I wonder," he continued, "if it's a bit prophetic?"[22] He determined, however, whether a "dug-out" or not, he would try to make the board work harder.

One of the primary issues the board would be addressing was submarine characteristics. On that issue, Tommy, as we know, had some very definite opinions and he had fought for them in front of the board in the early 1920s. Furthermore, he had continued to chair conferences of submarine officers and kept in touch via correspondence with many other submariners. He was hesitant at first to state his opinions from the chair, but as time went on he became more and more outspoken. His view was that, in the past fifteen years or so, U.S. submarines had become larger and larger simply to accommodate more and more sophisticated equipment, and that too many creature comforts were being included; to him it seemed "we overdo it—badly." He had doubts about whether some of that equipment and the additional space devoted to habitability really paid for themselves; he was firmly convinced that, for some missions, bigger was not better. He was probably still thinking in terms of the small, efficient U-boats which he thought could play an important role in the U.S. naval arsenal. What he wanted for the U.S. Navy was a small, simple boat suitable for coastal defense either off the U.S. coasts or off some of the U.S. island dependencies.[23] At first he was unable to convince his fellow board members of the wisdom of building some small boats, instead of concentrating exclusively on the standard, 1,500-ton fleet submarines, but he did not give up.

Having returned to the matter several times in 1937 without success, he started some interservice lobbying. The result was that in May 1938 the influential Submarine Officers Conference endorsed his general principle by calling for the construction of two 600–800-ton submarines in the 1940 program. These prototypes were to determine "the characteristics considered necessary for a wartime coastal or patrol type" of undersea craft.[24] What Hart wanted was a partially double-hulled 750-ton vessel with four bow and two stern torpedo tubes, a load of ten torpedoes, and two direct-connected diesel engines that would give it a 14-knot surface speed. Further specifications he suggested were: a hull designed for dives of 250-300 feet; two 34-foot periscopes; a diving time of 45 seconds; a range of 6,000 miles; submerged speed of 9 knots; and a submerged endurance of 48 hours.[25] Not all submarine officers agreed with Hart or with the Submarine Officers Conference, so there was considerable selling to be done and, in consequence, the 1940 date was allowed to slip by. There was also much correspondence with the Electric Boat Company in Groton, Connecticut, the firm Hart thought should build the 750-ton prototype. Finally, on 27 January 1939, the General Board approved specifications for an 800-ton submarine to be included in the 1941 building program. This design received final approval on 20 March 1939; consequently the Electric Boat Company laid down first the *Mackerel* and then the *Marlin* as the first, and last, realizations of Hart's desired small, relatively simple submarine for coastal defense.[26]

Hart followed a somewhat similar approach to the matter of cruiser design. He did not push immediately for what he wanted, but by June of 1937, when speaking for the board as chairman, he could put his requirements in terms of the board's requirements. Of primary importance, it seemed to him, was simplicity of operation and maintenance: automatic devices should be installed only when it was certain that they would increase efficiency. Second, the trend toward ships with "hotel accommodations" should be reversed: crews should be housed comfortably, but not luxuriously. Next, the 32-knot, 8,000-ton ship the board wanted should be designed primarily to work with destroyers and for fleet work and should incorporate considerable antiaircraft power. In other words, it was essential that the cruisers be good general-purpose ships.[27] Clearly, these specifications show that Hart had managed to sell the board on principles dear to his heart. He wanted simple, efficient, fast, maneuverable ships, capable of being handled by simple sailors who were willing to work and fight under spartan conditions and without a lot of help from fancy, but useless, gadgets. As with the submarines, he did not argue that these should be the navy's only cruisers, but at least some of them should fit these criteria.

The more he thought about it, the more wisdom he saw in an even smaller cruiser. On 30 December 1937 he laid before the board a seventeen-page proposal of characteristics for a medium-sized cruiser. What he there envisaged was a 6,000-ton ship armed with torpedoes and 5-inch guns and capable of making more than 32 knots. It was a well-thought-out proposal that reflected Hart's ability to deal knowledgeably with the kind of materiel matters some of the other board members found difficult. The years he had spent working with the Bureau of Ordnance paid off in this regard, and he found he even enjoyed some of this detailed, conceptual work. Despite his expertise, the board remained less than fully committed to what it called the Hart-class cruiser. In the estimates for fiscal 1940 the board called for laying down two 6,000-ton cruisers with 5-inch guns and two 8,000-ton cruisers with 6-inch guns; however, in their estimates for 1941 they went exclusively for more powerfully gunned vessels.[28]

In a sense, Hart's conservatism regarding size and simplicity was out of keeping with the times. When an attempt at the London Naval Conference, 1935–1936, failed to arrive at a new agreement with the Japanese on tonnage allocation, virtually all treaty limitations on navies were allowed to expire as of 31 December 1936. There were agreements between the British, the French, and the Americans, but they were so designed as to let each power do pretty much what it wanted. As one observer said, the "restrictions" were "like a bed without sheets"; in other words, the agreements bore very little resemblance to a disarmament treaty.[29] In February 1937 the General Board formalized this change by striking the clause "in conformity with treaty provisions" from its official statement of U.S. naval policy. Now, simply stated, that policy was "to create, maintain and operate a navy second to none."[30] The naval appropriation grew yearly, assisted by special measures such as the Naval Expansion Act of May 1938, which authorized a 20 per cent increase in overall tonnage. This meant 660,000 tons of capital ships, instead of 525,000 tons; 175,000 tons of aircraft carriers, instead of 135,000 tons; 412,754 tons of cruisers, instead of 344,000 tons; and so on down the line. Since it was now possible to build larger ships, the board in 1938 called for three 45,000-ton capital ships. Furthermore, at this time, funds were available for modernizing older ships and improving bases. In short, it was a "go-go" period in naval expansion. Hart was in favor of the general policy; he just had nagging fears that money was being wasted, and he worried whether, in its haste to expand and expend, the navy might not be overlooking simpler ways of doing things which, in the long run, would prove more efficient.

In a certain sense, he had the same reaction to the Washington scene. He was distinctly unhappy with the Roosevelt administration's method of solving problems by throwing money at them. He believed the government was being run more and more for the "mob," with Roosevelt acting from time to time like a power-hungry demagogue. Those feelings came to a head over the attempt to "pack" the Supreme Court, which caused Hart to write: "Well, he is my Commander-in-Chief but in my private capacity I can no longer be his faithful subject. I see Mr. Roosevelt now as a very dangerous leader and I can't go his way."[31] He was not a whole lot happier about Secretary of the Navy Claude A. Swanson. The secretary was a former senator from Virginia to whom, the admiral believed, the president was beholden for political support. Unfortunately, the secretary was quite frail and often incapable of fulfilling his duties for months on end. When he was in his office, Hart could not see that it made much difference. "He never writes," the admiral commented, "never reads anything, his voice is so weak and his diction so thick that he can scarcely be understood."[32] It was not very inspirational. Hart knew, however, that the navy was being run by a very vigorous man—Franklin D. Roosevelt. Indeed, it was his distinct impression that Swanson's infirmity was in no way displeasing to the commander in chief. He was virtually certain that the navy had never been so completely run from 1600 Pennsylvania Avenue as it was between 1933 and 1940.[33]

As things turned out, this situation did not redound to Hart's favor. When he returned from his tour with the cruisers, he had a fine reputation within the navy as a seaman, tactician, and leader. His class was at this time very well represented in the higher ranks of the U.S. Navy; seven of its members were flag officers. By mid-1937 there was a considerable body of opinion among high-ranking naval officers that Hart ought to go back to sea as CinCUS. In July Admiral Leahy told Hart that he intended to propose him for that billet when Admiral Hepburn stepped down, a move expected within the year. Chances looked extremely good although Hart privately asked himself, "Do I *want* the job?" The private answer came back, "not so much."[34] With FDR playing such a prominent role in the administration of the navy, Hart's answer to the question might not be the most important one.

Hepburn strongly backed Hart as his successor, yet when the new CinCUS was announced in November it was Admiral Claude C. Bloch who had been given the nod. What had happened? The simple answer is that FDR preferred Bloch or, put another way, did not prefer Hart; and that answer is what Hart believed at the time as well as later. He was told that the chief of the Bureau of Navigation, Rear Admiral Adolphus Andrews, class of 1901, hoped to increase his own prospects for high command by striking a blow at the class of '97 and supporting Bloch, of the class of '99. It also was suggested that Secretary Swanson had vetoed the choice of Hart because, while carrying out economy measures at the Naval Academy, Hart cut one of Swanson's Virginia constituents from the civilian faculty. How much that old score, which caused quite a furor at the time, entered into the decision is not known; in any case, Hart was to stay on the General Board.

His reaction? At first, he believed that his career had clearly come to an end, but as friends offered condolences and told him about how the choice was made, he became somewhat more philosophical and less angry. It was not so much that he wanted the job or that he had been unfairly treated—he contended that he did not have strong views on his own qualifications—but he was furious that the navy was being run on the basis of politics, personal favoritism, and jealousy. As far as Bloch was concerned, Hart thought him well qualified and a good choice. Naturally, though, he was hurt and for a while thought again of retiring, a prospect that he did not find totally unattractive. However, Leahy and others convinced him that all was not lost; higher commands would become vacant later, and anyway, the navy needed him now.

The fact that the navy needed him was driven home when on 12 December 1937 Japanese war planes attacked and sank the U.S. gunboat *Panay* on the Yangtze River. It was a clear act of Japanese aggression which resulted in a brief spate of war fever in the United States. Caroline anticipated that all her men would be in it, but guessed that she had at last had enough and was ready for war. Tommy's guess was that the "little brown brothers" would say it was a mistake and offer some phony excuse, which the government would meekly accept—as the weak democracies were prone to do when facing the aggressors.[35] Despite that phlegmatic response, it did appear to him that the world was drifting toward war. "Will I," he asked, "yet serve in a third one?"

Little did he know that plans being laid almost as he wrote would have a definite impact on his future and on the matter of whether the United States would be in yet another war. In direct response to the *Panay* incident and in recognition of the limited fighting ability of the understrength U.S. Navy, in late December FDR dispatched the chief of the navy's War Plans Division, Captain Royal E. Ingersoll, to London to consult with the British on possible joint action in the Pacific.[36] There had not been, nor was there then, unanimity among the Americans themselves on how best to fight a war in the Pacific. Naturally, there was a plan for a war against Japan, but there was not confidence in all quarters that it was realistic. Obviously it would be best if the British and the American navies could act jointly in the face of Japanese aggression, but neither of them was completely certain of the other's reliability. Roosevelt appeared to some Englishmen as something less than consistent; there always seemed to be more ideas than ability or intention to follow them through, more talk than action. From the American perspective, the British appeared too willing to compromise, too devoid of resolution, too crafty to be relied upon. Furthermore, in the Department of State and elsewhere there was a disinclination to help pull British chestnuts out of the fire, especially if that fire were in a colonial area. The only thing worse in the view of American naval planners would be going to help the British or becoming involved in some supposedly joint venture and suddenly finding that the British had pulled out, leaving the United States holding the bag. Part of Ingersoll's mission was subtly to survey the naval war planning landscape and determine the practicality of joint operations.

He arrived in London early in January 1938 and held a series of meetings, most of them with his counterpart in the Admiralty, Captain T. S. V. (Tom) Phillips. The British were not sure what Ingersoll wanted, but they needed help if they were to make realistic plans for the Far East, so various forms of cooperation were explored. Ingersoll made it clear that he could make no commitments, but he was ready to discuss American plans and to hypothesize about joint ventures. There was considerable talk about Singapore as well as about an impractical scheme proposed by Roosevelt for blockading the Pacific in some future emergency with a line of naval ships and converted yachts stretched from the Pacific coast of the United States to Australia. They also talked about American plans for reinforcing Hawaii and the Philippines, possible joint use of facilities, and the exchange of recognition signals, codes, ciphers, and intelligence. Little of a formal nature came out of the discussions, which ended on 17 January, but the very fact that they had been held was precedent-shattering and set in train a series of conferences on Anglo-American collaboration that was not concluded until Tommy Hart met with Admiral Sir Tom Phillips on 6 December 1941.

Hart's fate was already being sealed, but in 1938 it was not clear whether his son, Tom, would be doing his fighting as a graduate of the Naval Academy. He did not have twenty-twenty vision which, combined with the fact that he seemingly had never warmed to the school on the banks of the Severn, made his continuation there an on-again off-again affair. His father did not really care; as he had often said, it was Caroline's desire more than his that Tom should follow in his father's footsteps. Whether or not that was precisely true is difficult to say; from the number of entries on the subject in his diary during this period it seems doubtful that the father was emotionally uninvolved. In June 1938 Tom decided to resign from the academy. In July, after preparations had been made for him to enter Princeton, he changed his mind. Tommy was not much happier with this course of events than he was with his navigator's "jack rabbiting" into San Pedro Harbor, but at least Tom was back in Annapolis for better or for worse.

The rest of family life was flowing along smoothly during this tour in Washington. All the children were away, either in school or pursuing their careers, which left the parents free to pursue their social life. Or, to judge from Hart's comments, it allowed Caroline to give rein to her social instincts, which were unlimited, and the admiral contends that he was often left gasping after a round of dinners, dances, receptions, and so on. It was a good thing he kept in shape. The Harts had rented an apartment in the Shoreham Hotel, from which every day, rain or shine, Tommy walked the three miles back and forth to work in the old Main Navy Building on Constitution Avenue. He also continued his frequent sallies onto the links. In June 1938 he made this typical entry in his diary: "Been laboring off and on for ten days to teach a new set of golf clubs something about the game. Said clubs are hopeless."

Several times that summer, Rear Admiral James O. Richardson, chief of the Bureau of Navigation, discussed with him the possibilities of his getting command of the U.S. Fleet. Japy Hepburn hinted broadly that his contacts told him that Hart was still a very live prospect for the "Big Fleet."[37] Exactly how Hart reacted to these personal votes of confidence we do not know, but he admitted privately that he found the possibility of the fleet command immensely cheering. He must have been encouraged, because when he put down his preference for his next assignment in September 1938, he wrote, "Command, U.S. Fleet." January 1939 found him still unsettled, with Leahy sounding him out about assignment to some other fleet, possibly the Asiatic Fleet. Hart told his old friend that he did not think he would be too happy out in the Orient watching the "Japs throw their weight around."[38]

Naturally, he saw no reason to accept the Asiatic Fleet while he still hoped he would get the "Big Fleet." Then on 6 March 1939 came the word that, no matter what his feelings, his "fate" was to become commander of the Asiatic Fleet. "A 'full' Admiralcy," he wrote, "not a very large command though and relations with foreigners the most important part of the duties. Well such talents as I have lie with the main fighting fleet but that was just not to be. Perhaps I'm lucky to get what I am getting. At any rate I do not owe Palace Politics for it!"[39]

In a sense that was wrong. As Admiral Richardson recalled, Hart, for whom he had the highest regard, topped the list of admirals suggested to FDR for Commander in Chief, U.S. Fleet. The president took one look and said angrily, "Take that name off the list!"[40] So, palace politics had determined Hart's fate. Those politics, however, were set in train years earlier when Hart ran afoul of FDR's pro-labor policies. There may have been other reasons, but it is difficult to avoid the impression that FDR did not think he would find Hart simpatico, no matter what his qualifications. Hart did not question the president's right to appoint the officers he wanted, but there is little doubt that the admiral was disappointed.

Hart's impression was that, when he was offered the Asiatic Fleet, "I felt I saw between the lines the hope on the part of somebody that I would decline the job and simply retire."[41] All thoughts of retirement, however, had gone from his mind. The chance to go back to sea for two years was just too good to pass up, even though it was not what he had hoped for. It would mean serving a president whom he distrusted and one who apparently did not have the highest regard for him. There also was the chance he would have to go sans family, but at least it was back to sea, and he was very sure he was not going to let anyone force him out of the navy.

Letters of congratulation poured in, many of them bemoaning the fact that he had not gotten the "Big Fleet." They all were welcome, but none so welcome or touching as this one from Tom, who was nearing graduation from the Academy:

Dear Tommy Hart:

I suppose that isn't quite the way a lowly midshipman should address an admiral or quite proper for a very respecting son to use in connection with the object of his respect, but at present I am writing as a member of the Officer Corps of the Navy of which both you and I are a part; and to that part of the Navy which knows you best you are Tommy Hart. If my informant of this afternoon has not made a mistake you will be receiving countless letters such as this in the near future and I want to get mine on top of the pile so that it will be read. It may surprise you that one so far down the line as I have an ear to the undercurrents in Washington, but some of your best friends are mine, too.

Well, I join the rest of the Navy in my congratulations to Tommy Hart on receiving at the climax of his career his well earned four stars and perhaps the most important command that exists in the organization today. I am also of one mind with the rest of the Navy that a better man couldn't have been picked for the job. . . . Yes, Dad, it is really a terrific source of satisfaction to me. This job, as I see it, will require a great deal more than the qualities of a naval officer in which you have for forty-some years demonstrated your excellence. You must have that, of course, but also a great deal more. . . . I fear I sound like *your father* rather than your son, but I am only trying to say that I know you are the one man who is equipped to take this thing on and that I am awfully glad to see that others realize it, too. You are an awful lot more than so many stripes up ahead of your subordinates and associates, because you are known and respected and loved as Tommy Hart and it will take Tommy Hart to take this job over, rather than so much gold braid. Of course, we both know that your position will be, besides immensely important, both trying and interesting; and naturally I can think of no duty more to my taste. I envy you for having it and rejoice with you in your success. May you have all the good fortune there is in the world in your last command.

Tom
(who is flattered when referred
to as Tommy Hart, Jr.)[42]

There were a thousand details to deal with before leaving the country for two years. There were reports for the General Board to be completed, family business to be seen to, and, most happily, a graduation to attend. Tom, after various ups, downs, and uncertainties, graduated from the Naval Academy, ninety-ninth in his class, on 1 June 1939. Despite all previous comments about it mattering only to Caroline, Tommy admitted that "C [Caroline]—and I of course were very proud—and considerably emotionée." So with a new naval officer in the family and the news that at least the women of that group would be able to join the admiral in the Orient, the tour of duty in Washington was ending very satisfactorily. He had not enjoyed all his work with the General Board, often finding its slow pace and inefficient methods very difficult to live with. Yet he knew it had gone a long way toward designing the navy of the 1940s, and in that there was great satisfaction.

Hart's impact on the General Board has to be judged as something short of revolutionary. He probably did act as a brake on the big spenders, if there were any on the board, and as a constant reminder of the need for straightforward fighting ships. He got the prototypes of his small submarines and his light cruisers and he finally went along with the idea of putting more torpedo tubes on the larger submarines, which most of the younger officers wanted. However, while Tommy Hart is usually identified with those prototype small submarines, it should be remembered that many of the large fleet submarines with which the U.S. Navy started World War II were approved by the General Board during Hart's tenure as chairman. Moreover, previous and later models, many of which served throughout the war, have the stamp of his influence or at least incorporated many features of which he approved. In other words, Hart's impact on submarine design was not limited to one type or one size.

As probably the most influential submarine officer of the decade, he must be given credit for the generally excellent submarine designs adopted during that period. It never was established that the small submarine that he championed as a *part* of the U.S.

inventory was not a good design for some missions: true, it did not prove popular, but not enough units were ever built to properly test the concept. Nevertheless, the point still stands: Tommy Hart's contribution to U.S. submarine design was significant, generally enlightened, and more positive than negative. One of Admiral Hart's most valued possessions was a plaque whose inscription reads: "To Admiral Thomas C. Hart, USN, in appreciation, from submarine officers and men to whom he contributed so much in pioneering the development and preparation which made them tick during W.W.II."

Most intriguing about this period of Tommy Hart's life is the matter of his ambition. In the strictest sense of the word, he was ambitious. Regardless of how much he attributes his various successes to luck, some of that "luck" was the result of hard, conscientious work—he willed that and must have known it. Furthermore, no one rises to four-star rank in the navy without being competitive and eager for high command. It is very clear that Hart wanted to command the U.S. Fleet; he even put it in writing. When he did not get it, he forgot his intention to retire and took the Asiatic Fleet, partly to disappoint those who were hoping he would step down. Some officers undoubtedly, and FDR possibly, did hope he would retire, but others made it clear that they had the highest possible regard for him and sincerely wanted him to take the Asiatic command. In December 1941, for example, Admiral Leahy wrote the president: "Of all the flag officers known to me, I should, given a free choice, have selected Hart, King and Nimitz as the best. Of the three, I consider Hart the most reliable and the least likely to make a mistake."[43]

Yet, it would not be inaccurate to say that in relative terms Tommy Hart had very little ambition. He was not good at internecine politics or at self-promotion; that was partially because those traits did not come naturally to him and he did not deign to develop them. Admiral Richardson perhaps put it best when he wrote that Tommy Hart "was an extremely competent, although not a 'showy' officer. He had always sought to further the interests of the Naval Service, as he saw them, and never pushed hir self forward for any purpose."[44] What Tommy sought was to satisfy himself that he had done a good job; he cared some, but not greatly, for what others thought. Some of that attitude derived from the fact that he did not have much respect for the opinions of most people. It also was because he was fiercely independent. But why was he that way?

There is both a speculative, psychological answer to that question and a pragmatic one. Psychologists would say that, since he had far exceeded his father's success, Tommy Hart had no driving need to go farther. More practically and possibly more satisfactorily, what is known about his life leads to another entirely logical answer. By the time he reached the age of fifty, and possibly well before, he was a satisfied man. He attributed this to luck, but even that would be taken by some as being the most satisfactory way of explaining his ascendance over his father. "I am not responsible, luck is." First and foremost, he was married to a woman whom he both loved and admired. Second, although not completely satisfied with his children, he was a devoted family man who had found almost everything in this family that he missed when he was growing up in Michigan. Next, his somewhat cynical view of government and of the motives of most people did not make him hanker to wade into the center of the fray. Finally, money, creature comforts, and social position were not concerns of great moment to Tommy Hart. He had what most men wanted, he was wise enough to realize that, and it was not his nature to spend much time intriguing or wondering why he did not have more.

6

ASSIGNMENT TO
THE ASIATIC FLEET

On 25 June 1939 Admiral Hart set out on the first leg of his trip to China. He stopped in Flint to check on family there, then went on to Chicago, where Mrs. Hart, accompanied by Brownie and Harriet, joined him. They had decided to take the two younger girls out of school for a year so that they could have the experience of living in the Orient; the two boys remained in the States. Isabella was to join the family in China after she finished her job in New York. The Harts sailed from San Francisco on 1 July in the *President Coolidge*, and five days later landed at Honolulu, where they were entertained by their old friends Vice Admiral and Mrs. Murfin. On 7 July they left for Japan. In Yokohama they were met by the U.S. naval attaché, who informed Admiral Hart that the U.S. embassy in Tokyo wanted the new commander of the Asiatic Fleet to maintain a low profile while he was in Japan.[1] This did not mean confinement to the ship, but it did mean no uniform, no comments for the press, and no formal receptions. That was fine with Tommy, who was primarily interested in having his family see a little of Tokyo and Kyoto, which he had last seen in 1922. The attaché briefed him on Japanese-British relations, which Hart interpreted as being "more menacing than ever." After some sightseeing, they sailed from Kobe and by the evening of the nineteenth were installed at the Cathay Mansions Hotel in Shanghai.

This meant Admiral Hart had five days to get acclimated before formally assuming command. Admiral Harry Yarnell, whom Hart was relieving and for whom he had the greatest respect, spared no effort in bringing him up to date. Hart was amazed at the complexity of the issues and "more appalled than ever at the task ahead."[2] He had long realized that the stimulation of diversity was part of the navy's allure but, as he wrote, "this time, taking over the last job of the lot, I'm faced with things entirely new—the naval part is all quite secondary—and said 'stimulation' has magnitude enough!" Characteristically, he added, "I hope that 62 years is not going to be too great a handicap." He saw all the diplomacy, the formality, the international intrigue, as a heavy burden, and fervently hoped that his splendid luck would hold for another two years so that he might be equal to whatever was required. This was really not the way he had hoped to end his career; it was too little navy and too much strain but it was the assignment fate had sent his way, so he would just shoulder his heavy responsibilities and go forward. When the day of the change of command came, the ceremony was quite grand; both principals were four-star admirals and there was the panoply of flags, bands, and the press scrambling for photos. Hart admitted to a certain thrill on 25 July as his flag was broken on the cruiser *Augusta*, but what he felt most of all was sadness for Yarnell, who was leaving command and retiring after a long career during which Hart felt he had never received adequate credit for his fine mind, his flawless grasp of the naval art, and his selfless service on the Asiatic hot seat.[3] He must have wondered whether he would be retiring two years hence with the same inadequate credit. But for now he was Commander in Chief, Asiatic Fleet, with all the honors, perquisites, and responsibilities that went with the title.

As Hart clearly realized, his primary missions were to protect American interests, show the flag, and participate as a military diplomat in the many discussions that animated the international community in China. This last role was the reason for his high rank; the U.S. Navy wanted its representative to be equal, if not superior, in rank to the senior officers of the other navies on the scene. Prominent in China at this time were the British, the French, the Italians, and, of course, the Japanese. In terms of force, the U.S. Asiatic Fleet was small: it consisted of two cruisers, thirteen destroyers, twelve submarines, the necessary auxiliaries, and the 4th Marine Regiment. The Yangtze River Patrol, under the command of Rear Admiral William A. Glassford, Jr., which maintained contact with American missionaries and other interests far inland, was part of Hart's command, as were the naval installations at Manila Bay, more than 1,100 miles to the south. With a command so scattered over miles of river and ocean, supervision was very difficult. And the equipment with which he had to work left much to be desired; most of his surface ships, for instance, were of World War I vintage—Hart used to say they were old enough to vote. But geography and materiel would have been less bothersome had the international situation been less threatening.

Since at least the early 1920s conditions in the Orient had not been such as to induce complacency. With the Manchurian Incident in September 1931, things had gotten progressively more tense. As the Japanese slowly exerted control over more and more of China, it became clear that while winning their war against the Kuomintang was one phase of their program, driving the white man out of Asia was another. Any doubts about the extent to which some of the Japanese military were willing to go in exercising their aggressive instincts were dispelled in December 1937 when Japanese planes strafed and bombed British and American gunboats on the Yangtze River. The sinking of the USS *Panay* with the loss of two American lives not only shook many Americans into facing the Japanese challenge but also, and perhaps of greater long-range significance, prompted President Roosevelt to seek Anglo-American naval collaboration. For reasons too complex to justify analysis here, the first steps along this route were not productive. Captain Ingersoll of the U.S. Navy and Captain Phillips of the Royal Navy, as already noted, discussed a Pacific blockade, the exchange of information, and a regularized system of meeting, but little actually was done. The contact, however, was significant because, among other things, it led the British to anticipate that they might get some vital assistance from the U.S. Navy in protecting their interests in the Far East. Aware of this, the Americans were determined that, while seeking mutually desirable collaboration, they would not get drawn into fighting Britain's battles or protecting interests that were solely Britannia's. Hart shared this desire, but he would become much more intimately involved in later negotiations than he could even imagine and his fate would become inextricably bound up with that of the British Empire in Asia.

More was involved, of course, than British interests in Asia. The British government, and to a lesser extent the French government, insisted that if the Japanese were allowed to push one nonoriental power out of China, it would be only a matter of time before all nonoriental powers were squeezed out. At the same time, the British admitted that, the situation in Europe being what it was, they could not withdraw any naval forces from the Mediterranean to back up a militant reaction to Japanese squeezing. Therefore, in June of 1939, when the Japanese blockaded the French and British concessions at Tientsin and otherwise interfered in the affairs of British nationals, His Majesty's government appealed for direct American diplomatic intervention in their behalf. After lengthy discussions at the highest diplomatic and military levels of the U.S. government, it was decided not to grant the British request. Militarily, the reason was that any form of intervention might lead to an armed confrontation for which the United States was not prepared. The diplomatic thinking was similar, but more complicated. Secretary of State Cordell Hull and the U.S. ambassador to Japan, Joseph C. Grew, hoped that by avoiding provocations they could strengthen the hand of the more reasonable elements within the Japanese government at the expense of the militarists. Moreover, entering the crisis at this point might drive the Japanese into a closer association with Germany and Italy. So, since the military was weak and the State Department timid, it was decided not to take a firm stand against Japanese insults to the British or to declare an identity of Anglo-American interests. Instead, the U.S. government confined itself to the time-honored practice of issuing verbal warnings. The British responded by formally recognizing the authority of Japanese military officials in areas occupied by the Imperial Army. The United States saw this as appeasement, the Japanese saw it as a victory, and the British, incapable of facing down the Japanese singlehandedly, saw it as realism.[4]

This most recent diplomatic flare-up occurred while Hart was making his way east to take command. When he took over, the immediate and most provocative issues facing him, as they had done for Yarnell, centered around Shanghai. This teeming port city of three million was the locus of an international community that almost daily became more polyglot and bizarre. When the Japanese fought their way into Shanghai in 1937 they did not occupy the International Settlement, where the large foreign community lived, played, and conducted its business. Shanghai was no garden spot under the best of circumstances. Arnold Toynbee's reaction upon visiting it was:

> You Smyrna weeping London's tears
> You London racked by Smyrna's fears,

Busy, detestable Shanghai,
Our anchor's up. Thank God. Good-bye.

The impression of an old China hand, Joseph W. "Vinegar Joe"
Stilwell was similar but for different reasons. "This town would
ruin anybody in no time," he wrote. "The babes that twitch around
the hotels need attention so badly that it is hard not to give it to
them."[5]

The settlement was run by a multinational municipal council
which performed, or was supposed to perform, all the functions
and services of a city government. Although there was a police
force, the settlement was divided into defense sectors which were
patrolled by the military forces of Britain, France, the United
States, and Italy. Standing by to assist them was the Shanghai
Volunteer Corps, a group of professional men organized into a
parapolice force. The settlement teemed with Chinese refugees,
German Jews fleeing the Nazis, Russians fleeing the Soviets, various other refugees, spies, and the flotsam and jetsam driven there
by the tides of an international order coming apart; outside, lurked
the main Japanese army waiting for an excuse to take over the
settlement. There were endless opportunities for friction between
the Japanese and the foreigners and between the Japanese and the
Chinese, some of whom, hiding behind their foreign protectors,
did little to conceal their loyalty to the government of Chiang Kai-
shek.

A major part of Hart's mission was to find out what the Japanese
were up to—he had funds for hiring spies—negotiate with them
if a confrontation were to develop, and, all else failing, try to bluff
them out of denying American rights. Shanghai being the center
of American commercial interests in Japanese-occupied China, the
maintenance of American rights there was vital. It also, quite
understandably, was a likely scene for further troubles; there certainly had been many in the recent past. Hart was not sure what
help he could expect from the American consul, Clarence E.
Gauss, but advance information was not very encouraging, implying that Gauss would not support any resolute action. Indeed, the
few briefings he was given indicated that the Department of State
wanted to follow a course that many naval officers, Hart included,
thought bordered on the craven. Not that Hart thought the marines would have a chance in a showdown with the Japanese, but
he intended to pursue the same firm course Yarnell had pursued
and was prepared to be even firmer if the situation so required.

Some of this attitude arose because Hart respected Yarnell, some of it was because Hart generally favored firmness in response to pressure, some of it was because he believed the Japanese respected firmness, and some of it was racial prejudice. There is no question that Tommy had the racial prejudices common to his generation. Consequently, although he did not approve of everything the white man did in the Orient—he thought many of them were lazy or spoiled by high living—he believed that white men were superior to yellow men, whether those yellow men were Japanese or Chinese. One way to demonstrate that superiority was to be firm in the face of provocation. He did not have to wait long to test his theories.

The day after Hart assumed command, his Japanese opposite number, Vice Admiral Koshiro Oikawa, called on him. Even though they had to discuss the mistreatment of a naval warrant officer by a Japanese sentry in Hankow, Admiral Oikawa proved to be friendly and disposed to be agreeable. Indeed, to Hart's relief, the Japanese seemed to be making as much effort to avoid a major confrontation as the Americans were.[6] As he later said, "If anything, I thought I could see an easing up, although there was a continuance of all these incidents and disputes which went on through Yarnell's time and which I inherited. But I don't think handling them was ever as difficult for me as it was for Yarnell because they simply didn't push me as hard. I think the effect of Yarnell's firmness and acumen followed through to my incumbency, and since I tried to carry on in the same way he had, the Japanese didn't want to stir us up."

In the following days there were other callers to be received and calls to make, as well as a series of formal entertainments provided by the military, the diplomatic, and the commercial communities. Then, after reviewing the eleven-hundred-man marine detachment and each of the river patrol craft in Shanghai, he boarded his flagship, the *Augusta*, for the four-hundred-mile journey north to Tsingtao. That Japanese-run city on the Shantung Peninsula was the summer base for the cruiser *Marblehead*, the tender *Canopus*, which mothered six old S-boats, and two tugs. Mrs. Hart and the girls followed by commercial steamer. By 3 August they were all installed in an American-run hotel and ready for another round of calls and entertainments, this time put on by the Italian diplomatic delegation and attended by most of the local white community. The family had been in their hotel about a week when, on 10 August, Caroline came down with a serious case of

Admirals Thomas C. Hart and Harry E. Yarnell aboard the *Augusta*. The Shanghai waterfront is in the background. Courtesy of Mrs. T. C. Hart

food poisoning, apparently the result of eating tainted chicken curry served by the hotel. Her temperature shot up, she lapsed into delirium, and went through two weeks of very debilitating illness.

Since she seemed on the road to recovery, Admiral Hart took the opportunity to go up to Weihaiwei and return the courtesy call of Vice Admiral Sir Percy Noble, the British naval commander in Chinese waters. He also intended to have a "very confidential" talk with Noble about possible actions "if this situation develops into actual hostilities with the Japs."[7] When Hart arrived on 25 August he found that developments halfway around the globe had caused Noble to be more interested in the Germans than in the Japanese. Hitler was making menacing noises about Poland, and the Nazi-Soviet nonaggression pact signed just two days earlier made it easier to convert those words into action. In response to these developments, Sir Percy was going to concentrate his surface ships at Hong Kong. After coolly and matter-of-factly providing this disturbing news, Noble bid Hart good-bye and departed to lead the British ships, now battened down and in a state of war-readiness, south toward Hong Kong. The few remaining British naval personnel, in the best stiff-upper-lip style, insisted on following through with the full round of entertainments originally scheduled for the new commander in chief of the Asiatic Fleet. Hart was impressed and commented that the British "are admirable—even if they do exasperate."[8]

His next stop was Chefoo, where Destroyer Division 5 was based. While he was there a natural disaster struck—a typhoon with winds clocked at more than 70 knots. The ships in northern waters rode out the storm, but at Tsingtao, where the winds were higher, the submarine rescue vessel *Pigeon* was blown onto some rocks in the harbor. This event brought him back south, which is where he was on 3 September 1939 when war was declared in Europe. He immediately dispatched a destroyer division to Manila and sent the marines who were in summer camp to Shanghai where he thought trouble was most likely.

He followed his marines back to the hot, dirty city. When he arrived his spy system conveyed to him rumors that confirmed his suspicion of trouble. On the pretext that Asia should be kept neutral, the Japanese were going to attempt to force the British and the French military to disarm or get out of China. With that accomplished, Japanese forces would quickly take advantage of the vacuum created in Shanghai and elsewhere and move to replace the departed or disarmed Occidentals with Japanese forces. When this news was conveyed to Consul Gauss he seemed disinclined to take a strong stand. Hart, however, did not intend to accept passively "whatever Mr. Jap puts forth" or Gauss's pliant attitude.

Therefore, Hart moved on several fronts simultaneously. He arranged a series of meetings with his staff, with Gauss, and with the British and French military commanders. He found to his distress that the British and French were disinclined to take any strong stand against the Japanese; their governments were fully occupied in Europe and their orders were to do everything possible to avoid provocation. Hart also ordered his intelligence officer, Lieutenant Commander Redfield "Rosy" Mason, an able linguist, to reestablish contacts with "moderate" elements in the Japanese command. And so that the possibility of "incidents" or friction might be minimized, he ordered that special care be taken by all personnel who might come in contact with the Japanese. Finally, Hart ordered that a full set of plans for countering any likely Japanese power play be prepared for use in case his efforts to head off trouble did not work. Specifically, he wanted the U.S. gov-

ernment to "insist on participation [in the] protection of whites
here even to [the] extent of taking over *all* areas [defense sectors]
covered by British and French."[9] The commanding officer of the
4th Marines, Colonel Joseph C. Fegan, agreed, but Consul Gauss
remained less than enthusiastic. However, after lengthy joint discussions, Hart's forceful policy prevailed over Gauss's caution.
After recommending to the navy that the United States be prepared to take over for the French and the British, Hart left for
Tsingtao feeling that, at a minimum, his appearance on the scene
and his prompt action may have robbed the Japanese of the initiative. He left Glassford, who had a reputation for diplomatic
acumen, in Shanghai to handle any minor problems that might
arise, thus setting up a buffer and emphasizing his own position
as a court of last resort.

At Tsingtao he found an alarming situation. Mrs. Hart, not fully
recovered from the food poisoning, had come down with a serious
case of pleurisy. For two days the admiral faced the very real
possibility that his beloved Caroline might die. With two doctors,
two nurses, the girls, and himself in attendance, some improvement came, but only slowly. When Mrs. Hart was just barely off
the critical list, a request for his immediate return to Shanghai
came from Glassford and Gauss. Naturally, but with severe misgivings, he went.

A week of conferences on the deteriorating situation ensued
without much profit. It was all very frustrating; Hart believed the
best way to avoid trouble with the Japanese was to be tough and
resolute; others, including the British and the French, wanted to
be more pliant arguing that they could not afford the risks that
a tough stand entailed. Although Gauss was more helpful than
Hart anticipated, the diplomat was not eager to allow Hart to take
the dramatic military move of having U.S. forces take over the
British and French defense sectors, and that was about all that
Hart could propose. Fortunately, the Japanese seemed anxious to
assure him that they wanted no trouble, and there was none,
although rumors continued to fly. As he wrote Admiral Stark, the
new chief of naval operations, "The affairs of the white man in
Shanghai are in a poor situation, which seems daily to deteriorate
further."[10] As he had already indicated, the only salvation was for
the United States to fill the vacuum left by the evaporation of
British and French will. Tommy understood the State Department's hesitance, yet he was aware that, if initiative were not shown
and risks not taken, the opportunity might be lost. With the Eu-

ropean powers fully occupied by Nazi aggression, the United States was the only hope for tending the white man's interests in Asia; he feared that if it did not act "we or our children will eventually be sorry." The most obvious move was for the Americans to take over protection of the foreign defense sectors; the Japanese would protest, he supposed, but eventually go along. To his diary he confided his more private thoughts. "A sad mess," he wrote, "most complicated and ineffective governing organization, the various white nationalities working at cross purposes, even seeking advantages over each other in these times. . . ." It was a markedly inappropriate time for bickering among themselves since they were "confronted by the resolute, persistent and hard working Japs who are bent on throwing out all whites." In a way, he could understand how the Japanese felt; many of the foreigners lived in luxury, which they had acquired at the expense of the Orientals, and white malefactors took advantage of their extraterritorial status. Personally, he found it difficult "to enter into helping them [the whites] with the whole-heartedness that the situation demands."[11] But he did.

The trouble was that the Asian repercussions from the war in Europe demanded his whole-hearted help in many places at the same time. He was particularly uneasy about Manila. The difficulties in China had been so pressing for the past two years that Yarnell had not been able to visit the Asiatic Fleet's facilities in the Philippines. If war actually came, those areas would be more defensible than would any of the bases along the China coast. It seemed essential, therefore, that Hart go to Manila and survey the situation. Glassford had been set up as a buffer in Shanghai, and now Hart decided that his river patrol commander was ready for added responsibility. To prepare him to take over active command when Hart went to the Philippines, Glassford was integrated into a wider variety of negotiations regarding the city of Shanghai.

October proved to be a relatively quiet month as the Japanese seemed intent on what Hart called "appeasing us—for as long as such serves their purpose." It was not quiet for the British, however, as the Japanese military, obviously intending to force them out of their defense sector, put increasing pressure on them. When the pressure started, Major General Frank K. Simmons, the British commander, asked Hart to station some of his marines in the British defense sector. Hart considered this mixing of forces unwise because, at some flash point, the Americans might find themselves drawn into a conflict over which they had no control. Luckily for Hart and Glassford, the British came to see the complexities of a joint defense force and decided instead to demonstrate resolution on their own. Simmons dug in his heels, warned the Japanese that no further concessions would be made, and implied that the British were at last willing to fight to protect their interests. This posture, which Hart applauded, put a stop, at least for the moment, to the testing of the white community and, with that pressure relieved, the time seemed right for Tommy to make a long visit to the Philippines. Stark, who trusted Hart's judgment and knew from his letters how strongly he felt the need to visit Manila, agreed that he should go. Glassford, with one cruiser and the river patrol boats, was left in Shanghai, and the rest of the fleet's ships left for the Philippines in mid-November.

The Philippine Islands, which Hart was visiting for the first time in fourteen years, promised to be far less anxiety-producing than was the China coast. There were problems aplenty, as he soon found out, but the islands were American territory—at least for the moment—so the problems were American ones and thus, theoretically, more amenable to solution. The Philippines had made strides toward independence which, under the terms of the Tydings-McDuffie Act of 1934, was to be formally granted in 1946. The elected government was led by the flamboyant President Manuel Quezon, a "playboy" type much given to flashy clothes, gambling casinos, late hours, and elegant parties. Having been president since 1935, he had a lot to do with the islands' preparations for independence and how they would defend themselves once it had been gained. To assist in their defense, Quezon had hired one of the best professional soldiers in the world to train his National Guard, Douglas MacArthur, the recently retired chief of staff of the U.S. Army. MacArthur was given the rank of field marshal, a large salary, and the title of military adviser to the president. Theoretically superior to both these men, if he could be strong and tactful enough to exercise his authority, was the American high commissioner for the Philippines. Francis B. Sayre, a son-in-law of Woodrow Wilson and a prominent Democratic lawyer with considerable experience in the Orient, had just arrived to take up that post. Completing the hierarchy was Major General Walter Grant, an old friend of Hart's from Army War College days, who commanded the small garrison of regular U.S. Army troops in the islands. On an organization chart it would have looked neat enough except for the potential friction between the

Filipinos and the Americans, many of whom looked on the natives as "little brown brothers."

Naturally, Hart's primary interest was in his naval facilities and there he soon ran into complications. Within four days of his arrival he wrote: "I knew I would find difficulties and complexities in this Filippine Field but it's going to be worse than I expected. . . . I face a sad state of unreadiness."[12] In terms of a natural harbor one could hardly have asked for more than Manila Bay—it was probably the best in the Far East. Naval shore installations included the extensive facilities at the Cavite Navy Yard, where there was located an industrial plant, warehouses, repair shops, barracks and officers' quarters, a power plant and signal station, and the headquarters of the Sixteenth Naval District commanded by Rear Admiral John M. Smeallie. Close by, at Sangley Point, was the large communications facility capable of long-range transmitting. Mariveles, on the Bataan Peninsula, was the base for Patrol Wing 10, which was made up primarily of PBYs. Then, at Subic Bay, north and west of Manila, was the all-important dry dock, which was moored at Olongapo. Smeallie had only recently arrived and, as Hart informed Washington, found morale bad, equipment run down, and the staff organization in disarray at Cavite. Not helping Smeallie to deal with his service responsibilities were distressing family problems: his only son had recently died and, just before he arrived in Manila, he found out that his wife was going blind. Manila was a distant post "so far out of sight that it tended to be out of mind"; the result was that the Bureau of Navigation did not give its needs very high priority, and the men Smeallie had to work with tended to be, in Hart's words, "below naval standards."[13] As Hart saw it, "There were some good men in the 16th District, but there were too many officers there because they weren't wanted elsewhere." First impressions were not encouraging.

No doubt part of the problem was that the servicemen stationed in the Philippines realized that, in case of hostilities, the role assigned to them, literally and figuratively, would be that of hostages to fortune. The navy had anticipated war with Japan at least since the early 1920s, but it knew that, even given the 5:3 advantage in naval tonnage granted at the Washington Conference, such a war, at least in its early stages, would be a losing proposition. It was tacitly assumed that the Japanese would be allowed the luxury of striking the first blow and that the Philippine Islands would be on the receiving end. The question was, would the islands be able to absorb the Japanese strike and then hold out long enough to serve as a base for launching war-winning operations? The answer, given in successive plans for war with Japan, was yes.[14]

There were qualifications to that "yes." The Asiatic Fleet's war plan called for the major combatants, on the outbreak of war, to withdraw behind the Malay barrier, leaving only local defense components. The fleet was to base in the Indian Ocean and operate against Japanese shipping until the Pacific Fleet's westward advance from Hawaii allowed the two units to link up. Then, together, they would relieve the Philippine defenders. So, theoretically, the affirmative answer could be supported. And, as several scholars have recently pointed out, defending the affirmative answer was almost as important to the U.S. Navy as defending the Philippines because, in order to justify increased expenditures, it had to have a practical mission.[15] The Royal Navy had traditionally policed the Atlantic, and it was up to the U.S. Navy to find a mission for itself in the Pacific. As Admiral Richardson, Commander in Chief, U.S. Fleet, later wrote, the most important function of the plan for war with Japan was to provide justification for appropriation requests.[16] Once the logic of that position is accepted, it becomes clear how important it was to sustain the argument that the Philippines could be held, even though many naval officers doubted that they could be; the validity of the argument was, in this sense, of secondary importance.

As if this little exercise in sophistry were not enough, there was also the bothersome matter of the army, which did not have the same compelling reasons for maintaining that the Philippines were defensible. Since the early 1930s there had been the curious spectacle of successive groups of naval planners insisting that the islands could be held, while equally insistent groups of army planners argued that it would be impossible, unwise, and undesirable to hold them. The only thing that kept this dispute from being resolved was the fact that no one other than the commander in chief had the power, and he did not deign to do so.

In 1935, when Douglas MacArthur accepted appointment as field marshal of the Philippine Army with the assignment of building a creditable defense force for the islands, the U.S. Army's confidence increased, but only slightly. There were questions about the possibility of the natives being molded into a reliable force, about the time required and available, and about the determination of Quezon and his political confreres to resist, even if MacArthur did succeed in building a real army. Therefore, the U.S. Army continued to plan on slowly giving ground until it was finally backed into the fortress of Corregidor, where it would put up a heroic, but essentially hopeless, battle to the death. The navy continued to insist officially that the islands could be held, although later versions of its war plan ominously omitted any reference to *when* the naval relief force would arrive to save the army.

Aside from the fact that it was demoralized by being assigned an essentially defensive, retreating role, the Asiatic Fleet had, Hart believed, become soft by reason of insufficient activity. Time was too short for him to do much about war plans, but he did have a prescription for flabbiness: the application of what he called the "sharp stick" of maneuvers under wartime conditions.

This remedy he administered with characteristic energy. There were inspections, reviews of plans, even realistic fleet maneuvers, in which he and his staff went to sea with the fleet and put it through a series of drills, including running darkened at night, avoiding submarines, target practice, and signaling. "It's a long, long time," he wrote, "since I've seen a body of ships so sadly in need of drill."[17] When he put the destroyers through a night attack exercise, to his pleasant surprise, they turned in an adequate performance. Nevertheless, there was room for improvement and, as he said, "There's nothing so good for sailors as going to sea." After some days of practicing for "eventualities," he judged them to be still "a very green outfit" but "at least it now realizes . . . how low it had sunk."[18] Stuck as he was in Shanghai, Yarnell could not do anything about training, and the fighting efficiency of the Asiatic Fleet had sunk right off the chart. Hart left little doubt that he intended to bring it back.

The situation on shore also demanded his ministrations. Although he regarded Smeallie as an efficient officer, the affairs of the Sixteenth District were being handled in a far from satisfactory manner. As he analyzed the situation, there were two basic problems. First, the staff had a tendency to be sorry for themselves because they felt neglected by the powers in Washington. Second, the prevailing attitude seemed to be "if Washington cannot meet our requests for such and such equipment or facilities, we cannot do an adequate job; therefore, when we fall short it is not our fault."[19] Hart understood the feeling of neglect because he not only shared it but knew it to be partially true and was striving to combat it. However, he had little sympathy with the attitude of helplessness. He was frugal by nature and believed far too many people tried to solve problems by asking for fancy equipment or more money and, when it was not forthcoming, thought they had an alibi for inaction. He knew that Smeallie tended to think in "grandiose defensive terms" and was disappointed when his requests were not satisfied. Consequently, Hart's first task was to reeducate his senior subordinate. Getting him to accept things as they were was of primary importance; since war might come at any moment, wisdom dictated that plans to fight "as is" be made. Hart drew up a full set of "as-is" plans to illustrate what he meant. It took many months of meetings, discussions, even arguments, to convince Smeallie and his staff of the wisdom of this course but, by March, Hart thought he had succeeded in bringing them around to the approach they should take.

He did not unquestioningly accept the Navy Department's parsimony, but he did realize that, if hostilities were as imminent as they seemed, there was little time for building elaborate shore facilities and that the possibility of the navy having to evacuate the islands in 1946, anyway, made them impractical. He did, however, want certain things, one of which was $78,000 for the building of tunnels on Corregidor for the navy. The army had previously been only lukewarm on this undertaking, but Hart soon had General Grant's willing support. With that, he began urging, almost demanding, that Stark send the necessary money. "Send the money now," he wrote, "and pay the Treasury later."[20] With $78,000 and laborers from Bilibid Prison, he would be able to dig the tunnels and have a secure place for vital radio communications and decoding equipment, a command post, and storage for torpedoes, ammunition, and spare parts. Speed was essential because Grant was nearing retirement and with him might go army acquiescence.

It took Hart only a short time, and a personal inspection, to see the deficiencies in the much-heralded plan for mining the entrance to Manila Bay. Even if they worked, the mines to be used could not keep out such light surface craft as motor torpedo boats or submarines. The way really to protect the bay was with nets and booms.[21] Such a system would not only keep the Japanese out of the bay, but would allow U.S. warships to sally forth to attack the enemy. The fact that he viewed this consideration as a significant advantage is one of the first indications of Hart's shift from a defensive to an offensive posture.

It would seem that all this training and meeting and planning with his staff left little time for anything else. Not so. Hart found opportunities for an occasional game of golf, a little sightseeing with his family, and an absolutely stupefying number of social events. During one ten-day period in January, for instance, there was a reception and dance aboard the *Augusta*; a dinner for the navy, courtesy of Mrs. Sayre; a dinner for the Sayres aboard the *Augusta*; a *grande baillie* for the fleet given by President Quezon; a formal luncheon for General Grant; and a birthday ball in Manila. How Mrs. Hart, who was very slowly recovering from her illness, could stand all this activity is hard to imagine. But she was part of the team and did her best to keep up. One of the reasons Hart went to Manila was to meet the people he would work with if the

Admiral Hart and his flag lieutenant, Leo W. Nilon, Manila, 1940. Courtesy of Mrs. T. C. Hart

Asiatic Fleet had to fall back on the Philippines, and entertaining and being entertained was a relatively painless way to do so—or so it originally seemed.

As the situation actually developed, what Hart learned about his counterparts was not altogether reassuring, according to his diary entries and what he wrote to Admiral Stark. This correspondence with the chief of naval operations, which began as a continuation of a similar contact between Yarnell and Admiral Leahy, became increasingly personal. At first, the two men addressed one another as "Dear Admiral," but by this time it was "Tommy" and "Betty." Perhaps this degree of intimacy arose because of Hart's candor. On 4 January 1940 he wrote:

> I am quite cheerful and as healthy in mind and body as I usually am. I am not at all sore at not having been sent to that for which I thought I was best trained and am fully and exclusively interested in what lies before me.
>
> I am entirely subordinate to you and will be absolutely loyal to any decision finally made. BUT I will argue with you *until* I see that such decision rests on a comprehensive viewpoint and knowledge—including [my] estimate from here.[22]

He went on to say that he needed to know what was in Stark's mind and "must be kept in touch to the end that I may do the right thing if something surprising comes on very quickly." Stark responded with both candor and warmth and no doubt his openness helped the communication link. For instance, he wrote Tommy that the "only purpose of this job [CNO] is to support you all afloat. . . ."[23] Stark probably honestly meant what he said—he was that kind of person; he also probably thought it wise, in the face of various shortages and an uncertain future, to leave no doubt among his subordinates that he was trying to be their advocate. Stark was honestly trying to win the confidence of Hart and his other fleet commanders because moral support might be all he could offer. Hart was too old and too experienced to pull his punches, so if Stark wanted to hear from him he would respond very candidly and he was soon sharing very personal reactions with his superior.

Quezon, he said, he found to be "splendid as a playboy," extravagant "officially and also personally," wielding "almost dictatorial powers" in some areas. Yet he was "shrewd, with a quick and at times brilliant mentality, coupled with extraordinary political ability and understanding of the psychology of his people."

Furthermore, Quezon had been open with him, admitting among other things that talking of building adequate defense forces by 1946 was absolutely ridiculous. To sum up, Hart wrote, "I like El Presidente immensely—and admire him quite a lot. He can be laughed about but not laughed off."[24]

Sayre, he was afraid, did not like the new commander in chief of the Asiatic Fleet, apparently because he was disappointed that Hart was not "tied to the tail of his kite." Hart was not convinced that the high commissioner was going to make a success of his mission because, although Sayre had mastered its professional aspects, he was not able to handle social affairs to the liking of the Filipinos. Nor was he enough of a playboy to keep up with Quezon; he was simply too stiff, too formal, not "one of the boys," and Hart thought this would eventually undermine his effectiveness. Another unfortunate thing was that Sayre seemed to be inclined toward pacifism, which made him underestimate the possibility of war and led him to favor cutting the Philippine national defense budget.

The man responsible for that national defense was another matter. "Much has been said," Hart wrote, about General MacArthur's "salary and emoluments. Not so much gets said about the fact that his offices are most unpretentious and that he has a relatively small staff—with which he has accomplished a vast amount of work."[25] MacArthur was concentrating on training the Philippine Army in hopes that by 1946 he would have built a self-sufficient defense force. The field marshal was supporting this concept by pointing out how difficult it would be for the Japanese to land on a defended coast. His forces, he said, would soon be prepared for anything the Japanese could throw against them. "No authoritative opinion, least of all that of our Army out here, agrees at all with those statements," wrote Hart.

With the eloquent MacArthur, public delusion and even self-delusion was always possible because he was, oh, so persuasive. Tommy was in an advantageous position for judging Douglas realistically, and he was one of very few people in the islands who could call him by his first name. Tommy had known the MacArthurs for almost forty years. One of his closest friends was Douglas's brother Arthur; in fact, he was a pallbearer at Arthur's funeral in 1923; and, while he was superintendent of the Naval Academy, he dealt with Douglas over the Army-Navy football issue. None of that made Douglas's domineering, egotistical manner any easier to take, but Tommy could interrupt one of his

monologues by saying, "Come on, Douglas. Sit down and let someone else talk," and not many people could get away with that.
"Long talks with Walter Grant and Douglas MacArthur," Hart
recorded in his diary.[26] "I talked to Walter and listened to
Douglas." As he said, "Douglas knows a lot of things which are
not so; he is a very able and convincing talker—a combination
which spells danger," but still he liked the fact that Douglas was
a fighter.[27] It did not take long, though, to find that personal and
professional sensitivities might have an effect on that fighting
spirit. The U.S. Army, possibly because its war plan called for
abandoning everything but Corregidor and the lower end of the
Bataan Peninsula, made little effort to cooperate with MacArthur
and his Philippine Army. The lack of cooperation may also have
arisen from personality clashes or professional jealousies. For any
regular army officer to cooperate with a former chief of staff, let
alone MacArthur, and maintain the upper hand would be very
difficult. And then it was awkward to cooperate with a "native"
army, particularly one that was still largely a dream.

The awkward relations between the U.S. Army and Philippine
Army were apparent even in society. The Harts, who always preferred "mixed" to "single service" parties, naturally expected to
see the MacArthurs at social functions. But they soon noticed that
the MacArthurs, although often the topic of conversation, seldom
attended army parties.[28] The Harts set out to do what they could
to break down this social isolation of the MacArthurs by including
Douglas and his young wife Jean in all their social activities. Douglas seemed delighted; he accepted and contributed what Hart
called a "goodly share" to the conversation. Maybe, if there was
enough of this kind of contact between MacArthur and the other
U.S. Army officers, there would be a payoff at the more practical
level of military cooperation.

Social contact between the native and nonnative communities
was a more subtle matter. As already made clear, Hart respected
President Quezon. For very practical reasons, he made an effort
to meet, cultivate, and understand the Philippine president. The
navy needed the kind of help only the president could give—space
for an enlisted men's club, for instance—and Hart knew that, to
obtain such help, he would have to appear on the social scene
because Quezon put great emphasis on social and personal rela-
tionships. Consequently, Hart found himself spending more time
gambling, always for small stakes, and dancing with beautiful Filipino women than might otherwise have been the case. He found

that willingness to fraternize with the natives was rare among the Americans in the islands. As he wrote Stark, there was far too much social aloofness evident in the American community "which has too often gone to the point of drawing a distinct color line."[29] Doubtless the Filipinos regarded this aloofness as racism, doubtless they resented it, and there is no doubt that it made them less cooperative. Hart was not a social equalitarian—we know he believed in white supremacy—nor did he judge the Filipinos to be ready for independence; he admitted to being an "imperialist" who did not agree with "the white man's walking out."[30] Indeed, he regretted what had been done along that line, but he accepted the situation as it was, anticipated that the navy would move out in 1946, and saw full cooperation with the Filipinos as the only practical course. Furthermore, he found his contact with them, which was extensive, "pleasurable as well as profitable."[31] He hoped that his example might influence other nonnatives to invite Filipinos to their parties and their homes.

As March turned into April, which brought with it crushing tropic heat, Hart prepared to move his command back to China. Things seemed to be heating up there, too, after a fairly calm winter. "Thanks for the respite, Slant-Eyes," Hart wrote in his diary, "[we] needed this winter down here."[32] All in all, it had been a profitable five months. His most satisfactory accomplishments were the training of his fleet and the change in thinking that he had brought about at Cavite. He still did not have much to fight with but what he had was at least better prepared and those who had to do the fighting were mentally readier to go forward "as is." The facilities being built on Corregidor were also a big plus; in fact, he was inclined to regard them as his greatest contribution. Then, he had familiarized himself with the waters surrounding the islands, including sites for a harbor well south of Manila. Although he had made valuable personal contacts, he sensed the possibility of serious trouble in that area. Indeed it would be a lot easier to concentrate on the Japanese if all the Americans could get along among themselves and with their potential allies, the Filipinos.

Hart headed back to China with a somewhat clearer idea of his responsibilities as a result of his correspondence with Betty Stark. After numerous requests from Hart, a letter from Stark, written on 9 February but not received until 9 March, laid out in fairly straightforward terms his view of Hart's role. In China that role was to try to avoid war by countering Japanese probes with resolution. The theory was that the snake would not strike if you reacted in kind every time it stuck out its tongue at you. This practice was not likely to induce serenity, but as Hart noted, "They didn't send me out here to be serene."[33] What if the theory proved wrong and the snake struck, anyhow? Stark made the obligatory reference to the war plans, but hastened to admit that they were theoretical, based on anticipated action by the Japanese forces. Hart would, in whatever situation, have to act as his own best judgment dictated. In other words, he had wide discretion, which did not mean that he had a wide range of choices. In the event of a Japanese attack, cruisers and other major combatants could try to fight their way south into the Indian Ocean. Destroyers and submarines might base in the Philippines for a while and then, depending on events, try to fight east, eventually to link up with the Pacific Fleet. The possibility of cooperation with the British or the Dutch was being considered, but the chief of naval operations thought it unlikely that this would come about in the present chaotic world situation. One thing the Asiatic Fleet might be able to do was take shelter in ports controlled by European powers, thereby accepting internment for the duration of the war or until an alliance could be worked out. As far as the 4th Marines were concerned, Stark had talked with the commandant of marines, but he said that "he does not know himself just what the plan is. . . ." What happened "depends almost entirely on arrangements more or less under your control, as for example hooking up with the Chinese, removal, and in the last analysis, possible capture." Hart seemed to have the independence he liked even though it might appear that his independent state existed primarily because there was little else to do with a cat's-paw so far removed from the cat.

On his way back to Shanghai, Hart visited Swatow and Amoy. These two coastal cities were occupied by the Japanese, Swatow by the army and Amoy by the navy. At Swatow he conferred with the American consul and at Amoy with Captain Richard E. Cassidy, the commander of the American naval patrol that was stationed there aboard the river patrol boat *Asheville*. At Amoy there was an international settlement similar to the one in Shanghai. Hart had visited this part of his command only once before and the time seemed right for so doing again, especially because of recent developments. If the Japanese were going to use the European war as a pretext for squeezing out foreigners, and Hart believed they were, why not start in some place small like Amoy? Once they had established the principle, they would be able to apply it more easily to Shanghai. His caution and his customarily pessimistic outlook made him well suited for this kind of preemptive duty. In any case, he showed the flag in Amoy, briefed his naval commander on what to expect, and sailed on.

He arrived in Shanghai on 18 April 1940 to find the situation essentially unchanged. The Japanese had set up a puppet Chinese government in Nanking under the leadership of Wang Ching-wei. Using this as a cloak of legitimacy, the Japanese might mount a major push against the white settlements, or maybe Wang Ching-wei would just further complicate an already complicated scene. There were also rumors that this year it might be the Americans rather than the British who would be cast in the role of foreign devils.[34] The British and, to a lesser degree, the French had been trying to keep low profiles by reducing their garrisons in Peking, Tientsin, Hankow, and Shanghai. This looked to Hart like more British appeasement in an attempt to save themselves. In this instance, it would be at the expense of the Americans rather than the Czechs, as it was at Munich. Hart hated to think this about the British whom he admitted to liking perhaps unduly, but it seemed to be the case.[35]

These fears were confirmed when, shortly after Hart arrived in Shanghai, Major General Simmons called. After a bit of hemming and hawing Simmons got to the point. The British had decided that, if the Japanese Army demanded entry into their sector, rather than fight a losing battle with attendant civilian casualties, they would pull their troops out and accede to the demand. What, he wanted to know, would Hart do in similar circumstances? Hart, having thought long and hard about just such a development, replied that, if a strong Japanese force, responsibly led, demanded access to his sector, he would follow the procedure Simmons had outlined. If, however, it appeared that the Japanese move occurred under circumstances "involving or presaging a state of war," the 4th Marines would probably react quite differently and much more positively. Simmons took that in and then asked a more disturbing and probably the primary question that was on his mind. If the Japanese disarmed the British or shoved them out of their sector—an apparent act of war, had Hart considered accepting Simmons's force for internment? Hart said no. He had thought about taking over its defense-sector duties, but interning British forces . . . ? It was hardly a pleasant prospect.[36]

The possibility of developments such as Simmons worried about came closer on 10 May when the Nazi columns rolled into the

Low Countries. It was almost more agonizing to watch the collapse of Western Europe from the distant, isolated Orient than from Washington. Hart felt helpless, yet involved. To his horror, the Dutch crumbled in only four days. What did that imply about the resolution of the Netherlands East Indies, one of the refuges he might seek for his Asiatic Fleet?

That was a long-range worry with no immediate solution and, there being more immediate ones, Hart started to do what he called "intrigue." It was his guess that the Italians would enter the war sooner or later. When they did, the temptation would be very great, since the French Concession bordered their sector, for one side or the other to start shooting. And if that happened, the Japanese would have just the pretext they had been seeking to occupy the International Settlement in the name of preserving peace. So, Hart, without consulting Washington, got the British, the French, and the Italians together and persuaded them to agree not to let developments in Europe, no matter what they were, lead to fighting in Shanghai. Going beyond that, they agreed to cooperate in safeguarding foreign interests in Shanghai, including establishing joint military patrols if necessary. On 14 May Hart informed Admiral Shigetaro Shimada, commander of the Japanese fleet in Chinese waters, that the agreement was a fait accompli. Shimada, apparently caught by surprise, expressed willingness to cooperate but said that in his view the "best method would be withdrawal or disarming all belligerent forces."[37] Reaction by the foreign ministry in Tokyo was similar but included word that the Japanese government was "displeased" that Hart had broken precedent by not consulting the Japanese authorities before taking action.[38]

Hart was very pleased with himself, considering it quite the neatest bit of diplomacy he had yet accomplished. The Japanese could not complain if his scheme succeeded in maintaining the peace, because that is what they said they wanted. From a negotiating standpoint, his move strengthened his reputation as strong man within the foreign community. In fact he soon learned that he had a reputation for prescience and power out of all proportion to reality. Of course, that would not have been the case had Washington disavowed his action; as he often told himself, "Well, Hart, you're on your own, expected to do the best you can with what you have, as you see it, and if you spill the beans, your head will be regretfully cut off."[39] It tickled him not to have his head cut off *and* to get ahead of the "damn dwarf-slaves," as the Chinese called the Japanese.

His personal relations with some of the Japanese were quite good. It is strange how men presumably prepared to kill each other sometimes act. For instance, when Admiral Oikawa left Shanghai, Hart was sincerely sorry to see him go. He paid a good-bye call at Oikawa's office and presented him with a handsome cigarette case as a memento. Oikawa had ready a gift for Hart— a book of prints. But, wrote Hart, "I'll get the last word by sending him flowers just a few minutes before his ship leaves tomorrow," and admitted "I rather like the old savage."[40] By and large, he tended to like the Japanese naval officers better than the army officers, who, he felt, were provincial and given to unpredictable violence. Most of them, he said, he would like to kick. Part of his dislike may have stemmed from his anxiety lest some army sentry involve a member of his family in an incident. Those sentries roughed up his sailors on the slightest pretext, and they might make his family a target; his girls had explicit instructions on how to react in case of provocation.

That anxiety was soon to be removed. The two younger girls were going home to resume their schooling. Mrs. Hart was going with them and they would all leave in time to be present at Roswell Hart's wedding. Isabella was going with her mother and sisters as far as Japan, then coming back to take care of the admiral until Caroline returned in September. The year with the girls had passed all too quickly. "It's been grand to have them out here," he wrote, "it has brought them closer to me than I've been for years."[41] That island of familial happiness in the sea of strain was welcome, but, if he had to move, he would be able to do so more quickly and with fewer anxieties if unencumbered by the family.

When they sailed in the *President Cleveland* on 9 June he headed north for Tsingtao. Glassford, who had been out on patrol, had returned to Shanghai, and Hart wanted to keep himself in a "reserve" role as far as that city was concerned. If he could do so, his appearance in times of trouble would be more dramatic, and he would avoid getting tied to Shanghai, as Yarnell was.[42] The larger issue of having his entire force stuck in Chinese waters in case of trouble was much on his mind. He believed his fleet was still serving a useful purpose on the Asian coast; however, things were becoming more tense by the moment and the more ships he had there the greater the risk. There were several things he could do and he set about doing them. First, he sent some of the slow submarine auxiliaries to the Philippines. Next, he began consolidating his forces in northern China by bringing the destroyers down from Chefoo to Tsingtao. There was another liability much on his mind this summer—the two thousand dependents who followed his fleet around. He had asked Stark during the fall of 1939 to consider at least cutting off the funds available for bringing dependents to the Far East, yet still no action had been taken. The situation was brought pointedly to his mind as he watched the dependents swarm north from Shanghai in response to his movement of the fleet to Tsingtao. And then the British demonstrated their sensitivity on the issue by announcing that they were reducing their force at Hong Kong and sending the women and children home. It was another harbinger of things to come.

On 12 June he observed his sixty-third birthday without much pleasure. "Well, I'm definitely an old man now," he wrote. One unpleasant prospect the "old man" had to deal with was the continuing reduction of British forces in the Far East. Coupled with the prospect that the French were well on their way to being overrun in Europe, it likely meant more responsibility for the Americans. After a hurried visit to Shanghai, he decided the time had come to organize an international peace-keeping force. He again acted quickly and without orders. He established a patrol consisting of twelve American, British, and French marines, all in battle dress. They toured the International Settlement daily in ranks by nationalities. The American marines directed the operation but usually stayed in the rear of the formation. Despite some murmurs of protest from the Japanese, it seemed to work quite well.[43] However, Hart realized this was only a stopgap measure; what if the British and French were forced to leave? He had a recommendation for that contingency, too. He wanted, as he had said earlier, the Americans to take over their responsibilities, at least in Defense Sector B, the British sector. The Navy Department referred this recommendation to the State Department, which took its usual cautious approach. Hart was advised that only after working out a mutually acceptable agreement with the Japanese should he make any move toward taking over any other defense sector.[44] He realized that the Japanese were not likely to act cooperatively; they certainly had not given him any reason to believe that they would, and their past actions gave slight grounds for optimism. The State Department's attitude distressed him almost more than Japanese intransigence; it was supposed to be on his side. And it was not that State did not understand that the Japanese were trying to capitalize on the white man's troubles; internal memoranda showed that there were people in the Department painfully aware of the realities. It was just that the diplomats did not want to do anything precipitate while the American position was so weak. There was obviously some wisdom in this counsel, but, taken beyond a certain point, caution can easily be mistaken for weakness. Furthermore, there was no reason to believe that there was going to be any shift in the balance of power, at least a shift in the direction of the United States, any time soon. As if to underline this unpleasant realization, in the midst of the exchanges between Hart, Navy, and State, France gave a final shudder and collapsed. After brief negotiations the French agreed to let the Japanese occupy their sector.

On 25 July 1940 Hart marked the end of his first year as Commander in Chief, Asiatic Fleet. There is no better way to capture his thoughts than to quote his diary entry for that day:

> At sea, cabin dismantled and battened down, with the ship doing a shoot and its the anniversary of my taking this job over from Harry Yarnell: fitting state of things for such an occasion. Well:— Its been rather a hard and trying year. I haven't had too much work or experienced hardship and discomfort but my chafing gear feels that it has had a good deal of wear and tear; guess that I'm still sound underneath it. I suppose the year has been hard solely because of the nervousness of the work. Experience did not bear much on what I've faced, and I began with *no* knowledge whatever. Its been a case of the old dog *having* to learn new tricks; the dog's luck (and perhaps Yankee common sense) have carried him along all right for a year.
>
> And *now* I feel fairly well qualified, by experience and hard-won knowledge, to face my next and final year. So it should be a fairly easy and downhill ride. But I doubt that it is going to be. The white man's position out here has deteriorated at a rapidly increasing rate since the allied defeat on the continent. If the war *does* go on for a long time, as the British say it will, we will just continue to slip in the face of Japanese shoving at us. Am afraid that I'm not going to be holding very good cards in this game and that it may not be a very good year.

7

STRATEGY BY NEGOTIATION

The coming months were to bring important developments across the spectrum of Hart's command. There would be continued tensions with the Japanese on the mainland, a growing sense of urgency regarding the Philippines, personnel changes at the senior level, as well as a personnel policy that affected thousands from the lowest ranking seaman to the highest ranking officer. There also would be moves in the tangled diplomatic-military-political jungle of alliance-making, as Allies and Axis alike tried to make arrangements for protecting their interests in a world that was daily slipping closer to the precipice. This was supposed to be the last year of Tommy's naval career and in many ways it must have seemed like his first year of active duty when the United States and Spain were tugging and pulling each other toward war.

The "new" year started in a substantially different way from the last. For one thing, Hart was more sure of himself regarding the diplomatic aspect of his job. For another, he was more alone. Instead of the bevy of Hart women who helped initiate his Asiatic command, only Isabella remained to officiate with him at social functions and help fill his lonely hours. "Sisser" was a great companion who remembers quiet evenings, golf, walks along the beach, and day trips into the countryside. Hart was sorry she could not travel more, instead of being tied to the "old man."

Yet, things were very much the same. The Japanese were still causing friction at every opportunity. An "incident" was created on 7 July when U.S. marines arrested sixteen armed Japanese gendarmes "loitering" in the American sector, and it remained an unresolved problem after endless hours of haggling.[1] A more serious matter arose a month later when General Simmons announced that the British Army would be pulling out of Shanghai within ten days. This was not entirely unexpected, yet when it became a reality the American community was caught by surprise. Hart's strong views on this subject were already on record, so Colonel DeWitt Peck, who had taken command of the 4th Marines the previous January, decided to move quickly to put those views into action. Accordingly, he called a meeting of the Defense Committee for 12 August, stating as he did so his intention to propose that the Americans take over Defense Sector B and the southern part of Sector D, which were presently allotted to the British. When the committee, which was made up of the British, American, French, Italian, and Japanese military and of representatives of the Municipal Police and the Shanghai Volunteer Corps, met, the Japanese representatives refused to attend. They had asked that the meeting be postponed to the fifteenth, so, after hearing the details of Peck's proposal, the committee adjourned until that day.[2]

Fearing trouble, Hart, who was in Tsingtao, made for Shanghai in the submarine *Porpoise*. He figured, wrongly, that this would be his last trip in a "pigboat" and, rightly, that he was in for a worrisome time. He arrived the evening before the meeting; met with Peck, who was the active negotiator; and, acting as a "coach," set the strategy. Between 10:00 a.m. and 2:00 p.m. the next day that strategy was put in motion. As Hart said, "Our cards were none too good, but we mapped out the game well and I think got full value out of each card."[3] What the American delegation got at the meeting on 15 August was agreement by the Defense Committee for U.S. marines to take over Sector B and for the Japanese to take over British responsibilities in Sector D. That agreement won approval of the majority, with the Italians abstaining and the Japanese voting "no."[4] On 16 August 1940 *The New York Times* reported that the apportionment of Sector B, "formerly held by the British forces in Shanghai, to the U.S. Marines . . . was greeted with great relief by all Americans and Europeans." Since majorities carry decisions, this agreement went to the Municipal Council where it was approved, then on to the State Department which also approved. So the issue was settled. Or was it? At this point the Japanese decided to dig in their heels and show just how tough they could be as negotiators.

First, they protested Peck's presumption in calling the meeting for the twelfth; next, they took offense that the issue had been decided by a majority when they thought unanimity should be the rule; then, they proposed that the Shanghai Volunteer Corps, rather than the marines, should take over Sector B. The one thing they agreed with was that the Japanese should replace the British in Sector D. In all their communications with the committee they dropped hints that if the majority's decision were carried out, there would be a military clash. Negotiating with the Japanese required patience. They tended to present themselves as benevolent conquerors who were attempting to be eminently reasonable, as is illustrated in the opening paragraph of a memorandum handed to Glassford by a Japanese delegate:

> It is a sheer fact, which nobody in the whole world would deny, that Japan has, over the period of more than 3 years, in China, instituted *de facto* war and deadly fightings are going on. And it is also a fact that the whole Japanese nation have been making their utmost efforts in fighting out the incident in the earnest desire of restoring peace in the Far East without delay, thus contributing to the cause of peace and welfare of the whole world.[5]

However, as the reader makes his way through paragraph after paragraph of self-serving rhetoric, it becomes increasingly evident that the Japanese are maddeningly obtuse and totally inflexible. Hart let Glassford and Peck, assisted by the brilliant Rosy Mason, do the talking, but he made the decisions. By the nineteenth it seemed to him that his representatives had maneuvered the Japanese into a position from which agreement offered the only exit. On that day a message arrived from Washington telling him that the negotiations were being taken out of his hands and moved up to the Washington-Tokyo level. It directed him to arrange for the Shanghai Volunteer Corps temporarily to take over Sector B, which was what the Japanese had suggested.[6] Although disappointed, Hart saw this as a judicious move because had he won the argument and moved the marines in, as he fully intended to do, there might have been a confrontation.[7] He considered the issue significant and Sector B extremely important. "Those seven blocks along the British Bund," he wrote Stark, "constitute the last open chink in the 'open door' of China." It was the financial center not only of Shanghai, but of all China and, as such, it was, in Hart's opinion, more significant than even the Burma Road.[8] The Shanghai Volunteer Corps, which was made up of professional men on leave from their offices, was not much of an impediment to anything the Japanese wanted to do; however, it would have to take the responsibility at least until Washington was willing to take a firmer line.

This did not mean that the matter was settled; it would drag on, as did all these incidents. Nevertheless, there being little more that he could add to the proceedings, Hart headed back north. The interminable negotiations with the Japanese were distracting him from his primary responsibility: he simply had to get his fleet ready for war. So when he got back to Tsingtao, he took his destroyers out on training exercises. It was another disappointing performance. He "read the riot act" to some of his personnel and noted in his diary, "The long and short of it is that our people on this Station are not very efficient—and the condition has obtained for a long time."[9] They simply were not "tuned for war" and that was what he wanted them to be.

Hardly had he settled in ashore when he received an urgent request that he return to Shanghai. Washington had taken a strong position and agreed to let the marines move into Sector B but the message, in Hart's view, had been softened when it was delivered to the Japanese by Ambassador Grew in Tokyo. Hart was not much impressed by the toughness of the U.S. representatives in the Japanese capital; they seemed too ready to see the Japanese side of things. In any case, the ball had been bounced back to Shanghai, and he was needed there. A quick run south in the light cruiser *Marblehead*, meetings with Richard P. Butrick, who had replaced Gauss as consul, Glassford, Peck, and Mason, and then confrontation with the "yellow bellies," as he called them when they were being troublesome. He found that they were stiffer than before, apparently having received instructions from Tokyo to be so. They pointed to the fact that there had been no trouble in Sector B since the Shanghai Volunteer Corps had been patrolling it. The insinuation being, why not let the Volunteer Corps continue. Hart suspected that the Japanese garrison in Shanghai was under orders not to cause trouble for the corps. The goal of this good behavior was to use Sector B as proof that foreign troops were not needed and, eventually, to tell them all to get out.[10] Whatever its goal, no progress was made on getting the marines into Sector B, so there was little for Hart to do but agree to allow the Shanghai Volunteer Corps to continue patrolling it for the time being. It was time-consuming and not very fruitful for him to make emergency visits to Shanghai, he thought, especially since he had great confidence in Glassford's and Peck's abilities as negotiators. But stress and frustration were becoming a familiar part of his routine.

At Tsingtao, to which he returned, it was also the same old story: go out on training exercises, read the depressing dispatches on the war in Europe and anticipated events in the Far East, go to parties ashore, and play golf. One of his golfing companions was Vice Admiral Naokuni Nomura, his Japanese counterpart in Tsingtao. Nomura was a gentleman, in Hart's opinion, and their relations were quite good. The following story illustrates Hart's sensitivity to Nomura's status with his own officers and the lengths to which Hart would go to spare him embarrassment.

> There were about four golf tournaments, usually the Japanese Navy challenging us, always with the statement that their admiral would be playing, which meant that I was to play against him; we played fairly evenly,—he a little better, winning more often than I did. This is just to illustrate a queer trait in the military mind of young Japanese. In one match, we were even up to the last hole, Nomura having been ahead most of the time, and he lost the match by four-putting the home green. We were the last pair around, and the others were watching us. As I went on in to dress, I noticed a knot gathering around poor Nomura at once. It was his own team, and they were taking him to task most severely and very disrespectfully because he had putted so badly and had lost the match. Those young Navy men were so angry that I worried as to how far they would go. Had the result been reversed, my own young fellows would have grinned, said something about how bad it was, *old* man, that you could not have lasted the cut—and passed me a drink. The story's implications match some most serious acts by young officers. Young Admiral Nomura had been humiliated before us. But very soon I persuaded him to play golf with me privately—so much so that no one could see us. He won the match, we took several strokes on the 19th hole,—and all remained well as between us.[11]

In late September things began to heat up in a most alarming way. On the twentieth Hart received word that the Japanese were going to move on Indochina in force. It was not clear whether the French would fight or acquiesce, but it did not much matter; either way, the Japanese would end up with the "rich prize" of Indochina. Hart guessed the meaning of the invasion of Indochina to be that the "Japs have signed up in an alliance with the Germans, and with the Italians as well. . . ." He further speculated that the next move would be against Hong Kong and, if the United States decided to go to the aid of the British, there might be real trouble. "I'm not likely to be told in time to do any good in running my own show," he wrote, "but the luck is with me in timing, for many of the ships are already south and what I have with me are quick on their feet. . . ." The Tsingtao fleet was scheduled to go to Shanghai on 22 September anyway, so little remained to be done, yet his state of mind was "most uneasy."[12]

When he arrived in Shanghai he found the situation unchanged except that the Japanese were reacting badly to the U.S. government's announcement that the sale of scrap iron to Japan was to be stopped. The iron was important for the Japanese defense industry, but perhaps more important in the oriental world, where great emphasis is placed on symbolism, was the "meaning" of the U.S. embargo. Did it portend a reduction of commercial relations, or was it a step toward a total economic break that might lead to hostilities? To Hart it meant that he had to "turn somewhat from looking after lives and 'interests' in China and think more about *war*."[13]

Then like distant thunder on a summer afternoon came two rumbles that indicated that others read the threatening clouds just as he did. First, the Navy Department announced that it would send no more dependents to the Far East in tacit recognition of the growing danger. That was a satisfying partial response to Hart's repeated pleas. Then on the twenty-eighth came word that Japan, Germany, and Italy had signed the Tripartite Pact. Hart had anticipated that, but what he had not dared to hope for was the hard line the U.S. Department of State seemed to be taking in response. Secretary of State Cordell Hull said that the pact was clearly aimed at the United States and went on to say that the country would not be deterred from its course by threats or intimidation.[14] "Hooray to all of it," wrote Hart. He was not even dismayed when the Japanese responded by asking for a temporary suspension of U.S. Navy patrols on the Yangtze and using their military to make life more difficult for the Americans in China. Hart thought that by doing so the Japanese were merely showing their true intentions and the more Washington perceived reality the better. As for himself, he was "psychologically ready for war right now!"[15]

But his fleet was hardly ready, spread out as it was. The place for it was in the Philippines, out of Japanese reach. Also, even though no more wives and children were being sent to the Far East, there were more than two thousand already there. The first issue he resolved by ordering all his ships, except the two cruisers and the river patrol boats, to sail for Manila on 10 October. The other issue was resolved, more or less, by the Navy Department which, on 3 October, ordered that all naval dependents be sent home. The problem there was that he was told to keep the order and its point of origin secret. He wanted in the worst way to get rid of what he called his "hostages to fortune," but how could he do it secretly? The only way to keep the origin of the order secret was to accept full responsibility himself for issuing it. But what better way to alienate every married person in the Asiatic Fleet? Despite this consideration, on 10 October he issued the fateful order over his signature. Reactions were immediate and varied. Most of the fleet thought he "had his wind up," and was overreacting to developments; many wives were ready to claw his eyes out; and the Japanese worried about the implications of this American move.

What it meant for Hart was that, when Caroline arrived in Shanghai on 13 October aboard the *President Garfield* after a four-month absence and a long trip across the Pacific, he told her not to unpack. Naturally, she was shocked and disappointed; things had just not gone well in the Orient for the Harts; first the months of debilitating illness and now this. But Caroline was a professional, too, or, as Tommy wrote, "a thorough-bred." She knew that orders were orders and, in the course of the less than twenty-four hours they had together, he let it slip that this order was not his alone. She did what had to be done. She packed up Isabella and reboarded the *President Garfield* for the journey to the Philippines. If all went as planned, he would soon be joining them in Manila but, since the Philippines were not exempt from Hart's order regarding dependents, they could stay there only a short time. If naval families were to suffer the anguish of separation, he wanted it obvious that he and his family were suffering, too.

On 15 October he advised the Navy Department that he intended to take the *Augusta* and join the rest of the fleet in Manila. Glassford was obviously able to handle things in Shanghai, the world situation was tense and developments coming so fast he believed that war was just over the horizon and, if that were the case, the best, perhaps the only place for him to be was the Philippines. Furthermore, there were indications that things in the Sixteenth Naval District were not going well and some changes might be called for there.[16] The next day the reply came saying that the State Department "desired" him to stay in Shanghai and the navy "desired" that he comply with that desire. "Terrible Tommy" hit the roof. Who is running the navy, he asked himself? In his diary, he even relieved himself of a few unkind remarks about Admiral Stark. As he reread the message, he thought he saw some daylight between the lines; the navy did not say no, it said it "desired" him to comply. Well, he not only "desired" not to comply, he thought complying would be a mistake. "I have to do what I think is right," he wrote, "and since I am not definitely ordered to stay here I am going on to Manila, on the 18th, as scheduled."[17] He drafted another message telling the Navy Department that he was leaving within twenty-four hours unless definitely ordered to stay. He realized that this came close to insubordination, but he had decided that if he were prohibited from leaving he would resign. When word of his message to Washington got to his staff, they ran to his office saying "you can't send this, you'll lose your job!"[18] "I'll take the risk," he said and wrote in his diary, "I feel that my duty is quite plainly getting south where my Fleet is and helping it get ready for eventualities." And that is what he did.

The fall of The Netherlands and then France called for drastic changes in U.S. war plans. There was serious concern in some circles in Washington that the world balance of naval power had shifted or was about to do so. There also was a sickening realization that the field of potential Allies, in the Atlantic area at least, had shrunk to one. Several of the war plans drawn up originally in 1939 referred to the possibility of a U.S.-British-French coalition; now France had gone and the desirability of being less vague was vastly increased. As we have seen, after the *Panay* incident steps were taken toward closer contact with the British; in the summer of 1940 action was taken to formalize that contact.

On 29 August 1940, Admiral Robert L. Ghormley, assistant chief of naval operations and a former director of war plans, began a series of meetings with high-ranking British officers in London. Theoretically, he was conducting exploratory discussions but making no commitments because Washington was still reluctant to become too firmly allied with the British. In the first place, the United States was still a neutral, isolationist country whose president was engaged in a reelection campaign in which he was proclaiming his intent to stay out of foreign wars. Then there was the historic U.S. position of shunning alliances. And finally there was the possibility that Great Britain might well be in her death throes.

The British, on the other hand, faced none of these impediments to agreement. They were in a war that was going badly. They had a long history of alliances. Furthermore, they had a specific role in mind for the U.S. Navy. Not uncharacteristically, they started to plan for involving the United States before Ghormley arrived. On 20 July a special committee was established to plan for a U.S.-U.K. naval alliance. It soon became apparent to the committee that, aside from the general desirability of drawing the Americans to their side, it was most desirable to assign the U.S. Navy the role of policing the Far East. To the Admiralty it was reasonable; British preoccupation with the war in Europe gave Japan a perfect opportunity for aggression in the Far East. If she took advantage of that opportunity, it would mean, at a minimum, that Australia and New Zealand would not be able to provide the forces needed to maintain the perilous equilibrium in Europe and the Mediterranean. At a maximum, it would mean that British forces would have to be stretched so thin that they would lose in both the Atlantic and the Pacific. So, since the Americans also had a stake in the Far East, why not make them a partner, base their Asiatic Fleet at Singapore, and assign them the role of protecting British and American interests in that area?

Ghormley, who was operating with only vague instructions, was not sure he was authorized to agree to such a change in U.S. policy, but in any case he was not impressed by British logic. There was suspicion in Washington of perfidious Albion and a determination not to pull her chestnuts out of the fire. Furthermore, there was reluctance about being put in the position of protecting the British Empire. And that is certainly what the United States would appear to be doing if, in the event of hostilities, the Asiatic Fleet were to be based in Singapore. Ghormley refused to go beyond an exchange of views—but he stayed in London for more conversations.

Events in September reinforced British interest in an alliance. First the Japanese invaded Indochina, then they signed the Tripartite Pact. Unless something were done to stop the tide, surely Hong Kong's turn would come soon. Or maybe Japan would decide to take over the colonial possessions of some other defeated European country. That could mean tightening its hold on Indochina, or taking over the Netherlands East Indies, with their rich supplies of oil, or both. Either of these actions would place a Japanese force astride communications between Australia and Malaya. The French were in a hopelessly compromised position and the Dutch were questionable and questioning potential allies. The British asked the Dutch, "Will you fight? Will you form an alliance and fight beside us?" The Dutch replied, "We'll tell you whether we'll fight after you tell us whether you'll form an alliance." Since the answer to the latter question was in part contingent on America's willingness to join the team, the British deemed it best to avoid a response for the moment. With the world collapsing about them, however, a decision could not be long delayed. As is often the case, the immediate answer was to call a conference.

The British, the Australians, the New Zealanders, and the Dutch arranged to meet in Singapore in November to discuss contingency planning. At first, the Americans refused to send a representative but, in response to Ghormley's requests, the Navy Department agreed to send an "observer." The British wanted Admiral Hart, but in order to keep the visit less conspicuous and at a lower level his chief of staff, Captain William R. Purnell, was dispatched. Although no account of Purnell's reaction or role can presently be found in either American or British records it is safe to conclude that he did little other than observe proceedings. It is also reasonable, based on the records of those meetings, to make some suppositions about his reactions. The British and Dutch reached no conclusions about an alliance; that cannot have been encouraging, because without such an alliance might not the Americans find themselves fighting alongside the British and outflanked by a Dutch collapse? The British seemed convinced that Singapore was the best available base in the Far East; if the Asiatic Fleet were to base there, lines of communication between it and the Pacific Fleet in Hawaii would be dangerously extended. There was more discussion of convoying and protecting commerce than of striking at Japanese targets; that was unduly defensive-minded from an American perspective. Had Purnell been a participant rather than an observer there still would not have been much he could say effectively to counter the points raised by the British and the Dutch. Since American war plans, now organized into a series called Rainbow, were being reevaluated, nothing totally responsive to the situation was available.[19]

Back in Washington Admiral Stark, working first alone and then with a few trusted aides, set about reordering American strategic priorities. He drew up four alternative plans, A, B, C, and D, for America's response to crisis and, out of these possibilities, he chose Plan D, or Plan Dog. It called for preparing to fight a war in alliance with Great Britain in which the primary offensive effort would be expended in the Atlantic area. In other words, the navy should leave unresolved the ambiguities and contradictions in the old plan for war against Japan and turn its main attention to another ocean. This meant accepting the loss of the Philippines, as the army always had done. Previously the Pacific had been the only place where the navy could reasonably assume that it would play a major role; now, with the French gone and the British desperate, the Atlantic beckoned. Moreover, moving into the Atlantic would free the British for other tasks—such as protecting their possessions in the Far East. As for the U.S. role in that area, it was Stark's opinion that the United States should not "willingly engage in any war against Japan unless we are certain of aid from Great Britain and the Netherlands East Indies." Although by the time he had finished his reassessment, the Singapore conference was over, he called for series of joint staff conferences to formalize Plan D.[20]

The British were trying to draw the Americans into the war and use them in a way both wise and advantageous—for the British. The Americans were trying to avoid premature or unwanted commitments, yet to influence planning before events swept them past the point of leverage. The Dutch in the East Indies desperately needed assurances of help or they would have to capitulate, and the British could not afford to let the Dutch capitulate. The British, therefore, were willing to support the Dutch, but preferably not until the Americans agreed to come into the war if the British should be attacked by the Japanese. The Americans were hesitant to make such an agreement, especially in the absence of a British-Dutch alliance. Hart and his little fleet were pawns on this checkerboard. He wrote rather plaintively to Stark in August, "I *still* feel very much out of touch with 'the management' and that does not make my lot easier."[21] Unfortunately the fact that his involvement was going to increase immensely did not mean a commensurate increase in attention from "the management."

From the moment he arrived in Manila, he found there were more immediate problems to distract him. He had faced the issue of sending the dependents home; now he had to implement it. Getting two thousand women and children back to the United States on short notice would not have been simple even if there had not been hostility all around. Not making matters easier were the facts that the army had not yet ordered its dependents home and the high commissioner questioned the need for anyone to leave the Philippines. Naval dependents were going, though; that had been decided. A member of Hart's staff was detailed to the task and given sufficient help to get on with it promptly.

The first problem was shipping space. The Navy Department helped by chartering a vessel with a passenger capacity of ap-

proximately one thousand, and soon she was on her way to the
United States via Australia. Slowly other space was found, sched-
ules made, and families separated. One humorous incident illustrates the kind of complication such an undertaking runs into.
Early in the proceedings, the officer in charge of the evacuation
had to deal with the question of pregnant wives. After some discussion it was decided that women who were seven months pregnant would be allowed to remain in the Philippines until their
babies were born. For about forty women, that meant a significant
delay, but it seemed to Admiral Hart that some of them were
taking advantage of the situation, overstaying their welcome, as
it were. One morning "just after I'd had breakfast and was still
grumpy," Hart recalled,

> I sent for this staff officer and said, "I saw some more Navy wives
> on shore last night. I want to know about this delay, for it doesn't
> seem right to me. Doesn't look right. Bring the papers."
> He came back with a file about two inches thick, laid it down,
> waiting for my questions. I saw on the front of it a figure at the
> top, "1978." "Is that one number, 1978 women and children?"
> "That's what we began with." Well, then followed a lot of additions
> and subtractions, coming all the way down the sheet, at the end
> there, there was a number "14" with question marks after it.
> As I say, I was grumpy, and I don't think he'd had breakfast at
> all. I pounded the table and said, "Fourteen with a question mark!
> What is being done here? I want to know how many more there
> are left?"
> Then he pounded the table and rasped out, "All right, if you'll
> tell me whether the rest of these women are going to have singles,
> or twins, or triplets, I'll tell you how many!"[22]

Making no exceptions, Hart insisted that Caroline and Isabella
join the procession. He regretted the passing of each day that
brought them closer to departure. Why, he asked himself, with
so few months of service left, should he be denied the comfort
of having wife and daughter with him? But then again he reassured
himself by concentrating on how few those months before retirement and reunion were.

Finally the dreaded day came. Twenty years earlier, Caroline,
in a long blue cape and a broad-brimmed hat, had come to Union
Station in Washington to see him off for the Orient. This time,
dressed much as before, she boarded a Philippine clipper in the
early hours of 25 November and Tommy stayed behind. "Well,
its a splendid mind picture," he wrote, "she and Isabella—both

handsome and trim. I'll be seeing it vividly for a long time and watching the lights of the plane finally go out of sight—right into the rays of the rising moon." At 3:00 a.m. a saddened Tommy Hart boarded the recently arrived heavy cruiser *Houston*, his flagship and from now on his lonely home. He would miss them sorely, but at the same time he wanted them safe and, as he noted a few days later, "The time has come for single mind and purpose."

One area demanding immediate attention was the Sixteenth Naval District. When Hart had arrived at Manila he had found Rear Admiral Smeallie in a distraught state, "riding off in all directions." A number of projects were going on under Smeallie's authority in anticipation of hostilities: the industrial capacity of the Cavite Navy Yard was being increased and its submarine-battery-charging facilities were being improved; the dry dock at Olongapo was being overhauled; power lines were being laid at Mariveles; dredging was being done in Manila Bay; and, of course, tunnels were being dug on Corregidor. All of this apparently proved too much for the district's commandant. Hart liked Smeallie, felt sorry for him, and furthermore, could hardly afford to lose another commandant of the Sixteenth Naval District. So first he counseled him, reminding him of the British joke that the best way to beat the Americans would be to declare war, let them wear themselves out for a couple of weeks doing mindless activity, and then come in and pick up the pieces. Next he tried spending more time at Cavite, but that only served to make Smeallie more nervous. Finally, he tried doing some of the work himself. None of this helped much, as Hart learned on 12 December when he was at sea on a training exercise with the *Houston*. On that date, he got word that Smeallie had driven a Moro dagger into his stomach in an attempt to commit suicide. There was little to do but invalid him home and request a strong replacement. Hart believed it was a combination of family and work pressures, too little exercise, and the tropical climate. Ill health seemed to haunt the tropics; first he lost Rear Admiral George J. Meyers as district commandant; then Colonel Fegan; and his friend General Grant had to be invalided home before his time. It was enough to make one extremely cautious. Hart immediately increased his golfing.

General Grant's replacement was Major General George Grunert, whom Hart found quite easy to work with. He did not have the close personal relationship he had with Grant, but Grunert seemed almost more actively responsive to his requests. The immediate issue was the laying of a minefield in Manila Bay and the two officers soon agreed on a plan. When they deemed it necessary to lay mines, the army's mines, which were recoverable, would be laid and notices of the action would *imply* that the navy's mines, which were not recoverable, had also been laid. If the secret could be kept, and they thought it could, they would give the impression of protection without taking an irreversible step. In a period when tension went up and down like a yo-yo, such flexibility was desirable.

Hart was also pleased to find that, contrary to rumor, President Quezon was growing considerably more bellicose. The president and the admiral picked up their relationship where it had left off the previous spring, with Quezon apparently confiding his most secret thoughts to Hart. For instance, the president told the admiral that he believed the situation so critical that he should mobilize his army in the very near future. That kind of spirit warmed the admiral's heart.

He did not find the same bellicosity in High Commissioner Sayre nor did he find any improvement in the relationship between Sayre and MacArthur. Sayre was still inclined to minimize the possibility of war and to eschew any action that might "upset" the Filipinos. With a little effort, which he was willing to put forward, Hart thought he could change the high commissioner's attitude. He was not so sure that anything could be done about the bad blood between Douglas and Francis. One night when he dined with the MacArthurs in their "palatial penthouse apartment" in the Manila Hotel, he was treated to a lengthy "fulmination" against the high commissioner.[23] He had heard similar opinions expressed by Sayre about the field marshal. It was a little awkward being the confidant of two men who so heartily disliked each other. Douglas, it seemed to Hart, "seems to have sunk to an unenviable official position and relationship" in which "the dignified thing to do would be to resign." Probably both Sayre and MacArthur were somewhat wrong, but Hart determined that when the time came to choose sides, "I'll be with the A.H.C. [American High Commissioner]."

The possibility that he might be around when the "time to choose" came increased markedly on 19 December. In a letter from Rear Admiral Chester Nimitz, now chief of the Bureau of Navigation, he learned that Smeallie's replacement, Rear Admiral Bemis, his old friend and companion from World War I, was on his way out and that, in view of the current tense situation, it might be desirable for Hart to stay on beyond the age of retirement. Being asked to stay on in a sea command was a tremendous compliment, and one hardly ever paid. "Of course I can't reject such a feather in my cap, conceit or no conceit," Hart noted in his diary, "so I'm writing Nimitz that it will be okay with me provided that when the time for decision arrives I am in good enough condition *to* continue."[24] That afternoon he played golf and shot a 78.

Christmas he spent with the Sayres at Baguio, and next day was back in the *Houston*, opening presents and reading dispatches. On 30 December he wrote in his diary:

> The year is ending *and* the clouds seem to be shutting in on us— out here. There is more and more indication that the Japs are coming south and, for the first time, I really am seeing the loom of WAR, not so far over the horizon. No, I'm not ready, its impossible to be sufficiently ready; without precipitating something. So of course I am uneasy. One worries so much lest he miss a trick at such a time as this."[25]

The first big activity of the new year was dispatching Purnell to another conference. Ever since Purnell returned from Singapore, Hart had been aware of the increasing importance of steps being taken to form a fighting alliance with the Dutch.[26] It was crucial that their oil be denied to the Japanese and, as has been said, he was none too certain about the defensibility of Singapore. In any case, Purnell's meeting in November served to put the commander in chief of the Asiatic Fleet in closer touch with his British counterpart, Vice Admiral Sir Geoffrey Layton. Steps were being taken to exchange information on communication procedures and to keep track of construction and staffing at the Singapore base, and liaison officers were exchanged, Lieutenant Commander Wisden, RN, joining Hart's staff. There had been no such exchanges with the Dutch, which Hart considered a real deficiency. He was anxious to remedy this situation because preliminary plans seemed to call for American command of any combined force. As he wrote on 5 November, "I seem to be driving the team but without knowing what it is that [is] in the harness."[27] Purnell was sent to Java in January to look over the other horses.

As he was preparing to leave, a very important courier, Commander John L. McCrea, arrived from Washington with the navy's draft war plan, Rainbow 3 (WPL 44). His role was to collect the reactions of the senior naval officers in the Pacific regarding the plan and to answer what questions he could about particulars. He reported to Hart on 10 January and for the next nine days shared Hart's quarters in the *Houston*. Other errands McCrea was given were to ascertain Hart's views about remaining in command and to convey to him a personal and extremely confidential message from Admiral Stark: "Tell Admiral Hart," Stark said, "that consistent with a strong policy, there will be no backing down. The President, Secretary of State, Mr. Welles (Undersecretary of State) and Secretary Knox do not desire war with Orange [Japan]. However, there will be no weakening of our policy—nor appeasing."[28] Those were words Tommy was eager to hear, but their effect was somewhat diluted by the less bellicose concluding comment "pinpricks are to be avoided." That made it seem like a part of the same old story—the United States is tough and is not going to be pushed around, *but* let's not do anything that might make the Japanese mad. Nevertheless, maybe there was more muscle behind Stark's determination than previously.

The new draft war plan contained some indication of that muscle, and that was extremely welcome to Admiral Hart. The basis of Rainbow 3 was that the Asiatic Fleet would be reinforced by at least a cruiser division, a carrier, and a squadron of destroyers. This would approximately triple the size of Hart's force. The plan also contemplated an American-British-Dutch alliance. The British would be engaged mainly in the Atlantic and perhaps in the western part of the Indian Ocean. Therefore, Hart's force, whether reinforced or not, would have a major role to play along the Malay barrier.

On the other hand, McCrea brought some rather disturbing news about the possibility of actually reaching agreement with those allies. Shortly before leaving Washington, he met with the chief of the war plans division, Rear Admiral Richmond Kelly Turner, and the senior British liaison officer, Captain Arthur W. Clarke. The conclusion was that the Dutch were "exhibiting the same degree of reluctance about holding staff talks with reference to the Far East they exhibited last spring prior to the overrunning of the Low Countries by Germany." The U.S. Navy was willing surreptitiously to send liaison officers, in the guise of language students, to the Netherlands East Indies, but the Dutch resisted. Captain Clarke said that the British in Singapore were going to try again to draw them into staff talks and everyone wanted Hart to "do his utmost to establish satisfactory contact with the Dutch." The most that he would be able to offer as an inducement for them to join any kind of alliance was contained in Rainbow 3, namely, a reinforced Asiatic Fleet. Still, even Turner and Clarke anticipated that getting a "definite agreement to cooperate will be difficult." And, in Hart's opinion, even if that agreement were obtained, determining the actual mechanism for working together would be complicated. Hart told McCrea to report:

> I have given much thought to the Allied Command Areas. Air Marshal Brooke-Popham has command of all British land and air forces out here. These forces are defensive forces. Far and away the best set up would be unified command for the air and naval forces and the British have already set up something in the way of this as pointed out above. I feel that our war efforts in this theater would be considerably weakened if a *cooperative* principle is decided upon, rather than a *unified* command for air and naval forces. I wish to point out very strongly that I have no personal ambition in this regard. I view this matter with so much importance that I wish it to be pressed most strongly before the Navy Department.
>
> Are the territorial and naval forces going to help hold the Malay Barrier? If so, that is all right, but if they are to be utilized to defend Sydney and Auckland that is all wrong. I would like to get a definite agreement on this point. If their employment is to be restricted to a cooperative principle I would like to know it and I wish to impress that that cooperation will have to be damned whole hearted to be effective.[29]

Even as Hart and McCrea were discussing the subject, Purnell was meeting with the Dutch in Java, so possibly some specific command arrangement could soon be worked out.

There was a whole list of other issues to cover with McCrea, as Hart tried to give him a rounded picture of what was going on in his theater. He had arranged that the marines in China would take to the hills and fight alongside the Chinese, in case war broke out. Marine replacements were being retained in the Philippines rather than sent on to China. He was not taking Sayre into his confidence because he found him to be "leaky." MacArthur and Grunert did not get along and Hart guessed that, if it were not for his high salary, MacArthur would "duck out, because he doesn't appear to be too happy in the job." The army air corps was weak as well as improperly handled: Hart thought enough planes should be maintained on alert to punish an air attack at any time so severely that the Japanese would not attempt a second one. It was possible that the Philippine government would adopt an appeasement policy toward Japan. He wanted clearance to set up nets and booms at the entrance to Manila Bay. There was a strong possibility of espionage and sabotage. Hart doubted that "an ORANGE [Japanese] landing could long be held off on any part of the coast outside of the Manila Bay area." When the additional submarines he was supposed to get arrived, he intended to depart from the original concept of keeping them tied closely to Manila. The new boats would constitute the "punch" of the fleet and "we expect to use this arm aggressively." He had comments on various high-ranking Japanese officers, including Admiral Isoroku Yamamoto:

> Energetic. Highly able. Bold in contrast to most who are inclined to be cautious. Decisive. He has American viewpoint. Formerly Naval Attache in Washington. London Arms Conference delegate. Well versed in international affairs. A wounded veteran, having lost two fingers at Tsushima. Highly thought of by rank and file of ORANGE [Japanese] Navy. Personally *likes* Americans. Plays excellent bridge and poker. Alert in every way. Very air minded.

Hart worked long and hard on the war plan brought out by McCrea, even though he was at sea and on the flag bridge of the *Houston* during much of this period, supervising fleet exercises, which at least gave a sense of immediacy to his war planning. It was just as well that he spent time on his flag bridge; "it might happen," he noted, "that I will end my days right on that bridge; quite possible in fact. I suppose that after all, that would not be such a bad ending."[30] But, he added, "I'd like to see my wife and my offspring once more." It was not that he was sure that the Japanese were going to sneak up on him. He had found them to be very cautious and believed they "won't jump us unless they feel certain that in so doing they can attain a tremendous initial advantage. . . . I do not feel that the destruction of the entire Asiatic Fleet would be regarded by them as such an 'initial advantage.'" It was more likely that they would strike the British or the Dutch and try to keep the United States out. That was why he thought it so important for "the powers that be" to decide what to do in that contingency. However, if the Asiatic Fleet were reinforced as contemplated, he would be happy. "Give me these," he said in reference to the reinforcements, "and I am ready for war."

He made it quite obvious that he was not happy with the way he had been treated up to this point:

> I consider that the Asiatic Fleet should be given priority in all things. This is the front line trench. Above all I want *priority of attention* from the Navy Department. I do not want to have to send

follow-up dispatches. It goes against my grain and principles to do so. From my position out here I feel that the Department is altogether too slow in answering my dispatches. Some of my recommendations have evidently been completely ignored.[31]

McCrea's report might help remedy the situation. "In my judgement Thos. C. Hart was one of the Navy's best," McCrea writes, "and in my time I saw some good ones I can assure you." Hart "had brains and he knew how to use them." During this trip, as McCrea stood at the rail of the *Houston* and looked out at some of the Asiatic Fleet's large submarines lying at anchor, Hart remarked: "When the war comes, those boats are going to be of great value to us. They will be able to hit the enemy hard." After a pause, he added quietly, "When I was a member of the General Board I vigorously opposed the building of submarines of that size. I thought they would be too big." Another pause and then: "Fortunately for the country and the Navy wiser counsel prevailed!" Years later McCrea wrote: "I had long thought well of him. My regard for him at that moment moved up, if possible a few notches—he had character!"[32]

McCrea departed Manila on 20 January leaving Hart with much work to do in anticipation of the Asiatic Fleet being enlarged. Two days later came a dash of cold water. There would be no reinforcement of the Asiatic Fleet.[33] The ships were being sent to the Atlantic instead. Tommy would have to fight with what he had. Plan Rainbow 3 had already been superseded by events and, although Stark's Plan Dog had yet to be fully accepted, this latest change in force deployment was a harbinger of things to come. Hart was getting reverberations resulting from the naval bureaucracy's preparation for the Anglo-American staff conferences. That there should be reverberations, changes, and shifts was understandable; that confusion should result, and in this case disappointment as well, was equally understandable. Tommy could not tell what the master plan was behind these various adjustments, or whether indeed there was a master plan at all. The most awkward part was trying to negotiate with potential Allies, whose disappointment in the failure of the United States to reinforce the Asiatic Fleet would more than equal Hart's own. Washington would soon have to make up its mind about how the war, which Hart so clearly saw coming, was going to be fought.

A major step in that direction was about to be taken ten thousand miles east of Manila. On 29 January 1941 the first of a series of full-fledged U.S.-British staff conferences opened at the Navy

Department. These meetings, known collectively as the ABC Conference, did not end until March and, when they did, the strategic course of World War II had been set.[34]

Although not obvious from the results of the conference, the disposition of the Asiatic Fleet played a highly important role in the discussions. From the American perspective that role was pivotal; negative, but pivotal. The trouble arose because the British had had their original enthusiasm for a large American role in the Far East whetted by the war plan that McCrea had discussed with Hart. Captain Clarke, in Washington, had been shown a copy of that plan in November 1940. For the United States to augment the Asiatic Fleet and fight in an alliance with the British and Dutch sounded to Admiralty planners like an answer to prayer. Therefore, when the ABC Conference began, the British pushed hard for a specific commitment to reinforce the Asiatic Fleet and a guarantee that the United States would enter the war if the Japanese attacked British possessions in the Far East. The problem was that U.S. plans had changed. Plan Dog called for concentrating on the Atlantic, not the Pacific. And the harder the British pushed for a commitment in the Pacific, the more determined the American naval delegates became in their resistance. Rear Admiral Richmond Kelly Turner, whom one of the British delegates suggested was "rather liable to start from the assumption that he was right and everyone else either fools or knaves," was particularly adamant.[35] His attitude, which already bordered on Anglophobia, became so rigid that he threatened to break off the conference if the British did not stop pushing and conniving to get a U.S. fleet to base at Singapore. Finally, Prime Minister Churchill intervened. "Get the United States into the war," he ordered his delegation; after that arguments could be conducted on how to fight it. If they did not want to defend the Far East, and that was painfully obvious, let them play a larger role in the Atlantic. In short, do whatever was necessary to be conciliatory and do not dwell on topics that made Turner and his ilk cross or obdurate. Even while issuing this sound advice, the prime minister could not refrain from saying that "it would however be a wise precaution in our opinion if the American Asiatic Fleet were somewhat reinforced with cruisers"; but it was not an issue to be pushed.[36]

The Americans responded far better to conciliation than to what they perceived as coercion. Thus the major naval decision of the conference was that the Atlantic would be the primary focus of the Allied endeavor, with the Pacific relegated to a secondary role.

To effect this decision, the United States would shift units to the Atlantic and the British would redeploy their forces thus relieved to the Far East. The Americans were willing to do some things to support the British-American posture in the Far East; they agreed not to try to hold the Philippines but rather to have Hart fall back to either Surabaja, in the Netherlands East Indies, or Singapore. They would not agree to put him under British command, however, or to set a timetable for the fleet's movement. To flesh out arrangements, it was agreed to have further conversations in the Far East "as soon as practicable."[37]

By the time the ABC Conference began Purnell had already met with the Dutch between 9 and 18 January. It was anticipated that the Dutch would not be forthcoming, but quite the contrary, Purnell found them completely frank. They told him that if there was anything *naval* the United States wanted to know, all they had to do was ask. Unfortunately, what they found when they did ask was not reassuring. "It looks as if the N.E.I. [Netherlands East Indies] Navy," Hart reported to Stark, "is no stronger than we thought, and perhaps it is really weaker." Part of the trouble, according to Hart, was racial; their ships had mixed crews. "Purnell thinks even the submarines' crews are partly Malay, and the surface ships are thus diluted." The army was nine-tenths native, even the officer corps showing the effects of mixing the races. Hart's interpretation of this was that once the Japanese got on land they would cut through the Royal Netherlands East Indies Army like a hot knife through butter. The only restraining device available to the Dutch was that they could threaten to destroy the oil wells. That was a pretty good device, but not reassuring when it constituted the only line of defense.[38]

So the Dutch were more open, but possibly weaker, than had been thought. Nevertheless, what was needed was to arrive at some concerted plan of action. It was fine to come up with a plan in Washington for an area where agreement could be reached, in this case the Atlantic, and to let the people on the scene do the planning for the western Pacific, but how were they to resolve the dilemma of alliance and commitment that had stymied every earlier effort? In other words, there was still the old conundrum of "we'll agree to an alliance if you'll make a commitment to the third party first." Hart had a working premise to propose. As he wrote Stark on 7 February:

> Our position is that the two other parties should go right ahead
> with arangements for their own cooperation and we shall urge them

to that end; they know that *we* can, as yet, make no commitments in their favor. Therefore, it is only fair that when "the day" arrives for us, we should fit in with those plans which they have agreed upon as between themselves—at least in the beginning. I think that we can make a proper fit with them initially and can then adjust everything as becomes necessary as a campaign develops. I am led to that opinion by their apparent attitude, which is that if we will only help they will do most anything that we say! Possibly I am wrong, but anyhow I can see no other practical course for getting on with things at present.

Hart was obviously aware of the problems, but he suggested they be resolved in Washington. If you can do it, he wrote, "The greatest service toward the mutuality of the 'cause' would be your urging the N.E.I. into full commitments with the British. Our impression is that they are the more reluctant of the pair to come out and make real engagements along the one-for-all and all-for-one line."[39]

Since this issue bedeviled the alliance right up until 8 December 1941, it might be well at this point to examine a uniquely American part of the problem. Traditionally, Americans have made a distinction between "political" and "military" decisions. As a naval officer, Hart could plan *how to cooperate* with the British and the Dutch; that was a "military" matter. But he could not make any commitment *to cooperate*; that was a "political" matter. Wise as that division might have been, in this particular situation it seriously retarded progress. First, the other two parties had less potential power in the western Pacific than the United States had and, consequently, looked for the U.S. Navy to play a large role in decision-making. Second, neither of the others felt secure making a commitment in the absence of an American commitment. And third, Franklin Roosevelt, the "political" leader, was not about to make any commitment, even a secret one, while he was publicly pursuing a course of keeping the United States out of war. That, too, was probably wise, but it certainly did complicate alliance-making in the Far East.

Hart's solution to the impasse was to try to push the potential Allies into making an agreement onto which could be grafted American participation when and if it came about. It was to further this concept that, on 19 February, the redoubtable Purnell was again sent south to attend a full-fledged Allied conference. It was a delicate task, especially since Hart had been instructed on 7 February to propose that any Allied naval force be under American command, a strange aspiration for an "uncommitted ally"; but if anyone could succeed, Purnell should be able to. Hart thought him to be perfect for the assignment because of his "splendid intuition, ability to see what's under the paint" and his aptitude for setting forth his case effectively.[40] Despite these strengths and the efforts no doubt of the other participants, the conference was a great disappointment. The Australians, British, and Dutch failed to come up with a plan on which they could agree, even among themselves, and that was what Hart considered "the first step." It was a big meeting with all the services represented, and some agreements were made, but, in Purnell's and Hart's view, it ended "about where it was to have been hoped it would have started." Much remained to be done. Purnell was very frank, told them what they could expect from the Asiatic Fleet "if we do join up with them," and criticized their strategic attitudes and the defensive measures they favored.

Those strategic attitudes were another stumbling block. This time it was the Australians and New Zealanders who were the most outspoken. Apparently on instructions from their governments, they would consider using their naval forces only in "their own backyards" to protect their trade routes. The British seemed very reluctant to press their commonwealth partners on this subject, preferring to leave that to the Americans. Hart thought that someone in Washington should be able to show the Australian ambassador that "their ships should not simply settle down to a pure defensive role, if other naval forces get into the war to an extent that at least permits an offensive against the other fellow's [Japan's] trade routes." All the participants in the conference, it appeared to Hart, were entirely too defense-minded. In his view, there was a connection between this defensive approach and a U.S. commitment. "I am convinced," he wrote, "that we can get the Dutch and British local navies (not the Anzacs) to do most anything we say, IF they feel their own sea reinforcement lines are reasonably secure—because of our own, or the R.N.'s efforts. . . . Then they are likely to go along with us, accepting our naval command without hesitation and, I think, our strategic ideas." Some progress had been made and some seeds planted, but this diplomacy was a complicated business. "What Napoleon or some other Old Guy said about the unwieldiness with and low collective efficiency of Allies does come to mind," he wrote Stark.[41]

The strategic ideas he mentioned in this letter were a continuing source of controversy. In the first place, American war plans, as

well as Hart's inclination, called for an offensive role to be performed by any Allied force to which the Asiatic Fleet was attached.
Second, for several reasons, the Americans were interested in
denying the Japanese passage through the Malay barrier from the
east, whereas the British wanted to block it from the west. The
primary reason for the American attitude was that keeping the
eastern entrances closed to the Japanese would provide connection
with, and passage for, the Pacific Fleet. The British plan to block
the approaches from the west would keep Allied forces tied tightly
to Singapore, and that would divide U.S. forces while placing the
Allies in a blocking, rather than a flanking, position.

Differences of opinion on offense versus defense and east versus
west came out very clearly at the next Singapore Conference. This
was the conference called for at the ABC Conference and it
opened on 21 April. Purnell, in light of the ABC proceedings, was
able to say very definitely that the Asiatic Fleet would fall back
on Singapore or Surabaja. What he could not do was talk the other
participants out of using the U.S. cruisers and destroyers, at least
in the initial stages of the war, "in dispersed protection of Associated shipping on trade routes." Nor was he able to argue them
into denying the Japanese passage through the eastern part of the
Malay barrier. That, as far as Allied planning was concerned, was
"definitely out." Hart did not insist that that was definitely wrong
but he did want American naval officials in Washington to make
no mistake about the fact that the British were very "trade-and-
raider conscious," just as they were in World War I.[42]

Because procedures at this conference were influenced by the
personalities of the conferees, Hart included in his report some
insights on them:

> We don't think much of Brooke-Popham [Air Chief Marshal Sir
> Henry Brooke-Popham]. Our opinions are the result of his visits
> to Manila and what our people saw of him on his own grounds
> during two conferences; the latter of course were the more valuable
> observations. The Air Marshal is considerably a politico. He may
> be adequate in Air subjects but he is very little of an Army Officer
> when one tries to get him thinking of, say, a Brigade in an important
> area, his mind runs off on moving some small squadron of obso-
> lescent planes. He seems rather muddle-headed, personality is not
> that of a leader of large, diverse forces. He clearly shows his years,
> 62–63, dozes off when he should not, etc. Until recently, Brooke-
> Popham's Chief of Staff was an Army General, very good indeed,
> and with him on the job there was reason to feel fairly comfortable
> about that general picture. That General has recently broken down

and seems to be temporarily replaced by Derval, an Air Officer who has made a far from good impression on my observers. The British Army was not really represented at this last Conference at all! We don't "*hear*" that things, in general, go very smoothly under the "Commander in Chief, Far East"—that is Brooke-Popham's title—there appears to be a good deal of friction. Although it is not likely that our sea forces will touch him in any way, and our air forces won't actually have to do so—still there is the fact that Brooke-Popham is the senior officer in the area and that a large and important land, (and air), force is in his hands. Vice Admiral Layton has my people's entire liking and respect—as a fine example of the blue-water school of the Royal Navy. He is direct, frank and forceful. Inasmuch as he holds back on anything to do with long-range planning, there is the possibility that important decisions may not be reached soon enough. (This last Report recommends one Strategic Commander for the entire "Eastern Theatre" (see paragraph 34). Admiral Layton has mentioned that some senior Admiral may come out, perhaps only when Phase II begins—or three months afterward. Nothing known about who is to be the Commander of the Eastern Theatre in the meantime.)[43]

Despite the various problems, the ADB (American, Dutch, British) report was produced and forwarded to Washington. With that completed, little remained to do on the alliance front until the president, the prime minister, and the various officials in the service departments in America and England could react.

It was obvious from Stark's letters that the higher-ups had much on their minds in this spring of 1941. The perilous situation of Great Britain probably topped the list. The German campaign against her seaborne commerce was in high gear and she was still reeling from the Luftwaffe's bombing raids. At times, Stark gave her as little as ninety days. These concerns made the concept of drawing forces from the Pacific Fleet to reinforce the Atlantic Fleet and letting the British reinforce their naval forces in the Far East particularly attractive. As Stark wrote his senior commanders, "From the standpoint of U.S. national defense the proposed naval deployment gives adequate security in case the British Isles should fall."[44]

Following close on the heels of anxieties about Britain's fate was anticipation of Japanese actions leading up to the war Stark and others in Washington were increasingly sure was going to come. Avoiding hostilities in the Pacific for as long as possible was given added impetus by the decision to make the Atlantic the primary theater. The questions raised were: first, what to do that was strong enough to deter the Japanese yet not so strong as to precipitate hostilities? One thing that could be done was refrain from reinforcing the Asiatic Fleet. The logic that forced this conclusion was that a reinforcement taken from the Pacific Fleet at Hawaii might tempt the Japanese into attacking both Hawaii and Manila since neither U.S. force would then be strong enough to ward off the blow. On the other hand, substantial strengthening of the Asiatic Fleet might provoke the Japanese into making a preemptive strike against the Philippines.[45] No one made the point at the time, but obviously taking ships from the Pacific Fleet and sending them to the Atlantic would also have the effect of leaving two understrength fleets in harm's way. The second question Stark said he was pondering was: if, or when, the Japanese moved, against whom would they move? The answer to this was more difficult. As of April, Stark thought it distinctly possible that the Japanese would pass up attacking the United States and move instead against either the British or the Dutch. But if they did so, it still was unclear what the United States would do. It looked more and more likely that she would fight beside her semi-allies— not certain, but likely.

Hart was not reassured by this questioning and imprecise answering on matters that could well mean life or death for him and his men. For one thing, he did not like giving the Japanese the luxury of determining where and when to strike. "I do prefer the offensive to the defensive," he grumbled. Yet it was obvious that the United States was not going to strike the first blow and he did not have many better answers than Stark did.

8

CHAOS BEFORE DISASTER

Hart found living with all these uncertainties especially trying because, in a sense, one uncertainty led to another. From a practical standpoint the most difficult thing to do was decide how much alert was enough. Or, put another way, how long could he keep his forces in a state of readiness and how hard could he work them without dulling their fighting edge? He was convinced that war might come at any moment and was determined not to be "caught napping." On the other hand, he could not afford to work himself into collapse, as Smeallie had done, or work his men and old ships so hard in rehearsal that they would be incapable of meeting the challenge when the curtain went up.

With spring and the arrival of hot weather, Hart decided that, whatever the risks, he needed to take his fleet out for extended training. The logical place to go would be the waters of the southern Philippines, for it was there that part of the war might be fought. On 21 April 1941 the fleet set sail, ostensibly to get the men out of the heat and provide a change of scene, but actually to conduct war maneuvers. For the next several weeks the ships engaged in gunnery practice and night cruising, dodged mock submarines, and generally sharpened their fighting skills. When they returned to Manila on 12 May, Hart was satisfied that much had been accomplished; they were not totally ready, but they were more ready than they had been.

He had been assured by the Navy Department that he would get four days' warning of impending hostilities, so he based all tactical contingency plans on a two-day warning. He had been around too long to put much faith in official assurances.[1] Even though agreement had not been reached on particulars of Allied strategic plans, there were things that could be done to facilitate cooperation at the tactical level. To assist in this procedure, the various parties exchanged liaison officers. Joining Hart in Manila, in addition to Lieutenant Commander Wisden, who arrived in November, was Commander H. D. Linder, Royal Netherlands Navy. Disguised as shipping control officers, these men had as their primary responsibility the setting-up of joint communications. A comprehensive series of meetings was held on cryptographic aids, radio channels, radio procedures, and so on, to the end that the Allies would have a secure method for coordinating tactical movements.[2]

In spite of the preparations, Hart was still not entirely clear about which part of his fleet should be prepared for what. The new war plan that had grown out of Stark's Plan Dog memorandum and been endorsed at the ABC Conference—Rainbow 5 (WPL 46)—called for the major surface ships of the Asiatic Fleet to retire to the southwest where they would join the other Allied fleets. What had not been resolved was *when* in the course of the war they would do so. There were obvious conflicting pressures. Not surprisingly, the British and the Dutch wanted the Asiatic Fleet sent south with all possible speed as soon as war seemed imminent. Purnell, doing everything possible to encourage British-Dutch cooperation and, therefore, wanting to demonstrate American amiability, assured the conferees in Singapore that Admiral Hart still intended to send his cruisers, destroyers, and large auxiliaries to Singapore at the first signs of an "emergency."[3] However, being realistic, and possibly to retain some bargaining leverage, Purnell insisted that the conference report state specifically that Admiral Hart, and Admiral Hart alone, would determine when an "emergency" had arrived.

Even that provision did not appease Hart's army commander, General Grunert. Naturally, Grunert wanted all possible support from the U.S. Navy for just as long as he could get it. Since Rainbow 5 called for reinforcing the army in the Philippines, Grunert thought his prospects for holding out were improving, so it was logical to ask for more support from the navy even though the army was still planning for a limited, defensive campaign.

An appeal to Washington for help in resolving what Hart called these "quandries" brought word that it was up to him to decide them. He was given wide latitude as to the composition of the force sent south and the timing of its departure.[4] Tommy Hart probably wished that Stark and others had less confidence in him or at least gave him some better guidance.

There were factors inclining him toward accepting Grunert's view. There was, for instance, the use the British intended to make of the ships sent to them from the Asiatic Fleet. Hart was not enthusiastic about protecting trade routes. Then, the increasing reinforcement of the army's land and air strength made the prospect of holding Manila Bay brighter. Finally, at least in the short run, the rainy season of early summer worked to the advantage of any defending force. All these factors led Hart to restudy the possibilities of fighting the war from Manila Bay. When he calculated the power, ship to ship, he would be up against, it did not look "too promising," but the crux of the matter was to determine whether the "ultimate cause" would be better served by basing in Singapore or Manila. He tried to keep an open mind, yet, when he did so, the answer came back as it originally had, deploy in Singapore. So, he advised Washington that was what he intended to do, unless ordered differently.[5]

There was still the troublesome matter of what his surface ships and submarines could do once so deployed. The British were not the only impediment to his using them against Japanese shipping in what he considered their most effective manner. Under U.S. naval doctrine, submarine operations against merchant shipping must be conducted according to international law governing cruiser warfare. That meant approaching on the surface, giving warning, and making provision for disembarking passengers and crews. Hart considered this impractical, unwise and dangerous, but he could not allow his commanders to break the law. One official publication of particular interest to submarine captains was *Instructions for the Navy of the United States Governing Maritime and Aerial Warfare*, which contained many rules concerning engagement and included the reminder that any submarine violating these rules could be hunted down and captured or sunk as a pirate. Appeals to Washington for revision of these instructions were to no avail; therefore, he had to face the prospect that the operations of even his most effective weapon might be seriously hampered.

There were things he could do to ready his command for the move south. Aside from scouting out harbors and learning the waters, he could plan his logistics. Two merchant ships, the *Pecos* and the *Trinity*, and his large submarine tenders were loaded with

2,500 tons of ammunition, torpedoes, spare parts, and other stores. Not much in the way of spares for submarines could be included, only what could be carried in the tender *Canopus*. But with careful planning, they managed to get in even spare propellers and some shafting, and with the provision of these vital stores the fleet's readiness for any eventuality was markedly improved. Among other things, it was found that, since the 2,500 tons did not unduly deplete stocks in Manila, the fleet would now be able to operate out of either Singapore *or* the Philippines.

The next move was to make arrangements for command and control. In view of the fluid state of Allied planning, it seemed wisest to designate the forces sent south to cooperate with potential Allies as Task Force 5.[6] This would allow for tactical cooperation with the Allies on the spot. Strategic command and administration of the Asiatic Fleet could best be maintained from a base ashore in Manila. This arrangement would allow for secure and continuous communication as well as facilitate the close coordination with the U.S. Army that Hart thought desirable. For command of the task force Hart first thought of Glassford, but then settled on Purnell because of his experience in dealing with the Allies.[7]

But when war came, who would be the Asiatic Fleet commander? It was looking more and more as though it would be Tommy Hart. It will be recalled that as early as November this idea was discussed and when McCrea came to Manila one of his duties was to assess Hart's potential. Then on 28 March 1941 had come official word: "Department intends you remain present duty after normal date for retirement."[8]

Hart responded affirmatively, but not without reservation. The most significant of his reservations had to do with health. He had always considered health a significant, if often overlooked, factor in an officer's ability effectively to excercise control over his forces. More specifically, he considered his health, and his vitality, as critical in his role as commander of the Asiatic Fleet. He was very conscious of his age and of the fact that senior officers around him were dropping like flies. Moreover, his highly developed sense of responsibility decreed that he not risk lives or miss opportunities because of any mental lapse. Actually, his health had been quite surprisingly good over the past year and a half. He had had an occasional cold and at least one serious bout with anemia, but medication had quickly corrected that imbalance. He worked seven days a week, took regular exercise, and golfed enthusiastically. Still he worried. Hence it was logical that he would make his health a factor in his, and the navy's, decision about remaining in command; he wrote Caroline in December 1940, that it would be "no go unless I *am* sufficiently well preserved."[9] He made the same comment to McCrea. When the order to stay on came he confided his thoughts to his diary:

> I'm naturally pleased, satisfied and happy that I have engendered that much trust and confidence in those . . . who are of a mind to keep me on. But I don't contemplate the future with much delight. There is not going to be any happiness in it. There will be continuance of strain, worry, and the weight of great responsibility—most likely much more than I've lived through the last twenty months. Even that has been a fair burden and, though I don't think I'm tired very much, there is no doubt that the keenness has gone from my cutting edge. However, I'm in for it and now to continue to take the correct road and to do the right thing. One of those right things is to maintain a proper estimate of my own physical, mental and nervous state. There is no one else in position to do that so *I* must watch to see that these vastly important affairs do not drift into the grasp of a man too weak, too old. Guess just that is going to take some doing.
>
> Well, I'd been looking forward—despite all the "rumors" about my continuance—to getting home next summer—Caroline, my offspring, the Connecticut countryside, King House and the farm and the U.S.A. in general. Now to forget all about that until ? [10]

Aside from the references to health there are other refrains in this passage that help fill out a picture of Tommy Hart as he approached this summer of his sixty-fourth year. For one thing, he says that he will not find much happiness in the job, obviously in part because of the constant tension. Eighteen months after he took command of the Asiatic Fleet, he wrote, "I suppose I have had a normal amount of fun, sufficient relaxation, etc. But the worry, the feeling of thin ice, of a volcano even underneath that . . . has been pretty steady and constant. Have I *liked* my last year and a half? I don't know, yet; but at least I've been interested, and, I think, I find satisfaction in what it has meant. *That* is the most important part— of any man's feelings and consciousness."[11] There also is self-criticism in his comment about the keenness of his cutting edge having gone. Hart was hard on himself, unemotional in his self-evaluation, but even though he thought he was slipping, he was confident enough of his ability to perform satisfactorily to be willing to stay on.

He was less confident about the future. The world situation, admittedly, did not look bright and there was reason for doubts. Hart brooded about that future; he saw the democracies continually outguessed by the dictators and he worried about how the economic policies of the Roosevelt administration would affect his and his family's financial security. One night he became so upset he could not sleep, so he sat down and wrote out his thoughts for transmission to Caroline. He warned her that, when she read the short essay he included with his letter, she would be convinced she was married to a "cynical, skeptical, distrustful old man," but getting his thoughts on paper relieved him.

The essay is a diatribe against the various forces—ethnic, economic, and political—that had, in his view, sapped America's strength. In it, Tommy reveals himself as a true conservative, if that is one who reveres and would like to preserve the values of the past. He did not like many things that had happened in the immediate past and it was his impression that Washington was again filling with moneygrubbers and profiteers who saw defense primarily as a way to line their pockets. He also sensed that self-seeking groups were becoming more and more proficient at draining the public trough and doing so without reference to the long-range public interest.

Part of this lack of a common goal and common values he attributed to racial heterogeneity. Tommy's views on race are reminiscent of Theodore Roosevelt's or maybe even Herbert Spencer's, but wherever they came from they are distinctly nineteenth-century. It was not simply that he was a white supremacist for, although he was quick to note racial differences, he was tolerant of those differences and even condemned some of his colleagues for letting prejudice interfere with their professional obligations. It was more that Tommy was always looking for explanations for why people and organizations fell short of his expectations, and race provided one answer. He saw America as weakened in her unity of purpose by the infusion of too many disparate races. He saw the black population as unassimilable. The same was true of the Jewish population, one of whose "unamerican" characteristics he considered to be their internationalism. The rush for cheap labor brought in millions of Far Eastern and Mediterranean peoples. "To say that they are inferior to western and northern European stock," he wrote, "opens an unprofitable argument." But, he went on, "there is no doubt that they do not merge with the racial stocks which preceded them to the consequent improvement of the whole." He offered no solution for the situation, he simply worried that the United States was not the unified nation it once seemed to be. Clearly on his mind was the question of how well this disparate mass would pull together in the military contest he saw just ahead. And after that war, in the world his children would inherit, he wondered what kind of economic and political nation would emerge:

> Our melting pot may have melted the charge but the mass in the crucible is really a mess, with the good sound metal so cluttered with dross and slag that its effectiveness is badly compromised. And, the damage is probably irreparable.
>
> Self-seeking, particularly of groups and blocks, still and again is rife in the land. The home guards are again prominent in their demands on the purse. The demagogues and "leaders" of various sorts still exercise authority without responsibility. The racial melting pot glows dully through unsightly slag and the politicos are still hungrily politiking. It's been economically a tough old country, that America of ours. But, looking ahead a short time, what is "Our way of life" going to become like anyhow?[12]

Whatever the future might bring, it appeared that Tommy's role on the temporal stage would soon be phased out. On 12 June 1941 he reached official retirement age. In spite of the fact that his service was to continue past this milestone, the officers in his command staged a ceremony and presented him with an engraved silver tray. They probably did not notice, but "Tough Tommy" was twice on the verge of tears, as he tried to find the words to thank them. He was touched by their recognition, especially because he did not feel he merited their kind thoughts. "It seems to me," he wrote, that "I don't do anything for them at all, work them to death and only growl at them, with a lot of bad temper flying off me most of the time."[13]

That probably was how he felt, but the most revealing comment about himself and his attitude was contained in a letter written on his birthday. After reminding his wife about his old wish to end his career by being swept from the quarterdeck by a 14-inch shell, he wrote: "When I do arrive at the point, those are not my thoughts at all! Whereas ambition was a prominent part of me in the days B.C. (before Caroline) and up to now also, I don't feel the least vestige of that kind of urge now. Don't get me wrong now—there is no connection whatever with the 14 inch shell business; and being without ambition is all to the good, I think. No, my thoughts are quite healthy and normal. . . . Today, I just wish that nothing whatever were expected of me, in a public way. I just crave to be free of it all, to be with you and to be assured that I'll *always* be with you during such ever days as the fates will that I shall have left."[14]

Obviously he was lonely. It was particularly agonizing to suffer loneliness now that he no longer had any ambition for success or fame. Previous separations had occurred when he was on his way up, or at least was trying to solve some problem or merit a good fitness report. Now he was a fulfilled man, he felt no urge to continue in the "gold-fish bowl" of public life; in fact, he considered it in a way unseemly for an older man to conspire, or even aspire, to cling to power after his time had passed. His letter concluded:

> I'm sure that I don't need that big shell to round things out with. No, my thoughts are quite along other lines, and I see that one Caroline Brownson is the reason for the switch in basic ideas. She began the transformation in that way well over thirty years ago, and her influence on my irrelevant thought has been cumulative throughout those years.
>
> My uppermost thought today is decidedly with home sickness. I sort of feel finished as a public person. Feel that the so-called career can, or should, be considered finished. Feeling no further ambition whatever, along those lines, my thoughts turn entirely to what I, as a private citizen in full retirement, wish to do with whatever years are left to us. I've some fixed ideas therein: I firstly wish to be with Caroline—and with my children—for such hours as they feel like giving up to us. I wish to unpack my trunk and stow my kit, finally, and for all time, under that roof, up in Sharon. Wish to watch the crops, and the animals grow, on that farm. Wish to go off with Caroline to again look at some places which we were in, together, long ago; and to a whole lot of other places we've never seen but which for years we have promised ourselves we would see—and "do." I wish to be at hand whenever any of those important things happen to any of my children. Well, thanks to one Hitler, I don't see myself doing any of those things—yet. Tomorrow I'll turn over a new frame—even a new volume of this. It will scarcely be fitting to begin a new frame, on the first day of my 65th year with a continuance of being sorry for myself. So I suppose I'll succeed in going on with what is expected of me, with the best grace possible.

Whether he liked it or not, Hart was going to stay in the "fish bowl" and, if anything, become more, not less, of a public personality. He was also going to find the strain increasing rather than diminishing as he made new plans and new dispositions and implemented some decisions already made. He had decided, for instance, to detach Task Force 5, place it under Purnell's command, and send it into southern Philippine waters to be close to prospective British and Dutch allies. He also decided to move his fleet headquarters ashore, which meant finding suitable quarters. The best place was a building on the waterfront that the State Department was planning to use for the consul and the trade commissioner. The diplomats refused to relinquish their plans, even though their needs perhaps should have been given a lower priority than Hart's. In any case, after an unseemly squabble, which Washington was unwilling or unable to resolve, Hart gave up and moved his offices and communications center into rented space in the Marsman Building, at the end of Pier 7, on the Manila waterfront. This commercial building was far from satisfactory, security arrangements and so on had to be improvised, but it seemed the best solution available on short notice. Had he set up headquarters at Cavite it would have overshadowed Bemis, the commandant of the Sixteenth Naval District, which Hart did not want to do for personal as well as professional reasons. In fact, he was planning on increasing Bemis's responsibilities. As things appeared in June, Purnell would command the task force, Bemis would command operations in and around Manila, and Hart would exercise overall command either from Manila or from somewhere south with the Allies.

This arrangement seemed reasonable and looked good on an organization chart, but it was not easy for him to do. For one thing, he could not get over his feeling that the commander of the fleet should have his headquarters afloat, yet it was so much more efficient to command and communicate securely from ashore. For another thing, it was an emotional wrench to leave his seagoing home in the *Houston*. On the night of 28 June he paced the deck as he reminisced about all the other ships he had inhabited for so many years in so many different places and how he was leaving his last shipboard home. The walking gave him exercise, but the remembering made him blue; it seemed that everything he did he was doing for the last time now. The next day he moved out and into a small apartment in the Manila Hotel, just below the penthouse of Field Marshal MacArthur.

There also was the fact that the change in command arrangements meant installing Purnell in the *Houston* and actually sending him south. With a flurry and a bustle that was difficult to maintain between typhoons, that too was accomplished. The admiral's flag was hauled down and broken on the little converted yacht *Isabel*, good-byes were said, and on 9 July the *Houston* steamed out of Manila Bay. In harbors in the Sulu chain Purnell would improvise basing facilities, and familiarize his crews with the seas where they would probably be fighting. All that remained to be done was fly a few staff members south to join him when the time came to mobilize, and the Asiatic Fleet would be ready to fight World War II. There was a sense of satisfaction in being prepared for the war he expected any day, but there was also a sense of being left out, of sending others off to fight in what he called the "front line trenches," of playing observer rather than participant.

Not that there was not plenty to do on shore. Among other things, intelligence interception and interpretation activities were producing dividends. In the spring Hart had received a highly classified cryptographic decoding device known as a Purple machine which, installed in the Malinta Tunnel on Corregidor, allowed his team of code specialists to read certain Japanese messages. During one of Purnell's visits to Singapore intelligence specialists got together and exchanged information; the result was that, when he returned to Manila, the Asiatic Fleet's cryptanalysts were provided with "complete information on the make up of the Japanese Navy's code system that carried the heaviest volume, its idiosyncrasies, etc. and the keys they [presumably the British] had thus far broken down."[15]

Thus, Hart had access to some of the best raw intelligence available to anyone, as good as Washington's, better than Pearl Harbor's. Furthermore, in Rosy Mason he had one of the best intelligence officers in the U.S. Navy. But most important, Hart himself had a highly developed capability for evaluating intelligence. At least once a week he took the *Isabel* over to Corregidor, where he reviewed the most recent intercepts and went over anything that was giving the analysts trouble. This impressed one of the intelligence officers because, he said, "I had always thought of Tommy Hart as a rather stiff necked old disciplinarian who tolerated no nonsense in his fleet." But there he was "sitting informally on the edge of people's desks, picking their brains and putting it all together in a highly competent manner."[16]

In June, when news of the German attack on Russia came, Hart thought that the Japanese might take advantage of the situation and move north against Russia, rather than south. But in July the Imperial Army took over full control of Indochina, thereby gaining airfields within striking distance of Malaya.[17] In response, President Roosevelt issued an executive order freezing Japanese assets in the United States. A financial embargo had long been opposed by Stark and others in the Navy Department on the grounds that it would deny Japan the means to buy vital oil and make a Japanese move against the Netherlands East Indies inevitable. Hart agreed with the navy's logic and this meant that the mining of Manila Bay could no longer be delayed. Deciding to lay the minefield and laying it were two different things. The officers responsible over at Cavite did not move as efficiently as Hart would have liked, which raised doubt about the capacity of his friend, Cap Bemis. With more bravado than reality, however, on 31 July he announced that Manila Bay was sealed.

The other big news in July was that on the same day FDR froze Japanese assets, the War Department issued orders making Douglas MacArthur Commander in Chief, American Army Forces in the Far East.[18] Brought back into federal service and given the rank of temporary lieutenant general, MacArthur was in his element. His Philippine Army was also to be called into the service of the United States, so when mobilization had been completed he would be relatively free of local political interference. While he was field marshal, there had been friction between him and President Quezon, and speculation was rife that MacArthur himself orchestrated the change to avoid being fired. Now he was a general in the U.S. Army again and he began burning up the wires to Washington urging his friends there to send him planes, ammunition, guns, anything to help him arm his troops. MacArthur's change in status was not welcomed by many, including High Commissioner Sayre, who had grown both more tough-minded and less fond of MacArthur. Hart was surprised by the change, but not displeased; he even fancied that he might be able to serve as a "buffer" between the general and the commissioner. He estimated that "as soon as my friend Douglas gets to it," he would push hard for using all U.S. sea and land forces in "defense of Luzon"; however, Hart was confident that he could handle him.[19]

Before handling MacArthur he had to do some manipulating of his own command. As mentioned, the initial laying of the minefield had not gone well; progress on improvements was slow; a lot of mines exploded after being laid; and support from the Sixteenth Naval District did not seem to Hart as rapid or professional as he would have liked. Tommy Hart did not react passively to that kind of situation; he chewed people out, dispensed discipline where called for, and "leaned" on Cap Bemis. It soon became apparent to him that, contrary to his hopes, Bemis could not do the job whether leaned on or left alone. "Bemis a disappointment," he wrote in his diary on 10 August. Not only did he seem to lack managerial ability, but he had a tendency to get sick at the most inconvenient moments. Hart intended, once war started, to turn virtually complete control of forces in Manila over to Bemis; that now seemed impractical. After several days of thought, he came up with a solution.

If Washington had selected his replacement as Asiatic Fleet commander, why not send him out immediately? The replacement could temporarily take over command of the Sixteenth Naval District, with Bemis being given responsibility for the Navy Yard at Cavite.[20] Hart would stay on the scene until everyone was acclimatized and broken in, then, when a new commandant for the Sixteenth District had been found, Hart would go home. If this procedure were not followed, Hart and Bemis might have to be replaced simultaneously for reasons of health, and the Asiatic Fleet might go through a very difficult transition at a most inopportune time. It sounded logical, but Washington just could not seem to get organized to do anything logically or swiftly; therefore, Hart made on-the-spot adjustments. Since Bemis clearly could not take more responsibility, the plan for him to take over if Hart went south was scrapped. To fill gaps over at Cavite the only available flag officer around would have to lend a hand. That officer? T. C. Hart. The worst part of it was the increased worry it caused him to realize that he *must* stay fit since he had an unreliable number two. Perhaps for that reason on 29 August he took the day off. He had taken no leave since he arrived in July 1939 and generally worked seven days a week—in fact, this was the first day off he had had in eight months. Still, he felt a little guilty about it.

He also was feeling uneasy about the situation vis-à-vis his potential allies. Describing the ADB report that had come out of the last Singapore conference as "ineffective," Stark had informed Hart in early July that Washington would not approve it.[21] Unfortunately, both for Hart's peace of mind and for planners in the Far East, no one told the British. At the end of the month Hart felt he had to give Admiral Layton in Singapore some clue that all was not well, so he wrote him that he had heard rumors that ADB was running into opposition. Hart said he guessed the reason was the "failure to take proper measures to deny the Malay

Barrier." But the planners in Singapore continued to pour out operational plans called PLENAPs based on ADB. Hart wished that Washington would let London know what was going on in order to stop the planning machinery turning out stacks of useless plans, if for no other reason.

Not helping Hart's humor were two visits by the dunderheaded Brooke-Popham. It was bad enough that he fell asleep in meetings and kept mumbling about the presumed effectiveness of his obsolete aircraft, but he also insisted on talking with the press. In these interviews he left plenty of room for the deduction that a full-fledged alliance had been established. Hart, who abhorred the press, anyhow, thought it a bad idea to be implying an alliance, thereby inviting a Japanese attack, especially when planning was in such disarray. It was all too much, Washington dawdling, the British running off in the wrong direction in their planning, and a Blimpish air marshal, who once wrote that one of the worst things about the war was that it would finish fox-hunting, blundering around for comic relief!

Hart began a campaign to have Brooke-Popham replaced, or at least to have Washington make London fully aware of his shortcomings. Washington was at this same time trying to pressure the British into accepting a more offensive strategy in the Far East. The amount of muscle the American service chiefs could exert, however, was limited by the contradiction in their stance. They wanted a more offensive strategy, but were unwilling to make a commitment to fight unless American territory were attacked, nor would they reinforce the Asiatic Fleet. In other words, they wanted the British to provide the major surface ships to carry out the strategy *and* to conduct that strategy along the lines the Americans thought best. When ABC gave command of naval forces in the Far East to the British, the Americans lost virtually all their right of initiative. Now they could only disapprove plans they did not like and delay giving a precise date when Hart would send his forces to join up with British and Dutch forces. This negative posture did not provide much leverage, but Hart did not have much of a fleet either.

After more discussion, including conversations between Roosevelt and Churchill at Argentia, Newfoundland, in August, Stark advised Hart on 11 September that the latest PLENAP had been disapproved and it was suggested that he consider deferring a decision on whether to base ships in Singapore or the Netherlands East Indies until "after war comes."[22] Then came a long dispatch explaining the Navy Department's rationale for disapproving the ADB report and the PLENAP developed to support it: (a) British unwillingness to assign and use ships for offensive purposes, and (b) the tentativeness of British plans for sending a fleet to the Far East. Until the British were willing to take a "predominant part in the defense of the British position in the Far East," the U.S. Asiatic Fleet would not operate under their strategic direction. It was up to Hart to command his fleet, but he should coordinate with the British and the Dutch "by the method of mutual cooperation."[23] Hart underscored the term *mutual cooperation* and put two exclamation points behind it. As he had made clear earlier, he considered anything other than unified command was virtually useless. He was advised to think in terms not of American interests only, but of the whole Far East. "The security of the Philippine Islands is important to the United States," the dispatch went on, "but the naval effort devoted to this security should not be such as to jeopardize greatly the success of the associated powers in maintaining the security of the Malay Barrier." Hart interpreted this message to mean that he had been cut loose from the Allies. He saw what Stark was trying to accomplish by the maneuver, but it was, as he observed, "a slightly hazy situation."[24]

With strategic command of his fleet now back in his own hands, Hart informed the Navy Department on 17 September that he intended the "initial deployment" of most of his surface forces to be well to the southwest of Manila but still within the Philippine Islands area.[25] Within twenty-four hours the Navy Department approved this deployment and informed him that the American efforts at pressure had begun to bring success. The British had said that they would definitely reinforce the Far East, and in Washington they agreed "with your opinion that . . . [the] Philippines ought to be seriously considered as initial base for naval and air forces. . . ."[26]

These last several messages were a trifle confusing. In the first place, it was still not clear exactly what his relationship with his potential allies should be. He disagreed with the idea that a decision on where and how to base the ships he was going to send to cooperate with the British and Dutch be "deferred until after war eventuates." That seemed to him impractical.[27] He also considered "mutual cooperation" to be "much inferior to unified control." In the second place, he would not be able to use the Philippines as a base for long because he still doubted that Manila Harbor, the only one that could accommodate an allied fleet, could be adequately protected. Moreover, if the British were now sending reinforcements to the Far East, would it not be wise to return to the concept of sending the main body of the Asiatic Fleet to either British or Dutch bases? But whatever the answer, the imperative thing was to make some decision on where to base and how to cooperate. Time was running out, and it already was much too late in the game for deferring such fundamental determinations.

The hint from Washington that the Philippines might be considered as a main base, so foreign to all previous plans, reflected increasing confidence regarding defense of the islands. After literally years of writing the Philippines off in the opening stages of any war, official opinion had undergone a dramatic change. Previously, it will be recalled, in all debates on the plan for war with Japan, the navy argued, probably without much conviction, that the army would be able to hold out; now, ironically, the army, which had previously been negative, was the prime mover in the optimistic upswing. One reason for the change was an estimate that the B-17 bomber would be able to play a substantial role in defending the Philippines, but the most important factor was the infectious optimism of General MacArthur. He had apparently convinced himself, and was busy convincing others, that previous forecasts of doom resulted from improper or unimaginative perception. Under his leadership, MacArthur was convinced that given the time available—he doubted the Japanese would attack before the spring of 1942—adequate defenses could be devised. There is "plenty of time," he told a worried Hart.[28]

Although intimations of this thinking had reached Hart earlier, on 22 September he got the full benefit of a MacArthur soliloquy. The general told Hart that he was "not going to follow, or be in any way bound by whatever war plans have been evolved, agreed upon and approved." MacArthur had his own ideas about how the islands could be defended and he was going to put them in motion.[29] As Hart listened, MacArthur strode up and down, striking his palm for emphasis as he outlined how, with his proposed 200,000-man army and powerful air force, he would fight a "glorious land war." He professed not to care whether the navy stopped a Japanese landing or not; let them get ashore and MacArthur's army would crush them. When Hart interrupted to outline his plans for a defensive battle with most of the surface ships south of Manila, MacArthur said that the "Navy had its plans, the Army had its plans and that we each had our own fields."

Moreover, Hart wrote, "he had no questions whatever, made no suggestions and offered no objections."[30]

Hart began actively to dislike "friend Douglas." On previous occasions MacArthur had gone out of his way to belittle Hart's command. He was constantly seeking publicity, he was pompous, and Hart suspected that he prevaricated in his official reports.[31] But the general's bombastic display and cavalier dismissal of the navy's plans and role were apparently the last straw. In spite of the growing coolness between the two men, Hart was, perhaps despite himself, influenced by the confidence MacArthur exuded and by the presence of 130 modern fighter planes. Perhaps it would be possible for the Asiatic Fleet to fight it out from Manila.[32]

Other developments contributed to a two-month upswing in Hart's outlook. For one thing he was informed that he would receive reinforcements. Twelve new submarines and a tender were being sent from Pearl Harbor, along with six modern PT boats. Moreover, letters from Admiral Stark were filled with optimistic news about army air and ground reinforcements for the Philippines.[33] On a different tack, Brooke-Popham made another visit to Manila. MacArthur arranged considerable publicity for him, which Hart thought the British loved because they "like to have it appear that we are already in the war" but which he deplored because he thought time was on the Allied side and he did not want to give the Japanese any pretext for taking action.[34] MacArthur and "Brookem" had many long conversations, during the course of which the air marshal characteristically dozed off, but Hart talked only briefly with the British commander in chief. Hart had little respect for Brooke-Popham's strategic vision but, more important, he soon discerned that there had been little change in the British defensive inclinations. Since Hart was growing guardedly more offensive with every day and every reinforcement, there seemed little to talk over and slight reason to worry about how to work closely with the British. Better to concentrate on fighting the war where and how he thought best.

The final element contributing to Hart's optimism was personal. On 18 September he had a complete physical examination. As he recounted it, he kidded with the doctors, trying to convince them that he had something wrong but was trying to conceal it in order to keep his job. To further mystify them, he also pretended to have "suspicions of various kinds of disability." "Lots of fun," he wrote. To their relief, and one suspects to Hart's as well, the doctors found him "sound as a dollar, weight almost 135, blood pressure 112, and they had to go down into the forty band to pick out the various muscle tests, reactions, etc. Will live to be 100 and have to be killed by an axe."[35] This report could hardly help but relieve any anxieties he may have had about his health. He had told Stark repeatedly that he would advise Washington of any decline in his condition, emphasizing his willingness to pass over command "as soon as *you* say so; I'll not cling."[36] But this very positive medical report made it likely that he would remain on the job for the foreseeable future and, from his perspective, that meant he would be in the saddle when the war began. Although he continued to refer to himself as an "Old Man," he knew that he was an awfully tough old man. He would have to be. Within the week he learned that Bemis was to be invalided home because of "chronic colds and indigestion."[37]

The loss of Bemis threw the command structure he had so recently modified into disarray. Hart was advised from Washington that immediate attention would be directed toward finding a new commandant for the Sixteenth Naval District, the third in eighteen months, but until he arrived Hart would simply have to pick up the slack at Cavite. Stark had not decided on a replacement for Hart. He told Hart that he, Hart, had the "full confidence" of the president, the State Department, and the navy; furthermore, selecting a replacement was difficult because the commander in chief of the Asiatic Fleet had to be "the best man the Navy can produce."[38] That was very complimentary, but it did not sound as though much progress was being made in the search for that individual.

One possibility was to bring Glassford back from China. Hart was growing increasingly concerned about the vulnerability of the Yangtze Patrol and the 4th Marines. As he had informed the Navy Department, they should be withdrawn at the earliest opportunity. The State Department, however, did not agree and the navy went along with it. The department was afraid that pulling U.S. forces out of China would look like either panic or a move presaging war. Moreover, if the marines left, who would protect American interests? Hart's view was that there was little real protection for those interests, anyhow, and all the marines and the gunboats did was provide hostages to "Mr. Jap." If the Japanese wanted to interpret the withdrawal of the marines as a step toward war, let them; it might even have a restraining influence. But once again he was stymied by timidity and indecision from above. Everyone, supposedly, had complete confidence in Hart's judgment, yet when Washington and Manila did not see eye to eye, Washington exercised its veto power and stopped Hart from doing things he felt were vital to the security of his command. When that happened, all he could do was brood over his lengthening list of unmet priorities and speculate about the confusion that apparently reigned in decision-making circles in far-off Washington.

Letters from Stark, while welcome, tended to confirm Hart's speculations about confusion in Washington, but they did bring news of the "other" war in the Atlantic, where things were heating up. American ships were now escorting British convoys, and in September the president issued "shoot on sight" orders. Even before that, the chief of naval operations thought that "if the Germans want an excuse for war, they have plenty."[39] The war in Russia was going badly; the British were still hard pressed in the air and on the sea. The only good news was that the British did seem to be making plans to send those long-awaited capital ships to Singapore.

Meanwhile, Purnell and Task Force 5 had returned to Manila on 4 October for rest and refit. Given the vacancy over at the Sixteenth District, the uncertainty concerning dispositions since the Asiatic Fleet was not to be under British strategic command, and the fact that the task force had been away from base for three months, Hart decided to hold it and Purnell at Manila. His chief of staff would be a help in overseeing the forces joining the fleet and in filling the gap left by Bemis's departure. The new submarines and PT boats were not an offensive threat to the Japanese Navy and, while the Asiatic Fleet could hardly be called formidable, its defensive power had increased significantly.

Some new patrol aircraft had arrived, which was encouraging because Hart was becoming concerned about aerial reconnaissance. Surprisingly, his army counterpart, MacArthur, did not seem to be much concerned about the air; his primary interest was in the land battle he was going to wage. To be sure, MacArthur was impressed with the growing strength of his air arm, but he did not give much thought to its use. Hart anticipated trouble. To him it was axiomatic that, if the two services' air operations over water were to be mutually beneficial as well as efficient, they should be closely coordinated. If MacArthur was not interested, or did not want to cooperate, then Hart would ask for "full control of all air operations *over the water*."[40] He had emphasized his willingness to work closely with the army; he had told MacArthur that one of the reasons he moved ashore was to facilitate cooperation;

now, with the departure of Bemis, he informed the general that he, personally, would be coordinating operations with the Army. It was apparently to no avail; MacArthur would just nod and hurry on to his next soliloquy. Hart thought it best to put the air arrangement he proposed on paper, and volunteered to do that.[41]

Some decision was also needed regarding the permanent disposition of Task Force 5. The harbors in the southern Philippines were open to submarine attack, whereas Manila Bay derived at least a modicum of protection from the minefields. However, he did not want to be trapped in the bay and having the task force six hundred miles farther south would make surprise attack less likely. There simply was no perfect solution.[42] By mid-October, though, he was near to making a momentous decision over which he had been mulling since at least June.

On 27 October he informed the Navy Department that he was changing his plans dramatically; he had decided to exercise the latitude that Stark was constantly reminding him he had. The change was that he would keep the fleet together and fight the war from the Philippines. As he informed Stark, his reasoning was: (1) no agreed plan for joint operations had been possible with the British and Dutch except to furnish some destroyers *when* the British fleet had been reinforced; (2) operating the task force from

Admiral Hart's two flagships, the cruisers *Houston*, in the foreground, and *Augusta*, in the background, in Manila Bay, 1940. Courtesy of Mrs. T. C. Hart

improvised bases had proved difficult; (3) Manila Bay was a more secure and central base from which to operate both surface ships and submarines. As he put it, it was "now possible to envisage Navy task here as mainly offensive rather than supporting Army's defensive mission. . . ." The recently augmented squadrons of army P-40 fighters would protect the bay from sustained bombing attacks and, if MacArthur could do even part of what he implied he would do, all might yet be well. So, although he realized that there was no ideal way to solve the dilemma of having an under-strength fleet, keeping his whole force in the Philippines would at least have the virtue of concentration and provide a satisfyingly offensive posture.[43] Moreover, he felt a sense of relief in cutting loose from the nascent alliance that had proved so elusive.

Although, in the weeks that followed the news of his change of plans, Hart received dispatches from Washington, such as one on 14 November which said, "decisions as [to] basing surface forces in Philippines must be made by you," none of them gave specific approval.[44] Therefore, Hart could not put his plans into full operation. There was plenty to do, however, including further attempts to coordinate with General MacArthur. As he had promised, Hart drafted a letter that outlined air operations over water and, as he had indicated, called for naval control over them. He sent a copy to MacArthur, who, on 7 November, responded with what Hart called a "perfectly rotten" official letter. Essentially the general said that he found Hart's proposal "entirely objectionable." He went on, in Hart's phrase, "about as far as his active brain could take him toward being nasty to the Navy in general and me in particular."[45] He objected to putting his large air force under the control of a naval force "of such combat inferiority as your Command. . . ."[46] Not content with this insulting comment, MacArthur appealed to Washington for support. As a local matter, it was referred back to the commanders on the scene and several acrimonious discussions were held before, on 1 December, agreement was reached.

During this same period another dispute flared. Hart learned that several army transports had stopped at Shanghai and the officers in charge had given the passengers passes to go ashore. Since he was hoping to pull the marines out of China at any moment, the last thing Hart wanted was an "incident" wherein the Japanese roughed up some drunken soldier. If that happened, it would mean long negotiations during which the marines would not be able to leave without appearing to flee from Japanese militance.

Reacting quickly, too quickly perhaps, he issued an order about "shore leave precautions." By some unfortunate mistake, the information copies of the order became mixed up with the action copy and "that made it appear," wrote Hart, "that I was giving MacArthur orders!!" MacArthur reacted predictably; he telephoned Hart and the lines fairly sizzled. Under the influence of his white-hot anger, MacArthur seemed to think, Hart wrote, that he was "man enough to browbeat me."[47] Admitting the error, Hart apologized, but MacArthur would have none of it. He fired another appeal to Washington for help: the commander in chief of the Asiatic Fleet should learn military protocol, be advised about the limits of his authority, and so forth. Eventually a semblance of normality was restored, but it was obvious that there would not be the cooperation there was when Grunert commanded the U.S. Army in the Far East.

In retrospect neither of these incidents was important of itself. What was important was the maneuvering for ascendancy. Hart guessed, probably accurately, that MacArthur resented Hart's rank; as a full admiral, Hart wore four stars, MacArthur only three. "Small Fleet, big Admiral" was the way MacArthur put it, and the fact that, being an old acquaintance and friend of the family, Hart was not awed by him did not help things a bit. There seems little question that MacArthur was either insensitive to Hart's feelings, or tried to humiliate him, as on this occasion:

> The General came down to my living quarters, right under his own. Characteristically he had his wife telephone me for the appointment and he came down in his bathrobe. The occasion was a dispatch from the War Department about Army reinforcements on the way. . . . after extolling the Big Show which he would, eventually, have he said: "Get yourself a real Fleet, Tommy, then you will belong." "I listened to such patronizing talk," Hart wrote, "and under the circumstances it was not pleasant."[48]

And in fact Hart found he was, unwillingly, developing a deepseated dislike for the general. It was partially because MacArthur refused to keep him informed of plans, partially because the general gave cooperation with the "sister service" a low priority, and partially because his celebrated brilliance had lost some of its luster in Hart's estimation. MacArthur's mind seemed "erratic," Hart wrote to Stark, and "while knowledge has come wisdom tends to linger."[49] Or, as he more candidly informed Caroline, "The truth of the matter is that Douglas is, I think, no longer altogether sane . . . he may not have been for a long time."[50] Hart warned Stark that he should keep MacArthur's personality in mind when selecting a new commander for the Asiatic Fleet. As for himself, Hart knew he had earned the general's enmity and accordingly expected more trouble either directly or through MacArthur's contacts in Washington. The admiral was never more right.

Still, there had to be cooperation at the working level even if it was impossible at the highest level. To accomplish this, Hart assigned a young commander, Robert L. Dennison, as his representative at MacArthur's headquarters. Dennison was an engaging, capable officer who soon won the respect of the general's staff and finally of the general himself.[51] It was not as satisfactory a situation as direct liaison between the top men would have been, but it did provide for an exchange of information.

While all this was going on, Hart waited, in the torments of uncertainty, for Washington to approve the new fleet dispositions he had proposed. During the first week of November he again requested direction from the Navy Department.[52] The days crept by. He dared not be more than an hour's journey away from his office or take any more days off. He had complained to Stark repeatedly in personal letters and to the Navy Department officially about the slowness in communications, but this was more agonizing than anything before. He could virtually feel the world slipping toward war and, after all his effort, he still did not know for certain where his fleet would fight. But his visits to the Malinta Tunnel, where intelligence was correlated, told him he would soon be fighting. Finally he could wait no longer. On 19 November he called his senior officers together to announce his decision and the new dispositions it necessitated. The Asiatic Fleet would fight the war from Manila Bay.[53]

The next day—twenty-four days after he requested them—instructions came from Washington. Plan disapproved.[54] Hart immediately wrote Stark an extremely candid letter. He described his state of mind as "the worst possible" and went on to outline his frustration. He had tried dispersing his command and that had not worked; he personally favored moving all his ships to Singapore and going with them, but he knew Washington would not listen to that; he was even willing to put his command under British strategic command, but Stark had personally disapproved that; so, since he supposedly had so much discretion, he came up with something else and now Washington would not let him do that.[55] His idea may have been wrong, and he later admitted that it was, but the whole issue could hardly have been handled worse.[56]

Adding to this overall unhappiness was his personal loneliness; it was now a year since Caroline and Isabella had left Manila. On the anniversary of that evening when he watched their flying boat disappear into a rising moon, he wrote Caroline a letter in which he made it clear that he wished he had not been so tough on the subject of dependents. He told her that he often looked up at a third-quarter moon and said, "yes, that's where my Caroline went when she left me—she flew right into that moon. It's so very far up there that I fear she will never get back to me." It made him especially sad and homesick to think that a year had gone out of their life together, "a whole year . . . and now its gone, beyond recall." "It's not a pleasant thought, Old Dear," he continued, "with not such an awful lot left for our you-and-me life." The world was better for the job that she had done, but his "trade" never seemed to make the world better—perhaps just kept it from getting worse. "Well, Dear Girl," he concluded, "we have it to do, have had to live apart and all that; but at least we have stood up to our jobs—and there lies satisfaction."[57]

No matter what his feelings, the rush was now on to change dispositions and put things back more or less as they were before he made the decision to fight from Manila Bay. First, he would deploy some of his surface ships to the south. As advance units, four destroyers and the tender *Blackhawk* were sent to Balikpapan, and the cruiser *Marblehead* and four destroyers to Tarakan. Ostensibly, the ships were to fuel in those ports in east Borneo, but they were ordered to develop "difficulties" to justify remaining in the area.[58] Obviously, these were ships Hart was holding in readiness to furnish the British. The submarines—by this time he had twenty-nine of them—and their tenders would base in Manila Bay. These sleek S-class boats were seen as potentially the most effective part of the fleet; they also would be the greatest help in defending against Japanese attack on the Philippines, or so it seemed.

Task Force 5 was to be reactivated and, to command it, Hart chose Rear Admiral Glassford, who was due to arrive soon from China with the gunboats of the Yangtze Patrol. Hart was keeping Purnell at Manila as his chief of staff. His reason for doing this was that he intended to occupy the Manila command post and directly command the newly expanded Philippine coastal defenses. Since Hart would therefore be retaining personal command of the submarines, the air patrol wing, the motor torpedo boats, and some other small surface craft, he needed a chief of staff. The new commandant of the Sixteenth Naval District, Rear Admiral Francis W. Rockwell, had arrived at last; under his jurisdiction would come the sea defenses in and off Manila and Subic bays as well as the facilities at Cavite. Some other changes were made, as Hart ordered Captain W. E. Doyle, Commander, Submarines, Asiatic Fleet, to take some of the submarines south to help hold the Malay barrier but kept the former commander, Captain John Wilkes, in Manila "for eventualities."[59] Little was lost except the wear and tear on Tommy Hart. Nevertheless, it certainly appeared that, to say the least, the Asiatic Fleet did not enjoy a very high priority in Washington. In spite of his admission, at the time and later, that the department's final decision was right and his proposal to fight from Manila was wrong, Hart was aggrieved at how long it took Washington to make that decision.

It was during this critical period that *Time* came out with a cover story on "Tommy" Hart, the "indispensable oldster."[60] Clare Boothe Luce was among the reporters who interviewed Hart and provided an accurate description, if a little too clever and "Time-esque." He was the "man of the hour" and a "scrapper" who was spoiling for a fight with the Japanese. True, he was "no glib, soft-spoken naval diplomat," but it may have been a bit exaggerated to describe him as "weathered, wrinkled" and "tough as a winter apple." After indiscreetly suggesting that his role would be to attack Japanese convoys in the South China Sea, the article even more indiscreetly implied that there was an alliance between the British, the Dutch, and the Americans. It also mentioned Hart's family and his desire to get home to the farm in Sharon. It was clear that the author admired the commander of the Asiatic Fleet, even though he was said to have a mean temper and salty tongue and to be a tough taskmaster. One of Hart's officers was quoted as saying that during normal times he would prefer to serve under someone easier than Admiral Hart, "but in times like this . . . I would much prefer to be under him." On things such as military courtesy he was a stickler, but he defended sailors who got drunk when on liberty in Manila: he was said to believe that, after a long time at sea, they had a right to a "rough liberty," and anyhow, he added, only a hundred or so were reported for misconduct on any one night and that was not much worse than college boys on a football weekend. It was a laudatory article and, even though Hart did not normally welcome publicity, he thought it would please Caroline.

On 26 November and again on the twenty-ninth, Hart received

definite war warnings. This meant putting his final precautions into effect. He had waited, testing his nerve, so that he would not prematurely bring his people up to the peak of preparedness. "My people should be ready for the call now," he wrote.[61] They were sent scurrying about, moving explosives from the magazine at Cavite, rolling drums of aviation gasoline into clumps of trees behind the beach, building bomb shelters, and making other final preparations. Since his intelligence unit had picked up information that large Japanese Army units were moving down the Indochina coast, perhaps headed for Thailand, perhaps for Malaya, he authorized reconnaissance flights over their convoys.[62] He took personal, day-to-day direction of these PBY flights, instructing the pilots to avoid being spotted if possible and give no provocation. This was an extremely risky move, and even adherence to his instructions did not guarantee that there would not be an incident. The PBYs sighted large numbers of cargo ships and transports at sea and in port. In Camranh Bay there were more than twenty large-to-medium-sized ships accompanied by numerous auxiliaries, the whole fleet protected by air units that maintained patrol above them. This activity led Hart to conclude that strong Japanese amphibious operations were about to be mounted somewhere. He duly reported his information to Washington where, added to other intelligence, it was seen as increasing the probability that the Japanese would take action, soon.

On 1 December Hart received a most unusual message: it opened with the words, "President directs that the following be done as soon as possible."[63] What FDR wanted Hart to do, and do with haste, was form a "Defensive Information Patrol" to report Japanese movements in the "West China Sea" and the Gulf of Siam. Three small vessels were to be chartered, and the president was specific about how they should be manned and armed and insistent that they meet no more than the minimum requirements to "establish identity as United States men-of-war." The places where he directed that they be stationed were the precise latitudes where they would probably be run down by the southward-moving Japanese forces.

Why the president wanted this very dangerous mission undertaken has never been satisfactorily explained. Exhaustive research on the reason for the directive leads to the belief that the president was trying to provoke a *Panay*-type incident. Such an incident would provide enough provocation to justify an American declaration of war, in the event the Japanese bypassed U.S. possessions and attacked only the British. FDR's provocative actions in the Atlantic vis-à-vis German U-boats and comments by members of his administration lend credence to this theory. Rear Admiral Kemp Tolley, author of the best book on the incident, *Cruise of the Lanikai,* thinks that is what FDR was doing, but, since Tolley commanded one of the three ships, he may be viewed as other than an objective witness.

More objective witnesses contend that this was simply another reconnaissance mission and had no conspiratorial intent.[64] There are difficulties with that explanation. For one thing, Hart's air patrols were already bringing back detailed information on Japanese ship movements, and it was being relayed to Washington. Next, it was highly unusual, to say the least, for the president himself to give orders in such detail. Perhaps his defenders would say that this was just another instance of his sometimes harum-scarum interference in naval affairs. Perhaps. But at the very least, sending three ships on a mission of this nature in the volatile atmosphere then obtaining was unwise.

Finally, it is most instructive to see what impact the president's order had on Admiral Hart. Hart considered it "ill-advised" and did not like the fact that it "risked valuable personnel and ships to no legitimate end." Until his death, he was sure that FDR intended to provoke the Japanese into firing the first shot.[65]

Hart thought the mission so dangerous and provocative that he kept a detailed written record of what happened and what he did. He later said that he had thought the ships were "bait" tossed into a sea of Japanese sharks. And in the same interview said bluntly that the object of the mission was provocation "and I could prove it. But I won't."[66] He apparently never said officially what he thought about the mission. Given, however, what we know about Hart's attitude toward FDR and his views about the lack of support he was getting from Washington, it is not difficult to imagine what it was. The three small ships were only the first part of the "bait"; the Asiatic Fleet, its base, and its commander, would be the next bite. He could not have been overjoyed by that prospect, but he probably was not surprised by it, either. No one had been able to agree upon how his fleet could perform any other invaluable service and there were certainly those who considered him expendable. But Hart was trained to obey the orders of presidents, and obey he did.

On 3 December he personally briefed the commanding officer of his yacht *Isabel,* Lieutenant John Walker Payne, Jr.[67] The mission was top secret, no written orders were provided, and a story was made up about a lost patrol plane for which Payne was ostensibly searching. If necessary, the *Isabel* was to fight and under no circumstances should she be allowed to fall into Japanese hands. With that stirring message and several extra lifeboats, Lieutenant Payne steamed out of Manila Bay and possibly into the pages of the history books that already carried the names *Chesapeake*, *Maine*, and *Lusitania*.

By 5 December he was off Camranh Bay and, almost upon arrival, spotted by Japanese planes. They shadowed him all day thus getting ample opportunity to identify the *Isabel* as a U.S. naval vessel. By evening Hart decided to recall the *Isabel* to Manila; he then advised Washington of developments. "*Isabel* returning," he radioed, "was spotted and identified well off coast hence potential utility of her mission problematical."[68] In other words, the Japanese had chosen not to sink her; there would be no incident. Possibly, the other ships would be more difficult to identify and thus were more likely to fulfill what Hart thought were the president's desires. Fortunately, or unfortunately, they could not be prepared to put to sea before other events intervened.

On the same day the *Isabel* was spotted, the most important Allied visitor to date arrived in Manila. Vice Admiral Sir Tom Phillips, selected as the new Commander in Chief, Far East, had come to discuss war plans with Admiral Hart. The British were sending the battle cruiser *Repulse* and the battleship *Prince of Wales* to Singapore, soon to be followed by more reinforcements. The reversal of Hart's plan to fight at Manila had not reversed the Navy Department's order of October, which disapproved ADB-1 and ADB-2, as well as the current PLENAP. Therefore, in case of war the U.S. Asiatic Fleet would not be technically under the strategic command of the British. As will be recalled, that commitment had been withheld until the British substantially strengthened their fleet at Singapore. Phillips and his new ships were a step in that direction, but Hart still had considerable latitude in determining when and how he would cooperate with his potential allies.[69]

All negotiations were conducted in great secrecy, Phillips and his staff being put up at Cavite, far from the prying newsmen who had so lionized Brooke-Popham. To get the inevitable out of the way, Hart arranged that the first meeting would include General MacArthur. As anticipated, MacArthur talked at them at length about his plans and preparations for war after April 1942. As not anticipated, he ended his talk by saying "Admiral Hart and I operate in the closest cooperation. We are the oldest and dearest friends."[70] Hart's staff had trouble keeping their composure; the admiral maintained an impassive visage. After the general left, the two little admirals—neither one weighed more than 140 pounds and Phillips stood only five-foot-two—got down to discussing plans and sizing each other up. During their meetings, Hart received word from Captain John Creighton, U.S. naval attaché in Singapore, that the U.S. government had made the long-awaited commitment to enter the war under four sets of circumstances, one of which was an attack by the Japanese on British or Dutch territory, even if U.S. territory were untouched. Hart knew nothing of any such commitment and immediately cabled Washington for confirmation: "Learn from Singapore we have assured [the] British armed support under three or four eventualities."[71] He did not get a reply before Phillips left Manila.

Phillips urged Hart to send two divisions of destroyers to protect his capital ships at Singapore. Discussion of this request ranged on into the next day and apparently got rather heated. Phillips took the position that the PLENAP and Rainbow 5 called for U.S. destroyers to be sent to Singapore if the United States were to fight when the British were attacked. He submitted that these conditions now pertained: all indications were that British forces would soon be attacked; there was a U.S. commitment; and, since he was going to take his battle force north from Singapore to counter any landings by the Japanese, he needed the destroyers. Hart hedged. Why could the British not use the destroyers they had at Hong Kong? Phillips replied that that move was "politically" unpalatable. Hart was not convinced. In any case, he argued, he needed his destroyers to work with his submarines and cruisers. He did admit that Destroyer Division 57, at Balikpapan, was prepared to deploy toward Singapore when war came, but he was not yet ready to give it orders to move. Clearly, Hart was stalling for time and feeling out the offensive spirit of this new British naval commander. What he found he liked. Phillips was "good stuff," he wrote, "decidedly the intellectual type with a first rate brain." Moreover, Phillips agreed that Manila was a better base than Singapore for conducting offensive operations and said that he would plan on basing the British battle fleet there. He also agreed to form several "striking forces" whose primary role would be offensive and only secondarily the protection of convoys. As Hart advised Stark, Phillips's ideas were similar "in general" to those "previously encountered out here but perhaps less extreme."[72] The British were still of a mind to "disperse forces, guard everything and be so thin that nothing is really guarded."[73] The most encouraging things from Hart's point of view were Phillips's offensive spirit and his candor. "We were quite frank," wrote Hart, "laid our cards down and wore no gloves." Hart found Phillips a man whom he liked, respected, and would be happy to serve under.

As they were meeting on the afternoon of 6 December, confirmation came that Japanese amphibious forces had been sighted in the Gulf of Siam. Phillips prepared to leave for Singapore immediately, stating that he would collect such ships as he could and put to sea to meet the enemy. Hart ordered Destroyer Division 57 to sail west from Balikpapan. Virtually on the dock, Hart told Phillips that he was ordering the destroyers to Singapore where they were to be "under the orders of the British C in C." As Hart wrote, "the differences disclosed by the day's arguments were rapidly disappearing if still existent."[74]

Phillips was no doubt gratified, but Hart's action requires some analysis. Putting American ships under a British commander who is going into battle against a nation with which the United States is at peace is risk-taking of a very high order. Of course, the ships could be recalled and the orders rescinded at any moment, but as an indication of Hart's willingness to take initiative, assume responsibility, and cooperate with the British, his order is highly significant. Why was Hart willing to take such independent action? Neither the contemporary record nor that compiled in the past thirty-five years gives an answer, so one has to be extrapolated from what is known. For one thing, Hart had been edging toward increasingly risky action for ten days as a result of British requests, the president's message, intelligence intercepts, and his own anxiety. In fact, Washington had been encouraging him to take independent, possibly dangerously independent, action. Long-delayed replies to his messages, letters from Stark telling him that the navy had gotten into a war in the Atlantic without public or congressional assent, the war warnings, the freedom to coordinate relations with Allies that was virtually forced on him, all contributed to this encouragement. Not that Washington agreed with everything he did, but he could reasonably assume that he was supposed to read between the lines, interpret for himself, and, while not implicating the government, be in every way ready for an Anglo-American war against the Japanese. The "commitment" message from Creighton and the possibly significant lack of any confirmation or denial from Washington could well have been what drove him to action. But for whatever reason, Hart, encouraged by Phillips's combative attitude, gave the ultimate degree of cooperation that could be expected of a potential ally—he lived up to what he understood to be a commitment of honor.

In other words, it is at least possible that Tommy Hart was being manipulated into doing just what, from 1941 to the present, Roosevelt-haters have accused President Roosevelt of doing. That is, Tommy was providing the Japanese with a reason to attack U.S. ships so that the United States could enter the war via the back door. Had either of Hart's actions been public knowledge at an earlier date, when accusations about Roosevelt's conduct were political rather than historical matters, the president's fellow Democrats and his memory would have been seriously damaged. Attention instead was diverted to Pearl Harbor where even Roosevelt's severest critics had to stretch their credibility to believe that he demonstrated the Machiavellianism necessary to use the whole Pacific Fleet as bait. But Hart's little fleet? That would require risk-taking and pragmatism of a far smaller order of magnitude. And allowing a subordinate to make the decision about joining the war on the side of the British, a decision that he himself shied away from making for political reasons, seems like vintage Roosevelt. After all, Lord Halifax, at this time British ambassador to the United States, once observed that FDR had a "fatal gift of manipulation bestowed by a bad fairy which disposes him to manoeuvre."[75] In some ways it was all very neat, a distant commander informed of a commitment and then, because of communications difficulties, being unable to get confirmation or denial of that commitment before a decision had to be made. An added advantage was that this particular distant commander had already displayed tendencies that could hardly be called cautious. It was a pretty good bet that if Tommy thought there was a commitment he would act on the presumption that there was.

Several years ago a careful review of the evidence concluded that while Roosevelt had, in meetings with Lord Halifax on 1, 3, and 4 December 1941, "implied" a commitment, no commitment had, in fact, been made.[76] The opening of previously secret British records revealed little to contradict that analysis, if a strictly legalistic interpretation of "commitment" is adhered to. Actions after the Roosevelt-Halifax meetings, such as the conferences by Roosevelt's closest lieutenants up to the morning of 7 December, when they discussed what to do if only the British were attacked in the Far East, and Churchill's reported relief when the United States was attacked and thus rudely brought into the war as a British ally both tend to support the no-commitment thesis.

On two occasions, 1 December and 3 December, Roosevelt *implied* to Halifax that if Britain were attacked the United States would provide armed assistance. FDR appears to have been very cautious, stopping short of an unambiguous agreement to alliance. But what was the *effect* of his statement? Halifax informed London that Britain could count on U.S. armed assistance in certain eventualities; London informed Singapore of this fact—omitting any reference to the president's diplomatic hedging; Captain Creighton in Singapore confirmed the receipt of such a message from London; and the Navy Department did not respond to Hart's request for confirmation—possibly because no one could quickly determine precisely how the commitment had come about. "My Government has assured the British," wrote Hart in his diary on 7 December, "of armed support in any one of four contingencies. . . ." On the basis of that information, Hart placed a division of destroyers under British command before either a formal commitment or war had come. In other words, for all practical intents, there was a commitment. Had the Japanese limited their attack to British possessions, Hart's destroyers would have been there fighting beside Phillips's capital ships, with the virtually inevitable result that the United States would have been drawn into the war. Whether drawing the United States into the war was the intent of the British or of FDR, is not at this time known; it certainly would have fulfilled one of Churchill's fondest hopes and solved Secretary of War Henry L. Stimson's problem of "maneuvering" the Japanese into firing the first shot.

In fact what had happened was that Hart had been "maneuvered" into running the risk of being fired on first, initially when he sent the *Isabel* out and then when he sent Destroyer Division 57 to Phillips. He did not know the whole story, but by the evening of 7 December he knew that Washington was using him without keeping him properly informed. "In ordinary times," he wrote in reference to being informed by the British of the commitment, "such treatment as that would force me to ask for my immediate relief." He realized that his mistake had been his willingness to stay as Commander in Chief, Asiatic Fleet; now he knew it was too late. "Guess there is a war just around the corner," he wrote at the end of his diary entry on 7 December, "but I think I'll go to a movie."

This is a good point at which to assess Tommy Hart's performance during the year preceding U.S. hostilities. Of primary importance was how he prepared the Asiatic Fleet for any eventuality. Basing his actions on his intelligence officers' estimates of Japanese actions, which were more accurate than those of most analysts, he set out to prepare, but not prepare too soon, for the war he was sure was coming. His men and ships were exercising sufficiently to keep in fighting trim, but not so much that they were worn down or unnecessarily tired out. Considering the problems of command at Cavite, it is difficult to imagine how the Sixteenth Naval District could have achieved a higher degree of preparedness. Hart might have sent the dependents home a bit sooner than was necessary, but no one would suggest that it should not have been done. Conversely, the removal of the marines and the river gunboats from China was unduly delayed, but that was the State Department's, and not Hart's, fault. As he freely admitted, his plan for fighting his fleet from Manila Bay was not sound but, as in so many other instances, Washington compounded the error by not advising him of their dissent earlier. When that dissent did arrive, Hart performed a near miracle in changing his dispositions and preparing his fleet to fight a war that was at that point less than three weeks away. All things considered, he did an excellent job with what he had and many naval officers believe that, had Tommy Hart been in command at Pearl Harbor, the fate of the Pacific Fleet might have been far different.

Hart's record on alliance-building is less positive. There is no question that he and his chief negotiator, Captain Purnell, worked assiduously, but there was little concrete result from their labors. This was partially because Hart disagreed with the strategy of his potential Allies—and here he reflected the views of his superiors. It was also in part the fault of those same superiors who, seemingly, found it difficult to give him prompt answers and unambiguous instructions. The biggest gap was the absence of a clear-cut political decision to make a commitment to the Allies. The result was that when the war began little had been definitely settled, as the meeting with Phillips on 5–6 December illustrated. There was plenty of room for misunderstanding, recrimination, and confusion. As we shall see, the Allies used every inch available. Most critical, from a tactical standpoint, was the Asiatic Fleet's lack of familiarity with the waters in which they would have to fight. Hart and his commanders knew that at some point they would go to the southwest and fight in cooperation with some combination of Allies, possibly under British command, but as to the configurations of the shores they would fight along or of the seas beneath them, they knew nothing. The lack of knowledge exacted a high price.

Relations with MacArthur were lamentable but not critical. It would appear that Hart tried harder than did MacArthur to be cooperative and to meet his military counterpart more than halfway. It was Hart who established personal liaison, he who initiated most of the contacts; furthermore, he moved ashore so as to facilitate working with the army. MacArthur, on the other hand, appears to have been closed-minded regarding naval affairs, to have been petty in matters touching upon his dignity, to have been unpleasant in the extreme when crossed, in brief to have been vain, pompous, and difficult. It seems as though Hart enjoyed needling friend Douglas; he certainly was determined that MacArthur was not going to walk over him. Be that as it may, it was Hart's firmly held conviction that the personal feud between the two of them in no way affected war preparations. The admiral considered himself far too professional to let petty quarrels distract him from his duty. Indeed, it should be remembered that Hart was impressed enough by MacArthur's fighting spirit—and his reinforcements—to consider changing his own war plans and joining in defending the Philippines. It was Washington, not the Asiatic Fleet commander, that directed the fleet to withdraw from Manila, an event that evoked the general's enduring enmity toward the admiral.

Little can be added to what has already been said about Hart's mood during 1941. He had ups, when he believed his fleet would be reinforced, and downs, when he believed he was being neglected by Washington. He came to feel that he had made a mistake by staying in command. He missed his wife. He was under considerable strain but remained, in *Time*'s phrase, "sprier than most of his juniors." It was not a happy year; his health held up, yet he was depressed by being constantly exposed "in the front line trench," as he called it, and consistently last on the priority list. We can almost sense his frustration, or is it resignation, as he strides off alone on the evening of 7 December to take in a movie.

9

M-DAY AND AFTER

At approximately 3:30 on the morning of 8 December (7 December in Hawaii) Marine Lieutenant Colonel William T. Clement handed a rudely awakened Admiral Hart word of the attack on Pearl Harbor.[1] Hart had already deployed Task Force 5 and his submarines but had not completed all the arrangements necessitated by Washington's recent change in his plans. "Timing was bad for us," Hart wrote in a classic understatement, "still evacuating from China; setting up Glassford in command of Cruisers and Destroyers—with his outfit scattered over a thousand miles. Reorganizing the Submarines, incident to my last reinforcement. A new—and very slow—District Commandant, etc."[2] Supplies had to be hurriedly loaded in auxiliaries, submarines started on new missions, Glassford put on a plane bound south to meet his task force, and innumerable other details taken care of. Official notification of hostilities did not come in from the Navy Department until after nine o'clock, but it made little difference. Hart and his command knew what to do and by then were busy doing it. So well prepared were they that Hart's initial order simply stated: "Japan has started hostilities . . . govern yourselves accordingly." It was a "long unhappy day," on which the Asiatic Fleet's losses were minimal, two PBYs and the gunboat *Wake*, but "the Army Air was mauled." The worst of that story was "it was no surprise by a matter of 18 hours." The army air forces made a poor showing, but it had to be admitted that the Japanese "were highly efficient." They certainly had "a grand Round One," concluded Hart.

What happened to MacArthur's vaunted air force is still a subject of controversy. Having performed reconnaissance missions in the morning, his bombers and fighters returned to Clark Field and other army bases around Manila before noon. The crews disposed themselves variously; some ate lunch, some helped to prepare the three B-17s that were to perform reconnaissance, others were briefed on the bombing raid that was to be delivered against Formosa later that day. At approximately 12:45 p.m. twenty-seven twin-engine Mitsubishi bombers appeared over Clark Field and began dropping their bombs among the fueling planes and incredulous crews. Another wave of bombers followed and then came thirty-four Zero fighter planes which delivered a devastating low-level strafing attack. The attack on Clark Field lasted more than an hour during which time similar raids were being delivered against the fighter base at Iba. By the time the 108 Japanese bombers and 77 fighters—only 7 Japanese fighters were lost—turned back toward Formosa more than 50 per cent of the Far East Air Force had been destroyed, most of it knocked out on the ground. Only seventeen of the original thirty-five B-17s remained; of the seventy-two P-40s, at least fifty-six were lost. In addition, some twenty-five to thirty older military aircraft were destroyed. Total casualties for the day were more than two hundred and twenty-five killed and wounded. How did such a devastating loss occur? The latest biography on the "American Caesar" concludes that "the key to the riddle is the General himself."[3] MacArthur blamed his subordinates, while some of them blame MacArthur. After the explanations, or alibis, have been heard, the fact remains that, with one blow, the Japanese acquired virtual control of the air over the Philippines with easily predictable results.

Throughout 8 and 9 December Hart was busy analyzing developments. Clearly Admiral Husband E. Kimmel's Pacific Fleet was not going to begin fighting its Rainbow 5 war westward for "quite a time"; nor was the Far East Air Force going to provide much cover for the submarines and other small ships in the Philippines. The islands, as Tommy saw it, were going to have to be defended by those submarines "helped by my grand little air force as long as it lasts" and whatever the ground troops could do. The strength of his "grand little air force" was concentrated in Patrol Wing 10 and its twenty-eight lumbering PBY patrol bombers, which were no match for Japanese fighters but were excellent for reconnaissance and could perform limited offensive missions. The outlook was far from promising, but he determined "we have to do our best and we shall."

To compound the gloom, on the tenth the *Repulse*, the *Prince of Wales*, and Admiral Sir Tom Phillips were lost to Japanese aircraft off the coast of Malaya. The destroyers Hart had sent south arrived in time to help pick up survivors. The only bright note was that the Navy Department had sent not a single dispatch in the past twenty-four hours. As Hart read the news of Phillips's loss, Cavite was under air attack.

The Japanese came in high at about 12:30 p.m.; there were fifty-four two-engine bombers with fighter escorts. Since they were hardly molested at all either by U.S. planes or by the fire of .50-caliber machine guns and other antiquated antiaircraft weapons on the ground, they took their time selecting their targets. It was terrifying yet fascinating to watch them divide into groups, make a pass or two, and finally release their bombs. The minesweeper *Bittern* was set afire and direct hits were made on the "power plant, dispensary, torpedo repair shop, supply office and warehouses, signal station, commissary store, receiving station, barracks and officer quarters." As it became clear that the antiaircraft fire was having no effect on the attackers, ships at the wharves tried to cast off and head for open water. The destroyer *Pillsbury* was hit before she could get under way and a bomb landed square on the conning tower of the submarine *Sealion*. Smoke followed the flames, with secondary explosions adding to the chaos; prisoners in the brig were turned loose to join the fire-fighting brigades. It was a hellish scene.[4]

Tommy watched the two-hour attack as long as he could stand it from the roof of the Marsman Building. He noted resentfully the absence of any U.S. Army fighter protection, as the Japanese once again efficiently wreaked destruction. "At least one group of airmen were performing well," he reflected bitterly. The industrial and supply part of Cavite was left a burned-out, smoking shambles, which he judged to be "utterly ruined." For all practical purposes, Admiral Rockwell's command was out of business. Many Filipinos were killed, along with some twenty-five "of my young men"; the *Sealion* was lost; the *Pillsbury* and *Bittern* were damaged, and other small craft suffered from the blast effects of nearby hits. It was a crushing blow and it led Hart to the reluctant conclusion that "we are bound to lose the war in the air and we shall be blockaded here, for a long time."[5] Consequently, he was "bouncing out" all the tenders, except the *Canopus,* seven small craft, including the *Isabel,* and some two hundred thousand tons of merchant shipping that had stacked up in the harbor, in hopes that they would be able, by moving soon, to slip past the Japanese surface ships. He advised Washington that he considered Manila "untenable as [a] base [on] account of air situation," but that he would continue submarine and reconnaissance operations as long as possible.[6] He ended his diary entry "a bad day and an awfully hard one. But poor Rockwell!"

The next few hectic days were filled with the details incident to getting combat and merchant shipping out of Manila. Hart loaded as many essential personnel as he could, said a prayer they would get through, and watched them slip out of the bay. The few licks that Patrol Wing 10 got at Japanese ships and planes were little more than pinpricks. Then on 12 December Patrol Wing 10 got its turn when Japanese fighters followed its planes back to base and destroyed seven PBYs on the water. Hart had two meetings and appeared at a press conference with MacArthur although there wasn't much left with which to cooperate or about which to talk. The Japanese had not yet attempted to land, and the general was still confident that his defense plan involving Philippine troops and American regulars would "stop them on the beaches." He was not pleased with the support he was getting from the navy; in particular he wanted Hart to escort a convoy of supply ships from Brisbane to Manila. This convoy, escorted by the cruiser *Pensacola*, had already caused considerable controversy in Washington, where the pessimists argued that it either could not get through to the Philippines or that its cargo was needed more elsewhere, while the optimists argued that it probably could reach Manila. Not surprisingly, in Washington the "political" argument was that for morale and symbolic reasons it was essential at least to try. Hart was seldom much impressed by political arguments and he told MacArthur that there was very little available with which to protect the convoy; furthermore, it was his opinion that, by the time the convoy was ready to move north from Brisbane, the Japanese would have blocked access to the Philippines. This reply was distinctly unsatisfactory to MacArthur who, in a tone that was to become familiar, complained to Washington about Hart's attitude, the "inactivity" of the Asiatic Fleet and the consequent "freedom of action" enjoyed by the Japanese Navy.[7]

When the air force was caught napping on 8 December, Hart was convinced that the Philippine campaign was lost. He was reporting that harsh truth to the Navy Department in spite of the fact that he knew his pessimism would not be welcome. Even less welcome was the reality he lived with. On 13 December he sent most of his pilots and most of their remaining planes south to form the nucleus "upon which, in time, something in the way of a force may be built up." Two days later he sent off the majority of the splendid staff he had created so laboriously, including his "strong right arm," Purnell, who in November had been promoted to acting rear admiral. He realized, painfully, that he was "passing the ball" to Glassford and Task Force 5, while himself staying in Manila as little more than a symbolic presence. Things had moved very fast, but Hart took some comfort and pride in the fact that he and his staff had "pretty well kept up with the march of events and acted fast" in response to them. Getting his auxiliaries, merchant shipping, and vital personnel out safely may not seem like much of a victory, but under the conditions existing at the time it was quite a feat.

He was left with two destroyers; six PT boats; the tender *Canopus*, which he ordered to anchor in shallow water so that if hit, she would settle on the bottom and still be usable; twenty-seven submarines, which when in Manila Bay had to remain submerged during daylight, much to the discomfort of the crews; a salvage ship; three river gunboats; three minesweepers; and one tug. It was not much of a command.

On 11 December he and Rockwell decided to evacuate the industrial plant at Cavite, which was still burning, and move the personnel, as well as whatever could be salvaged, to Sangley Point, Manila, Corregidor, and Mariveles. The gasoline reserves and some communications equipment had to be left behind. The Marsman Building was bombed almost daily and the planes and ineffectual antiaircraft guns available could do little to protect it. Having his command so spread out, temporarily housed, and constantly under attack made Hart, he admitted, a little "blue." Even so, he took time out to watch beautiful sunsets, remembering when he and Caroline used to watch them together, ate regularly, and slept in his "own little bed" despite the air raids.

Word came on 17 December that Purnell, whom Hart considered the most valuable man the navy had in the Far East, and the others had gotten through to Surabaja safely. As Hart saw it, his fabled luck was holding. Then on the nineteenth the bombers came back; this time they concentrated on Sangley Point, where they got the big gasoline dump, knocked the high-powered radio station out of commission, and killed some fifteen to twenty peo-

Rear Admiral Francis W. Rockwell in his "headquarters" after the Japanese raid on Cavite. Naval Historical Center

ple. It was "another bad set-back and the devil of it is that the Japs can do the same thing anywhere and any time they wish to," Hart recorded.[8]

As if the Japanese were not enough, trouble was brewing in two other areas. The first controversy to flare was with the Allies, the second had to do with MacArthur. The issue was the same: how the Asiatic Fleet's surviving ships could be most effectively used.

On 11 December Washington ordered Hart to withdraw the destroyers he had sent to Singapore and send them toward Darwin, Australia. He was further directed to send his surface forces and any submarines he withdrew from the Philippines in the same general direction, i.e., southeast rather than southwest. The Navy Department figured that if the Philippines fell, as it expected, and if Singapore fell, which it also anticipated, the Japanese would turn their fury on the Netherlands East Indies and the trade routes to Australia.[9]

Neither the negativism of these assumptions nor the reality of the movements were appreciated by the British. Indeed, Vice Admiral Sir Geoffrey Layton, who had again become commander in chief of the Far Eastern fleet upon Phillips's death, was quite shaken by the turn of events. Not helping the situation were the loss of wireless and cable contact with the Philippines between 10 and 12 December and the fact that the U.S. destroyers were withdrawn from Singapore without "warning or reference" to the British naval commander.[10] When the reasoning behind that move and the plan for future dispositions were made known to Layton, he observed that it was "a complete departure from all I had been led to expect, that it inevitably gravely prejudiced our chances of holding Malaya . . . the announcement of it had a considerably depressing effect on the War Council in Singapore."[11]

Layton had expected that Hart's cruisers, destroyers, and submarines would be available for the defense of Malaya "as soon as Manila was untenable as a base." If they had been, he reasoned, the Japanese landing on the east coast and infiltration on the west coast of Malaya could have been made "costly and hazardous," thus lessening the pressure on the land force and taking some of the momentum from the Japanese drive. In any case, the withdrawal of the U.S. forces was seen as a failure to act in good faith and was a "bitter disappointment."[12]

The Dutch, while undoubtedly pleased that the Americans were retiring in such a way as to reinforce their positions, had other complaints. Rear Admiral Glassford was not nearly as communicative as Vice Admiral Conrad E. L. Helfrich, commander in chief of the Royal Netherlands East Indian Navy, had hoped. He advised the Dutch of his movements, but Helfrich could get no satisfactory explanation of why he was making the movements or what his plans were. Consequently, Helfrich asked Layton to suggest that Hart order the U.S. ships to cooperate with the Dutch forces "instead of moving around in Indian waters without aim and without a fixed program."[13] He also wanted to consult with Glassford and settle upon some plan of operations. Hart readily agreed and told the Dutch commander that Purnell, who had met with the

Rear Admiral William A. Glassford, Jr. Naval Historical Center

Allies often before, would meet with him in Batavia. The meeting between Helfrich, Purnell, and Glassford was held on 18 December, but it proved a disappointment. The Dutch had been urged by the British, with whom they presumably agreed, to suggest that American forces should meet Japanese forces in the Makasar and Malacca straits or the Celebes Sea rather than allow them to approach Java. When this course was pressed on Glassford and Purnell they declined to discuss strategy or even command of their forces, saying that they were getting their orders from the chief of naval operations in Washington. They were willing, however, to agree on areas of responsibility and minor operational matters, including the assigning of Glassford to Batavia to facilitate cooperation. When Glassford got there on 22 December he told Helfrich that U.S. forces were definitely not going to operate in the Celebes Sea because they were needed to protect convoys coming from the mainland United States toward Australia and from Australia toward the Philippines. That was why Washington wanted him to be in Darwin, a move that all parties on the scene considered a mistake. But, as Glassford explained, while he disagreed with his orders Washington had tied his hands.[14]

All the bickering and maneuvering of the past two years had not produced a cooperative chain, but it might have been hoped that adversity would forge a stronger link. Instead, relations deteriorated and the blame that was laid seems somehow irrational. In all likelihood, for instance, Layton was wrong in thinking the Asiatic Fleet would have been more effective in staving off defeat in Malaya than it was in staving it off in the Philippines. Moreover, he overlooked the political ramifications of American ships protecting British possessions while the Philippines were falling, especially when that collapse was accompanied by cries from MacArthur that ranged the scale from calls for help to accusations of pusillanimous abandonment.

More logical criticism could be directed toward Washington. After months of finding it expedient to leave strategy to Hart's discretion, the Navy Department now found it desirable to orchestrate his strategic, and even his tactical, movements. Apparently the concatenation of defeats had shaken the naval establishment so badly that it dared not give local commanders much leeway. The result was a constant changing of plans that resulted in the aimless movement of American forces decried by the Dutch. But, despite the fact that these developments were beyond Hart's control, their unsatisfactory resolution impaired his prospect of eliciting cooperation. The bickering over commitments that marked the months before the war was reinforced by poor performance and by what was interpreted as bad faith.

The second controversy to flare up had to do with General MacArthur and his feeling that he was being deserted by the navy. Apparently forgetting his lack of interest in Hart's plans and operations, he began to find it increasingly desirable to remind his superiors, especially General George C. Marshall and Secretary of War Stimson, of the navy's failures. Marshall's reaction was sympathetic, but since MacArthur's messages were also filled with pleas for more supplies, manpower, and a higher priority, the chief of staff directed most of his attention to meeting, or trying to meet, those immediate needs. Stimson, however, had the time, the energy, and the experienced bureaucrat's sense to see the benefits inherent in blaming the navy for past and impending disasters. By reading between the lines, Stimson realized that MacArthur was saying that Hart's ships and submarines were ineffective, not because the Japanese controlled the air, but because Hart had lost his courage. "Hart (in conversation with General MacArthur) took the usual Navy defeatist position and had virtually told MacArthur that the Philippines were doomed instead of doing his best to keep MacArthur's lifeline open," Stimson recorded in his diary. He attributed this attitude to the fact that Hart and the navy were "rather shaken and panic stricken" after the disaster at Pearl.[15]

There is little question that in Admiral Stark's view the Philippines, and Singapore as well, were doomed. His orders to Hart concerning the *Pensacola* convoy are one clear indication of this attitude. Even though by 14 December the president had indicated his desire that no effort be spared in getting the convoy through to Manila, Stark's messages to Hart reveal considerable ambivalence on this subject. Hart was told that the convoy would arrive in Brisbane and that he should get in touch with MacArthur about the disposition to be made of the vital supplies on board. In his message of 14 December, far from ordering Hart to bring the convoy into Manila, Stark pointed out that the military stores in the convoy might be useful in the defense of Port Darwin. Then, on 17 December, after further prodding from the White House, Stark advised Hart to make an "effort when appropriate to pass through such support as may be practicable." By giving what has been described as such a "lukewarm injunction," Stark left Hart with great latitude while certainly implying no urgency and leaving it reasonable to deduce that the chief of naval operations wanted no risks taken to reinforce disaster.[16]

Even so, the Navy Department was sensitive to the criticisms being directed its way by MacArthur and Stimson. Furthermore, it naturally wanted to defend Hart, so he was advised of the "heavy pressure" being brought to bear and asked for a full account of "naval operations in support of the Army."[17] Hart anticipated his selection for the role of scapegoat, and on 19 December recorded in his diary: "He [MacArthur] is inclined to cut my throat and perhaps of the Navy in general. So I have to watch the record and keep it straight lest I wake up some morning and read that T. Hart lost a war or something." Part of the problem was that his submarines were not as effective as they should have been: Japanese destroyers infiltrated coastal waters at night, and when U.S. submarines sighted them they either missed their targets or their torpedoes failed to explode. In one two-week period, ten such episodes were reported:

12 December 1941. Lieutenant Wreford G. Chapple in the *S–38* sighted a transport and fired one torpedo at her. He either missed his target or the torpedo exploded prematurely.

13 December 1941. Lieutenant James W. Coe in the *S–39* fired four torpedoes at a 5,000-ton merchantman. Although he reported a solid hit, no damage could be verified.

19 December 1941. Lieutenant Commander Barton E. Bacon in the *Pickerel* sighted a Japanese patrol craft and fired five torpedoes without result.

20 December 1941. Lieutenant Roland F. Pryce in the *Spearfish* encountered a Japanese submarine. He made a submerged approach and fired four torpedoes, all of which missed.

21 December 1941. Lieutenant Commander William L. Wright in the *Sturgeon* made a surface attack on a large freighter. He fired four torpedoes but got no hit.

22 December 1941. Lieutenant Commander Theodore C. Aylward in the *Searaven* made a surface attack on a good-sized freighter and fired two torpedoes at her, both of which missed.

22 December 1941. Lieutenant Commander Hamilton L. Stone in the *Snapper* fired two torpedoes at a cargo ship, but neither scored a hit.

23 December 1941. Lieutenant Commander David A. Hurt in the *Permit* made a submerged attack on a Japanese destroyer. Neither of the two torpedoes he fired hit their target.

25 December 1941. Lieutenant Commander Charles L. Freeman in the *Skipjack* made a surface attack at night on a heavy cruiser. Not one of the three torpedoes fired found its mark.

25 December 1941. Lieutenant Commander Aylward in the *Searaven* fired one torpedo in a submerged attack on a merchantman but missed his target.[18]

It was not learned until 1943 that the Mark VI magnetic exploder, which Hart had helped develop at the torpedo station in 1929, was part of the problem. He did not know why the torpedoes were not exploding—all he could do was rage at his hapless submarine skippers, replace some of them, and hope for better results. He did know that his most modern submarines were not suited to work in shallow coastal waters where, during daylight hours, they were easily visible to air reconnaissance. The only surface ships with which he could confront the Japanese Navy in the Manila, or even Luzon, area were two destroyers, one of them damaged, six PT boats, and some small patrol craft. He had sent his most powerful ships south in accordance with prewar plans and, after the bombing of Cavite, used his own discretion in sending the rest of his fleet, with the few exceptions mentioned above, in the same direction.

The Navy Department, which was worried lest the Japanese mine the entrance to Manila Harbor, agreed with his action, and on 17 December advised him "when in your judgment you can from elsewhere more effectively direct the operations of your Fleet, CNO approves your departure from Manila." It also ordered that, when that moment came, he was to "place all remaining naval and marine personnel under MacArthur's command."[19] This order was repeated three days later even more explicitly: "Not only marines but all naval personnel remaining in Philippines should be made available to MacArthur through Rockwell for such use as might be profitable."[20]

On 22 December Japanese forces under Lieutenant General Nasaharu Homma landed, as expected, on the Lingayen Gulf, north and west of Manila. Instead of "meeting them on the beaches," as he had avowed, MacArthur made sporadic stabs at the enemy and then retreated in what has been described as "pell mell confusion."[21] Despite this turn of events, which was repeated again and again during the hours that followed, he stuck to the illusion that his poorly equipped, ill-trained army of Filipino scouts and American regulars could fight defensive battles far from Manila. He had called the earlier plan for war against Japan, with its planned withdrawal to Bataan and eventually to Corregidor, "defeatist" when he replaced it with his more grandiose design.[22] Now MacArthur could not bring himself to accept the consequences of the victory he had won concerning planning; for several days a curious lethargy reigned at army headquarters.

There had been few personal contacts between Hart and MacArthur since 8 December, most liaison being carried out by Commander Dennison from Hart's staff. Hart and MacArthur had held a joint news conference and otherwise there had been only brief meetings. On 22 December, the day the Japanese landed at Lingayen Gulf, Hart had his final contact with his army counterpart. The occasion was MacArthur's elevation to four-star rank and Tommy called to congratulate him. The conversation was short, Douglas allowing that he finally had his "rightful rank back."[23] With the landings, which Hart's submarines proved powerless to oppose, MacArthur hit a new high in outrage. "What in the world is the matter with your submarines?" he demanded of

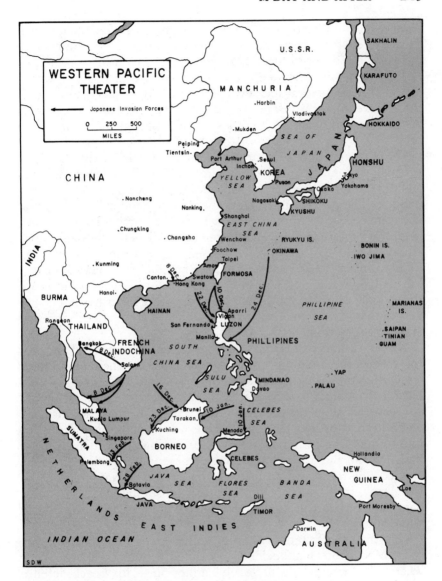

Hart. "The Jap ships are coming in here in the Lingayen Gulf, landing, and your people haven't sunk a single solitary ship."[24] Hart had to admit that what the general said was true and the horrible thing was he had no defense to offer for his beloved submarines. Some of his skippers were so frustrated they were even requesting relief. They would fire their torpedoes, wait in vain to hear indication of a kill, fire again, fire again, until the Japanese destroyers spotted them. Then there was nothing to do but dive to the bottom of Lingayen Gulf, which in some places is less than 120 feet deep, and ride out the destroyers' depth charges. After several such episodes, one officer said, "You'd better relieve me. I'm afraid my nerves are too bad to take this submarine out again, and I may lose it, through no fault of the crew."[25]

Some of the best submarines in the U.S. Navy, skippered by officers who later found their names in naval histories, sortied, sighted targets, fired their torpedoes, and came home empty-handed. The *Sargo*, under Lieutenant Commander Tyrrell D. Jacobs, made eight submerged attacks on her first wartime patrol, fired thirteen torpedoes, and scored zero. Virtually the same story could be told by the *Sailfish*, the *Seawolf*, and the *Swordfish*. On 22 December the *S–38*, with Lieutenant Chapple, got a confirmed kill in Lingayen Gulf, the only one registered against the more than eighty ships in the Japanese invasion force. It has been suggested that "Lingayen Gulf was a crucible of frustration," and that is no exaggeration.[26]

Direct contacts between the admiral and the general did not increase as the enemy poured ashore, but Hart knew MacArthur was going to be looking for someone to blame. The general would have little sympathy with Hart's "long range view" that he should conserve his ships for the drawn-out war he foresaw, hoping that, when he had proper air cover, there would be opportunities for him to meet the Imperial Navy on something other than a suicide basis. While pursuing that strategy, the admiral realized that he would have to "guard against it being said that Navy ran out on the Army, in its defense of the place, so submarines and I must hang on from here as long as we can. We have to guard the Navy's white plume."[27]

Guarding that plume was going to be increasingly difficult, because MacArthur had decided on a suitably dramatic action. After what is described as "stubbornly" adhering to his beach-defense plan for forty hours, while Japanese soldiers scrambled ashore, he decided on 23 December to revert to War Plan Orange.[28] This meant retreating to Corregidor and Bataan, where he had allowed few "defeatist," defensive preparations to be made. Among other things, he decided it would be wise to declare Manila an open city as of 25 December. This was an issue of some moment to Hart, whose base and headquarters were on the city's waterfront. Thus, the admiral was naturally distressed when, at 9:00 a.m. on 24 December, MacArthur sent Commander Dennison to tell him that the army would be evacuating the city within twenty-four hours.

Why MacArthur did not inform Hart of his intention sooner is hard to understand: on the twenty-second he advised the War Department that he anticipated being overwhelmed by superior numbers—he, in fact, had the numerical advantage—and that, when he was, he would "release Manila . . . by suitable proclamation."[29] Hart did not disagree with the general's decision, but he was plenty irritated that MacArthur had not "deigned" to consult or inform him earlier. The fact that he had to leave Manila made an utter wreck of his headquarters, communications, and supply organization, and made it impossible to operate his submarines out of Manila Bay. "The jig is up," he wrote, admitting at the same time that he felt "old" and "disspirited."[30]

He met with his staff and discussed whether he should go to Corregidor or south with his ships. The opinion was unanimous: staying would serve no useful purpose, he must go to Java. As they talked, bombs from three separate air attacks rattled the windows of the Marsman Building.

It was quite a Christmas. Some of his neighbors had decorated his apartment at the hotel but there was only time for the minimum of observances. Most of the day was spent arranging last-minute details, not the least troublesome of which was finding transportation for him and his people. The first plan was to use the three PBYs that were left in Manila, but the Japanese got there first, destroying two of them at their concealed moorings. That left one plane and one submarine as the only options. Literally thousands of naval officers and men would have to be abandoned to their fate. For Hart this was the most painful part of the whole business and something for which he held himself personally responsible. He could have sent many of his people to safety in the merchant ships that left Manila immediately after Cavite was bombed, but that would have been viewed as abandoning the army. The time he had for making preparations and the speed of the Japanese advance ensured an unhappy denouement, and unhappy it was.

Key members of the naval staff flew out in the remaining PBY on the evening of the twenty-fourth. MacArthur and his entourage left for Corregidor the same day. Hart's preparations for departure were not completed until noon on Christmas Day and late that night he boarded the submarine *Shark*. As he stood on the deck at midnight, a hellish sight met his eyes. Manila was ablaze and explosions were rocking the bay area. Figures could be seen scurrying through the gloom, looting, while reflections of the buildings flickered on a sea turned red by flames. At 2:00 a.m. on 26 December the *Shark* cast off and the last high-ranking American official left Manila.

As the *Shark* moved into Manila Bay, beginning her arduous 1,000-mile journey, Hart had ample reason for reflection. The war he expected had come with devastating suddenness and the collapse of his base had come almost as quickly. Aside from the future and the reception he might receive from his fractious Allies, two thoughts might well have filled his mind as the submarine plowed the dark tropic sea. One would have been his relations with Washington, and the other his relations with MacArthur.

As far as Washington was concerned, he had some ground for complaint and anxiety. The complaints would have centered on the Navy Department's recent predilection for running the war in the Far East. Long content to neglect Hart, the department now seemed obsessed with checking up on him and directing his every move. The reasons were more or less obvious, but the change was striking and was complicating Allied cooperation. The anxiety he felt would have stemmed from the rumors swirling about courts-martial for Lieutenant General Walter C. Short, commander of the Hawaiian Department, and Admiral Kimmel at Pearl Harbor. Although he was not caught flat-footed, as they were, the performance of his fleet could scarcely be hailed as a victory. His major surface units, as well as much merchant shipping, had gotten safely south, but retreats did not breed the kind of public enthusiasm the navy badly needed. Furthermore, it could not be denied that the submarines were a great disappointment. Hart had few illusions about the depth of his political support in the capital. If more sacrificial lambs were sought, he would not appear unattractive.

Nor had his relations with General MacArthur been such as to fill him with either satisfaction or security. Hart could logically defend all his actions, but still he was uneasy about the indications of ill will and even vindictiveness he had seen. The general, obviously eager to find reasons why his optimistic predictions had proven so wrong, settled upon the navy's lack of support as a major contributing factor. Though Hart could not have known it, even as he sped south through enemy-infested waters, his former comrade in arms was busy spreading rumors. "Enemy penetration resulted from our weakness on the sea and in the air," MacArthur cabled the army chief of staff on 26 December. "Surface elements of Asiatic Fleet were withdrawn," he continued, "and effect of submarines was negligible." "I wish to emphasize the necessity for naval action," the general concluded.[31] As Stark somewhat frantically tried to inform Hart, who was out of communication until he got to Java, this and other dispatches from MacArthur supported "unfortunate impressions." The impressions, indeed, were so persistent that Stark urged Hart to take greater "calculated risks."[32] But the fact was that no risk taken by Hart was going to save MacArthur, nor was Hart ever going to erase the impression fostered by the defeated general: that the navy had run out on the army.

In fairness to both sides, it must be said that the strategic precepts of the two services contributed to the basic misunderstanding. Ground forces do not have the mobility of naval forces; therefore, dramatic, last-ditch defenses, even defenses that end in defeat, have much greater legitimacy for the army than for the navy. MacArthur's lack of sympathy with the navy's strategy was a prelude to similar disputes in the future. As for other differences with Hart, all pale by comparison with the failure to coordinate operations. Even though Hart was not the easiest person to work with, this failure must be laid at MacArthur's door. Hart moved his headquarters ashore, he tried time and again to discuss plans, and he initiated the exchange of liaison officers. MacArthur greeted these efforts with boredom, disinterest, or strong indications of independence. It is in this regard that the failure to coordinate the evacuation of Manila assumes real significance. The lack of communication on that vital subject was indicative of a deep and endemic misalliance.

The most obvious example of lack of communication was MacArthur's failure to realize, if indeed he did fail to realize, that the Asiatic Fleet was going to be based far south of Manila and might very well be involved primarily in operations with the Allies. Had he not seen Task Force 5 leave the area in September? And what did he think those conversations with Brooke-Popham and Phillips were about? Certainly, there was confusion about precisely when and where and how the alliance would fight, but for almost a year the constant theme was that the Asiatic Fleet would be fighting with Allies well south of Manila. And, as far as is known, MacArthur did not raise a single objection to that plan. Once the war began and Hart's forces were joined with the British and Dutch, there was no possibility of their being unjoined, unless

Washington so decreed. On this point, then, Hart is not the culprit; he was simply following orders.

Alliance or no alliance, the withdrawal of the Asiatic Fleet from the Philippines in time of war had been a feature of army-navy joint war plans for at least a decade and a half. If MacArthur did not know that, he had himself to blame. The only naval officer who at this time suggested fighting a war from Manila was Hart who, as we have seen, was overruled. Ironically, on this issue MacArthur was out of step with his army predecessors and planners. Since the 1920s the army had been insisting that anything other than a citadel defense was impossible, and some army planners were none too optimistic even about that. As for the stepped-up naval evacuation, a tour of the destruction wrought at Cavite on 10 December would have made it obvious that if Hart wanted to save his ships he would have to evacuate them, and fast. And when MacArthur declared Manila an open city, Hart could not refrain from informing the general that his action would only shorten the period in which the submarines could provide even their imperfect defense.

Hart, it would appear, was the more realistic of the two men. MacArthur regarded this realism as defeatist and so advised his superiors, thus critically undermining Hart's credibility. He continued to believe that the navy's nerve was another casualty of Pearl Harbor; that an attack on the Japanese naval forces might have "cut through to relieve our hard pressed forces."[33] But the personalities of the two men were at the root of the matter. Hart was blunt, taciturn, and precise; MacArthur expansive, verbose, and imaginative. In this case, MacArthur's imagination and optimism, possibly leavened by ambition, led him to make incorrect estimates. When events ran counter to his hopes, he could not admit his mistakes. When he finally did accept reality and revert to what he called the "defeatist" war plan, he moved too swiftly to allow supplies on Corregidor to be built up. As past and future events show, the magisterial MacArthur was "predictably" incapable of budging from his stated position when matters of honor or personal pride were involved. Hart had no difficulty in admitting his mistakes. He had been preparing for disaster for months, and neither his career, self-esteem, nor reputation led him to deny reality.

Heroic stands that end in death for thousands will continue to be meat for mythmakers; those who wish to understand the past should be more discerning. Thus it is unfortunate to find that even

The power plant at Cavite after the Japanese raid. In the foreground is an exploded warhead that landed on top of a piling. Naval Historical Center

recent accounts award plaudits to the general who, perhaps intentionally, misled his government about his prospects, was found almost criminally unprepared eight hours after war had begun, who time after time made errors of omission or commission, but who remained optimistic in the face of calamity.[34] Those same accounts have only contempt for the admiral who correctly estimated the prospects of his force, who was fully prepared for hostilities, who made few strategic or tactical errors, but who counseled prudence rather than bravado. It was not that Hart's handling of himself or his forces was above reproach; his failure to get more personnel out of the Islands, for instance, was something he himself bitterly regretted; however, he had been repeatedly ordered by Washington to leave nonessential personnel with MacArthur. One can only wonder how vindictive MacArthur would have been had Hart tried to further drain his defense forces. But whether he could have gotten more men out or not, his overall performance

The devastated supply sheds, machine shop, foundry, and ways at Cavite, as seen from the end of the pier at the submarine base. Naval Historical Center

was more constructive than that of his chief detractor and his assessment more accurate. Unfortunately for Hart, however, it was MacArthur's assessment of his performance that was going to cast the longer shadow.

Two more points remain to be made about the denouement in the Philippines. First, despite the obvious ill will between the two men, Hart never publicly criticized MacArthur, nor did he ever contend that the general's actions before or during the war were responsible for any of his problems. Although it made him furious at the time, he never complained publicly about the declaration regarding Manila. Furthermore, he remained until his death adamant in his contention that the bad blood between himself and MacArthur in no way affected his, or MacArthur's, performance of duty. It was Tommy's enduring belief that the ultimate fate of the Philippines would have been the same no matter who was there.

The other point relates to speculation about Hart's actions had he been in command of the U.S. Fleet. Many observers have suggested that had Tommy Hart been at Pearl Harbor, rather than with the Asiatic Fleet, the Japanese would not have caught the navy so unprepared. If true, President Roosevelt's decision to give Hart the Asiatic, rather than the U.S., Fleet was fateful indeed. Obviously, speculation on this subject is fruitless, but it does raise an interesting point. Hart had a Purple machine and Admiral Kimmel did not. Hart knew what Washington knew about Japanese moves and although Rosy Mason and his team in Manila may not have interpreted all the messages in the same way Washington did, they had the relevant data. In one sense this fact, coupled with the fact that the Asiatic Fleet was not caught in as exposed a position as the Pacific Fleet, supports the contention of those who, like Kimmel, argued that had data available in Washington been transmitted to Pearl Harbor the tragedy would not have occurred. On the other hand, the presence of a Purple machine on Corregidor while there was none on Oahu shows that Washington considered the Philippines a more likely target than Hawaii and therefore in greater need of forewarning. But all of that begs the question of Tommy Hart's performance. What Tommy Hart did right was not to wear his men out with premature preparation. He was painfully aware that even great boxers often leave their fight in the dressing room. His task and his agony was to know a Japanese attack was coming but to reserve the highest degree of readiness until the last possible moment. It still must remain purely speculative, but had someone with Hart's sense of pace been available at Pearl Harbor there might indeed have been a different result.

10

TRAPPED IN A
SINISTER TWILIGHT

On 2 January 1942, displaying the flag of a full admiral, the *Shark* drew alongside the pier and there was a flurry of activity. She had completed a hazardous, five-day, 1,000-mile passage from Manila and, when lines had been secured, the man who rated those four stars jumped spryly ashore. Admiral Hart had arrived in Surabaja, Java.

It had been a harrowing journey. With sixty-six passengers in addition to her crew, the *Shark* was overloaded and, to avoid detection, spent much of the time submerged. The temperature aboard rose above 100 degrees and some of the passengers, including the corpulent Commander Linder, the Dutch liaison officer with the Asiatic Fleet, suffered considerably. Admiral Hart confided to his diary that the voyage was hard on him, too. Added to his discomfort were anxieties about what he had left behind and what lay ahead. But the worst aspect of the journey was being out of touch at this critical juncture in the war. "Damn the Japs for getting those planes at the last minute," he wrote.[1] Well he might lament, for events that transpired during his journey shaped the rest of his naval career.

Reporters crowded around the admiral, and when one of them asked about the rigors of the passage just ended, Hart answered that it was not hard on the experienced crew but was very hard on the passengers. Then, making light of the melodramatic aspect of his adventure, he added that one of the passengers, himself, was too old, and another, pointing to the 250-pound Linder, was too big.[2] He got his laugh and continued on his way along the pier. The reporters had their story.

Soon after his arrival at the command post in Surabaja that Glassford and Purnell had established for Task Force 5 and the Asiatic Fleet, Hart was handed a sheaf of messages that had piled up while he was at sea. Among those from Washington was one from Stark detailing MacArthur's criticism of the Asiatic Fleet's performance.[3] By careful choice of words, Stark implied that MacArthur was attacking Hart as well as the Asiatic Fleet and he gave the impression that the general's blows were having a telling effect on official opinion. He closed by imploring Hart to undertake greater "calculated risks."

Hart was angry and hurt, with good reason. As he pointed out in his reply, he had long suspected that MacArthur would blame the navy and, consequently, had acted with circumspection and kept a detailed record. In his diary, he referred several times to keeping the record straight and among his private papers is a detailed narrative of his personal relations with MacArthur. Moreover, in his opinion, if the Philippines were lost, it would be because control of the air was lost, and that had happened by 2:00 p.m. on the day of the first attack. Without air protection, he had no choice but to send his surface ships and most of his submarines out of Manila. Furthermore, since that withdrawal was in compliance with what Hart referred to as Stark's own plan, he felt that the Navy Department should provide "full defense against criticism." Finally, Hart said he was already taking great risks with his submarines, but could see no purpose in expending his surface forces "except on chances of large results," of which there did not seem to be many at the moment.[4]

His mood was not improved by another out-of-date message in the pile. "Steps are in hand to create [a] supreme command in Southwest Pacific," it read, "under which will be unified command naval forces under U.S. Admiral probably yourself."[5] Hart interpreted this to be asking whether he wished to be assigned the unified command. Moreover, he thought he read between the lines a request for a report on his health such as he promised to give periodically when he agreed to forgo retirement in June 1941.[6] Whether that was the intent of the message or not, Hart reacted to his own interpretation. "In view of my doubtful endurance," he cabled back, "advise you choose another for command."[7] He was still upset about MacArthur's criticism, especially his reference to the poor record of the submarines. That irritated him, partly because of his career-long connection with submarines, but mostly because he was already despondent about their performance and did not need to have an army officer complaining to Washington about it. Unfortunately, that irritation flowed over into his comments about his fitness for the naval command: "being mad probably had something to do with the wording of my reply about putting in another man," he wrote.[8]

In all probability Hart honestly did not want the command, but that had nothing to do with his health. As he could have pointed out, he had long held that no American officer could work satisfactorily with the Allies in the Southwest Pacific unless a truly unified strategy were determined. One reason why his meetings with Admiral Phillips were so gratifying was that he got the impression that Phillips was moving closer to an American "offensive" strategy. Furthermore, Phillips agreed to work with Hart on the principle of "mutual cooperation," although Hart was willing to work under Phillips's command. Unfortunately, all those prospects went down with the *Prince of Wales* on 10 December. The weeks since that date were filled with bickering and recriminations, no strategy had been determined and there was scant hope that combined command would prove easy or even possible. Hart might have cited these reasons for not wanting the task, but he chose instead to cite his health.

With the subject of his role in a supreme command apparently disposed of, Hart spent the afternoon and part of the next day sorting out problems at his headquarters. On 3 January he took the noisy, uncomfortable night train to Batavia. His mind was filled with details that needed attending to, and, as a result, he got little sleep. That was unfortunate, because he was going to need all of his reserves for the conferences to come. Vice Admiral Helfrich met him at the station and accompanied him to the capitol for a conference with the governor general of the Netherlands East Indies, Alidius van Starkenborgh Stachouwer, and the lieutenant governor, Hubertus J. van Mook.

Immediately upon being ushered into the governor general's presence Hart realized that he was being "set up." Wasting few words, the governor read Hart a press release announcing the formation of a unified Allied command to be known as ABDA (Australian, British, Dutch, American), whose naval commander would be Admiral T. C. Hart, USN. It soon became apparent that Admiral Helfrich knew of this announcement, although he had not mentioned it, thus heightening the shock of the governor's

Admiral Hart arriving in Java and greeting Vice Admiral C. E. L. Helfrich.
Courtesy of Mrs. T. C. Hart

announcement. It also was apparent that the Dutch admiral and
his civilian superior resented the fact that the Americans and the
British were going to dominate the new command.[9] The Dutch
naturally and probably rightly, believed it was essential for
whoever was to be in command to be familiar with the area, particularly the waters around the Netherlands East Indies. They also
made it clear that events in the Philippines and the failure of Hart's
submarines gave them little reason for confidence in U.S. leadership. Hart understood how they felt and sympathized, but still
it was galling when, taking advantage of his lack of knowledge and
obvious surprise, they asked him for a detailed plan of operations.

Hart stumbled for an answer. How could he be expected to have a plan when he had just been informed of his new command? Conscious of Dutch resentment and the manner in which the announcement had been staged, he felt ill at ease and on the defensive. He pointed out that he had neither sought nor been informed of his appointment. In fact, he said, he had just cabled Washington saying he was too old for the job and thought someone else might better serve Allied interests. Furthermore, he said he did not like the idea of being in command over Helfrich in waters that the Dutchman knew far better than he did. As for strategy, he suggested that it would be best not to make any specific plans pending the arrival of Field Marshal Sir Archibald Wavell, who had been named in the same press release as Supreme Commander, Southwest Pacific. The governor was not happy with Hart's reply and made note of the comments he made about his age.

Admiral Helfrich had already made up his mind that Hart was unduly cautious. As soon as war broke out, he tried to learn what American forces were going to operate in the Netherlands East Indies area and what their strategic mission would be. Neither Hart nor Glassford, who was in command of Task Force 5, which Hart had sent south from the Philippines, could provide an answer that Helfrich considered satisfactory. Consequently, the Dutch officer appealed to the British for help in getting the Americans to cooperate rather than "moving around . . . without aim and without a fixed program."[10] This caustic comment led to the meeting on 18 December between the Dutch, Rear Admiral Glassford, and Rear Admiral Purnell, who had just arrived from Hart's headquarters. Helfrich wanted the Americans to form a blocking force to keep the Japanese out of the Makasar and Malacca straits or the Celebes Sea. As will be recalled, neither of the American officers would commit himself to this strategy, both saying that they were getting their orders from Washington. This displeased Helfrich who seemed insensitive to the American concern with the Philippines and the obvious confusion that still reigned ten days after Pearl Harbor.[11]

When Hart and Helfrich met, they found themselves almost immediately at cross purposes. Describing their first meeting, Helfrich wrote: "The charming 65-year-old [Hart was 64] admiral was not optimistic and seemed somewhat downcast by Pearl Harbor and his rapid departure from the Philippines. . . . What disturbed me more was his opinion that the defense of the Dutch

East Indies was a lost cause and that retreat to Australia was the next step to be taken." He went on to describe Hart as "the prototype of a naval officer of a great sea power, thinking in terms of battleships, aircraft carriers and heavy cruisers, in terms of superiority in the classic sea battle. With a shock I realized that my colleague had never thought in terms of a holding action against a much stronger enemy, or of how to make something out of particular geographical and hydrographic conditions."[12] In other words, Helfrich thought Hart had no spirit for the unique kind of battle that lay ahead. In making these observations, Helfrich implied that it was he who had the spirit and know-how to fight the war that circumstances demanded.

Hart probably was unaware of the bad impression he had made on Helfrich, although he was surely aware that the Dutch were unhappy. Given this atmosphere, while granting that Hart's reaction when asked about taking the naval command was ill considered, he cannot be blamed for being somewhat taken aback by the situation. Aside from his longstanding objection to the establishment of a "combined" headquarters before firm agreement had been reached on strategy and his recent reply to Washington about serving in any such organization, there was the matter of precedent. Late in World War I, a supreme command was established, but neither the American navy nor the Allied naval forces were a part of it. Thus, anyone might shrink from the prospect of accepting responsibility in an innovative organization that was being established in the midst of a war that was going badly. And, after his recent experience with interservice cooperation, when a fellow countryman and old family friend had tried to stab him in the back, Hart may even have had reservations about serving under a British field marshal.

Field Marshal Wavell was no ordinary, garden variety army officer, either. Noted before 1939 equally for his intellectuality and for his strategic thinking, he had, since June 1941, become a controversial figure within the British military establishment. Appointed commander in chief of British forces in the Middle East in 1940, a time when things looked grim, he succeeded in sustaining a fighting advance of five hundred miles in two months and destroying an Italian army six times the size of his own. Early the next year his troubles began when Churchill detached badly needed men and material from his command to fight the ill-starred campaign in Greece. At this time, Wavell's opponent in the Middle East was General Erwin Rommel, and he proved to be a far tougher foe than his Italian predecessor. When the indecisive struggle in the desert had gone on for months, the prime minister decided to change the leadership and, in the controversial shake-up, Wavell was relieved of his command. That move and his subsequent designation as commander in chief in India were real blows to his reputation. Though hotly defended by many fellow officers and generally conceded to have been treated badly, Wavell was definitely under a cloud. Clearly, he was chosen to head the ABDA only because he was available; he had yet to assume his post in India and there were few unemployed field marshals drifting about. Appointing a failed officer to a unique command organization in an area with which he was not familiar could hardly be expected to inspire unbounded confidence.

It is relevant to inquire how the decision to establish the ABDA command came about. A partial explanation can be found in the records of the Arcadia Conference on Anglo-American strategy which began in Washington in late December 1941. At the meeting on Christmas Day, General George C. Marshall, chief of staff of the U.S. Army, surprised his guests, and possibly some of his colleagues as well, by suggesting that "experience in the last war" demonstrated the need for unity of command over naval, land, and air forces. The first area where this concept should be applied, he said, was the Southwest Pacific, and he was eager to reach agreement on the principle and the personnel.[13] At first, the British delegation was not enthusiastic nor was it prepared for the strong pressure that Marshall and Roosevelt exerted. On 27 December Churchill met with his staff and announced that not only did the president and the chief of staff want a supreme commander, but they wanted Field Marshal Wavell to have the honor of being that person.[14] Instead of being more enthusiastic, as Marshall had hoped, the British reacted to this seemingly generous offer with profound suspicion. General Sir John Dill, one of Churchill's advisers at the conference, wrote General Sir Alan Brooke, chief of the imperial general staff, "It would, I think, be fatal to have a British commander responsible for the disasters that are coming."[15] Were the Americans volunteering a British officer for assignment to catastrophe, asked several members of the delegation. Ambassador Halifax replied that he *thought* the offer was being made in good faith, while Churchill said that he doubted an attempt was being made "to shift the responsibility for disasters on to our shoulders." There was no way to be sure, but the prime minister thought it would be very bad to appear suspicious or to "shirk" the responsibility offered. Moreover, if the honor and the responsibility were rejected, the Americans would take over the command themselves and that might make them "unduly Pacific minded." Since the idea that the Americans might shift attention away from the Atlantic was one of Churchill's darkest fears and since establishing a cooperative atmosphere was one of his most heartfelt desires, there was little to do but graciously accede to the U.S. suggestion. This was the course that Churchill followed at his next meeting with the president.

Of considerable interest also is the question of how Wavell's naval commander, Admiral Hart, was chosen. The surprising answer is that very little consideration seems to have been given to either the duties of the naval command or to the man to be assigned. There was, however, considerable discussion within both the American and the British delegations about the desirability of placing the naval forces of ABDA under an army commander. The noteworthy thing is that Marshall and a young colonel named Dwight D. Eisenhower, who had been brought to Washington because of his familiarity and close relations with General MacArthur, led the fight to have the man in command of the naval forces under Wavell's direct command.[16] Marshall, armed with a staff study prepared by Eisenhower, fought with the U.S. admirals, who were not willing to see a naval officer under army command. Admiral Ernest J. King, who had just been appointed Commander in Chief, U.S. Fleet (CominCh), accepted Marshall's argument, but according to Secretary of War Stimson "the bulk of the admirals have evidently been pretty stubborn."[17] An attempt was made to "effect a compromise," but Marshall "insisted that Hart be placed under Wavell's command" and Roosevelt accepted that arrangement.[18]

The Royal Navy proved more obdurate than the U.S. Navy. Never had a senior naval officer had to serve in such a position. How could any army officer have mastered the complexities of the "senior service," British naval officers asked. In brief, they "kicked like bay steers," according to one participant.[19] Admiral Stark finally saved the day by observing that a unified command could be established and, if it did not work, revisions could be made.[20] On that note of positive tentativeness, the British dropped their opposition and the deal was sealed. Although, apparently, no one raised the point, the British were influenced in their agreement by the fact that Wavell's naval counterpart would be an American. This meant that no officer of the Royal Navy would suffer the indignity of serving under an army commander, and there were prospective benefits in the arrangement. No American raised any question about those benefits, but since the British were quick to suspect American ulterior motives, it might have been wise for the Americans to be similarly questioning. Events proved that it would have been wise, because the British did have ulterior motives.

Ever since Anglo-American naval cooperation began to be discussed, there had been a running debate over which country would provide the most naval force in the Far East. The Admiralty delegation went to the ABC staff conferences in Washington, January–March 1941, determined to convince the Americans that Singapore was a better place for their capital ships to be based than was Pearl Harbor.[21] When the Americans proved adamantly opposed to that suggestion, Churchill intervened: "Get the Americans into the war," he cabled from London, "then we will determine where and how they exert their power."[22] Far better to agree to almost anything, he believed, than to stubbornly support a concept that would prevent the nascent alliance from being born. This view was reluctantly accepted by the Admiralty, but that did not mean that the Royal Navy, the British government, or even Winston Churchill ever gave up hope that the Americans would assume a major share of the responsibility for protecting the Far East. The British backed down for the moment, hoping that "events would teach the Americans the best way to dispose their forces."[23] As a token of good faith, Churchill dispatched the *Repulse* and the *Prince of Wales* to Singapore in November 1941. By Christmas these two magnificent ships had been lost, and it was more desirable than ever before that the U.S. Navy begin to learn its proper role. What better advocate for that role than a four-star U.S. admiral?

Another inducement to British acceptance of Wavell's assignment was the realization that not only would it be logical and "fair" for him to have an American as his naval counterpart, but, as Admiral Sir Charles Little, the chief of the British naval liaison group in Washington, said at a meeting on 28 December, such an appointment would be "useful" because it "might secure additional U.S. forces."[24] In other words, the British quickly and without discussion accepted the appointment of an American naval officer because they agreed with their joint planners that he was "more likely to get support from his compatriot, i.e., the Commander-in-Chief of the Pacific Fleet, than any other officer."[25] Of course, if that support were not forthcoming, the British could be expected to direct their disappointment toward the American officer assigned, but Stark had already said changes could be made.

Why was Hart chosen for this difficult assignment? The primary consideration seems to have been his availability. He was very highly regarded within the U.S. Navy, but no one asked whether it was wise to assign a man who, after almost a year of negotiation, had not been able to reach agreement on an Allied plan of operations. Nor did anyone wonder whether an officer under a cloud of suspicion, at least within the hierarchy of the U.S. Army, should be given this political-military assignment. Indeed, the selection of Hart raises the question of whether Marshall was more interested in the principle of having naval officers serve under army officers than in the specific case at hand. MacArthur's critical reports could hardly have made Marshall and Eisenhower confident that Hart would cooperate unless he was forced to do so. Moreover, since the British and the Dutch had already criticized him for what they saw as his lack of cooperation, someone might have asked whether he was likely to be given wholehearted support. But, since no one did, it would appear that Hart was being assigned to a delicate and complex task of Allied coordination without his superiors having taken full account of his assets and liabilities, on the grounds that if it did not work out adjustments could be made. Well might he have felt trapped when confronted, in the Dutch governor general's office, with the news of his appointment.

In spite of the foregoing, many people still had full confidence in Tommy Hart. Admiral Stark, for one, and Hart might have been cheered had he known what Stark was writing to him at about the time he walked out of the governor general's office into the tropic heat of Batavia. Stark had just received Hart's message defending the conduct of the Asiatic Fleet. "As to the substance of your dispatch," he wrote, "I agree with it all one hundred percent."[26] Furthermore, Stark said he had "perfect confidence in whatever you were doing." Indeed, he said he could virtually get down on his knees and "thank God you didn't stay in Manila too long and that you have done everything just as you have done it." That was very comforting, but Stark's letter contained some disturbing notes as well. The chief of naval operations said that some day he would reveal to Hart just why the message questioning Hart's operations in the Philippines had been written and his regret for having sent it. A clue was provided immediately, because Stark continued, "I am not 'Boss of the Show' and there are times when we all have to say 'Aye, aye, Sir.' " Stark asked that Hart destroy this evidence of support.

It took that letter six months to reach Hart, so it was without benefit of these friendly lines that he made the journey back to Surabaja.

The first problem he had to deal with was command structure. Now that Hart was in Java and still in command of the Asiatic Fleet, Purnell would revert to his role as chief of staff. But if Hart were to become Allied naval commander, he could hardly be expected actually to command the Asiatic Fleet as well. The solution would be to reinstate Glassford in command of the surface ships of Task Force 5 and allow Purnell to make the day-to-day decisions for the Asiatic Fleet in Hart's name. This meant that Purnell, whose headquarters would be at 15 Reiniersz Boulevard on the Surabaja waterfront, would be acting fleet commander. Glassford's flagship would be the *Houston* from which he would command the task force which, when opportunities arose, would be reconstituted as a striking force. The Asiatic Fleet's auxiliaries, at the insistence of the Navy Department, had been sent to Port Darwin, Australia, and Captain W. E. Doyle was put in command of the base there.

This rather confused and irregular command arrangement is illustrative of the problems confronting Hart and requires some explanation. The auxiliaries were based at Port Darwin, despite Hart's and Allied objections, because of pessimism on the part of the U.S. naval high command about the future of Allied resistance in Malaya and Java. The improvised arrangement concerning command of the Asiatic Fleet arose because no one in Washington had apparently thought far enough in advance about how the fleet would actually be run while Hart was moving into the Allied command structure. As will be recalled, Purnell had originally commanded Task Force 5. When Hart proposed that the Asiatic Fleet fight the war from Manila, Task Force 5 was temporarily deactivated and Purnell resumed his duties as chief of staff while Hart awaited instructions from Washington. By the time those instructions came, Admiral Glassford was available for command of the task force. Since he was the senior officer, he was flown south to take command immediately after the war began. But Glassford apparently thought that Hart, by putting Purnell in nominal command of the Asiatic Fleet and sending him, Glassford, to sea, was denying him his rightful preferment. To some extent that was true but, as Hart saw it, Purnell, who had worked closely with

Rear Admiral William R. Purnell. Naval Historical Center

the Dutch and the British since 1940, was the logical person to retain on shore where he would be available for conferences. Furthermore, Purnell, as a result of two years as chief of staff, was far more familiar with the workings of the Asiatic Fleet.[27] The task force/striking force dichotomy arose in part from Hart's ambivalence about the role the Allies wanted the surface ships to play. As a result of American and—to a lesser degree—Dutch insistence that the navies play an offensive as well as a defensive role, the Allies had agreed that when the U.S. ships were performing convoy duty they were Task Force 5; when they were performing the role that Hart preferred—engaging in offensive operations—they were the striking force. The Americans and local Dutch forces had responsibility for striking forces to protect the eastern approaches to Java, and the British and the Dutch had responsibility for protecting the western approaches.

Hart worked out these various arrangements between 4 and 7

January. Then on 8 January, he received official word that he was to accept the naval command, but he was not given any detailed instructions concerning procedures and responsibilities.[28] That was frustrating enough, but he also had to contend with the desire of the chief of naval operations to second-guess him on the command arrangements for his fleet.[29] From 7,000 miles away, it seemed to Stark better to have Glassford as acting fleet commander and Purnell with the task force. Since Hart had already made other arrangements, he chose to ignore this advice, but the issue was not resolved and Samuel Eliot Morison has suggested that for some time "even the admirals themselves hardly knew what their status really was."[30] But, while it advised freely, the Navy Department could not provide any word of reinforcements, which Hart urgently requested, or even of diversionary action by the Pacific Fleet. Thus, Hart came to realize, if he had not done so before, that he was going to have to fight it out with what he had, and that Washington, while wanting to control details, was not going to give him much help.

And, although he did not realize this immediately either, the war was not the only fight he was going to have on his hands. Shortly after he arrived in Java, he received a communication from CominCh telling him to get some ammunition to Corregidor by whatever means he could.[31] It was obvious that this dispatch was sent in response to pressure MacArthur was putting on Washington for assistance. It must have stirred memories of the *Pensacola* convoy and the controversy over its practicality. The fastest ships in that convoy were not prepared to leave Brisbane until 28 December 1941, by which time, just as Hart had predicted, the Japanese had established bases in Borneo, which led to abandonment of the plan to send supplies by surface ship to the Philippines. Hart did not immediately respond to this latest call for help but, after receiving two more directives, each more urgent than the last, he discussed the matter with Lieutenant General George H. Brett, U.S. Army, who had been designated as deputy supreme commander under Wavell. The two officers agreed, according to Hart, on the impracticability of the mission and Hart so informed CominCh.[32] When General Marshall saw that message and forwarded it to MacArthur, things really began to happen. Questioned about its contents, Brett gave the impression that, while Hart considered the mission impractical and did not intend to carry it out, he, Brett, did not agree.[33] In MacArthur's view, Hart's refusal was a clear indication that the naval officer still had the "defeatist attitude" that, in the general's opinion, marked his performance in the Philippines. If further evidence were necessary, which the beleaguered general obviously did not think was the case, this latest refusal to obey orders was sufficient to prove that a new commander was needed, one who "would provide a more aggressive and resourceful handling of naval forces."[34]

At this juncture the Navy Department advised Hart that Brett was not supporting his arguments and stated that "conditions" in Washington made it "imperative" that he send the ammunition.[35] Hart, who unwisely was not giving the subject the attention it demanded, replied that he was now under Wavell's command and that the "impression is that general situation for entire command does not justify diversion of effort which would be required."[36] Nevertheless, he said, he was trying to collect the needed ammunition, although he did not believe that the relatively small amount a submarine could carry would make any difference. He did not say so in his message, but he had the impression that "Douglas" was "sitting in his tunnel dreaming up suggestions of how the Navy could help him win the war that he actually had lost in the first 24 hours."[37] That impression did not stir a sympathetic reaction nor was he unhappy that all he got from Washington were suggestions concerning an obviously minor operation while he was struggling to organize a new Allied command without a word of instruction.[38] The next cable he got from the navy told him that Wavell was not yet in operational command and that the directive to get ammunition to MacArthur was now an ironclad order.[39] These exchanges could hardly have helped Hart's mood— or given Washington the impression that he was cooperative.

The more immediate problem was cooperation within his new command. At 11:00 a.m. on 10 January 1942, Field Marshal Sir Archibald Wavell arrived in Batavia, and the combined staff of Allied officers turned out to greet him. It was quite a show, marred only by the fact that the Dutch musicians could not find the score for "The Star-Spangled Banner." With the ceremonies concluded, the field marshal—El Supremo, as the British called him—held a full-dress staff conference to review developments and lay plans. A disturbing pattern soon emerged: the command structure was going to be dominated by the army; attention was going to be focused on Malaya and Burma; the naval forces were to concentrate on convoying supplies into those beleaguered countries; and optimism was the order of the day. Hart found himself out of sympathy with every phase of the pattern.[40] Although he thought

Wavell "quite a man" and someone with whom he could work, he could not bring himself to be disingenuously optimistic; in his view it was essential that all members of the Supreme Commander's Council be "entirely factual lest we be simply fooling ourselves." It was also his opinion that in attacking Java the Japanese were going to use the same rapid, leapfrogging, amphibious tactics, which army officers did not understand, as they had in the Philippines. Air superiority would be a key factor, but in lieu of that it was necessary that there be very close cooperation between all air force units, both army and navy, and that a close working relationship be established between sea and air forces. Furthermore, there was little hope of organizing a combined naval striking force capable of falling on targets of opportunity if large numbers of ships were to be diverted to convoy work. In that regard he asked that some determination be made about the division of effort between striking forces and escort of convoys. Wavell implied that the two missions were of about equal importance.[41] Aside from the fact that this view ran counter to his inclinations, it seemed to Hart that the British were asking the Dutch for help in saving Singapore but were not willing to recognize the immediacy of the threat to the Netherlands East Indies or to help counter it. This show of British high-handedness made him pessimistic about the chances for real Allied cooperation and sympathetic toward the Dutch.

British reaction to the Americans, most particularly to Hart, was not entirely positive, either. It seemed to Wavell's chief of staff, Lieutenant General Sir Henry Pownall, that the Americans were a "little difficult and had to be put in their place."[42] And Wavell and Pownall both made it clear that they were, as Hart suspected, far more interested in Singapore than they were in Java. Moreover, they regarded Hart's expressions of respect for Japanese efficiency as founded more on his recent experiences in the Philippines than on the future, and hence out of place as well as bad form.[43] Pownall, and possibly Wavell as well, was on the way to concluding that Hart was a burnt-out case.

Wavell wanted to establish his general headquarters at Lembang, ten miles up in the hills above Bandung, which was seventy-five miles from Hart's command post in Surabaja. Hart objected at first, but eventually concurred on the principle that Wavell certainly had the right to establish his headquarters where he wanted.[44] The proposed structure of the ABDA command was:

Field Marshal Sir Archibald Wavell, Supreme Commander
  General Sir Henry R. Pownall, Chief of Staff
  Lieutenant General George H. Brett, USA, Deputy Commander
  Admiral Thomas C. Hart, USN, Commander, Naval Forces
  Rear Admiral Arthur F. E. Palliser, RN, Chief of Staff
  Rear Admiral Karel W. F. M. Doorman, RNN, Commander,
    Combined Striking Force (from 2 February)
  Lieutenant General Hein ter Poorten, Netherlands East Indies
    Army, Commander, Ground Forces
  Air Chief Marshal Sir Richard E. C. Peirse, RAF, Commander,
    Air Forces

Hart was not displeased with the composition of the high-level staff. His chief of staff, Palliser, was an experienced naval officer, whom Hart immediately decided to let handle affairs that related directly to the Royal Navy. He had six other officers on his staff and, aside from the Americans, he found himself particularly drawn to the capable and reliable Captain John Collins, Royal Australian Navy. The attraction was evidently mutual because, in 1975, Collins wrote: "I had the greatest admiration for Admiral Tommy Hart from the moment I met him."[45]

Hart delegated to Admiral Helfrich the difficult task of dealing directly with the Dutch naval commander, Rear Admiral Doorman. As he recognized immediately, it was going to be hard to convince Helfrich that he had not coveted the ABDA command and behind that tough personal problem, there lurked a murkier and more sensitive political issue. As commander in chief of the Royal Netherlands East Indian Navy, Helfrich was not only operational head of that navy, but also minister of marine in the Royal Netherlands government. In other words, he held a civilian as well as a military billet, which made the fact that Hart had superseded him more awkward than was at first recognized.[46] As if that were not enough, while Helfrich's counterpart, the commander in chief of the Dutch army, was on a command level equal to Hart, he himself was not even part of the command.[47] Helfrich reacted to his exclusion and to Hart's precedence over him by constantly needling the American about the performance of American submarines and commenting caustically about the amount of time U.S. ships spent in port.[48] The resentment never went beyond verbal exchanges, although Hart was convinced that

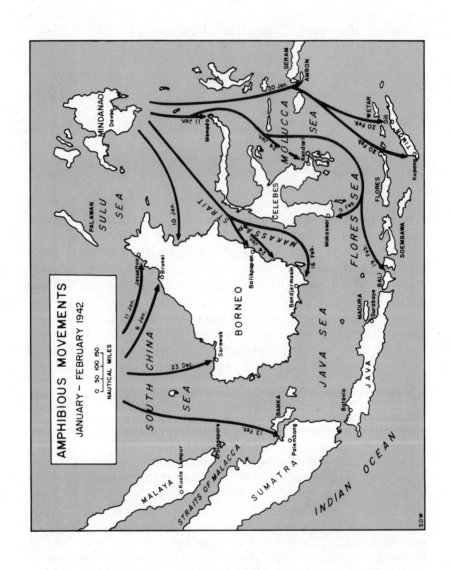

AMPHIBIOUS MOVEMENTS
JANUARY – FEBRUARY 1942

0 50 100 150
NAUTICAL MILES

MINDANAO

Davao

SULU
SEA

PALAWAN

SERAM

AMBON

30 Jan.

MOLUCCA
SEA

WETAR

20 Feb.

Oiti

TIMOR

20 Feb.

Kupang

11 Jan.

Menado

23 Jan.

Kendari

CELEBES

FLORES

9 Feb.

FLORES
SEA

SOEMBAWA

10 Jan.

MAKASSAR
STRAIT

24 Jan.

Mokassar

9 Feb.

BALI

19 Feb.

Jesselton

Brunei

11 Jan.

6 Jan.

Balikpapan

Bandjermasin

16 Feb.

BORNEO

MADURA

Surabaya

SOUTH
CHINA
SEA

23 Dec.

Sarawak

JAVA
SEA

Batavia

JAVA

BANKA

13 Feb.

Palembang

Singapore

Kuala Lumpur

MALAYA

STRAITS OF MALACCA

SUMATRA

INDIAN OCEAN

SDW

Helfrich withheld vital information from him and, on at least one occasion, misinformed him about the availability of Dutch ships.[49]

Situations like that made smooth relations difficult, but more worrisome from a military point of view was an awkward five-day interregnum during which Hart was nominally under Wavell's joint command but actually had authority only over his own ships. This came about because, almost immediately after his arrival in Batavia, Wavell took off for Singapore—without telling Hart that he was doing so—and creation of the ABDA command, which was supposed to have taken place on 12 January, was delayed.[50]

During the first two weeks in January, the Japanese were taking advantage of Allied confusion by moving on two widely separated fronts. The western wing of the offensive, the one directed toward Singapore, was undoubtedly the stronger and was given primary attention by the Allies, particularly by the British. The central and eastern wings, the ones directed toward the Netherlands East Indies, were the most important to the Americans and the Dutch. The Dutch naturally worried about survival, while Admiral Hart worried about keeping open the supply lines to Australia and communications between his fleet and the U.S. Fleet in Hawaii. By 15 January, when ABDA was formally constituted, the tentacles of the Japanese octopus were probing for weak points and routes through the treacherous straits northeast of Java. Action had to be taken soon—or never. On 13 January Hart had sent out a U.S. cruiser-destroyer striking force to pounce upon a reported Japanese movement along the coast of Borneo. After the force had completed two-thirds of the tortuous passage, word came on 16 January that the "game had flown." In other words, either the report was false or the Japanese had been and gone.[51]

News of this disappointment came as Hart was preparing to move to his new command post, ten miles from and 4,000 feet above salt water, in the resort town of Lembang. When he surveyed his surroundings in the cool morning light of 19 January, he found them pleasing to the eye, but, though better than some other places that had been suggested, far from ideal.[52] There was room enough for staff meetings, but the army, the air, and the naval components each occupied one of the bungalows that were spaced around a central compound. Hart and Palliser shared a small house, in whose living room they worked and met with their staff. Communications were extremely complicated. The codes and ciphers were British, but Dutch equipment and channels were used. This local system was sufficient for Dutch needs, but it proved very difficult to expand. To supplement it, the U.S. Navy set up its own radio and coding system for communication with the Asiatic Fleet headquarters in Surabaja. Then the U.S. Army asked to use the navy's system and for a while that worked all right, but finally the army had to use Dutch commercial facilities. In addition, there was the language difficulty; however, given sufficient time and luck, perhaps all would come right.

But the Japanese would not allow time, and luck was in extremely short supply. No sooner had Hart arrived at Lembang than word came from Dutch Intelligence that a Japanese expedition was bound south through the Makasar Strait. He immediately ordered the American Striking Force into action again on 20 January.[53] It was a difficult passage through the Flores Sea, made no easier by the inaccuracy of the English-language charts. The Dutch charts were better, but none of the Americans could read them and the Dutch claimed they had no extra pilots available. Hence, first the virtually inevitable happened: the cruiser *Boise* ripped her bottom on an uncharted reef and the submarine *S–36* ran hard aground on a coral shelf. Then, on the twenty-first word came that the Japanese were not coming down the Makasar Strait—yet. None of this enhanced the view of the American commander entertained by the British Army. "Poor old Hart," recorded Pownall in his diary, "[he] is quite unfitted for his job, he has no kick in him at all."[54]

The next day, 22 January, Hart made the four-and-one-half-hour flight to Surabaja and back to deal with personnel matters. Despite the fact that he had made other arrangements, the Navy Department insisted that Glassford, rather than Purnell, be given command of the Asiatic Fleet which would on 30 January be designated U.S. Naval Forces in the Southwest Pacific. There was considerable embarrassment on the part of all three officers: Hart at being overruled by Washington; Glassford at being placed over the more experienced Purnell; and Purnell at being bumped from a billet he occupied for only two weeks. As Hart understated, it was a "difficult change to carry out in the face of an advancing enemy."[55] His own mood probably did not improve when, upon returning to Lembang, he learned that an American submarine had reported that the Japanese were definitely mounting their offensive strike down the Makasar Strait.[56]

"Oh, for a little LUCK!" wrote Hart, as he ordered his striking force out again.[57] He needed luck because his ships were low on fuel and their crews were tired as a result of their recent abortive run north. He could scrape together only four destroyers, the *Pope, John D. Ford, Parrott*, and *Paul Jones*, and the cruiser *Marblehead*, which had shaft problems and could make only 15 knots. Hart spent the twenty-third worrying and praying that the night attack the destroyers were to launch against the Japanese fleet at Balikpapan would be successful.[58]

For the first time in weeks, his prayers were answered. In a fiery, confusing, jumbled melee, the four destroyers scattered and shot up the surprised Japanese invasion force. It was the first major surface action for American warships since the Battle of Santiago de Cuba in 1898, in which Hart participated. More important than this historical fact, or than its overall military significance, was the boost it gave to American morale. Hart was elated and termed it the best day of the war for him. "Now if I could only hear of some bags by the submarines," he wrote, "my bowl of happiness would be overflowing."[59]

Such reports did not come and within two days, when he again visited his ships at Surabaja, it was clear that the destroyer action had done nothing to slow the Japanese advance. Moreover, viewed in retrospect, he and his destroyermen realized that their bag should have been much bigger. Those facts, coupled with the total exhaustion and poor health of Commander Paul Talbot, the destroyer force commander, were sufficient to dampen his enthusiasm and to put things in perspective.[60] His crews were feeling the strain of six weeks of war preceded by months of training and tension. Reports from Malaya indicated to Hart that, despite the continued optimism of Wavell and his staff, all was soon to be lost, and before long it seemed the Japanese would be severing the lines of communication with Australia. Hart, in agreement with John Collins, now promoted to commodore, that there was a "very great probability" that the Japanese would succeed in driving through the Malay barrier, decided to bring the auxiliaries west from Port Darwin and stop trying to cover the 1,500 miles of sea lanes between Australia and Java.[61] When he announced that decision at a staff conference on 28 January, he got a distinctly chilly reaction from the British members.[62] Thus, although less than two days before he was in high good spirits, when his first two weeks as commander of the ABDA naval forces ended, he realized that his situation had eased hardly at all.

He was frustrated at having to carry out a strategy with which he did not agree in company with a group of fractious allies. On 28 January he wrote in his diary:

We Americans are exasperated because, for three days now, there has been an opportunity for a Cruiser-Destroyer Foray, to the N.E. and we are unready because of the ships having been at sea so long. They are run to death and simply must have some time in port to get tuned up. At the conference this morning, (I tell too many blunt truths for my own popularity), I said that we had made the mistake in all three Navies of convoying and escorting interminably. That there would have been no losses if we had done none of that whatever, and that by exhausting our ships in that purely defensive work we had robbed ourselves of the power of offensive work, by Cruisers and Destroyers, just at the time when [a] good chance for it arrived. That attitude has been the main point of difference between the British and ourselves for a year back. I raised it at one of Wavell's early meetings but saw that I had to accept convoying as being the primary mission.

As Hart was well aware, the Dutch and, to a lesser degree, the British army representatives had been dissatisfied with the naval command arrangement for some time. The question was what action would Wavell take. His path would be smoothed by both Washington and Admiral Hart himself. Negative reports on Hart had been accumulating in the American capital since the opening days of the war. So long as they were coming only from General MacArthur, they could be partially discounted, but the gloom created by the general began to be augmented by others. Shortly after Hart's strained meeting in Batavia with the governor general of the Netherlands East Indies and his deputy, van Mook, the latter journeyed to the United States. Even before he arrived, the Navy Department began receiving indications of the conclusions van Mook drew from the governor general's meeting with the American admiral. In Melbourne, Australia, he told the U.S. naval liaison officer that Hart had described himself as "inadequate" to serve as commander of ABDA's naval forces because of his advanced age. Van Mook implied that he shared that view and he obviously wanted it reported; the comment was soon on its way to Washington.[63]

At least partially in response to these reports, on 12 January Admiral King sent a message to Hart asking for his estimate of Admiral Helfrich's qualifications for command. Hart replied that he considered Helfrich entirely competent to command ABDA's naval forces.[64] Sensing what was happening, Hart decided that he should brief Field Marshal Wavell on the affair, in case the supreme commander wanted to take some action before the ABDA headquarters were formally organized.[65] Accordingly, he told Wavell the whole story of the Dutch unhappiness. Wavell noted what Hart said but seemed disinclined to take any action; however, he did have some mental reservations about his naval chief and wired Churchill: "Hart is quiet attractive character and seems shrewd. But he is old and openly says so and gives me the impression of looking over his shoulder rather too much. His experiences at Manila seem to have given him exaggerated ideas of Japanese efficiency. Palliser will help to keep his eyes to the front. Hart should be easy to work with but may be over depressed if things go wrong."[66]

Roosevelt was distinctly unhappy with his ABDA naval commander. Indeed, he was so unhappy that, on 24 January, the day after the news of the destroyer attack in the Makasar Strait arrived, he was still concentrating on Hart's deficiencies rather than praising him for this success. Harry Hopkins, special assistant to the president, dined with Roosevelt that evening and came away with the impression that FDR was going to have some of the same problems Lincoln had "with generals and admirals whose records look awfully good but who may turn out to be the McClellans of this war." Hopkins thought, however, that Roosevelt would move more swiftly than did Lincoln. The president had heard that Hart was telling Wavell and the Dutch that he was not up to the job. This disturbed Roosevelt and made him think that Hart was "too old" to carry out his responsibilities; Hopkins guessed that "before long there will be a change in our naval command in the Far West [East ?]."[67] If victories could not win the support of the American president for an American commander, the other partners in the alliance could hardly be expected to restrain their ambitions.

Van Mook had arrived in the U.S. capital and made no secret of his dissatisfaction over Hart's appointment or of his desire to have him replaced by Helfrich. On 25 January Admiral King sent another dispatch to Hart, saying that "they"—presumably the administration—were disquieted to hear that the Dutch were unhappy that Admiral Helfrich was not included in the command structure. Admitting that he could not see how he "could help the dear boys' disquietude on my little own,"[68] Hart showed the message to Wavell, again explained that he had not tried to get the ABDA command for himself, and ran through the history of the case. Again Wavell gave no indication that the situation disturbed him, nor did he imply that he was going to take any action, so

Hart left with the impression that the subject was closed. Two days later, after having talked with Dutch officials in Batavia, Wavell called Hart in for a talk.

It was all a little awkward. The field marshal, obviously ill at ease, began the conversation with, "You told me that perhaps you are too old," whereupon Hart remarked that he often joked about his age, but that his relative capabilities would have to be judged by others. After again reviewing the history of his appointment, he said that he had given Wavell every opportunity to remove him before the ABDA command was set up but, since he had not been removed, and had reluctantly accepted a very difficult task, he did not think that he should be removed "in a manner which reflected adversely upon me." He went on to suggest, and Wavell agreed, that now the best thing to do would be to resume the conversation after he had settled into his job.[69]

Wavell chose to renew the conversation twenty-four hours later, on 29 January, the day after Hart announced that he was bringing his auxiliaries back from Australia. At this meeting, Hart told Wavell that if, as supreme commander, he felt a change in naval command was needed, he should ask the Dutch governor general for a letter requesting that Helfrich be made commander of ABDA's naval forces. This would be the logical procedure since, in Hart's view, it was a political rather than a military issue and should be openly handled as such. According to Hart, Wavell was "embarrassed by this suggestion," and Hart left the office with the impression that Wavell would not take any action.[70]

Had Wavell chosen not to act, it would have been understandable. He had little basis for judging Hart's capabilities. He had arrived in Java only eighteen days before this last conversation and although he had assumed the supreme command thirteen days before it, he had been out of the country on reconnaissance missions in Malaya and Burma for six of those days. Thus, he had had approximately a week in which to appraise Hart's performance of duty.[71] There should have been little reason to question Hart's offensive attitude, given the fact that he had ordered three separate naval strikes. Through no fault of his, two of them were abortive, but the third resulted in the victory at Balikpapan. Wavell, however, had apparently gotten bad reports on Hart even when his forces were enjoying success. On 25 January, Wavell's chief of staff, General Pownall, wrote in his diary regarding the American victory: "It was a good show on the part of the U.S. destroyers and should put their tails up, which they need. Moreover, it should do something towards activating old Admiral Hart, a nice man but with very little guts who always finds good reason for not doing things." He went on to say that the Americans were very "odd" to deal with. "Their knowledge of naval staff work seems to be nil," he wrote, and added, "Hart doesn't give decisions—he puts it to the vote of his assembled staff officers, and what action is taken depends on the result of the ballot."[72] This final comment was not true, but Pownall thought all along that the Americans were difficult to deal with and his background in the British Army scarcely inclined him to be generous. Moreover, he worked closely with the supreme commander and may well have helped poison Wavell's mind against his naval subordinate.

Whether he had adequate opportunity for a firsthand appraisal of Hart's capabilities or not, Wavell decided to seek political advice on the Hart-Helfrich affair. On 29 January, he sent Churchill a "private and most confidential" wire asking for help in sorting out the thorny problem. Wavell said Hart was a "charming personality" and knew his job, but he always took the "pessimistic view" and referred frequently to his age. The Dutch were saying openly that they wanted Helfrich to fill the post and van Mook had gone to Washington to make similar representations. Wavell was convinced, and Hart had said, that the American officer would be willing to step down "if it can be done in some way that will save his face." There was, however, another aspect to the matter. It was doubtful that the Americans would serve happily under Helfrich because the Dutchman was prone to "express himself caustically" about the U.S. Navy. Perhaps another American admiral could be sold to the Dutch if, and only if, he came with the assurance of a strong U.S. naval reinforcement. In essence, Wavell wanted Churchill's advice on how to "substitute [a] younger more energetic man than Hart without offending either Americans or Dutch or throwing stigma on Hart."[73]

If Churchill had simply given his advice, all might have been worked out smoothly but, because he felt his "relations with the President [were] so close," he sent Wavell's private telegram to Franklin Roosevelt. The president immediately replied that indications had already been received in Washington, presumably from van Mook and MacArthur, that Hart "felt that he was too old to handle that important command." If a change were to be made, FDR thought Helfrich would be ideal because he seemed to be a "very good naval officer." However, Roosevelt did want the United States to have command of some service, possibly the air forces. Perhaps Brett could be given that job, even if it meant leaving the post of deputy supreme commander temporarily vacant.[74] Churchill, for some reason, interpreted these last comments as implying that MacArthur was going to be withdrawn from Corregidor and sent to Java as Wavell's deputy. Since this move would put the "whole force and enthusiasm of the United States" behind Wavell's command, Churchill thought it far outweighed "all secondary considerations," one of which was presumably the feelings of Hart.

Roosevelt meanwhile showed Churchill's telegram to Admiral King, who in turn wired Hart to ask him whether he had in fact said he did not feel able to carry on. Hart, knowing nothing of Wavell's message, went to him for an explanation. Again, the supreme commander appeared to Hart "much embarrassed," but he explained what had happened. Wavell told him that the Dutch had no confidence in him, a fact that Hart could easily accept "since they have, all along, desired to give the job to Helfrich." Wavell offered no personal criticism of Hart or of the manner in which he had handled his job, but did mumble something about age. Hart resented Wavell's unwillingness to admit that it was a political, rather than a military, problem and stand out against it.[75] As Wavell recalled the meeting, Hart was "charming" but seemed hurt.[76]

Not realizing that Roosevelt had already agreed to his replacement, Hart sent King a telegram describing what had happened. After repeating the now familiar series of events, he told King that he had better assume that, for whatever reason, Wavell did not want him to continue.[77] This naturally placed King in a quandary. He did not want to relieve Hart, particularly because he, King, was quite disturbed by the Dutch behavior, but Roosevelt had already agreed that he should be relieved and now Wavell had fallen into line.[78]

Hart lay awake on the night of 1 February, his mind going over and over the developments. He was very unhappy, not about losing the command, if that was going to be the outcome, but because he was afraid he was going to be cast "in a bad light." His conscience was clear: he had dealt candidly and openly with all sides and could see no area "wherein I've made any considerable mistakes." He was determined not to be unhappy, although he felt that Wavell was not being forthright and that something was going on beneath the surface.[79]

Despite these personal preoccupations, the next day, 2 February, was unusually busy. Hart called all his commanders in and tried to organize another cruiser-destroyer strike into Makasar Strait. The Dutch could supply 40 per cent of the force, the British none, so it fell to the Americans to come up with 60 per cent. Even though this was not the division of effort he would have preferred, Hart decided to form a combined striking force under command of Admiral Doorman and go at the Japanese again. Doorman sailed out of Bunda Roads at 0000 on 4 February and in less than twelve hours all Hart's plans had gone awry. Within minutes of Japanese aircraft spotting the striking force, there were no seaworthy cruisers left in the Asiatic Fleet. Both the *Houston* and the *Marblehead* were hit hard and that, combined with damage to the Dutch cruiser *DeRuyter* and obvious Japanese control of the air, convinced Admiral Doorman that he should turn back. Hart was furious. "Too late," he wrote, "that has been generally the case all this war and particularly so since the surface ships reached the N.E.I. waters." He was unhappy with Doorman, but actually he blamed Helfrich and the reports he had provided about the preparedness of Dutch ships because, Hart wrote, "if he had not misled me we could have had this joint force set up two days earlier."[80]

The next blow fell on 5 February when Hart received a telegram from Admiral King saying that an awkward situation had arisen in Washington and, while he was reluctant to lose Hart's services, it might be best if Hart were to ask for detachment on grounds of health.[81] Hart did not wish to do so, but, as an officer who had been trained early to say "aye, aye," he followed orders and sent the requested wire. Thus, it was arranged that on 15 February, one month after he reluctantly accepted the command, Admiral Hart would be replaced by Admiral Helfrich. These were not exactly the circumstances "under which I would have wished to terminate my services," he wrote. Then, in a philosophical mood, he added, "It's all on the laps of the gods and, whatever happens, I don't now see any forks over the long road back there [where] I feel that I took the wrong turn."[82]

On the night of 14 February 1942 in a dining room of the Savoy Hotel in Bandung, Java, there occurred a most unusual retirement ceremony. At the conclusion of the meal and the toasts, the guest of honor rose to speak, struggled for the proper words, and gave up. "Well, boys," he said, "we all have a busy day tomorrow, so we'd better break this up." Then he walked to the door and stood there ramrod-straight in his high starched collar and bid a formal good-bye to the sixteen younger officers. The first three or four filed past in silence, then came Lieutenant Commander Redfield Mason's turn: he grasped the older man's hand in both of his and said, "Good-bye, Sir, you are the finest man I've ever known." The admiral's eyes clouded with tears and he was incapable of speaking to or even seeing the faces of the remaining men. "Oh it was hard," he wrote that night, partings were always sad, but doing it in wartime and "leaving them out here in the face of a dangerous enemy and commanded by God knows whom or how" was almost too much to bear.[83]

Speculation about the real reasons for Hart's removal from command of ABDA's naval forces began almost immediately. "Hart's replacement: a pat on the back or a kick," was the headline over one newspaper story, which recounted the growing tide of criticism among the Allies about Hart's performance.[84] Samuel E. Morison, in his monumental and generally authoritative history of U.S. naval operations in World War II, inaccurately wrote: "Finally President Roosevelt, Secretary Knox and Admiral King, on the ground that Java could not be held much longer anyway, decided it would be better to let a Dutch commander take the rap," and therefore agreed to Hart's being replaced.[85] Helfrich wrote in his *Memoirs*, "I believe that the advanced age of Admiral Hart was the direct cause of his replacement."[86] In his book on the six months after Pearl Harbor, John Toland came close to the attitude of the times when he said that Roosevelt was convinced that Hart was "too tired and unaggressive to command the ABDA Navy."[87] And the official Australian history of the period summed it up: "For Hart . . . the command was an unsought and heavy—apparently too heavy—responsibility."[88] The British war diary is perhaps the most damning—from the long list of commanders, Dutch, Australian, American, and British, who are praised for service in a losing cause, Hart's name is conspicuously absent.[89] In short, the common implication is that Hart's leadership was uninspiring, that he was not aggressive enough, and that his removal for "health reasons" was a convenient way to get rid of an unsatisfactory commander. Is this implication accurate? Most of the record now being available and the passage of time giving perspective, it may be possible to answer that question and to comment with certainty upon this unusual man, his performance of his duty, and the circumstances that led to his replacement.

Hart's personality has to be considered first. His blunt, outspoken, often less-than-tactful manner, was accepted and respected by his American colleagues, but it was not likely to go down well in an Allied headquarters. Moreover, his concept of honesty would not allow him to mouth platitudes about victory when all looked black, nor could he countenance those who talked of brave moves to be made months hence. But he was sensitive to the feelings of others and his sensitivity concerning Admiral Helfrich contributed to his downfall. It was because he understood Helfrich's disappointment at not being given the naval command that Hart emphasized the fact that he was merely carrying out an unsought duty. Sadly, by emphasizing this point, he gave Helfrich just the lever he needed to wedge the American officer out of the post.

In other ways, too, Hart did not serve his own interests well. One obvious case of his playing into the hands of his enemies was his handling of the request that he send supplies to MacArthur on Corregidor. By insisting that the supplies he might provide would not alter the final outcome in the Philippines and that the mission of getting them there would create a diversion from the central effort, Hart gave indirect support to MacArthur's case against him. Army authorities in Washington were already accusing the navy of being inefficient, timorous, and uncooperative; Hart's messages fit perfectly into the mold Stimson and others had constructed. Far better for Hart to have bowed to the inevitable, said nothing, and sent MacArthur what he could spare. The same was true on the question of his age.

Hart and his comments and attitude concerning his age would provide the material for an article on psycho-history. There is no doubt that he really did consider himself an old man. But why did he constantly talk about it? The answer must be speculative, but the most obvious suggestion is that he wanted his auditors to reassure him. Since he was legitimately concerned lest he be called upon to perform some critical duty and be found wanting because of infirmity, what support would be better than constant reassurance that he was not an old man? He must also have known that he looked frail, especially in a summer uniform complete with shorts, and perhaps he hoped to head off a negative comment by prompting a positive one. It might also be that, anticipating his unseating from his perilous position, Hart provided his enemies with the weapon for his destruction so as not to force them to seek potentially more damaging ones. One thing is certain: no one will ever know what prompted this man, who lived to be ninety-four, so candidly to refer to his advanced years.

A review of Admiral Hart's duty performance might be divided into two parts, actual performance and perceived performance. There can be no question but that Hart arrived in Java tired, tense, and unhappy. However, there is very little evidence to suggest that his physical condition impaired his judgment or his ability to command. He assimilated as quickly as could reasonably be expected a series of bewildering developments, and in four weeks set up an American command; changed it at the behest of authorities in Washington; helped organize the headquarters of the recently conceived supreme command; moved his own headquarters; and kept in touch with his operational commanders by flying to visit them at their bases. His anticipation of Japanese moves, his recognition of the flexibility and speed of amphibious warfare, and his realization that air control was vital, all indicate that he had a firm grasp of the situation.

The accusation that he hesitated to take offensive action is especially ironic. In fact, Hart argued for more than a year that the Allied naval forces should concentrate on offensive strikes rather than on convoying. He opposed British insistence that escorting convoys into Singapore be given priority, primarily on the grounds that such missions made it impossible for his ships to be available to strike targets of opportunity. In retrospect, since the Japanese never tried to disrupt the convoys that the Allies organized, it would appear that Hart was right about priorities and the British wrong. If he voiced pessimism as to the ultimate effectiveness of the strikes he advocated, he did so in conferences with other senior officers, where he felt that truth took precedence over pose. It is difficult to fault Hart's duty performance. He got most of his ships safely out of the Philippines; he established a new base of operations in reasonably short order; he organized three strikes against Japanese forces, one of which resulted in the American victory off Balikpapan. Few officers would have done as well under the circumstances, and since all authorities agree that no one could have changed the ultimate outcome, Hart must be given at least above average marks.

After all the positive things have been said, there is no denying that Hart was not the man to inspire confidence in the hearts of his British and Dutch allies. For this reason, and for this reason alone, he should not have been assigned as the ABDA naval commander. First, his inability to reach agreement on a coordinated plan in the months before the war prejudiced his future effectiveness. Second, the disappointment that greeted his inability to send surface ships and submarines to Malayan waters when war broke out, branded him in the minds of some British naval officers as uncooperative and possibly undependable. Some went so far as to blame him for the early losses in Malayan waters and the ultimate loss of Singapore, obviously biased and illogical contentions. Third, the circumstances of his journey to Java were not propitious. Fleeing the Philippines in a submarine could be viewed by the cynical as a fear-inspired retreat, especially when the army commander left behind was loudly protesting that he had been deserted. And then meeting Hart, who looked frail, whose handwriting wobbled like an octogenarian's, and who called himself an "old man," must have been very disillusioning to his new comrades. These circumstances explain, in part at least, why van Mook, after one meeting, and Wavell, after barely one week's contact, came to the conclusion that Hart was not up to the job.

That is not to say that there were not other motives for British and Dutch displeasure with Hart. The Dutch understandably wanted their own man to have the naval command, and they planned, pressured, conferred, and cajoled until they got it for him. It is difficult to understand why, after the appointment of Hart became a fact, they did not see the wisdom of pulling together rather than intriguing to change commanders in the midst of a battle that was going badly. The lack of British support is as easy to understand as is the Dutch. The fact that the command was army-dominated was the first strike against Hart. Furthermore, the British hoped that the appointment of Hart would ensure more American naval support for the Far East. When that support was not forthcoming, the argument for having an American in command of the naval forces collapsed. Hopes then turned to the possibility of Hart being exchanged for MacArthur, who quite likely would bring more American support. In the British view, the value of an American commander was in direct proportion to the priority of attention he could attract.

And that brings up the matter of Hart's relationship to his own government. Having leveled criticism at the Allied governments involved, it must be admitted that the greatest mistakes were made by the U.S. government. The first mistake was in appointing Hart. The second was in failing to support him. The American high command needed an American naval officer to balance the appointment of Wavell as supreme commander; thus, Hart became a pawn in an international game of chess. The high command forgot that the Dutch had players on the board, also, and when the Dutch brought pressure and found that no one was really supporting Hart, his removal was as simply accomplished as was his appointment.

Why was no one, with the exception of some in the higher echelons of the navy, supporting Hart? The answer is that his effectiveness had been slowly eroded by chance and circumstance. The president had not had much confidence in him for years; MacArthur had done his best to saddle Hart with responsibility for the disaster in the Philippines; the army hierarchy was inclined to be suspicious of him because a bitter battle was raging in Washington over which service was responsible for the debacle at Pearl Harbor, and he was a naval officer; and at the Navy Department, Hart's greatest confidant and defender, Admiral Stark, had become virtually ineffective because of his role in the events that culminated around 8:00 a.m. on 7 December 1941. In view of these circumstances, in view of his clearly stated objection to British naval strategy in the Far East, in view of his age, Hart should not have been chosen as commander of ABDA's naval forces. But once he had been chosen, he should have been supported. It was bad enough to be trapped in the "sinister twilight" the Japanese masterminded in the Far East, but for Hart it was no brighter in Washington than in the Makasar Strait.[90]

11

LIVING WITH DISASTER

The war was over for Tommy Hart, at least his active role in it. Now he had to go home and face the ignominy of being replaced at the critical point in the battle. There are many ways he could have reacted—with anger, shame, pique, or he might have struck out in several directions to prove that he had been shabbily treated. But that was not Hart's way. He believed that his reputation, his honor, had been sullied by the impression that he was guilty of misconduct or even cowardice, but he was an officer acting under orders given by superiors who saw fit to remove him from command. He did not question their judgment, though he could not accept the logic or fairness of their action. In his view, he had done everything he could. He must try to bring others to that realization, but he must do it without excuses, rancor, or whining. He was prepared to accept what came. He would go home and conduct himself, as he had always done, with reserved dignity.

The night of 14 February 1942 was a restless one indeed. To say that Tommy Hart was haunted by the knowledge that he was leaving thousands of naval officers and men to face certain defeat by a ruthless enemy would be no exaggeration. Adding to his unhappiness was the fact that men who had demonstrated every confidence in him would have to face their future under foreign command. Not that his own future looked bright, but at least he was supposed to be heading home. What awaited at home? The signs, which he had been watching carefully since the day the war began, indicated that in some quarters in Washington his arrival was awaited with malevolent eagerness.

The next morning, accompanied by one young lieutenant, he traveled the forty miles to Batavia in a battered sedan; a small four-star flag fluttered from a makeshift mounting on the fender. His "staff" left him on a pier in Batavia, wished him luck, and surreptitiously slipped the small four-star, "haul-down" flag into the pocket of the admiral's raincoat.

Standing on the pier is where the commanding officer of a destroyer from the Asiatic Fleet found him. D. A. Harris, skipper of the destroyer *Bulmer*, who was in Batavia to attend a conference, tells of the meeting:

> On returning from the conference I noted, as the only other individual in sight, an elderly man in civilian clothes. He was tall, thin, erect, white headed, and resembled Admiral Hart. But it could not be. You do not dump a four star Admiral, particularly one who within the past few days had been Commander of ABDAFLOAT, on the dock in a strange country where little English is spoken, and leave him to fend for himself like the newest recruit.
>
> A closer look proved that it was Admiral Hart, now reduced to the status of a seaman second—waiting on the dock. What to do? I was scared of the old devil. It was a well known fact that he could shrivel an individual to a cinder with but a single glance of those gimlet like eyes. By leaving him to his own devices—who would expect him to be in civilian clothes?—I might well escape the dressing down of my life, for in that field he also excelled. On the other hand, there was our Navy's most senior officer for thousands of miles in any direction, one for whose military abilities I had, and still have, the utmost respect and admiration, and he was being treated like a leper, being kicked when he was down.
>
> Letting my sympathy get the better of my good judgement, throwing caution to the winds, and with considerable trepidation, I went over to the old S.O.B. and addressed him about as follows: "Admiral, please excuse me for not saluting but I see that you are in civilian clothes and might not want to be recognized. My gig is alongside the float. May I be of any service?" He replied in effect that he wanted "to go out to a ship in the harbor." As he was boarding the gig I gave the coxswain the following orders: "Jones," (name forgotten but a fine young man), "take this gentleman wherever he wants to go. Return here and pick me up." With that they shoved off and were soon lost to sight in the mass of shipping which crowded the roadstead.
>
> "Jones" returned in somewhat less than an hour. I never asked him where he had been nor did he ever mention where he had taken his passenger. Insofar as I know, there was no scuttlebutt circulated on the *Bulmer* about that trip. I did not particularly like

waiting on the dock, having spent many long hours engaged in that pastime in previous years. But I had much rather have waited all day than to have been in the gig with Admiral Hart for two reasons. First and foremost, I detested him as an individual, while respecting and admiring his military abilities. Second, I did not want to know anything at all about his destination because what you do not know, you cannot tell, no matter what means of persuasion might be used."[1]

The ship Tommy went out to was the bomb-damaged British cruiser *Durban.* In her he made the first leg of his journey home. During most of the four days it took to get to Colombo, Ceylon, he stayed in his cabin analyzing what had gone wrong during the past two months. Most of that analysis was extremely objective— estimates of the Japanese command structure, suppositions concerning the ability of their pilots, and so on, and contained no evidence whatsoever of self-pity. Indeed, starting from the assumption that no one could have done much, he tended to give himself high marks. He wrote, and it was one of the few times he used the third person in his diary: "I can't find any great and serious fault with Hart. He *did* function pretty well for an old fellow during those three weeks in Manila; they involved the losing side all through but nothing that Hart could have done would have turned the scale."[2]

Not that he was totally pleased with his performance. He deeply regretted leaving so many people in the Philippines. He blamed himself for having put too much trust in the army air corps and what he called their "Pee-40's." Most interestingly, he did think he made a mistake in not bringing the cruisers and destroyers back to the Philippines for a raid or two on the Japanese transports supporting the invasion, even though Japanese control of the air would have made it extremely risky. Having said those things, he seemed content to let the dead past bury the dead. He realized that not enough time had passed to give him perspective, so he did not brood about his performance or possible repercussions.

The rest of his route home was from Ceylon to India and then in progressive hops to Cairo, Khartoum, Lagos, Brazil, and eventually the United States. Along the way he met a strangely mixed bag of generals, admirals, and diplomats—among them General Sir Claude Auchinleck, Admiral Sir Geoffrey Layton, and Ambassador John G. Winant—and in Basra, Iraq, he inspected a 500-man Polish battalion. It all came to an end on 8 March when he arrived in New York City without a cent or an overcoat. Caroline drove down to meet him. The papers were filled with pictures of his arrival, speculation about his removal, and questions about the campaign. For Tommy Hart the first stage of the war might have been over, but another was about to begin.

Caroline brought word that Admiral Stark, along with his regards, sent orders that Hart was to take as long as he needed to rest up. In light of the press coverage given his relief for reasons of health, and despite the exhausting twenty-five day, eight-thousand-mile journey he had just completed, Tommy and Caroline decided an appearance in Washington without delay was in order. Caroline was especially eager that the record be set right, at least as far as that could be done by actions and appearances.

So, the next day the Harts arrived in Washington where they spent the night with the Starks. Betty had aged, which Hart did not find surprising, in light of the burdens he was carrying. Hart guessed that, when the history of the period was written, Stark would be judged a "great man" for what he had been able to achieve under adverse conditions "political and administrative." Now, however, Stark was being ditched, not so much as a scapegoat as because having him around was a "constant reminder of all the sound advice which Betty has given and which F.D.R. did not take."[3]

His first calls were on Secretary Knox and Admiral King. He had a pleasant thirty-minute conversation with Knox, and his meeting with King was very reassuring as well. King was still angry with the Dutch about their behavior regarding Hart, and he was determined not to take any action that might allow them to infer that the U.S. Navy agreed with their evaluation of Hart. The best way not to give that impression was not to follow the normal practice and have Hart revert to his permanent rank of rear admiral. Therefore, King was going to allow Hart to retain his four stars and his title as commander in chief of the Asiatic Fleet. Whether he told Hart of his full plan at this meeting is not known, but he did greet Tommy warmly and, as Hart said, let him know "that he [King] had been sure that I was not sick or too decrepit for my job in ABDA and expressed regret that he had to act as he did in my removal."[4]

After these sessions, King and Knox escorted him to the White House to see the president. FDR "turned on all his charm," greeted Hart as "Tommy," and showed considerable interest in the Far East. In the course of the conversation, he implied that he did not have complete confidence in MacArthur's judgment,

Admiral and Mrs. Hart at King House just after the admiral's return from Java in 1942. Courtesy of Mrs. T. C. Hart

but the most shocking revelation was the president's comment that General Marshall had assured him the Philippines were capable of absorbing a Japanese attack as early as 1 December 1941. According to Hart, FDR said, "If I had known the true situation, I could have babied the Japanese along quite a while longer."[5] The president had only supportive words for "Tommy," but he did say he thought Hart should face the press at the earliest possible opportunity, the following day, for example. Thus it was arranged, although Tommy sensed considerable nervousness in the Navy Department about how he would fare. He did not usually like plays for press coverage—blah, he called them—but he was not the least bit opposed to this one. No doubt the press wanted to hear his story; "Let Hart Talk" was the title of an editorial in the *Washington Post* on the day of his press conference. The country was eager for news, any real news, about what was going on.

He was less happy with it on 12 March, when he actually had to face the lights, cameras, and questions, but the coverage and the comments by the navy's public relations officers indicated that he did a good job. He answered questions simply and straight-forwardly, he did not dodge issues, nor did he alibi for the per-formance of his fleet. In short, his remarks had the stamp of candor. For the navy, which at this point was getting very little positive coverage, Hart was a godsend. Not that all the papers were happy. The *Washington Post,* for instance, said it had hoped that Hart would do more to let people in on the overall picture in the Pacific. "No such light was shed," it groused. "He restricted himself mainly to the operations under his own command."[6]

From the navy's point of view, what Hart said was fine; at first, there was apparently some anxiety that he would say something damaging about either the Allies or the administration, an indi-cation of how little the public relations officers knew about Tommy Hart. He was willing to be outspoken inside the department either when speaking before the General Board, as he did on 12 March, or in conversation with Secretary Knox, but his sense of propriety did not allow for criticizing his commander in chief, his service, or his allies in the press. He even refused to be drawn into the debate over air power versus sea power. In his view the argument was "just plain silly." "Both ships and planes are needed," he said. He suggested that amphibious warfare, of which the hallmark was cooperation with continuous training together of the naval and air arms, was the warfare of the future in the Pacific.[7]

His candor, coupled with restraint, no doubt was a relief to many. It also showed that he was eminently suited for the role of "showing the flag" before various audiences. Interservice bickering over Pearl Harbor and over the general course of the war was still going on, and the idea of having the highest-ranking veteran run-ning interference for the navy was distinctly welcomed in the corridors of the Navy Department. Therefore, he soon found himself making radio talks, traveling to Chicago, and, horror of horrors, being considered as a kind of spokesman for the navy. Enough was enough. As he said, he never had been in love with the sound of his own voice and, while he agreed with Caroline that he owed it at least to himself to let people see he was not senile, no one was going to turn him into a public relations spe-cialist, a term he claimed he had never heard before.

He did consent to appear before the Senate Foreign Relations Committee, whose chairman at that time was Democratic Senator

Thomas T. Connally of Texas. Hart's immediate impression was that the chairman was hostile, while the Republicans on the committee scented that they might get some ammunition to use against the administration. Tommy carefully fashioned his replies so as not to conceal anything vital and at the same time not confirm Connally's prejudices, whatever they may have been, or play into the hands of the Republicans. It must have been a taxing hour and three-quarters, but when it was over he apparently had won seventeen valuable allies. King had convinced Roosevelt that, to protect Hart, a law should be passed allowing a three- or four-star admiral to retain that rank if he had held it for a year or more. Congress would have to agree and Hart had clearly done himself only good before the committee. Even before he arrived home, the *Army-Navy Journal* recommended that he be allowed to retain his four stars.[8] Most of the press presented him as a hero despite the questions that swirled about his removal from command. In that regard, the consensus seemed to be that, since he quite obviously was not seriously ill, he had been removed for "political" reasons. Still, some very cutting things were said. For example, Hanson W. Baldwin, military correspondent of the *New York Times*, commented that replacing the "old and ill" Admiral Hart would probably see the "defensive naval dispositions" that were responsible for U.S. "limited naval achievements" replaced by "more aggressive tactics."[9] But on that issue events served to mitigate the criticism.

On 25 February, Rear Admiral Doorman took a combined striking force out to intercept a reported Japanese landing expedition. Unable to find the enemy, he was returning to Surabaja on the morning of the twenty-seventh when he got word that the Japanese were nearing Bawean Island. He immediately ordered his five cruisers and nine destroyers to come about and prepare for battle. The Allied force was outnumbered, outgunned, and without air cover. The result, therefore, should not be surprising. In what became known as the Battle of the Java Sea, Doorman lost two cruisers and one destroyer, and another cruiser was damaged. Thus ended any realistic prospects of Allied interference with the Japanese advance. As if that were not bad enough, in attempting to escape, all three of his remaining cruisers, including Hart's *Houston*, were sunk.[10]

Many senior officers, Stark, King, and Hepburn included, were pushing for the bestowal on Hart of permanent rank of full admiral, as "my reward," Tommy said with a touch of irony. After a few fits and starts, the "honorables" on Capitol Hill devised the required legislation and Thomas C. Hart became a permanent full admiral by act of Congress. That did not quiet all his detractors, but it helped. The citation that accompanied his second Distinguished Service Medal reads in part:

> For exceptionally meritorious service as Commander in Chief, U.S. Asiatic Fleet. In that position of great responsibility, he exercised sound judgment and marked resourcefulness in dealing with the difficult military and diplomatic situation prevailing prior to December 7, 1941, and upon our entry into war with Japan, disposed and handled the Asiatic Fleet in a manner which left nothing to be desired. . . . His conduct of the operations of the Allied Naval Forces in the Southwest Pacific Area during January and February 1942 was characterized by unfailing judgment and sound decision coupled with marked moral courage in the face of discouraging surroundings and complex associations.

As Hart saw it, these words were well and carefully drawn and the award was ample for what he had done. His only regret, and he said he was really "hot" about this, was that time was not allowed for getting Caroline to the White House for the presentation.

The time was coming, though, when the Navy Department would have to decide what to do with him. He was busy enough; he was making speeches, writing his Narrative of Events which, since many official papers were lost, proved to be an invaluable record of what took place in the Far East, and writing, somewhat against his better judgment but at the urging of Secretary Knox, a two-part article for the *Saturday Evening Post*.[11] In that article, only those familiar with the facts could discern clues to some of Hart's true feelings.

He was, he thought, something of an enigma to "them," that is to say to the powers in Washington. He had more or less called their bluff. They said he was relieved because of ill health, yet here he was alert, spry, and full of sound advice. Helfrich, on the other hand, had lost the final battle before the Japanese invasion of Java, losing in the process the *Houston*, the destroyer *Edsall*, the tender *Langley*, the tanker *Pecos*, and gunboat *Asheville*, all remnants of the Asiatic Fleet. The press was suggesting that probably Hart would have done better, and those who saw him or read about him, for which there was ample opportunity because of Knox's desire that he engage in public relations, would at least have to wonder whether that might not be so. Since King privately told him that he had opposed his removal, which was dictated from the

White House for "political" reasons, Hart could assume the "professional" navy was still on his side.[12] Because there were many nonpolitical things that needed to be done, his peers thought his experience should be put to good use.

The solution was to send him back to the General Board. In August he reported to the chairman of the board, Admiral Hepburn. As a full admiral, Tommy outranked his old friend and former commanding officer, Japy Hepburn, so he could have stood on his dignity and requested the chairmanship, but he saw no need, personal or other, for thus humiliating Hepburn, and was content to serve as just another member. *Content* may be too strong a word. He expected to be retired; when he learned that he was to stay on the active list he hoped to be sent to submarines. When that was blocked, he gladly sidestepped a job proposed by Undersecretary of the Navy James V. Forrestal handing out "Navy E's." As interpreted by Hart, this "incentive" awards program was intended to inspire lazy workers to do what they should be doing anyhow, so he demurred. For these reasons he was content to serve on the General Board, although what he really wanted to do was get actively involved in the war in the southwest Pacific. Thus, three years, innumerable miles, a lost campaign, and if not a triumphal at least not an embarrassing homecoming later, he was back at the General Board.

The board was not engaged in vital work during this period. It still had a say on ship design and, since masses of ships were being called for, it was kept busy during late 1942 and early 1943. In this area, Tommy had some real credibility. Those 6,000-ton cruisers he favored back in the late thirties were coming into service. Their performance trials and their strong antiaircraft capability brought forth enthusiastic comment, so the father of the cruisers popularly known as the Hart class was in favor as a ship-design specialist.

Assignment to the board required that Hart be in Washington and that meant apartment-hunting in a city gone war-crazy. Finally, he found smallish accommodations which he shared with Isabella, who was working at the Navy Department as a cryptanalyst. Ros had resigned from his job in Hartford and wangled a naval reserve commission, which eventually landed him in the Atlantic on anti-submarine duty. Brownie entered the navy as a WAVE. Tom had various assignments, and ended up in command of a destroyer escort in the Pacific. Harriet came down with tuberculosis, so at this point she and Caroline were the only members of the Hart family not engaged in government activities. Actually Caroline was fully occupied in trying to turn parts of the dairy operation in Sharon into a food-producing truck farm. Among other things, this meant that there were often long separations when either crisis or routine required her presence in Connecticut.

Tommy did a considerable amount of traveling. The functions of the General Board were such that its members were often detached on special duty. In Hart's case, this meant frequent trips to shipyards for on-site inspection of production facilities. While on those trips, he was often sought out by the press who seldom were disappointed, for he answered their questions, if not colorfully, at least fully. As things developed, he had not been entirely successful in getting out of making "Navy E" presentations. When plants in Connecticut were to be so honored, Hart, who by this time had established residency in Sharon, was given that detail. He never did come to enjoy the short speeches, publicity, and hoopla that went with these ceremonies, but the occasions did serve to get him before large numbers of the Connecticut electorate with results that only later became clear.

All in all, these months in Washington were pretty dull; after a hectic start things slowed into a plodding routine. Hepburn's monologues to the General Board were tiresome; then Admiral Sexton, one of the better brains, retired. There seemed little pur-

Members of the General Board, 1942–1945. Left to right, Admirals Edward C. Kalbfus, Arthur J. Hepburn, Thomas C. Hart, and Claude C. Bloch, and Captain William D. Chandler. Courtesy of Mrs. T. C. Hart

pose in meeting just to be meeting or traveling just to be traveling. Hart's diary during this period proves that he was active, but generally unhappy with the manner in which his talents were being used. Often there were reminders of unhappy experiences in the Far East. Queen Wilhelmina of the Netherlands insisted on award- ing him the Order of Orange and Nassau with swords, which he thought rather odd considering the "shoddy" way the Dutch in Java treated him. When Admiral Helfrich showed up at the Dutch embassy in Washington, so as not to cause an incident, Hart went to greet him: the Dutch diplomats who were there looked at him "sort of cross-eyed" because by then they knew that he had tried to sidestep Queen Wilhelmina's decoration. Wavell also came to town and invited Tommy to visit him at the British embassy. He did. As Tommy put it, this was a time for "making the best of things," and that is precisely what he did. The hardest part was corresponding or otherwise communicating with the relatives of men in the Asiatic Fleet who contacted him for help or just for information. Overwhelmingly the letters were favorable regarding his performance or in reporting comments made about him by his men, but a few were bitter or recriminating. It made no difference; he answered all requests and wasted little time trying to defend himself.

Nineteen forty-two turned into 1943 with the tide of war shift- ing as the months went by. In February Guadalcanal was finally won. MacArthur, Commander in Chief, Southwest Pacific, began his advance up New Guinea. At Tarawa the marines learned bloody lessons about amphibious war. Meanwhile Tommy fidgeted in Washington. Numerous publishers approached him about writ- ing a book on the opening stages of the war. To all he gave a negative reply. He had read too many memoirs after the first world war that just turned into apologies; furthermore, he believed it was immoral to make money out of service for which he had already been paid. In any case, he was not sure that men in high places saw things quite "straight." Everything was colored by re- sults or self-interest. No, Tommy did not want to write about the war; he badly wanted to be back in it.

In early 1944 he got his wish—almost. As the campaign in the Pacific picked up momentum, some legally inclined minds in the Navy Department realized that important witnesses with infor- mation about the opening of the war were being jeopardized on the battlefront. Therefore, late in January Admiral King ap- proached him about taking on a tedious, sensitive assignment. As initially envisioned, the object was to assuage, in part at least, the desire of Rear Admiral Kimmel, who had been summarily dismissed from his post for his role in the Pearl Harbor debacle, for a court-martial which he hoped would clear his name. The navy was not eager to hold such a court while the war was going on. It feared that the proceedings would degenerate into a brawl in which reputations would be damaged, and would do nothing to improve the reputation of the U.S. military for interservice cooperation. Furthermore, in such a brawl there would be plenty of opportunity for political backbiting that might embarrass the current administration, and for any investigation to be complete it would have to include reference to classified information, most notably information on cryptanalysis. Balancing these factors was a desire to be fair to a fellow officer—Kimmel. There also was the point that, with the campaign in the Pacific heating up, there was a chance that some vital witnesses might be lost along with the information they could provide. The solution was to establish a "board" to take testimony from and cross-examine witnesses who were on the war front so that a record could be compiled for future use. The board was to be composed of Hart, who was chairman, Captain Jesse R. Wallace, USN, and Lieutenant William M. Whittington, Jr., USNR, who were to serve as legal counsel, and Ship's Clerk Charles O. Lee, USNR, as reporter. It was, to say the least, a large job for a small board.

Tommy was not sure at first whether or not he liked the task ahead; its enormity was one thing, the fact that it was "full of dynamite" was another.[13] If the "dynamite" was sensitivity concerning the issues involved, his anticipation was borne out when Admiral Kimmel came to Washington shortly after Hart officially accepted the task. Kimmel, aged but still forceful, was "bitter toward the powers that be," felt as though he had been treated "unjustly," and was "very distrustful." He was even somewhat distrustful of this board, one of whose objectives was to protect his interest. He would talk only with Hart, off the record, and seemed to be stalling. Secretary Knox's order setting up the board expressly stated that Kimmel, as an interested party, had the right to be "present, to have counsel, to introduce, examine, and cross examine witnesses, to introduce matter pertinent to the examination and to testify or declare in his own behalf at his own request."[14] Nevertheless, Kimmel, who stated he had full confidence in Hart, would not cooperate. At first his lawyers stalled for time, but on 6 March he informed Hart that he would not participate;

he gave no reasons for his attitude, so Tommy was advised to go ahead without him.

The actual taking of testimony began on 7 March with Admiral Claude C. Bloch in the witness chair. Bloch commanded the U.S. Fleet from 1939 to 1940, but in December 1941 was commandant of the Fourteenth Naval District, commandant of the navy yard at Pearl Harbor, and commander of the Hawaiian Sea Frontier. Admiral Bloch was followed by Rear Admiral William Ward Smith, who had been chief of staff to Kimmel; Rear Admiral Walter S. DeLany, assistant chief of staff for readiness and operations officer for Kimmel; and Rear Admiral Arthur C. Davis, Kimmel's fleet aviation officer. The pattern of procedure by this point was fairly well set. Hart and his counsel acted as examining officers, attempting to allow the witnesses to talk as freely as they liked on the subject at hand. There was cross-examination of the witnesses but, without Kimmel or his representatives present, there was nothing approaching an adversary proceeding. Within four days of beginning, Hart believed that the board was getting "highly important testimony" that would likely be "useful to someone who is bent on writing an honest-to-God history of this war."[15] It is difficult to disagree with this judgment. The issues emerging were those that loomed large in later, full-blown investigations of what happened at Pearl Harbor. How much warning was there and was it sufficient? How close was cooperation between the army and the navy, and why was it not closer? What was the degree of preparedness and why was it not higher?

One thing Hart soon learned—he was happier when he conducted the examinations himself. Whittington was pretty good, but Wallace he found a bit ponderous. So, for the next two weeks Hart did much of the examining. By the end of that time they had heard from witnesses in the area of Washington, D.C., who were thought to have relevant information. The next step was to go to the Pacific and interview witnesses on or near the battlefront. This phase of the process kicked off on 27 March when Hart's little cavalcade left for San Francisco. Hart informed Kimmel of this movement, advising him that since he and his colleagues did not know exactly where their witnesses were to be found, he would be unable to keep him informed as to the time and place of meetings.[16]

With that rather vague indication of things to come, it was off to war. The first stop, appropriately enough, was Pearl Harbor, where Hart was the guest of Admiral Nimitz. There were innumerable other old friends, many of whom Hart had helped to "rear," scattered around the sprawling, pulsating naval establishment on Oahu. The social contacts and memories of when he was in Hawaii before the first war filled him with nostalgia and rekindled his desire to play a more active role in this war. Instead, he settled down to interview more officers. At Pearl the most important witnesses were Captain Edwin T. Layton, an astute intelligence officer who reminded Hart of Rosy Mason, and Vice Admiral Richmond Kelly Turner, who was Stark's war plans officer in 1941. Hart himself handled Turner (as well as anyone could), and found him to be an extremely good witness. Turner, considered by many to be one of the best minds in the navy, naturally supported Stark's actions in late 1941, partly because, basically, Stark was acting in concert with Turner's advice. Turner said he had fully anticipated a Japanese attack, but against the British in Malaya or the Philippines. The warnings that were sent to Pearl Harbor, however, he deemed sufficient to have alerted Kimmel if Kimmel had interpreted them as broadly as Turner thought he should have. Specifically, he did not believe that the Office of the Chief of Naval Operations should get involved in how a commander reacted tactically to general strategic information or instructions.[17] Turner also revealed that it was he who added to Stark's message of 27 November 1941 the phrase "this dispatch is to be considered a war warning." That phrase he regarded as sufficient to alert all detachments "to act in every way as if we were actually at war. . . ."[18] Turner's overall testimony was hurtful to Kimmel's case. It was Turner's view that Stark did everything necessary and, even though Washington was wrong about the place at which the Japanese blow would fall, there should have been no doubt that war was coming momentarily.

After six days at Pearl, Hart's team took off in a cargo-laden plane bound for Tarawa. On 6 April they arrived at that island so dearly won from the Japanese by Kelly Turner's adolescent amphibious force and the 2nd Marine Division. Hart cleaned up, had dinner, and took off for a rendezvous with the battleships *Iowa* and *New Jersey*, which Admiral Raymond A. Spruance had brought to base at Majuro after pounding the Japanese in the Palaus. Among the witnesses to interview was Captain John L. McCrea, who had brought him news of current war plans back in January 1941. After completing his court's business Tommy got back into a PBY for the return trip to Tarawa.

Everywhere he went he was struck by the massive buildup going on. As soon as an island was taken the Seabees set their giant earth-moving machines fighting against the coral and palms. It was impressive, yet he could see that island after island was being spoilt as a "South Sea Gem" and the lives of the natives were being changed forever. "Poor devils," wrote Hart, "they had nothing to do with this war which is on and all around them."[19]

The next day it was on to where the U.S. offensive had started, Guadalcanal. Personal memories were painfully present there because he could look out the windows of his quarters and see where his old friend Rear Admiral Daniel J. Callaghan had died on the bridge of his ship in the titanic cruiser action on the night of 12–13 November 1942. The war had moved on past Guadalcanal, as the nightly movies, plush accommodations, and extensive facilities testified. The island now served as a key link in the navy's logistics chain and as a rest and recreation area. Almost anything was available on Guadalcanal, including testimony from two witnesses whose contributions a "skeptical" Tommy Hart considered valuable. The more important of those witnesses was Rear Admiral Theodore S. Wilkinson, who as former director of naval intelligence, had copious information on the processes by which information was collected and distributed. Unfortunately, since information regarding the breaking of the Japanese diplomatic code was still a closely held secret, there were obvious gaps in Wilkinson's account.

Hart spent 9 April at Espiritu Santo, where he was flown by Lieutenant Commander James C. Nolan, who was with Patrol Wing 10 when Hart had the Asiatic Fleet. The highlight of this stop was a long visit with his son Tom. Lieutenant Hart was commanding officer of the destroyer escort *Osterhaus* and, from all the admiral could tell, was doing a fine job of it. Throughout their visit young naval reserve officers kept popping in to ask questions of Tom. Noting this, the admiral said to one of them something to the effect that they seemed to rely heavily on Tom's advice. "You know what we call him in the flotilla?" the man asked. "No," said Tommy. "We call him 'The Naval Officer.' He's the only regular in these six vessels, and that's fifty-odd officers, which means that he is the only thoroughly trained officer of the lot. So we all have to come and ask The Naval Officer."[20]

This pleased the old man no end, as did the impression that his son's "outlook and thoughts for the future are very sane—if progressive."[21] It seemed as though all the pain of getting him through the academy was paying off; he was a credit to his family, his service, and his country.

Tom put to sea the next day, and the Hart team moved on. Its next stop was Nouméa. Almost as he got off the plane, Admiral William F. "Bull" Halsey, Jr., whisked him off to the Beach Club for a swim. Hart's impression was that things were pleasant in Nouméa, the comforts including some very pretty New Zealand girls who worked on the base. Halsey, who was in command of the carriers at the time of Pearl Harbor, turned out not to be a very good witness. He was more of a "fighting man," wrote Tommy. More productive was Vice Admiral John H. Newton, Jr., who in December 1941 was Commander, Cruisers, Scouting Force. He told of a secret mission to Australia and New Zealand he had been sent on in March of 1941. In that instance, Newton took a division of cruisers and a squadron of destroyers out of Pearl under conditions so secret that even Admiral Kimmel did not know the purpose of the voyage, nor did Newton ever learn, although he suspected it had been initiated at the request of the State Department. He also took a task force comprising the carrier *Lexington*, two cruisers, and five destroyers out of Pearl on 5 December 1941. The mission was to ferry planes to Midway, but it took him within striking distance of where the Japanese launched their attack on Pearl Harbor. When questioned, he said that he felt that he had not been kept adequately briefed on the war warning messages or other indications of seriously heightened tensions between the United States and Japan. The Roberts Commission, which had conducted an investigation immediately after the attack, missed these points, so here at least Hart felt he was augmenting the historical record.[22]

The visit also gave him a chance to get an overview of the navy's strategy for the Pacific area, at least as seen through Halsey's eyes. Hart liked Halsey and was dismayed when he learned that there were moves afoot to break up his fine fighting fleet and go forward with a three-pronged advance on the Philippines and Japan. Hart saw MacArthur's hand in some of it, but also thought that the "powers" in Washington were playing too prominent a role. "Success will probably ensue," he wrote, "but it will be at the cost of much more time, money—and perhaps more lives as well." In Hart's view it was a "plain crime on the part of 'they' and it's hard for one who realizes it to sleep."[23] He got what sleep he could,

however, and that was not too easy since Halsey had as a pet some
big ground bird that started waddling around the grounds barking
like a dog as soon as the sun came up.

The next stop was back at Pearl Harbor where he was again the
guest of Admiral Nimitz. He interviewed several witnesses at
Pearl, but Hart had decided that he and his board had just about
worked the field over. He did welcome the opportunity to talk
with old friends like Admiral Spruance, with whom he was often
compared. "Physically we *decidedly* are [alike]," Hart wrote, but
otherwise he could not see the similarity "in that *his* most predominant quality is shyness and reserve." Hart also got to travel
around the base a little and visit the spot where he had established
the first "hand-made" submarine base. In recognition of this pioneering work, Nimitz had had the central plaza named Hart
Circle. Such recognition and the nostalgia induced by old haunts
and familiar faces was almost as good as being a part of the war,
but not quite.

When he ran out of witnesses who could be really contributory,
Tommy felt he should get back to the States. As much as he
wanted to see Caroline, he hated to leave the war front where he
had gotten an opportunity to participate, at least vicariously, in
the action. But by 18 April he was back in San Francisco, having
covered some 20,000 miles in less than four weeks. He gave an
interview to the press, and tried to discount the theory, prevalent
at the time, that drinking may have contributed to the blunders
at Pearl. Then it was back to Washington where he reported to
Admiral King. There still were some witnesses to be included in
the proceedings and, since King seemed satisfied with the way
things were going, Hart pushed on to the end. The inquiry officially concluded on 15 June 1944, after forty-two days of formal
testimony. The Hart board recorded the testimony of forty witnesses and accepted into evidence some forty-two informational
exhibits; in total there were almost six hundred pages of printed
material. Hart freely admitted that there were a few other witnesses he could have called; however, it was his conviction that
he had gotten all necessary information to fulfill his orders. By
the time he completed his task he clearly sensed that others—with
political motives—were going to want to keep the pot boiling. He
was relieved to be getting out of it.

But he was not getting out of it. Admiral Kimmel had called
for and the navy had agreed to hold a formal court of inquiry on
the Pearl Harbor attack. One of the interested parties to appear

before the court was Admiral Stark, who was serving at this point
as Commander, Naval Forces, Europe. Betty Stark asked Tommy
to serve as his counsel and there was little Tommy could do other
than agree. Not that Hart wanted to become further involved; on
the contrary, "it's distasteful and I fret at being thus occupied,
rather than at something or other which I conceive that I might
do and think much more important." He wanted to be involved
in the conflict that was going on rather than rake over the history
of events long past. It must have been ironic for him to be defending his former commanding officer against charges that he had
not kept Kimmel adequately informed, when Hart had had the
same feelings himself.

The immediate practical problems were that preparing for the
hearings took many hours and that Stark's acuity did not improve
as those hours dragged by. He was "hard to handle" because he
"tends to wander off into unimportant bypaths all the time and
fags himself instead of sticking to the main issue."[24] That was
during preparation for the witness stand by Hart and Stark's lawyer; on the witness stand he was worse. Hart found that Stark did
not do well under cross-examination—he "is rather puzzle-witted,
doesn't watch the track or even stay on it himself." Hart was
disappointed; Stark was not well, worn out, Tommy thought, by
the strain of wartime responsibility, and Kimmel had a sharp lawyer
who skewered him at every turn. A week after the inquiry began,
Hart was worrying that censure of Stark seemed not unlikely. Part
of the problem was the composition of the court. It was made up
of Admirals Orin G. Murfin, Edward C. Kalbfus, and Adolphus
Andrews, two of whom, and he didn't say which two, were "not
very promising as regards their judicial ability."[25]

By 21 August he found himself even less pleased by the "brutal"
treatment to which Stark was being subjected. Tommy was "developing a rather *general* Contempt of Court!!"[26] This attitude was
not improved when he was ordered to go back to Pearl Harbor
and interview several more witnesses. That took ten days and,
while personally interesting, accomplished little, as far as he could
see. What he called the "Battle of Washington" resumed upon his
return and ran through 27 September. On that day Tommy made
a closing argument and summed up his view:

> It looks to me as if "my client" is in for criticism, on one vul-
> nerable point in particular, but there is no telling what this Court
> will "find." Two are basically pretty ignorant and one of them, I

think, is quite untrustworthy to boot. He indicates that he is out
for revenge on Stark, because he did not get elevated sufficiently.
Well, I'm glad it is over with.[27]

Tommy's anticipation proved correct. The court found that Admiral Harold R. Stark

> failed to display the sound judgement expected of him in that he
> did not transmit to Admiral Kimmel ... during the very critical
> period 26 November to 7 December important information which
> he had regarding the Japanese situation and, especially, in that, on
> the morning of 7 December 1941, he did not transmit immediately
> the fact that a message had been received which appeared to indicate
> that a break in diplomatic relations was imminent, and that an attack
> in the Hawaiian area might be expected soon.[28]

That was a strong indictment, but it was softened by the court's
conclusion that "no offenses have been committed nor serious
blame incurred on the part of any person or persons in the naval
service."

Interestingly enough, Tommy made no entry in his diary regarding the verdict. Despite the fact that no charges were brought
against Stark, this judgment left him sullied but not condemned.
It cast a pall over his remaining career, and even over his life. Hart
later said that he thought Stark had been too harshly judged,
particularly since no such blame was attached to his counterpart,
the army chief of staff, George C. Marshall. For now, however,
the issue was closed.

By December 1944 it appeared that Hart's active military career
was drawing to a close. There were fewer and fewer important
duties occupying his time and it was quite obvious that his talents
would not be put to use in the victory drive shaping up in the
Pacific. He was being edged into the shadows on the periphery
of the war; it seemed to him that the decline in his status had been
determined, but it would be slow; it would be relatively painless.
On 1 January 1945 he decided, therefore, to change the manner
of maintaining his diary: he would make no more daily entries
because he doubted that his remaining years were likely to bring
"anything of importance to anyone other than myself; and my
immediate family." Thereafter, he would write "only when events
have transpired, developments have occurred, or perhaps thoughts
are entertained which I feel are very well worth recording."

Twenty-seven days later there occurred an event that met at
least one of those criteria. On 28 January, Ellery Allen, a repre-

sentative of Connecticut's Governor Raymond E. Baldwin, met him in New York City by appointment to ask whether he would consider filling out the term of Connecticut's Republican senator, Francis T. Maloney, who had died on 16 January 1945. A hasty conference with Caroline was called, after which Hart gave a confidential, guardedly affirmative response. Since it appeared that the navy had little of significance for him to do, he and Caroline had agreed that he would be far better employed in the U.S. Senate. However, he did not want his name batted around in the political controversy brewing in Connecticut; Governor Baldwin could privately test out the idea of Hart for senator, but all should remain very tentative.

The political controversy arose over the constitutional question of whether Baldwin, a Republican, should appoint the new senator or whether the state legislature, in which the Democrats had a majority, should call for an election to fill the unexpired term. A good deal hinged on whom Baldwin wanted to nominate: if it were a Republican plow horse or someone controversial like Congresswoman Clare Boothe Luce, Hart's old friend from Manila days, the legislature would balk. After seven days of rampant speculation, it became clear to Hart that his imposition of secrecy was not fair to Baldwin, so he authorized the governor to broadcast his proposal.

On 6 February Baldwin dropped his bombshell. Declaring that it was not time for partisanship, he proposed that Hart, "one of the outstanding Naval heroes of this war" who had a "wide grasp of international affairs," be Connecticut's new senator.[29] With his name now out, endorsements quickly followed. Clare Boothe Luce led the list. She said "no man available" knew more about "America's post war needs in both the Atlantic and the Pacific," while at the same time being "a man of considerable vision."[30] Democrats countered by speculating that Luce was actually thinking of the prospects of a woman who would benefit from having Hart hold the seat for her until 1946. Luce denied the insinuation while the papers generally opined, as did the *Hartford Courant*, that the Democrats "could not afford to give the impression that they opposed the appointment of a man of Admiral Hart's standing and reputation."[31] The Democratic leadership seemed to agree. Said one: "He is such an outstanding man that we are sure that his views are all right. . . . He is a veteran of three wars and he must be all right."[32] The fact of the matter was that Baldwin had pulled off a coup of significant proportions that caught the Democrats flatfooted. No one knew anything about Hart's views on anything but naval matters. Because he had traveled about the state presenting Navy E's, he had fairly wide name recognition, but he was not affiliated with any party. So, partially on the grounds that there was nothing on Hart's record to oppose, the Democrats acceded to the governor's initiative. The major papers lent editorial support to the selection and thus a political career was launched, even though most observers were not sure whether he was a Republican or a Democrat.

There was not much doubt on that point in Hart's mind. He did have some misgivings about his abilities to pick up a new career at the age of sixty-seven as well as some pangs of nostalgia at laying aside the uniform he had worn for almost fifty-two years. He could see a lot of work ahead but was appreciative of what had been done for him and "fully realized that these two years will mean a much better end to Thomas Hart's career than would otherwise have been the case. My lucky star came back!"[33]

Few Naval Academy graduates had ever sat in the U.S. Congress. Thus, when Hart entered the chamber on 15 February, the third anniversary of his removal as ABDA commander, he became one of a small band. Numerous army officers had served in the Congress and in the White House, but naval officers seemed to move in different circles. In the case of submarine officers, maybe being members of the "silent service" automatically disqualified them. As for Hart, he had never even been in the chamber when the Senate was in session. He announced, however, shortly before entering, that he would sit on the Republican side of the aisle because "there was more room" there.

Actually, Hart was a Republican by conviction. Therefore, on most issues he would be opposing the senior senator from Connecticut, Brian McMahon. This would be especially true in domestic affairs where Hart looked with disfavor on the big spender, New Deal, left-leaning, labor-oriented policies of the Roosevelt administration which he thought were leading the country to financial ruin. On foreign policy, a subject in which he promised to take an "intense interest," he would sometimes find himself on the same side as the Democrats. It was his firm conviction, for instance, that there should be a world security organization in which the United States should play a leading role. He also opposed the permanent partition of Germany.[34] On the other hand, he did not wish to get too involved in questions of national security because he feared that he would be seen as simply a spokesman for the navy. To make it crystal clear that he was not, he determined to cut himself off from naval society while in Washington so that like Caesar's wife he would not only be, but seem, incorruptible. He asked not to be put on the Naval Affairs Committee for the same reason. Not that the Republican leadership took either his wishes or his talents too much into consideration, anyhow. His assignment to committees on commerce, small business, and civil service were based on considerations of "seniority, political and sectional balance," and so on; not at all on his qualifications or lack of them.[35] Well, as he said, he was the "lowliest" of the senators, the "veriest plebe possible," so he had scant grounds for complaint about his assignments.

The immediate need was to get prepared to do whatever had to be done in that Senate chamber. He was being thrown in in the middle of the session; his colleagues had had time to study the issues and get themselves prepared in the months preceding the Christmas recess; he had to catch up as things were going forward. He decided to pay particularly close attention to the attitudes and actions of the senator sitting next to him, Leverett Saltonstall, a Republican from Massachusetts, to whom he became quite attached professionally as well as personally. Staff was a problem at first, but he solved that by simply keeping all of Maloney's people. Maloney's papers, accumulated over almost ten years, posed another difficulty, but he solved that by getting rid of all of them. Still, he found that the trouble with being a senator was that there was more to do than time to do it in, and consequently he always had a feeling of being behind. "I'm in a high speed outfit," he wrote, "things happen fast at times, right in the midst of the eternal flow of oratory, and one has to be alert." President Roosevelt addressed a joint session of Congress on 1 March 1945 after returning from meeting with Churchill and Stalin at Yalta. Hart thought it was nice of him to come "but it's hard to find anything in the address which we did not already know!" Later events proved there was a lot about the Yalta Conference that Hart did not know, or like. Next came the nomination of Henry A. Wallace for secretary of commerce. Hart was one of only ten Republicans to vote "aye"; "I couldn't do otherwise," he wrote. Obviously he was not a captive Republican. Then, a little over a month after entering the Senate he made his maiden speech. In this case he again supported FDR by speaking in favor of a war manpower act that would provide for a form of universal military training. It will be recalled that Hart did not like speech-making, he even promised himself upon entering the Senate never to speak for more than fifteen minutes, so he had to feel deeply on the subject before he would get to his feet. The reception of his effort was positive, but he reiterated to his diary his intention to "keep quiet unless I have something to say that will be worth saying and worth listening to."

A few days later he reached a momentous decision. He would not be a candidate for any other public office. Having been in the Senate long enough to know his mind, he decided he should let Governor Baldwin in on his thoughts. To keep his political effectiveness as a senator from being totally vitiated, he asked the governor to keep his intentions secret until approximately a year hence. It took just two months for Tommy to be convinced that he certainly was "no politician."[36]

Meanwhile the war was raging to its conclusion. In March the American First Army had crossed the Rhine at Remagen; in April the Russians began battering Berlin; and on 8 May the conflict in Europe ended. There was still bitter fighting ahead in the Pacific. After absorbing heavy marine losses and substantial ship damage at the hands of Japanese kamikazes off Iwo Jima in February, the American offensive moved on to Okinawa. Here, the amphibious war reached its climax as marines from the 1st and 6th divisions were joined by soldiers from the 7th and 96th infantry divisions who poured ashore under gunfire support provided by the Fifth Fleet. Japanese suicide planes took their heavy toll again, as dedicated oriental warriors sacrificed themselves as of old. In another type of warfare Hart's favorite weapon, the submarine, was running out of targets, so successful had it been in 1944. In October of 1944 U.S. submarines sank sixty-eight Japanese ships for a total of 328,843 tons. In April 1945, they sank only eighteen merchant ships for a bag of 60,696 tons. Targets were getting so scarce that in June U.S. submarines resorted to a daring mission into the Inland Sea where they preyed on some of the few remaining Japanese merchant ships. After the rocky start they had, it was gratifying for Hart to see the submariners, many of whom he still considered his "young men," finishing on such a high note.

Fighting out there in the Pacific were Hart's two sons: Roswell, a lieutenant in the naval reserve, was in a minesweeper, and Tom, a lieutenant commander, was commanding the destroyer *Bullard*. After participating in Operation Iceberg off Okinawa, the *Bullard* withdrew to a rear area. Rest would not be enough for her young commanding officer. Tom Hart was grievously ill with what was diagnosed as leukemia myelogenous. For the past several months he had not been well, but had neither realized the extent of his illness nor been willing to take the time for proper treatment. During some of the later actions, he commanded from a cot he ordered placed on the bridge.

On 9 June, while on the floor of the Senate, Hart was informed that his son's condition was grave. The navy was flying Tom back to the West Coast as soon as transportation was available. He arrived on the twelfth and two days later the senator was advised that Tom was not responding to treatment. Caroline and Tommy caught the first available navy plane west, arriving just in time to be with their son as he died. It was a shattering blow. "The first person that I have ever seen or heard gasp his life out in a bed was my much loved son," he wrote. Tommy could not bring himself to acceptance; he rebelled, obviously in vain, against the horrible truth. The constantly recurring thought and haunting theme was why Tom at twenty-eight and not him at sixty-eight. This is, of course, a common reaction, but for Tommy with his sensitivities about age and health it was especially poignant. How ironic that it should be his son, not himself, who would physically collapse while in command. Then there was disappointment that if death had to come to a warrior it had not come in battle rather than against such an unfair foe. How much better had he died in the "glory of combat." But always, always, there was the loneliness. Tom was a "most satisfactory son," one in whom he took great pride, one who had the qualities that made for success and "usefulness in this world." Moreover, Tommy had been looking forward to "understandingly talking things over with [him] during my remaining years." Now he had gone and Tommy would never get over missing him. Year after year there would be references to how the blow was just as fresh as it was on 17 June 1945. It was the great personal tragedy of Tommy Hart's life.

As sad as he was he realized that he must resume his Senate duties. On 17 July he even mustered the spirit to make one of the three real speeches he made in 1945. The issue was the Bretton Woods agreement by which the United States would be the chief underwriter of an international loan fund of $8.8 billion to stabilize currencies and facilitate payments across international boundaries. A companion piece was the establishment of the World Bank capitalized at $9.1 billion to provide loans to war-torn nations for reconstruction and economic development. Supporters of the principles embodied in the United Nations were pushing the Bretton Woods agreement as an essential economic counterpart to a world political organization. Hart was fully in favor of the UN, but he had serious reservations about Bretton Woods. As he explained in his Senate speech, his worry was that the United States, which had already seriously depleted its resources in a long war, would make commitments that would ultimately be beyond its capacity to meet. As he saw it, "the nations which look to us for further help would do well to be moderate in their demands upon us." They would also be wise, he thought, "if in their own interest they will try to aid us in maintaining our strength in all fields" because a powerful America was the hope of the world. Hart was supported in his views by such Republican stalwarts as Robert A. Taft of Ohio, and the Republican National Committee distributed several thousand copies of his speech. It was all for naught, as Hart and his conservative colleagues were buried in a 61–16 vote. That result did not bother Tommy Hart one bit; he continued to believe that his counsel on that issue was wise although he hoped he was wrong about America's future capacity to pay.

Then, a little over a week later, he made another speech. "I wouldn't have thought it was in the simple old sailor" to make what some described as a powerful speech, Hart wrote, but the record proves that it was. In this case he spoke primarily in favor of the United Nations, a subject on which he agreed with the majority. But Hart conditioned his approval with a characteristic warning. The United States should be cautious not to overextend itself; Britain was weak and war-weary; Japan remained to be defeated. In conclusion he returned to a familiar theme: "We shall ratify the charter and loyally fulfill our commitments thereunder. But above all we must remain a strong America. We must not break the back of America in ill judged attempts to carry the burdens of all the rest of the world."

Within days some of Tommy's worries were allayed. The atomic bomb, plus the tightening grip of U.S. military and naval might, was bringing the war in the Pacific to an end. Another power had entered the war in that area to help the United States carry its burdens—the Soviet Union. Tommy wrote that he was "rather inclined to like" the first part, the dropping of the bomb, because of the American lives he assumed would be saved thereby. Moreover, he had known about the Manhattan Project for more than a year and feared that the Germans might produce a fission weapon first. As to the second part of the equation? "I'm inclined to be sorry," he wrote, "that the Ruskies could not be kept out of the Pacific War."

When news of the peace finally arrived the Harts were enjoying a short vacation at Little Moose Lake. "Caroline and I became pretty emotional," he recorded. "At last C's tears came as she stood by Tom's picture after the first news came in. Unfortunately for her she had stayed dry eyed up [till] then!! Yes, the grand news of the end of the war had a strong note of sadness for Caroline and me—if only Tom could have survived. . . ." It made it no easier for them to be at Little Moose which throughout Tom's life had been a safe harbor, a playground, a retreat from the world. Memories of him running through the woods, fishing in the lakes, laughing by the fire, were all around them.

It was almost a relief to get back to Washington where, because he was a military expert, the reporters descended on Hart to get

Thomas C. Hart as U.S. senator from Connecticut, 1945–1947. Courtesy of *The Hartford Courant*

his views on the atomic bomb. In Senator Hart's opinion, the ideal thing would be to establish an international peacekeeping force under the UN and allow it to control the atomic bomb. The problem, of course, was that the Russians would be in the United Nations and he was dead set against sharing atomic secrets with them. Senator McMahon, a Democrat, differed with Hart in regard to relations with the Russians. Both senators from Connecticut were appointed to the newly created Senate Atomic Energy Committee, a move almost surely calculated to cancel out each other's vote on the matter of the Soviets. Appointment to such a prestigious, significant body was a real honor for Hart, and he approached the complicated work enthusiastically.

In addition to McMahon, who became chairman, the Democratic senators on the committee were Thomas T. Connally of Texas, Harry Flood Byrd of Virginia, Richard Russell of Georgia, Edwin C. Johnson of Colorado, Millard E. Tydings of Maryland, and Eugene D. Milliken of Colorado; the Republicans were Warren R. Austin of Vermont, Arthur H. Vandenberg of Michigan, and, of course, Thomas C. Hart of Connecticut. It was a strong committee charged with drawing up the legislation for control over and development of atomic energy. A primary concern for most of the members was maintaining the American atomic monopoly, at least until some way could be found to control atomic weapons through international agreement. They knew the Russians were working on the bomb and there was fear lest through careless talk or poor security the Russians, or anyone, for that matter, learn the secret of atomic fission. Unfortunately, of the ten members of the committee, only one had any experience with technological matters; except for Vandenberg, who was a newspaper man, the rest were lawyers. Tommy Hart, the sailor who had learned engineering and physics at the academy almost fifty years earlier, was the sole member with technological expertise. Consequently, it was he who was sometimes delegated to talk with the scientists on the secret, technical details. This was all very nice for Hart's ego, but the responsibility was worrisome; he even worried that he might talk in his sleep! Not a hint of his secret discussions can be found in his diaries.

Hart was appointed also to the Military Affairs Committee. At first he objected, saying that while it might not be as inappropriate for him to serve on this committee as it would be on the Naval Affairs Committee, he doubted the army would welcome his membership. Warren Austin, a close friend by this time, anticipated this objection and, as senior Republican on the committee, solicited the views of the secretary of war. The secretary responded that he would be pleased if Hart were to serve as a member of the committee, so he was forthwith assigned. On some issues Hart proved a valued ally of his Republican colleagues and supporters like Austin, on others he eschewed strict party lines. For instance, he strongly supported universal military training, one of President Harry S Truman's pet projects, and his longest Senate speech, delivered just before he retired, was in opposition to one of Senator Austin's pet projects.

By the fall of 1945 Hart was finding the strictly political aspects of his job rather hard to take. As he later recalled, "all those legislators view . . . questions through a sort of transparency, and written on that glass is a word: V-O-T-E-S. For some, those letters conceal little on the other side of the transparency and for some of them the glass transparency is a bit opaque most of the time." In November 1945 he recorded in his diary "I find I'm not at all on the Republican 'party line.' I am considerably incensed at the demagoguery which many Republicans Leaders (?) have been practicing on 'get the boys back'—irrespective of anything else—on the Pearl Harbor Inquiry, etc." On that latter issue, it was almost foreordained that he would be drawn into the fray, and when he was he did little to make those on the less crowded side of the Senate chamber happy.

Clearly Hart was his own man, as he proved in December when he spoke up on the question of a Palestinian homeland for the Jewish people. In this instance, he believed that for most senators the word *votes* pretty well covered the transparency to which he had referred. He wanted to help the Jews who had suffered under Hitler, he said, but he did not want the United States to undertake an obligation to impose a Jewish homeland on the people who lived in Palestine without accepting at the same time the reality that the Arabs, and the rest of the world's two hundred million Moslems, would resent it. He also anticipated that there would be war and he wondered whether the United States was really willing to go to war to protect a Jewish state. What he wanted was to help the Jewish "remnant" left in Europe to resume their lives in their native lands and to establish in Palestine a "democratic commonwealth . . . in which all men, regardless of race or creed, shall have equal rights." But if possible he wanted that done in a way that would avoid hostilities. Therefore, he offered an amendment to Senate Concurrent Resolution 44, which related to the opening of Palestine to free entry by Jewish immigrants. His amendment would have watered down the resolution and allowed the British, who controlled Palestine, greater latitude in determining immigration policy.

Regardless of what one may think of Hart's view, and his previous comments make it clear that he was not free of racial bias, it must be admitted that his action took courage. Although he knew that he could expect help from neither Republicans nor Democrats, he probably did not anticipate that he would be virtually alone, receiving only one vote in support of his amendment. However, the chances are that he would have offered it, anyway. When, years later, he looked over his speech, he commented that it did not appear to be a good one and "probably looked quite bad then." Furthermore, he did not conceal that, when presenting it, he was "more scared than I ever was on the Hill." Even friends like Robert Taft attacked him virulently, so it turned out to be a brave, but totally fruitless, effort.

He demonstrated those same qualities in a different way in February of 1946 when he was called before the committee investigating Pearl Harbor. As already mentioned, Hart was not fully in sympathy with the motives of the Republicans in conducting the investigation. He thought they were trying to rake up dirt to sully the reputation of President Roosevelt and thereby, indirectly, the Democrats. Hart had his own grievances against FDR, but he was not about to do anything to contribute to dragging the name of his former commander in chief through the mud. As he put it years later, "I had to forget that I was a Senator and figuratively put my uniform on again. . . ."[37] What that meant in practice was that he was going to be extremely careful not to provide his Republican friends with any information that could be used in a partisan way; in the process he became a somewhat "difficult" witness.

When Hart was called to testify on 18 February, Senator Homer Ferguson, a Republican from Illinois and a vocal critic of the administration, was eager to question him about the message he sent to Washington on 6 December 1941, which read: "Learn from Singapore we have assured [the] British armed support under three or four eventualities." It will be recalled that when he received word from Captain Creighton, the U.S. naval attaché in Singapore, to the effect that the United States had assured the British of assistance in certain contingencies, Hart was greatly disturbed and sent the message in question in order to find out what Washington had done without his knowledge. In "normal times," he wrote in his diary, such action by his superiors would have caused him to resign immediately; Senator Ferguson would get no inkling of those feelings. Senator Hart explained who Creighton was, but said he could recall few other details. Then this exchange took place:

Senator Ferguson: I am trying to find out if you had any information either from the British or from America as to what we were supposed to do if there was an attack on the British and not upon the American possessions.

Senator Hart: You mean did I have? You said "we." Do you mean "me?"

Senator Ferguson: So you were at that time seeking information as to what we intended to do because you had the information from the British; is that correct?

Senator Hart: No, no; I don't think so. Will you repeat the question?

(The question was read by the reporter.)

Senator Ferguson: When I use the word "we" I mean the country here, the Government here in Washington. The British had told you, as I understand it, that there were eventualities [sic] that we were to give them armed support.

Senator Hart: Well, you don't understand it correctly. I had not been told that by the British.

Senator Ferguson: You learned from Singapore. Was that an American that gave you that information?

Senator Hart: I have told you two or three times, Senator, it came from Capt. J. Creighton, United States Navy—

Senator Ferguson: Did he tell you where he—

Senator Hart: Who said that Brooke-Popham had told him—

Senator Ferguson: So the information from Brooke-Popham was the British, was it not?

Senator Hart: Yes.

Senator Ferguson: Or the Dutch?

Senator Hart:	British.
Senator Ferguson:	British. So the information did come from the British, isn't that correct, even though it was hearsay?
Senator Hart:	The information to whom?
Senator Ferguson:	To the captain that gave you the message.
Senator Hart:	Yes, yes.
Senator Ferguson:	Now, did this armed support include an attack upon the British or the Dutch, that one of the eventualities was an attack upon the British or the Dutch?
Senator Hart:	I have told you that I do not remember what those eventualities were.[38]

The senators got little out of Hart, although they did touch on a subject that made him distinctly nervous. Senator Ferguson had come across the dispatch in which the president ordered Hart to send out three small ships to form a "defensive information patrol." Hart believed at the time, and later, that that order was intended to provoke a confrontation, or an "incident," between the U.S. ships, which would be "sitting ducks," and the Japanese invasion force.[39] He did not, however, care to give that impression to sensation-hunting, partisan Republicans, so he was distinctly relieved when Ferguson was satisfied with his statement that he remembered few details about that incident also.[40] Later he learned that the committee counsel knew all about the three small ships but had not deigned to ask him for details. The admiral was "greatly relieved that I didn't get into the mess."[41] But, after most of one day on the stand, Hart was excused, and that was his last official contact with the Pearl Harbor Investigation, which, in his view, aside from being an exercise in political scandalmongering, was an attempt to resurrect "long dead cats."

During late 1945 and early 1946, influential Republicans in Connecticut had been urging Hart to run for a full term in the Senate. They told him that the nomination was his for the asking, but he had to give the word before they could proceed. Actually, he had already given the word back in April of 1945 when he wrote Governor Baldwin declining to run. That letter had been kept secret lest by too early an announcement Hart would decrease his potential effectiveness in the Senate. By February of 1946 he could resist the pressure no longer and announced that he would not be a candidate in the fall election. When queried about his reasons for declining, the sixty-eight-year-old Hart said: "For years it has been true that men of too advanced age have held seats in the United States Senate. I shall not be one of that category." The remark about age did not go down very well with the numerous septuagenarians in the Senate. Hart noted that several of his older colleagues "are still nice to me but are no doubt resentful." Not uncharacteristically he concluded, "well, I had to say that."

Now it was officially all downhill but Hart did not seem to slacken his pace. In fact, he seemed to be burdened with more and more committee work as the session moved along. The most important of his committees was still that on atomic energy, where the finishing touches were being put on proposed legislation. The Atomic Energy Act was signed into law by President Truman on 1 August 1946. It transferred control over all materials, production, facilities, research, and information on nuclear fission from military to civilian authority. The controlling body was to be the Atomic Energy Commission composed of five civilians nominated by the president and confirmed by the Senate. The act of 1946, modified in 1954, has been the basis for handling nuclear development in the United States, and was undoubtedly Hart's most important contribution during his term in the Senate.

For him personally the greatest challenge was in his opposition to the National Science Foundation Act. He said he entered the Senate with the idea of never holding the floor for more than fifteen minutes, but in April 1946 he did so for three or four times that long as he tried to block this "statism project." It was not that he opposed federal support for the basic sciences—quite to the contrary—but in his opinion the proposed legislation had grown out of all proportion to the task; too much money administered by too many people in too complex a bureaucracy. After two days of debate, he and his supporters were voted down, yet all was not lost. The House voted against the bill partly on the basis, Hart thought, of information that he and his fellows in the Senate had brought out.

His last significant act on the Senate floor came on 25 July when he rose to speak against merger of the armed forces. His position on this subject was somewhat of a disappointment to Senator Austin who, it will be recalled, had wanted him to serve on the Military Affairs Committee. Austin hoped that Hart would be with him in supporting unification of the services, but he was disappointed. Hart did not oppose the creation of a defense department, but he "definitely did not believe in beginning the *unification* with a *separation*," that is to say with the establishment of a separate air force. When Hart rose on 25 July his purpose was to speak "ostensibly" in opposition to a service merger, but he "made it the occasion to find plenty of fault with the Army Air Corps—the real villain in that play." It was a well-composed, well-delivered speech, a fitting valedictory effort.

The next week the Senate session came to an end. On 2 August Tommy Hart wrote in his diary: "Yes, it's over. I'm relieved and glad but I am carrying some nostalgia with me tonight. I've had a good time, lived in an extremely interesting atmosphere and come to be friends with some dozens of very likeable gentlemen. I shall miss my surroundings and my associates. And now to carry on, as a leisurely Senator, for about three more months and, at the same time, to begin turning myself out to pasture. It's a satisfactory feeling."

Although the second session of the 79th Congress ended in August 1946, Hart served until the end of the year. This meant he had plenty of time for closing the apartment, preparing to leave Washington for the final time, tying up loose ends at the office, and bidding adieu to his new friends in the Senate. For the most part, the Harts followed through on their intent to cut themselves free from naval society while Tommy was a senator. This was particularly difficult for Caroline because that society had been "home" to her for more than half a century. Tommy found plenty of new friends in the Senate and later said that as a group he liked his colleagues there as well as or better than any other men he had ever met. Naturally, on brief association the Harts did not become intimate with the nation's political movers and shakers, but Tommy's assessment of some of them is of interest.

Senator Alben W. Barkley of Kentucky, the Democratic majority leader: "I finished the two years with a very high regard indeed for him. He was a politician but statesmanship ruled most of the time and he was a powerful leader. His politicking on the Senate floor was always done with absolute fairness, insofar as the other side was concerned. Barkley played politics, yes, but he was never petty or small about anything."

Senator Robert A. Taft, Republican minority leader: "Senator Taft was mentally one of the most powerful men in the entire Senate. His brain was remarkable. . . . He was the most knowledgeable man, I think, but at the same time, that old saying, 'knowledge comes but wisdom lingers' was to a certain degree applicable to Bob Taft. He would know all about something, but he was not good at picking the right answer to a problem, his judgment was not commensurate with the rest of his ability."

Senator Arthur H. Vandenberg: "Vandenberg was a man of lesser mentality [than Taft], but he was an extremely intuitive man. Without a great deal of knowledge on a subject, he would reach up and pick the correct answer out of the air, where Taft might miss it."

Senator Harry Byrd: "For Senator Byrd, I had the highest regard possible. Politican, yes, and you hear around Washington all kinds of stories about the dirtiness of Virginia politics, and the horribleness of his machine. But knowing the man as I did, I never believed very much of it. Harry Byrd possesses and manifests very high political courage. What he thinks wrong he opposes and he has no hesitation in advocating unpopular issues. I often wish he could cast a dozen instead of just one vote."

Senator Theodore G. Bilbo, a Democrat from Mississippi, with whom Hart and George Radcliffe, a Democratic senator from Maryland, served on a subcommittee: Hart and Radcliffe were awaiting Bilbo in the committee room. When the Mississippian arrived, he declined to sit down and said: "You, George, know all about drawing up bills. None can do that any better. You, Tommy, you know all about shipping (the issue at hand), at least you know or should know more than the rest of us. I'm just a hillbilly who doesn't know much of anything and can't be of use on this job. Now, go ahead and chaw up the bill between you, and for God's sake don't disagree and call me in to vote a decision. I would be feeling that as a Democrat I had to vote with George and at the same time I might think that Tommy was right." Adds Hart, "Bilbo was no great shakes as a Senator, but one has to like his honesty."

The Republican Party leadership: "From the political angle my impression is that the Republicans have not been very clever. . . . I've not acquired unbounded respect for the Republican leadership on Capitol Hill. The democrats seem abler—even if warped."

In August 1946, the veteran Connecticut political reporter, Robert D. Byrnes, wrote a long analysis of Senator Hart in the *Hartford Courant*. It was his impression that the admiral was a conservative "if being in favor of reduction of government expenditures and opposed to the aggrandizement of the central government constitutes conservatism." Byrnes learned that the short-time senator worked as diligently on committee assignments as any veteran, a fact that was duly noted and appreciated by his colleagues. Senator Hart was known for his independence and the "dry, crisp character" of his mind. Most members of the press corps had to admit, however, that Hart did not make very "good copy," even though they thought that more men like Hart would make for a better Senate. For one thing, he was not political, nor did he try very hard to achieve that distinction. One clear indication of that was how he handled constituents who came to see him over some piece of legislation; he listened to what they had to say, then told them how he was going to vote, whether they liked it or not. Byrnes found out about Hart's style of politics quite early. After voting for Henry Wallace as secretary of commerce, Hart was surrounded by the press eager to know why the new Republican senator had broken ranks on his first important vote. Hart told them that, while he did not think Wallace was very capable, he had always believed that a president had a right to name his own cabinet. Wrote Byrnes: "After just winning a lot of democratic voters to your side by your independence, you blow it by knocking Wallace. You've got a lot to learn."

The correction that needs to be made here is that Hart actually did not have a thing to "learn." He knew exactly what he was doing—he had been conducting himself in much the same manner for some fifty years. In summation, Tommy Hart made the same kind of senator that he did sailor: direct, conscientious, independent, a trifle insubordinate, possibly a little narrow, but the soul of integrity. He worried a lot about the state of the nation, about foreign relations—especially relations with the Soviet Union—and although he favored the United Nations, he was essentially isolationist. He continued to oppose waste, bureaucracy, indulgence, and catering to special interests. He never ceased to be the "simple sailor" he prided himself on being; he preferred the title "Admiral" to "Senator." As he sometimes said, "it took me thirty years to earn the one—the other was given to me."

He had enjoyed the experience, though, and those who thought him to be so tough might have been surprised to see him conduct his own little retirement ceremony all by himself. One November day, just after election, he packed up what personal effects remained in his Senate office, carefully unscrewed the nameplate from the door, kissed the outside of the door, and slipped into full retirement.

So Tommy Hart slipped into retirement. Caroline had put in long hours preparing the lovely old house in Sharon for this day. At the end of the village green and on a rise overlooking the rolling hills of the Harts' dairy farm, the eighteenth-century house provided a comfortable harbor for the old admiral. Now there was the time to spend with his family and on various projects and travels long delayed. In the village there were new local interests to pursue such as improving the golf club and getting a historical society established. In the wider world there were old interests and old haunts to revisit. Together they went to Europe and to England, where he visited with his British commander from World War I, Vice Admiral Sir Lewis Bayly. They sailed the waters of the southwest Pacific where the Asiatic Fleet had fought its last, desperate battles.

With his vow of abstinence no longer applicable, he rekindled old ties with naval comrades. As always, the academy exerted a tug at his heartstrings. Whenever possible he returned there for football games or other events, and he took great interest in the completion of several of the Memorial Hall murals he and Caroline donated in memory of Lieutenant Commander Thomas Comins Hart. After completing his oral history in 1962, Hart became very close to the director of the U.S. Naval Institute's oral history program, John T. Mason, Jr. On one visit to Annapolis, Hart was touring Mason around some of his old haunts. When they got to the room where the portraits of the past superintendents are displayed, the two men drifted apart as they studied the various paintings. When Mason rejoined Tommy, the veteran of Coxey's Army was standing before the portrait of Admiral Willard H. Brownson—with a full half-inch of his tongue stuck out. "That's my father-in-law," Tommy explained to the startled Mason.

There were other naval memories and associations he kept alive, as when he wrote members of his old command. In March 1959, for instance, he wrote to the officer who was his flag lieutenant with the Asiatic Fleet, Leo W. Nilon. He told Nilon that leaving him and the others in Java was "absolutely the worst experience" and "hardest thing that I ever had to do." He knew, he wrote, "that before Java fell we would have to come to grips with the Japanese, hopeless as was the prospect. I wanted to be there in it and it was in my mind that I would be in the front of it, on shipboard, when the time came." That, of course, was not the way it was for Hart, but that fate befell numerous others and Tommy never stopped regretting that fact.

But life went on; grandchildren were born, years passed, and some memories dimmed. There was always plenty to do around the farm and the old house to absorb endless hours. Yet there was time during these years to do some of the things he loved. There was quail-shooting in the broom-sage fields of Georgia, until his eyes weakened and he put away his shotguns. And there was trout-fishing in some of the fine waters that flowed through the Connecticut hills and bisected the lake country around the Adirondack League Club in upstate New York. Well into his eighties Tommy pursued the wily trout, opening the season every April even if it meant wading through snow and pushing past bushes that dropped cold globs down the back of his neck. Finally that, too, had to be given up as his wrists got stiff and he could no longer deliver the fly with the same deft touch.

In Sharon he was very much the local personality, probably feared by the children and by some adults who were apprehensive about facing a hurtling automobile driven by a determined white-haired man approaching not only them but ninety years as well. By most citizens of the village, however, he was beloved and respected; he and Caroline became more or less the venerable aristocrats. On his ninetieth birthday, the whole village turned out to see him be driven around the green in a golf cart. He wanted to drive himself, but cooler heads prevailed.

Time was running out, though. The "old man" could not deny the fates forever. In 1971 he and Caroline took their last trip south. Their first night out, Tommy insisted on carrying their dinner trays back from their rooms to the main lodge. In the dark he turned the wrong way at the head of the stairs and fell five and one-half feet into some pyracantha bushes. X-rays determined that his back was broken, and the chief of naval operations sent a navy plane to fly him to Bethesda Naval Hospital. At first his recovery seemed almost miraculous, but some months later he had a heart attack, after which he began to sink fast. On 4 July 1971 he died. Some might suggest that it was fitting and appropriate for Tommy Hart to die on Independence Day.

During the last twenty-five years of his life, which were lived in private, he seems to have been much the same kind of person that he was in his more than fifty years of public service. No doubt he mellowed. More humor showed through the crusty exterior. Yet, although he listened closely to what his grandchildren said, clearly wanting to learn about and understand their world, he was still "formidable" in their eyes. Those who listened to him found him to have very strong feelings and opinions, but he did not wish to force them on others. When his children traveled around with him, and he still preferred the company of young people, they observed that he was the same attentive listener whether talking with a gas-station owner, a farm hand, or an elevated personage in the village. Everyone got the same fair hearing; everyone was approached on his own ground. As the following story told by one of his grandsons suggests, he was even willing to approach on their own grounds those who fell short of his standards:

> Granddad's loyalty and respect for others sometimes outweighed his own sense of right and wrong. Duty to others arose over his own principles. Several times in my juvenile years, I ended up in serious legal trouble. On one occasion I was forced to call Granddad to obtain bail, my parents being on vacation. He drove several hours in the middle of the night to assist me. He must have been embarrassed, yet he silently listened to me and took me home. My actions must have appalled him, yet he earnestly listened. His level-headed, even-handed sternness and neutrality was a greater incentive for my reform than dozens of judges and jails. His personal dignity insured that I felt the full effect of my actions, guaranteed that I learned my own lesson. His manner was not one of punishment. Yet his stern, quiet support embarrassed me, caused me to deeply question my conduct, and was more rehabilitative than any coercion of our criminal justice system.

Tommy counseled his grandson to find inner sources of strength and to recognize the power of motivation which, he trusted, existed beneath the careless exterior of this callow youth. What Tommy said had so much impact that it moved the culprit "off the mesa I'd left myself on, moving me back to school and a law degree," he wrote. He went on:

> My life had been a mass of disjointed actions. That talk showed me that the secret to our actions, our conduct was the spirit in which the work is done. He basically taught me to lead with my mind, that mental images can be a job half done. Since that morning, I have come to believe that Granddad expressed in a word what our social philosophers and theologians have sought to describe since the Renaissance. For he was setting forth the essence of Western man, that our life was up to us, that we were given a free will and the determination to make the world as we dreamed, so long as we accepted our personal responsibility.

Maybe Tommy saw something in this "bad boy" that he recognized, or maybe his years of counseling midshipmen and sailors after "rough liberties" was coming through.

Tommy's grandson attributes to him a philosophical bent that was not apparent in his earlier life. Perhaps it was always there. Caroline can remember how during his years in retirement, at the end of most days, when the house was quiet and the family had moved toward bed, Tommy would go outside and stare up into the darkened sky, as he smoked one last cigarette. He never talked about what he was thinking, but he seemed to gain strength from those quiet moments under the stars.

He no longer used the diary for recording his actions or thoughts during these years in retirement. There just was not enough of importance to justify the time it took to keep up the running account. On 12 June 1952, he made his last formal entry. After filling in the events of several years, most notably the births of grandchildren, he entered a summary of his life:

Well—today I'm seventy-five years old—five years beyond the old allotted span and that means living a long long time. Its been a good life, in fact a wonderful life, wonderful, at least, as viewed from what would have been the outlook of my boyhood.

That boyhood, on farms and in Michigan's country villages, was lonely, narrow, and proscribed. My Mother's death, not long after my birth, was a sad circumstance. I had step-mothers, two of them, but the first one, while I most needed a mother, did not have it in her to be one. She died when I was ten. My Father was a grand person and he did his best by me—if he had any fault as a father, it lay in over-indulging me. His own life was a difficult one, and I mostly grew up just by myself, with young associates who were not always estimable.

Looking back, I think I excelled most of them mentally but not physically or always in character. Upon the whole I don't think that I was at all an admirable child or youth. I must have come from good stable stock, and heritage rather than environment governed my growth and development.

Then, at age fifteen, began my wonderful good fortunes. By the blindest sort of chance, I went into the Navy, and that has made my life. As an officer, I have been industrious, and I've been a worrier who never could sit back and coast until whatever was in hand was tied down and double-rivetted. Perhaps I haven't had enough fun in life—I never could play whole-heartedly until the job in hand was finished.

I suppose my mentality fitted my Profession fairly well. It was never anything out of the ordinary but it was helped along by a good sense of values, some acumen and pretty good horse sense—above all by being a good guesser. I don't know why I've written the foregoing for the major reason for my success in the Navy has been also perpetual good luck. I must have used up the family allottment for my namesake—who was much the better man of the two of us—just never had good luck. The other kind pursued Tom to his early grave and therein lies the one real tragedy in my life.

The last four years of the Navy, covering my third war, were not so good. I was licked in the Far East but seem to have come out of it without impairment of reputation. However then followed three years of rather chewing my fingers in the Navy Department:— no work or duties of primary importance, looked upon as just another Admiral too old for war. Then a final stroke of good fortune sent me to the U.S. Senate. That meant two years of very hard work in a strange new world but it was one of the most interesting times in my life, and I came to know some very estimable men to whom I shall always be devoted. Above all my own performance, under the difficult circumstances, was good enough for some personal satisfaction and that constituted a fitting end to the active career—at age 69.

So—it's been a good and a full life. . . .

Now I've had nearly six years, settled in at home with my wonderful wife, with my activities as sketched in this final volume. Caroline and I look back upon a grand life, in a very satisfying, interesting, and comfortable world, as far as concerns our own America. She also, eight years younger than I, is still healthy and probably with many years ahead of her. Yes, both of us are still busy but we are no longer important as far as the big outside world goes. So we shall be settled back, *watching* it go, unable to do much about it.

The world is rapidly changing. We have numerous descendants who add up to good stuff. What kind of a world they are going to have is a grave question and my oversize capacity for worrying is pointed in their direction. Upon the whole, it is unlikely that there is going to be a great deal that Caroline and I can do to help.

In any case, there is no sufficient reason for keeping this record any longer, and so—after forty years—

Finis

Thos. C. Hart

NOTES AND
ACKNOWLEDGMENTS

Of primary value in composing this biography was the Hart Diary. These twenty-one volumes, comprising approximately 3,000 pages of handwritten notes, allowed me to keep in touch with Tommy Hart's attitudes and feelings. Of almost equal value was the oral history done by Dr. John T. Mason, Jr., of the U.S. Naval Institute. The Hart Papers are in the Operational Archives, Navy Yard, Washington, D.C. However, there are numerous letters, scrapbooks, and other memorabilia at King House, Sharon, Connecticut, where Hart lived for more than forty-five years. The Narrative of Events, Asiatic Fleet, and Supplement, both written by Admiral T. C. Hart at the request of the Navy Department, were very useful in reconstructing events between 1940 and 1942. Numerous war diaries, notably those by Rear Admiral Francis W. Rockwell and Rear Admiral William A. Glassford, Jr., were also useful, as were the Admiralty papers in London.

As far as published material is concerned, Samuel Eliot Morison's *History of United States Naval Operations in World War II* was the most useful. For general background I relied on E. B. Potter's and Chester W. Nimitz's *Sea Power* and Harold and Margaret Sprout's *The Rise of American Naval Power, 1776–1918.* Also useful were E. B. Potter's *Nimitz,* Kemp Tolley's *Cruise of the Lanikai,* Louis B. Morton's *The Fall of the Philippines,* Clayton James's *The Years of MacArthur,* and Theodore Roscoe's *U.S. Submarine Operations in World War II.*

For personal assistance there is none to compare with that received from Mrs. Thomas C. Hart and members of the Hart family. But also of great help were Dr. John T. Mason, Jr., Vice Admiral Redfield Mason, Vice Admiral John L. McCrea, Rear Admiral Henry Eccles, Commander Thomas B. Buell, B. Mitchell Simpson, Paolo E. Coletta, and the hundreds of Naval Academy graduates who responded to my questionnaire.

For help with research materials, I am much indebted to the staff of the Operational Archives at the Washington Navy Yard, most particularly Dr. Dean Allard, Ms. Leslie Grover, and Ms. Martha Crawley. I also received courteous assistance from the staff of the Nimitz Library in Annapolis.

Finally, it would have been impossible to complete this work without the help of my editor, Mary Veronica Amoss, and a number of people here at Chapel Hill. My special thanks go to Robert Miller, Steven Baxter, George Mowry, Ron Maner, and Julie Perry.

After all is said and done, there is one person whose help, counsel, and support have been invaluable. I refer to my assistant, Mrs. Helen Wilson.

Naturally, as author, I am solely responsible for any errors, omissions, or interpretations.

ABBREVIATIONS

AFD	Asiatic Fleet Dispatches, Operational Archives, Navy Yard, Washington, D.C.
CH	Caroline Hart
CinCAF	Commander in Chief, Asiatic Fleet
CNO	Chief of Naval Operations
CominCh	Commander in Chief, U.S. Fleet
FR	*Foreign Relations*
GB	General Board
GBF	General Board Files, Operational Archives, Navy Yard, Washington, D.C.
HD	Hart Diary, King House, Sharon, Conn.
H-MM	Memorandum entitled "Relations between General Douglas MacArthur and Admiral Thomas C. Hart during the latter half of 1941," HP
HP	Hart Papers, Operational Archives, Navy Yard, Washington, D.C.
NA	National Archives, Washington, D.C.
NAA	Naval Academy Archives, Annapolis, Md.
NE	Narrative of Events, HP
OA	Operational Archives, Navy Yard, Washington, D.C.
OH	Admiral Hart's Oral History, Operational Archives, Navy Yard, Washington, D.C.
OPD	Operations Division, World War II Records Branch, NA.
OpNav	Office of the Chief of Naval Operations

PHA   *Hearings before the Joint Committee on the Pearl Harbor Attack*
PRO   Public Record Office, London
SDF   State Department Files, NA
TCH   Thomas C. Hart
TCHP   Hart Papers, King House, Sharon, Conn.

N. B. All unattributed quotations are from the Hart Diary.

1   CHILDHOOD AND YOUTH

1. Information about the Hart family prior to the advent of Thomas C. Hart is scarce; they were farming, working people who apparently kept few records or letters. What is incorporated in this study about Tommy's early childhood is pieced together from TCH papers, the Oral History, and conversations and correspondence with the Hart family.
2. A description of a childhood in Michigan has been provided in Bruce Catton, *Waiting for the Morning Train: An American Boyhood.*
3. OH, p. 3.
4. Ibid.
5. Record supplied by School Board, Flint, Michigan; TCH's comments from OH, pp. 2–3.
6. Information on the academy in the 1890s came from a variety of sources, including: Park Benjamin, *The United States Naval Academy*; John Crane and James F. Keiley, *The United States Naval Academy*; *The First Hundred Years*; Ralph Earle, *Life at the U.S. Naval Academy*; Peter Karsten, *The Naval Aristocracy*; William D. Puleston, *Annapolis: Gangway to the Quarterdeck*; also useful were the *Report of the Board of Visitors* and *Journal of the Naval Academy*. Specific information on Hart's class and record came primarily from the *Annual Register of the United States Naval Academy*. The last three items are in NAA.
7. Benjamin, *The United States Naval Academy*, p. 335.
8. OH, p. 7.
9. Thomas C. Hart, "A Cruise in the Old Navy," *Trident*, Vol. 5, Winter 1931.
10. *Lucky Bag*, 1894, NAA.
11. Ibid.
12. The best account of this incident and of other early contacts between TCH and Brownson is in *From Frigate to Dreadnaught*, compiled by Mrs. Thomas C. Hart from her father's papers with the help of Thomas C. Hart. Also a reference in *Lucky Bag*, 1895.
13. Benjamin, *United States Naval Academy*, p. 336.

14. Ibid., p. 337.
15. TCH wrote the section on the cutter crew in *Lucky Bag*, 1897.
16. H. Wayne Morgan, *America's Road to Empire*.
17. A recent analysis of the disaster suffered by the *Maine* concludes that, in fact, the *Maine* sank as a result of a fire in a coal bunker adjacent to a magazine. *See* Admiral Hyman G. Rickover, *How the Battleship Maine Was Destroyed*.
18. For general background and details on the Spanish-American War, *see* E. B. Potter and Chester W. Nimitz, *Sea Power*; D. B. Chidsey, *The Spanish-American War*; Frank B. Freidel, *The Splendid Little War*; Walter Millis, *The Martial Spirit*.
19. OH, p. 10; F. E. Chadwick, *Relations of the U.S. and Spain: The Spanish-American War*, Vol. I, pp. 383–84.
20. TCH later, at his wife's request, wrote out a brief narrative of this action and included it in TCHP.
21. Letter, 4 July 1898, in TCH Service Record, U.S. Navy Department.
22. OH, pp. 18–20.
23. John Bowlby, *Attachment and Loss*.

2   TOMMY HART'S SECOND WAR

1. All comments on performance come from the TCH Service Record, U.S. Navy Department.
2. Thomas C. Hart, "They Sent a Boy," *Shipmate*, April 1953, p. 6.
3. Caroline Hart, comp., *From Frigate to Dreadnaught*, p. 199.
4. Ibid., p. 210.
5. The text is in the Naval Academy Museum.
6. A description of this building plan is given in Jack Sweetman, *The U.S. Naval Academy: An Illustrated History*, pp. 142–47.
7. Memorandum, TCH apparently to the commandant of midshipmen, 6 February 1904, HP.
8. Author's interview with CH, May 1978.
9. Correspondence in HP.
10. OH, p. 15.
11. Letter, CH to author, 1 October 1979.
12. Hart, *From Frigate to Dreadnaught*, Chapter XIII. This chapter was written by TCH.
13. *Washington Post*, 31 March 1910.
14. *U.S. Naval Administration in World War II: Bureau of Ordnance*. 3 vols. Naval Torpedo Station, Newport, Rhode Island, Vol. II, Chapter XVI.
15. Frank Freidel, *Franklin D. Roosevelt*, Vol. I: *The Apprenticeship*, p. 197.
16. Ibid., p. 192. *See also* Alfred B. Rollins, *Roosevelt and Howe*, Chapters 7–10.
17. Undated note in HP, Box 1. There is no explanation regarding how

it got there but on the back, in TCH's squiggly writing, is the note, "A souvenir of which I've always been *very* proud."

18. For fuller coverage on Veracruz incident, *see* Robert E. Quirk, *An Affair of Honor.*
19. Letter, TCH to CH, 20 October 1915, TCHP.
20. HD, 12 June 1915.
21. Ibid., 26 June 1915.
22. Ibid., 4 December 1915.
23. Ibid., 12 December 1915.
24. OH, p. 24.
25. HD, 31 August 1916.
26. Ibid., 8 November 1916.
27. Ibid., 9 November 1916.
28. Ibid., 17 November 1916.
29. Ibid., 30 November 1916.
30. Hart, *From Frigate to Dreadnaught*, p. 275.
31. Some information on this early period in submarines taken from a long letter from TCH to James Fife, 25 April 1939, HP, Box 3, in which TCH provides some submarine history.
32. Admiral William S. Sims, *The Victory at Sea*, pp. 274–75.
33. For description of this inspection tour, *see* E. B. Potter, *Nimitz*, p. 130.
34. HD, 25 June 1918.
35. Letter, TCH to Fife, 25 April 1939, HP, Box 3.
36. Ibid.

3   THE 1920'S

1. Background, and some specific information from letter, TCH to James Fife, 25 April 1939, HP, Box 3.
2. *See* John D. Alden, *The Fleet Submarine in the U.S. Navy*, p. 10.
3. Letter, TCH to D. Foxvog, 21 May 1965, HP, Box 4.
4. Views from copy of letter to the *Army-Navy Register*, n.d., but probably 1919, and from his lecture to the Army General Staff College, 28 October 1919. Both items in HP, Box 4.
5. Copy in HP, Box 4.
6. For information on the unilateral scrapping of U.S. submarines, *see* Harold and Margaret Sprout, *Toward a New Order of Sea Power.*
7. Memorandum, TCH to CNO, 4 February 1919, copy in HP, Box 4.
8. Letter, TCH to Fife, 25 April 1939, HP, Box 4.
9. TCH Service Record, U.S. Navy Department.
10. HD, 3 June 1919.
11. Much information on the *S–5* accident in HP, Box 4.
12. Copy of Lieutenant Commander Gibson's report and TCH's endorsement in HP, Box 4.

13. Yates Stirling's letter, 21 March 1921, and TCH's endorsement, April 1921, in HP, Box 4.
14. HD, 3 February 1922.
15. Ibid., 6 March 1922.
16. Ibid., 15 July 1922.
17. OH, p. 36.
18. HD, 23 August 1923.
19. Copy of lecture in HP, Box 4.
20. OH, p. 43.
21. Letter, TCH to Commandant, Army War College, HP.
22. Donald W. Mitchell, *History of the Modern American Navy*, p. 279.
23. OH, Vice Admiral Joseph J. ("Jocko") Clark, pp. 179–82, OA.
24. OH, p. 46.
25. HD, 4 October 1927.
26. *History of the Naval Torpedo Station, Newport, Rhode Island*, Vol. VI, "Evolution of the Torpedo," Newport, R.I., January 1946, p. 88.
27. Ibid., p. 91.
28. *United States Naval Administration in World War II*: Bureau of Ordnance, Naval Torpedo Station, Newport, Rhode Island, Chapter 23.
29. HD, 10 December 1927.
30. Ibid., 21 November 1928.
31. TCH Service Record, U.S. Navy Department.
32. From *United States Naval Administration in World War II*, Chapter 23, but obviously a reflection of Hart's thinking.
33. HD, 5 January 1929.
34. Letter, William Ward Smith to TCH, 18 September 1939, HP, Box 1.
35. HD, 8 March 1929.
36. Ibid., 2 July 1929.
37. Ibid., 4 September 1929.
38. Ibid., 30 December 1929.
39. Ibid., 4 September 1930.
40. *New York Times*, 12 October 1930.
41. Alden, *Fleet Submarine*, pp. 20–21.
42. Ibid., p. 21.

4   BACK TO THE ACADEMY

1. A variety of sources have been used to provide a picture of the academy during TCH's tenure as superintendent. Most useful were: Jack Sweetman, *The U.S. Naval Academy: An Illustrated History*; John Crane and James F. Keiley, *The United States Naval Academy: The First Hundred Years*; Leland P. Lovette, *School of the Sea*; William D. Puleston, *Annapolis: Gangway to the Quarterdeck*; and Felix Riesenberg, *The Story of the Naval Academy*. Also useful was the *Annual Report of the Superintendent, United States Naval Academy*, 1931–1934, NAA. The Superintendent's Files and Naval Academy Archives

proved to be something of a disappointment partially because of their content and partially because the arrangement made them inconvenient to use. The *Log* magazine and the *Lucky Bag* annual were fun to read and useful.

2. *Annual Report of the Superintendent*, 1933.

3. For Sims's view, *see* Elting E. Morison, *Admiral Sims and the Modern American Navy*, pp. 521–25.

4. Naval Academy questionnaire sent out by the author.

5. Ibid.

6. Ibid.

7. OH, p. 65.

8. Puleston, *Annapolis*, p. 126.

9. *Report of the Board of Visitors*, 1931, NAA.

10. Memorandum, TCH to D. F. Sellers, 12 June 1934, HP, Box 2, hereafter referred to as Sellers Memorandum.

11. Letter, TCH to Frank Brooks Upham, 1 July 1931, HP, Box 1.

12. *Annual Report of the Superintendent*, 1932, p. 8, NAA.

13. Letter, TCH to William H. Standley, 19 September 1932, Superintendent's Files, Athletics, Box 2, Folder 9, NAA.

14. Sellers Memorandum.

15. Ibid.

16. *Annual Report of the Superintendent*, 1932.

17. Naval Academy questionnaire.

18. Ibid.

19. Ibid.

20. Ibid.

21. Letters in Superintendent's Files, Box 2, Folder 1, NAA.

22. Naval Academy questionnaire.

23. The issue of the Army-Navy football game was put together from information in the Superintendent's Files, Athletics, Box 2, Folder 9, NAA, newspaper clippings, and the Sellers Memorandum.

24. *New York Daily News*, 7 January 1928.

25. Letter, TCH to William D. Connor, 15 December 1931, Superintendent's Files, NAA.

26. HD, 25 August 1932.

27. Letter, TCH to Standley, 19 September 1932, Superintendent's Files, Athletics, Box 2, Folder 9, NAA.

28. Superintendent's Files, Athletics, Box 2, Folder 9, NAA.

29. HD, 2 September 1932.

30. Sellers Memorandum.

31. Naval Academy questionnaire. The same story is told of Rear Admiral Henry B. Wilson when he was superintendent.

32. HD, 4 March 1934.

33. For Sims's views, *see* Morison, *Admiral Sims*, pp. 521–25.

34. HD, 30 April 1934.

35. Sweetman, *U.S. Naval Academy*, p. 191.

5   CRUISERS AND THE GENERAL BOARD

1. HD, 17 July 1934.
2. OH, p. 74.
3. HD, 27 July 1934.
4. Fitness report, TCH Service Record, U.S. Navy Department.
5. HD, 1 January 1935.
6. Ibid., 16 May 1935.
7. Ibid., 12 June 1935.
8. Ibid., 14 December 1935.
9. Letter, Harry E. Yarnell to TCH, 24 January 1936, HP, Box 2.
10. HD, 10 January 1936.
11. Ibid., 20 January 1936.
12. Ibid., 23 January 1936.
13. Letter, William W. Smith to TCH, 18 May 1936, HP, Box 2.
14. Manuscript in HP, Box 2.
15. Letter, John W. Wilcox, Jr., to TCH, HP, Box 2.
16. *New York World Telegram*, 18 May 1941.
17. Naval Academy questionnaire.
18. Ibid.
19. Stephen Roskill, *Naval Policy between the Wars*, Vol. I: *The Period of Anglo-American Antagonism, 1919–1929*, p. 26.
20. Letter, TCH to GB, 24 February 1936, HP, Box 2. For Sims's view, *see* Elting E. Morison, *Admiral Sims and the Modern American Navy*, pp. 526–28.
21. HD, 9 November 1936.
22. Ibid., 1 December 1936.
23. Hearings, GB, 1937, Vol. I. Especially relevant are Hearings for March 1937; *see* pp. 102, 114, GBF.
24. Letter, Submarine Officers Conference to CNO, 12 May 1938, in GBF #420–15, Serial 1795.
25. Specifications put before GB on 21 June 1938, in GBF #420–2, Serial 1798. *See also* GB #420–15, Serial 1795, papers dated 12 July 1938.
26. The final specifications can be found in GBF #420–15, Serial 1795, and the final approval of the design is in Serial 1843.
27. Hearings, GB, 1937, Vol. 1, 9 June 1937.
28. For 1940 estimates, *see* GBF #420–2, Serial 1790 of 3 May 1938; for 1941 estimates, *see* GBF #420–2, Serial 1928 of 26 April 1939.
29. Comment made by Senator Hiram W. Johnson (D. California) to Captain Royal E. Ingersoll, who was one of the U.S. naval representatives at the conference. Author's interview with Vice Admiral Ingersoll, 1966.
30. GBF #420–2, Serial 1724, 18 February 1937.
31. HD, 5 March 1937.
32. Ibid., 15 September 1937.

33. OH, p. 87.
34. HD, 26 July 1937.
35. Ibid., 13 and 17 December 1937.
36. For a full description of Ingersoll's mission, *see* James R. Leutze, *Bargaining for Supremacy*, pp. 21–27.
37. HD during this period is liberally sprinkled with hints from fellow officers that he is in line for the "Big Fleet."
38. HD, 6 January 1939.
39. Ibid., 6 March 1939.
40. Richardson repeated this story to TCH. Author's interview, with CH, 20 September 1980.
41. OH, p. 86.
42. Letter, Tom Hart to TCH, 15 March 1939, HP, Box 2.
43. Admiral William D. Leahy, *I Was There*, p. 471.
44. Admiral James O. Richardson, *On the Treadmill to Pearl Harbor*, p. 8.

6   ASSIGNMENT TO THE ASIATIC FLEET

1. OH, p. 96.
2. HD, 20 July 1939.
3. Ibid., 25 July 1939.
4. William L. Langer and S. Everett Gleason, *The Challenge to Isolation*, Vol. I, pp. 148–57.
5. Barbara Tuchman, *Stilwell and the American Experience in China*, p. 88. Tuchman also provides some good background on the fighting for Shanghai in 1937.
6. OH, pp. 103–4.
7. HD, 24 August 1939.
8. Ibid., 25 August 1939.
9. Ibid., 6 September 1939.
10. Letter, TCH to Harold R. Stark, 19 September 1939, HP, Box 4.
11. HD, 19 September 1939.
12. Ibid., 28 November 1939.
13. OH, p. 110–11.
14. Most useful for reconstructing the complex story of planning during this period is Louis B. Morton "War Plan ORANGE: Evolution of a Strategy," *World Politics*, Vol. 11, pp. 221–50; and the same author's *War in the Pacific* in the U.S. Army's official history series.
15. Waldo H. Heinrichs, Jr., "The Role of the United States Navy" in *Pearl Harbor as History*, edited by Dorothy Borg and Sumpei Okamoto, pp. 197–223.
16. Notes given by Admiral J. O. Richardson to Secretary of the Navy Frank Knox, 12 September 1940, PHA, XIV, pp. 958–68.
17. HD, 3 January 1940.
18. Ibid., 5 January 1940.

19. Letter, TCH to Stark, 4 January 1940, HP, Box 4.
20. Letter, TCH to Stark, 9 February 1940, HP, Box 4.
21. Ibid.
22. Letter, TCH to Stark, 4 January 1940, HP, Box 4.
23. Letter, Stark to TCH, 1 December 1939, HP, Box 4.
24. HD, 4 April 1940.
25. Letter, TCH to Stark, 25 March 1940, HP, Box 4.
26. HD, 28 March 1940.
27. Ibid., 7 February 1940.
28. OH, pp. 112–13.
29. Letter, TCH to Stark, 25 March 1940, HP, Box 4.
30. Letter, TCH to Stark, 11 December 1939, HP, Box 4.
31. Letter, TCH to Stark, 25 March 1940, HP, Box 4.
32. HD, 3 April 1940.
33. Ibid., 7 March 1940.
34. Letter, TCH to Stark, 12 April 1940, HP, Box 4.
35. Letter, TCH to Stark, 9 February 1940, HP, Box 4.
36. Letter, TCH to Stark, 27 April 1940, HP, Box 4.
37. Cable, TCH to OpNav, 14 May 1940. Repeated to State. SDF 893.0146/782.
38. Japanese Ministry of Foreign Affairs to State Department, 11 June 1940. SDF 893.0146/786.
39. OH, p. 102.
40. HD, 6 May 1940.
41. Ibid., 8 June 1940.
42. TCH to Stark, 24 July 1940, HP, Box 4.
43. OH, p. 125.
44. Cable, Navy to State, 25 June 1940, SDF 893.1025/2091 1/2, and cable, Navy to TCH, 2098A, SDF.

7   STRATEGY BY NEGOTIATION

1. The gendarmes incident is mentioned in *FR*, 1940, Vol. IV, p. 752. Other relevant information appears in *FR*, Japan, 1931–1941, Vol. II, pp. 101 and 106. For more detailed coverage, *see* SDF, 893.1025/2122. The lengthy negotiations also rate many mentions in the Hart Diary.
2. *FR*, 1940, Vol. V, pp. 762–63.
3. HD, 15 August 1940.
4. *FR*, 1940, Vol. IV, p. 767.
5. Ibid., p. 772.
6. Ibid., p. 770.
7. HD, 19 August 1940.
8. Letter, TCH to Harold R. Stark, 20 August 1940, HP, Box 4.
9. HD, 27 August 1940.
10. Letter, TCH to Stark, 3 October 1940, HP, Box 4.

11. OH, pp. 125–26.
12. HD, 20 September 1940.
13. Ibid., 26 September 1940.
14. Cordell Hull, *The Memoirs of Cordell Hull*, Vol. I, pp. 908–9; HD, 28 September 1940.
15. HD, 29 September 1940.
16. Letter, TCH to Stark, 30 October 1940, HP, Box 4.
17. HD, 16 October 1940.
18. OH, p. 132.
19. *See* James R. Leutze, *Bargaining for Supremacy*, Chapters X and XI.
20. Ibid., p. 194.
21. Letter, TCH to Stark, 20 August 1940, HP, Box 4.
22. OH, p. 142.
23. HD, 12 November 1940.
24. Ibid., 19 December 1940.
25. Ibid., 30 December 1940.
26. *See*, for instance, ibid., 2 November 1940.
27. Ibid., 5 November 1940.
28. Letter, John L. McCrea to author, 22 December 1976. Admiral McCrea included with this letter a copy of a lengthy memorandum he delivered to Admiral Stark.
29. McCrea Memorandum.
30. HD, 16 January 1941.
31. McCrea Memorandum.
32. Letter, McCrea to author, 22 December 1976.
33. Cable, OpNav to CinCAF, 18 April 1940, AFD.
34. For an official account of the meetings, *see* Mark S. Watson, *Chief of Staff, Prewar Plans and Preparations*, pp. 367–82.
35. Air Marshal Sir John Slessor, *The Central Blue*, pp. 325–70.
36. Leutze, *Bargaining*, p. 241.
37. Ibid., p. 263.
38. Letter, TCH to Stark, 19 January 1941, HP, Box 4.
39. Letter, TCH to Stark, 7 February 1941, HP, Box 4.
40. Letter, TCH to Stark, 4 March 1941, HP, Box 4.
41. Ibid.
42. Letter, TCH to Stark, 29 April 1941, HP, Box 4.
43. Ibid.
44. Secret Serial 038612, CNO to all Commanders, 3 April 1941, AFD.
45. Stark argued this case very persuasively in a memorandum dated 11 February to President Roosevelt that he included with a 24 February letter to TCH, HP, Box 4.

8   CHAOS BEFORE DISASTER

1. HD, 28 January 1941.
2. Ibid., spring 1941, and NE, p. 3.

3. Letter, TCH to Harold R. Stark, 7 June 1941, HP, Box 4.
4. Cable, CNO to CinCAF, 9 May 1941, AFD.
5. Letter, TCH to Stark, 7 June 1941, HP, Box 4.
6. HD, 28 April 1941.
7. NE, p. 12.
8. Cable, CNO to CinCAF, AFD.
9. Letter, TCH to CH, 26 December 1940, TCHP.
10. HD, 28 March 1941.
11. Ibid., 25 January 1941.
12. Essay "Way of Life" included in letter, TCH to CH, 26 February 1941, TCHP.
13. Letter, TCH to CH, 15 June 1941, TCHP.
14. Letter, TCH to CH, 12 June 1941, TCHP.
15. Confidential statement by a naval officer who worked in intelligence on Corregidor.
16. Ibid., and OH, Rear Admiral Charles Adair.
17. William L. Langer and S. Everett Gleason, *The Undeclared War*, pp. 641–45.
18. Clayton James, *The Years of MacArthur*, Vol. I, pp. 590–91.
19. HD, 28 July 1941.
20. Ibid., 14 August 1941; and letter, TCH to Stark, 19 August 1941, HP, Box 4.
21. Letter, Stark to TCH, 3 July 1941, HP, Box 4.
22. HD, 11 September 1941.
23. Dispatch, CNO to CinCAF, 13 September 1941, AFD.
24. Supplement to NE, p. 4.
25. Dispatch, CinCAF to OpNav, 17 September 1941, AFD.
26. Supplement to NE, pp. 5–6.
27. Cable, CinCAF to OpNav, 19 September 1941, AFD.
28. HD, 2 September 1941.
29. Ibid., 24 September 1941, and Supplement to NE, p. 7.
30. Supplement to NE, p. 7.
31. *See also* H-MM.
32. In a letter written in response to a midshipman doing research for an essay, Hart wrote: "*Possibly* I was a bit misled by our Army's optimism—but not much." The primary factor was that "I allowed myself to become convinced that the 130 fighter planes . . . could control the air, at least in the vicinity of Luzon." Letter, TCH to Midshipman Smiley, 26 January 1956, HP. A more speculative, but more intriguing, prospect is that *because* TCH had come to dislike MacArthur so much he overcompensated for any natural distrust he might have. For instance, in his memorandum on relations with MacArthur, TCH recounts an incident where MacArthur insults him, and writes: "I listened to such patronizing talk, off and on, and under the circumstances it was not pleasant . . . It was all childish—

which I fully recognized but I did fear that its effect on me might be to warp my own judgment in important matters." H-MM.

33. *See especially*, letter, Stark to TCH, 22 September 1941, HP, Box 4.
34. Letter, TCH to CH, 7 October 1941, TCHP.
35. Letter, TCH to CH, 20 September 1941, TCHP.
36. Letter, TCH to Stark, 19 August 1941, HP, Box 4.
37. HD, 25 September 1941.
38. Letter, Stark to TCH, 22 September 1941, HP, Box 4.
39. Letter, Stark to TCH, 28 August 1941, HP, Box 4.
40. Letter, TCH to Stark, 4 October 1941, HP, Box 4.
41. NE, p. 23.
42. Ibid., p. 24.
43. Dispatch, TCH to Stark, 27 October 1941, AFD.
44. Dispatch, CNO to CinCAF, 14 November 1941, AFD.
45. HD, 8 November 1941.
46. Kemp Tolley, "Divided We Fell," *U.S. Naval Institute Proceedings*, October 1966, pp. 37–51. Very useful in reconstructing developments from MacArthur's perspective is James, *MacArthur*.
47. H-MM.
48. Ibid.; author's interview with CH, August 1975; and letter, TCH to CH, 9 November 1941, TCHP.
49. Letter, TCH to Stark, 20 November 1941, HP, Box 4.
50. Letter, TCH to CH, 9 November 1941, TCHP.
51. OH, Vice Admiral Robert L. Dennison, p. 23ff., and author's interview with Dennison, January 1978. Dennison now tends to see the situation more from MacArthur's than TCH's perspective; *see* OH, p. 39.
52. Dispatch, CinCAF to OpNav, 7 November 1941, AFD.
53. HD, 19 November 1941.
54. Dispatch, OpNav to CinCAF, 20 November 1941, AFD.
55. Letter, TCH to Stark, 20 November 1941, HP, Box 4.
56. NE, p. 25, and Supplement to NE, p. 6; letter, John L. McCrea to author, 2 January 1976.
57. Letter, TCH to CH, 25 November 1941, TCHP.
58. NE, pp. 29–30.
59. Ibid., pp. 31–32; Theodore Roscoe, *U.S. Submarine Operations in World War II*, pp. 61–62.
60. *Time*, 24 November 1941.
61. HD, 29 November 1941.
62. Supplement to NE, p. 34.
63. Kemp Tolley, *Cruise of the Lanikai*, p. 265.
64. Author's interview with Vice Admiral Redfield Mason, July 1977.
65. Kemp Tolley, "The Strange Voyage of the Lanikai," American Heritage, 24, pp. 56–95.

66. Ibid., p. 95.
67. For John W. Payne's recollection of TCH briefing, *see* Tolley, *Cruise of the Lanikai*, p. 269.
68. Ibid., p. 271.
69. NE, pp. 34–36. There is also a long summary of the sessions sent as a dispatch to Washington and London on 7 December 1941: the American copy is in AFD; the British copy in File, CAB 122, PRO.
70. Ibid.
71. PHA, Part X, p. 4802.
72. Dispatch, CinCAF to OpNav, 7 December 1941, AFD.
73. HD, 6 December 1941.
74. NE, p. 36.
75. Frederick Winston Furneaux Smith, Lord Birkenhead, *Halifax*, p. 525.
76. Raymond A. Esthus, "President Roosevelt's Commitment to Britain to Intervene in a Pacific War," *Mississippi Valley Historical Review*, pp. 28–38.

9   M-DAY AND AFTER

1. NE, p. 36.
2. HD, 8 December 1941.
3. William Manchester, *The American Caesar*, p. 206. The most straightforward treatment of MacArthur's campaign in the islands is Louis Morton, *The Fall of the Philippines*, Chapters 5–9. A very readable treatment is in Clayton James, *The Years of MacArthur*, Vol. II, Chapter 1.
4. Descriptions can be found in many places, including: Samuel Eliot Morison, *History of United States Naval Operations in World War II*, Vol. III: *Rising Sun in the Pacific*, pp. 171–72; Edwin P. Hoyt, *The Lonely Ships*, Chapter 19; Admiral Francis W. Rockwell, "Narrative of Events"; and War Diary, Sixteenth Naval District, OA. Admiral Redfield Mason added color in an interview.
5. HD, 10 December 1941.
6. Dispatch, CinCAF to OpNav, 10 December 1941, AFD.
7. Dispatch, MacArthur to Chief of Staff, 13 December 1941, OPD.
8. HD, 19 December 1941.
9. Dispatch, OpNav to CinCAF, 11 December 1941, AFD.
10. "General Review of First Week," in War Diary, Far Eastern Fleet, ADM 199/1185, Admiralty Records, PRO. This record was written by Vice Admiral Sir Geoffrey Layton.
11. "General Review of Second Week," ibid. During this period Admiral Ghormley, in London, was furnishing the Admiralty with copies of the CNO's telegrams to TCH. *See* File CAB 122, PRO.
12. Ibid.
13. Telegram, Helfrich to Layton, 15 December 1941, ibid.

14. Ibid.
15. Diary of Henry L. Stimson, 14 December 1941, Yale University Library, New Haven, Conn.
16. Morton, *Fall of the Philippines*, pp. 149–51.
17. Dispatch, OpNav to CinCAF, 23 December 1941, AFD.
18. Theodore Roscoe, *United States Submarine Operations in World War II*, p. 34.
19. Dispatch, OpNav to CinCAF, 17 December 1941, AFD.
20. Dispatch, OpNav to CinCAF, 20 December 1941, AFD.
21. James, *MacArthur*, Vol. II, p. 24. James, a generally friendly biographer, refers to MacArthur's plan as an "illusion" and quotes one of the general's own officers as calling it a "terrible thing." Ibid., p. 27.
22. Ibid., p. 26.
23. H-MM.
24. OH, Admiral Charles Adair, Vol. I, p. 32. This conversation was apparently repeated to Adair, as he was not actually present at any TCH-MacArthur meetings.
25. Ibid., p. 33.
26. Roscoe, *Submarine Operations*, p. 38.
27. HD, 22 December 1941.
28. James, *MacArthur*, Vol. II, p. 28.
29. Letter, TCH to MacArthur, 24 December 1941, TCHP. *See* CinC USAFFE to Adjutant General, OPD.
30. HD, 24 December 1941. The description of TCH's departure and his feelings is taken from HD.
31. Dispatch, CinC USAFFE to Chief of Staff, 26 December 1941, OPD.
32. Dispatch, CNO to CinCAF, 29 December 1941, AFD.
33. Manchester, *American Caesar*, p. 213.
34. Courtney Whitney, *MacArthur: Rendezvous with History*, pp. 14–15; Clark G. Lee and Richard Henshel, *Douglas MacArthur*, pp. 168–69; Frazier Hunt, *MacArthur and the War Against the Japanese*, p. 24.

10 TRAPPED IN A SINISTER TWILIGHT

1. HD, 28 December 1941.
2. Letter, TCH to Samuel Milner, 10 January 1959, HP, Box 3.
3. Message, CominCh to CinCAF, 29 December 1941, Dispatches, ComSoWesPac, January 1942-December 1943, OA.
4. Message, CinCAF to CominCh, 2 January 1942, ibid.
5. Message, CominCh to CinCAF, 25 December 1941, ibid.
6. Supplement to NE, 12 March 1948, p. 37.
7. Message, CinCAF to CominCh, 2 January 1942, Dispatches, ComSoWesPac, January 1942-December 1943, OA.
8. Letter, TCH to Milner, 10 January 1959, HP, Box 3.

9. HD, 3 January 1942.
10. Telegram, C. E. L. Helfrich to Sir Geoffrey Layton, 15 December 1941, "General Review of First Week," in War Diary, Far Eastern Fleet, ADM 199/1185, Admiralty Records, PRO.
11. Admiral C. E. L. Helfrich, *Memoirs*, Vol. I, p. 214.
12. Ibid., p. 247.
13. Forrest C. Pogue, *George C. Marshall*, Vol. II: *Ordeal and Hope, 1939–1942*, pp. 275–82. For the British side, *see* Minutes of 25 December 1941 meeting in CAB 99/17, War Cabinet Office Papers, PRO.
14. Minutes of 27 December 1941 meeting in CAB 99/17, PRO.
15. Arthur Bryant, *The Turn of the Tide*, pp. 235–36.
16. Stephen Ambrose, *The Supreme Commander*, pp. 12, 25–26.
17. Diary of Henry L. Stimson (MS), 27 December 1941, Yale University, New Haven, Conn.
18. Robert E. Sherwood, *Roosevelt and Hopkins*, p. 458.
19. Diary of Henry L. Stimson (MS), 28 December 1941, Yale University, New Haven, Conn.
20. Pogue, *Marshall*, p. 279.
21. Ibid., pp. 126–28.
22. Memorandum, Winston Churchill to First Lord of the Admiralty and First Sea Lord, 17 February 1941, ADM 116/4877, PRO.
23. Minute, Churchill to Chiefs of Staff and First Lord of the Admiralty, 12 February 1941, ibid.
24. Minutes, meeting of 28 December 1941, CAB 99/17, PRO.
25. Memorandum and recommendation by Joint Planning Staff to Chiefs of Staff, 2 January 1942, CAB 99/17, PRO.
26. Letter, Harold R. Stark to TCH, 5 January 1942, HP, Box 4.
27. NE, pp. 48–51.
28. Message, CominCh to CinCAF, 8 January 1942, Dispatches, ComSoWesPac, January 1942-December 1943, OA.
29. HD, 9 January 1942.
30. Samuel Eliot Morison, *History of United States Naval Operations in World War II*, Vol. III: *Rising Sun in the Pacific*, p. 279.
31. Message, CominCh to CinCAF, 5 January 1942, Dispatches, ComSoWesPac, January 1942-December 1943, OA.
32. Message, CinCAF to CominCh, 9 January 1942, ibid.
33. Memorandum, George C. Marshall to CominCh, 9 January 1942, enclosing Brett's message; and message, CominCh to CinCAF, 10 January 1942, pointing out that Brett's messages gave "no indication of agreement," ibid.
34. Message, Douglas MacArthur to Marshall, 9 January 1942, ibid.
35. Message, CominCh to CinCAF, 10 January 1942, ibid.
36. Message, CinCAF to CominCh, 10 January 1942, ibid.
37. HD, 11 January 1942.

38. Message, CinCAF to CominCh, 12 January 1942, Dispatches, ComSoWesPac, January 1942-December 1943, OA.
39. Message, CominCh to TCH, 12 January 1942, ibid.
40. Supplement to NE, 12 March 1948, p. 25; and NE, pp. 54–55.
41. NE, pp. 54–55.
42. Brian Bond, ed., *Chief of Staff: The Diaries of Lieutenant-General Sir Henry Pownall*, Vol. 2: *1940–1944*, p. 77.
43. Pownall Diaries (MS), 13 January 1942. Parts of the Pownall Diaries have not been published but were made available by their editor, Brian Bond.
44. HD, 10 January 1942.
45. Letter, John Collins to author, 2 October 1975.
46. Supplement to NE, p. 38.
47. *See also* F. C. Van Oosten, *The Battle of the Java Sea*, p. 15.
48. HD, 30 January 1942.
49. Ibid., 27 January 1942.
50. Ibid., 13 January 1942.
51. Ibid., 16 January 1942.
52. Ibid., 19 January 1942.
53. Ibid., 20 January 1942.
54. Bond, *Chief of Staff*, p. 83.
55. NE, p. 66.
56. HD, 21 January 1942.
57. Ibid., 22 January 1942.
58. Ibid., 23 January 1942.
59. Ibid., 25 January 1942.
60. Ibid., 26 January 1942.
61. Ibid., 27 January 1942.
62. Ibid., 28 January 1942.
63. Message, U.S. Naval Attaché, Melbourne, to OpNav, 9 January 1942, OA.
64. Message, CominCh to CinCAF and CinCAF to CominCh, 12 January 1942, Dispatches, ComSoWesPac, January 1942-December 1943, OA.
65. HD, 28 January 1942.
66. Message, Sir Archibald Wavell to War Office for Prime Minister, 12 January 1942, PREM 3, PRO.
67. Sherwood, *Roosevelt and Hopkins*, pp. 491–92.
68. HD, 28 January 1942.
69. Ibid.
70. Ibid., 29 January 1942.
71. Wavell's schedule has been reconstructed by comparing information from John Connell, *Wavell: Supreme Commander*, and from Bond, *Chief of Staff*.
72. Pownall Diaries (MS), 25 January 1942.

73. Message, Wavell to Churchill, 29 January 1942, PREM 3, PRO.
74. Roosevelt's reaction is quoted by Churchill in his cable to Wavell, 2 February 1942, PREM 3, PRO.
75. HD, 1 February 1942, and Supplement to NE, p. 39.
76. Message, Wavell to Churchill, 2 February 1942, PREM 3, PRO.
77. HD, 1 February 1942.
78. Ernest J. King and Walter M. Whitehill, *Fleet Admiral King*, p. 368. *See also* Thomas B. Buell, *Master of Sea Power*, p. 173.
79. HD, 1 February 1942.
80. Ibid., 2 February 1942.
81. Message, CominCh to CinCAF, 5 February 1942, Dispatches, ComSoWesPac, January 1942-December 1943, OA.
82. HD, 5 February 1942.
83. Ibid., 15 February 1942, and author's interview with Rear Admiral Redfield Mason, June 1975.
84. *The Daily Oklahoman*, 6 May 1942.
85. Morison, *Rising Sun*, p. 312.
86. Helfrich, *Memoirs*, Vol. I, p. 345.
87. John Toland, *But Not in Shame: The Six Months After Pearl Harbor*, p. 220.
88. G. Herman Gill, *Australia in the War of 1939–45*, Vol. I: *Royal Australian Navy, 1939–42*, p. 556.
89. War Diary, ADM 199/1185, PRO. The British official history, *The War at Sea*, Vol. II: *The Period of Balance*, by Captain Stephen Roskill, makes no mention of Hart's replacement; Hart just disappears.
90. Winston Churchill, *History of the Second World War*, Vol. III: *The Grand Alliance* (Boston: Houghton Mifflin, 1950), p. 587.

11   LIVING WITH DISASTER

1. Naval Academy questionnaire.
2. HD, 21 February 1942.
3. Ibid., 9 March 1942.
4. Thomas B. Buell, *Master of Sea Power*, pp. 320–21.
5. HD, 10 March 1942, and OH, p. 188.
6. *Washington Post*, 12 March 1942.
7. *New York Herald Tribune*, 16 March 1942.
8. *Army-Navy Journal*, 14 February 1942. For background, *see* Buell, *Master of Sea Power*, p. 321.
9. *New York Times*, 14 February 1942.
10. The best account is in F. C. van Oosten, *The Battle of the Java Sea*. *See also* Edwin P. Hoyt, *The Lonely Ships*, pp. 263–73, and Samuel Eliot Morison, *History of United States Naval Operations in World War II*, Vol. III: *Rising Sun in the Pacific*, Chapter XVIII.
11. "What Our Navy Learned in the Pacific," 3 October 1942, and "Amphibious War Against Japan," 10 October 1942.

12. HD, 10 March 1942. *See* Ernest J. King and Walter M. Whitehill, *Fleet Admiral King*, p. 368.
13. HD, 27 January 1944.
14. PHA, Proceedings of the Hart Inquiry, Part XXVI, p. 4.
15. HD, 11 March 1944.
16. PHA, Part XXVI, p. 58.
17. Ibid., p. 275.
18. Ibid., p. 280.
19. HD, 6 April 1944.
20. OH, p. 209.
21. HD, 10 April 1944.
22. PHA, Part XXVI, pp. 339–48.
23. HD, 12 April 1944. Hart was not correct in his suspicions, *see* E. B. Potter, *Nimitz*, pp. 282, 293–94.
24. HD, 5 August 1944.
25. Ibid., 11 August 1944.
26. Ibid., 21 August 1944.
27. Ibid., 27 September 1944.
28. PHA, Part XXXIX, p. 321.
29. *Bridgeport Post*, 6 February 1945.
30. Ibid.
31. *Hartford Courant*, 6 February 1945.
32. *New York Herald Tribune*, 6 February 1945.
33. HD, 14 February 1945.
34. *New York Times*, 13 February 1945.
35. HD, 28 February 1945.
36. Ibid., 5 April 1945.
37. OH, p. 273.
38. PHA, Part X, pp. 4808-9.
39. OH, p. 162.
40. PHA, Part X, pp. 4807-8.
41. OH, p. 163.

BIBLIOGRAPHY

I. UNPUBLISHED SOURCES

GREAT BRITAIN

London

Public Record Office
  Admiralty Records: Far Eastern Fleet
  War Cabinet Office Papers

UNITED STATES

Annapolis, Md.

Naval Academy Archives
  Lucky Bag (Academy Yearbook)
  Superintendent's Files

New Haven, Conn.

Yale University Library
  Henry L. Stimson Diary

Washington, D.C.

National Archives
  OPD Files. World War II Records Branch
  U.S. Department of State. State Department Files
  U.S. Navy Department. Personnel File.
Operational Naval Archives, U.S. Navy
  General Board Files, 1900–1951

Privately Held Papers

  Thomas C. Hart Diary. Among his personal papers at King House, Sharon, Conn.
  Pownall Diaries. In the possession of Brian Bond, Medmenham, England.
  Records supplied by School Board of Flint, Michigan, in letter to author, 6 March 1977.

II. INTERVIEWS AND ORAL HISTORIES

Adair, Rear Admiral Charles. Oral History, Operational Archives, Washington, D.C.
Dennison, Vice Admiral Robert L., Interview, Washington, D.C., January 1978.
Hart, Caroline, Interview, Sharon, Connecticut, May 1978.

Ingersoll, Vice Admiral Royal E., Interview, Washington, D.C., December 1966.

Mason, Vice Admiral Redfield, Interview, Manassas, Virginia, July 1977.

III. PUBLISHED MATERIALS

Alden, John D. *The Fleet Submarine in the U.S. Navy.* Annapolis: Naval Institute Press, 1979.

Ambrose, Stephen. *The Supreme Commander.* Garden City, New York: Doubleday and Company, 1969.

Annual Report of the Superintendent, United States Naval Academy. Naval Academy Archives. Naval Academy Press, 1922, 1933.

Benjamin, Park. *The United States Naval Academy.* New York: G.P. Putnam's Sons, 1900.

Birkenhead, Lord, Frederick Winston Furneaux Smith. *Halifax.* London: Hamish Hamilton, 1965.

Bond, Brian, ed. *Chief of Staff: The Diaries of Lieutenant-General Sir Henry Pownall.* London: L. Cooper, 1972.

Bowlby, John. *Attachment and Loss.* 2 vols. New York: Basic Books, 1969–73.

Bryant, Arthur. *The Turn of the Tide.* Garden City, New York: Doubleday and Company, 1957.

Buell, Thomas B. *Master of Sea Power.* Boston: Little, Brown and Company, 1980.

Bulkley, Robert J., Jr. *At Close Quarters: PT Boats in the United States Navy.* Naval History Division, Washington, D.C., 1962.

Bureau of Ordnance, Naval Torpedo Station. *United States Naval Administration in World War II.* Vols. I–III, VI. Newport, Rhode Island: 1946.

Catton, Bruce. *Waiting for the Morning Train: An American Boyhood.* New York: Doubleday and Company, 1972.

Chadwick, F. E. *Relations of the U.S. and Spain: The Spanish-American War.* 2 vols. New York: Charles Scribner's Sons, 1911.

Chidsey, Donald B. *The Spanish-American War.* New York: Crown Publishers, 1971.

Connell, John. *Wavell: Supreme Commander.* London: Collins, 1969.

Crane, John, and Keiley, James F. *The United States Naval Academy: The First Hundred Years.* New York: McGraw-Hill, 1945.

Dyer, Vice Admiral George. *On the Treadmill to Pearl Harbor.* Washington, D.C.: Naval History Division, Department of the Navy, 1973.

Earle, Ralph. *Life at the U.S. Naval Academy.* New York: G.P. Putnam's Sons, 1917.

Esthus, Raymond A. "President Roosevelt's Commitment to Britain to Intervene in a Pacific War." *Mississippi Valley Historical Review* (June 1963), 28–38.

Freidel, Frank. *Franklin D. Roosevelt.* Vol. I: *The Apprenticeship.* Boston: Little, Brown and Company, 1952.

————. *The Splendid Little War.* Boston: Little, Brown and Company, 1958.

Gill, G. Herman. *Australia in the War of 1939–1945.* Vol. I: *Royal Australian Navy, 1939–1942.* Melbourne: Australian War Memorial, 1957.

Hart, Mrs. Thomas C., comp. *From Frigate to Dreadnaught.* Sharon, Connecticut: King House, 1973.

Heinrichs, Waldo, Jr. "The Role of the United States Navy" in *Pearl Harbor as History,* edited by Dorothy Borg and Sumpei Okamoto. New York: Columbia University Press, 1973.

Helfrich, Admiral C. E. L. *Memoirs.* 2 vols. Amsterdam: Elsevier, 1950.

Hoyt, Edwin, P. *The Lonely Ships.* New York: McKay, 1976.

Hull, Cordell. *The Memoirs of Cordell Hull.* 2 vols. New York: Macmillan Company, 1958.

Hunt, Frazier. *MacArthur and the War Against the Japanese.* New York: Charles Scribner's Sons, 1944.

James, Clayton. *The Years of MacArthur.* 2 vols. Boston: Houghton Mifflin Company, 1970.

Karsten, Peter. *The Naval Aristocracy.* New York: Free Press, 1972.

Kimmel, Husband E. *Admiral Kimmel's Story.* Chicago: H. Regnery Co., 1955.

King, Ernest J., and Whitehill, Walter M. *Fleet Admiral King.* New York: W.W. Norton, 1952.

Langer, William L., and Gleason, S. Everett. *The Challenge to Isolation.* Vol. I. New York: Harper and Row, 1970.

————. *The Undeclared War, 1940–1941.* New York: Harper, 1953.

Leahy, Admiral William D. *I Was There.* New York: Whittlesey House, 1950.

Lee, Clark G., and Henshel, Richard. *Douglas MacArthur.* New York: Holt, 1952.

Leutze, James R. *Bargaining for Supremacy.* Chapel Hill, North Carolina: The University of North Carolina Press, 1977.

Lovette, Leland P. *School of the Sea.* New York: Frederick A. Stokes Company, 1941.

Manchester, William. *The American Caesar.* Boston: Little, Brown and Company, 1978.

Millis, Walter. *The Martial Spirit.* Boston: Houghton Mifflin Company, 1931.

Mitchell, Donald W. *History of the Modern American Navy.* New York: Alfred A. Knopf, 1946.

Morgan, H. Wayne. *America's Road to Empire.* New York: Wiley, 1965.

Morison, Elting E. *Admiral Sims and the Modern American Navy.* Boston: Houghton Mifflin Company, 1942.

Morison, Samuel Eliot. *History of United States Naval Operations in World War II.* Vol. III: *The Rising Sun in the Pacific.* Boston: Little, Brown and Company, 1948.

Morton, Louis B. *The Fall of the Philippines.* Washington, D.C.: Office of the Chief of Military History, Department of the Army, 1953.
————. "War Plan ORANGE: Evolution of a Strategy." *World Politics* 11 (October 1958–July 1959), 221–50.
Pearl Harbor Attack: Hearings before the Joint Committee on the Investigation of the Pearl Harbor Attack. Washington, D.C.: U.S. Government Printing Office, 1946.
Pogue, Forrest C. *George C. Marshall: Ordeal and Hope.* New York: Viking Press, 1966.
Potter, E. B. *Nimitz.* Annapolis: Naval Institute Press, 1976.
Potter, E. B., and Nimitz, Chester W. *Sea Power.* Englewood Cliffs, New Jersey: Prentice-Hall, 1960.
Puleston, William D. *Annapolis: Gangway to the Quarterdeck.* New York: D. Appleton-Century, 1942.
Quirk, Robert E. *An Affair of Honor.* Lexington, Kentucky: University of Kentucky Press, 1962.
Report of the Board of Visitors. Washington, D.C.: U.S. Government Printing Office, 1863–.
Richardson, Admiral James O. *On the Treadmill to Pearl Harbor.* Washington, D.C.: Naval History Division, 1973.
Rickover, Admiral Hyman G. *How the Battleship Maine was Destroyed.* Washington, D.C.: Department of the Navy, 1976.
Riesenberg, Felix. *The Story of the Naval Academy.* New York: Random House, 1958.
Rollins, Alfred B. *Roosevelt and Howe.* New York: Alfred A. Knopf, 1962.
Roscoe, Theodore. *U.S. Submarine Operations in World War II.* Annapolis: Naval Institute Press, 1949.
Roskill, Stephen. *Naval Policy Between the Wars.* 2 vols. New York: Walker, 1968.
————. *The War at Sea, 1939–1945.* 3 vols. London: Her Majesty's Stationery Office, 1954.
Sherwood, Robert E. *Roosevelt and Hopkins.* New York: Harper, 1948.
Sims, Admiral William S. *The Victory at Sea.* Garden City, New York: Doubleday, Page and Company, 1920.
Slessor, Air Marshal Sir John. *The Central Blue.* New York: Praeger, 1957.
Sprout, Harold and Margaret. *Toward a New Order of Sea Power.* Princeton: Princeton University Press, 1946.
Sweetman, Jack. *The U.S. Naval Academy: An Illustrated History.* Annapolis: Naval Institute Press, 1979.
Toland, John. *But Not in Shame: The Six Months after Pearl Harbor.* New York: Random House, 1961.
Tolley, Kemp. *Cruise of the Lanikai.* Annapolis: Naval Institute Press, 1973.
————. "Divided We Fell." *U.S. Naval Institute Proceedings* (October 1966), 36–51.

————. "The Strange Mission of the Lanikai." *American Heritage* (October 1973), 56–61, 93–95.

Tuchman, Barbara. *Stilwell and the American Experience in China.* New York: Macmillan, 1970.

U.S. Department of State. *Papers Relating to the Foreign Relations of the United States.* Washington, D.C.: U.S. Government Printing Office, 1862–.

Van Oosten, F. C. *The Battle of the Java Sea.* Annapolis: Naval Institute Press, 1976.

Watson, Mark S. *Chief of Staff, Prewar Plans and Preparations.* Washington, D.C.: Historical Division, Department of the Army, 1950.

Whitney, Courtney. *MacArthur: Rendezvous with History.* New York: Alfred A. Knopf, 1955.

IV. NEWSPAPERS AND MAGAZINES

Army-Navy Journal
Bridgeport Post
Daily Oklahoman
Hartford Courant
New York Daily News
New York Herald Tribune
New York Times
New York World Telegram
Time
Washington Post

INDEX